returns of the

"french freud"

freud, lacan,

and beyond

LA CARTE POSTALE DE SIGMUND FREUD A JACQUES LACAN (recto/verso)

returns of the "french freud"

freud, lacan, and beyond

edited by

Todd Dufresne

Routledge
New York and London

Published in 1997 by

Routledge
29 West 35th Street
New York, NY 10001

Published in Great Britain in 1996 by

Routledge
11 New Fetter Lane
London EC4P 4EE

Printed in the United States of America
Design: Jack Donner

Library of Congress Cataloging-in-Publication Data

Returns of the "French Freud" / [edited by] Todd Dufresne.
    p.   cm.
    Includes bibliographical references.
    ISBN 0–415–91525–2. — ISBN 0–415–91526–0.
    1. Psychoanalysis—History. 2. Freud, Sigmund, 1856–1939.
  3. Lacan, Jacques, 1901–1981. 4. Psychoanalysis—France.
  I. Dufresne, Todd, 1966–   .
BF173.R452   1996
150.19'52'09—dc20

95–53176
                                                                      CIP

contents

acknowledgments

A PROJECT OF THIS SORT DEPENDS UPON THE DIRECT AND INDIRECT GOODWILL of many people. Without the kind support of Mikkel Borch-Jacobsen this collection would not have materialized. My deepest appreciation to Clara Sacchetti for reading and correcting parts of the rough manuscript. My thanks also to Tony Greco, Johannes Mohr, Raymond Dufresne, Kenneth Little, and Paul Roazen for their support and helpful comments, and to Maureen MacGrogan and the very capable staff at Routledge. I am indebted to Julian Patrick, Sophie Thomas, John Caruana, and Charles Dudas for their thoughtful and painstaking works of translation. Most of all it is my great privilege to acknowledge each of the contributors for their generosity towards, patience with, and (compound) interest in this project. Without their participation this could not, echoing Freud, have become a valuable part of reality. Parts of this project developed while I was funded by a Social Science and Humanities Research Council grant, and a Queen Elizabeth II Ontario Scholarship.

The following contributions first appeared in these journals: Paul Roazen (based on), "Nietzsche and Freud: Two Voices From the Underground," *The Psychohistory Review* (Spring 1991): 327–49; Daniel Bougnoux, "Lacan oui, et apres?" *Revue Esprit* (July 1993); Jacques Derrida, "'To Do Justice to Freud': The History of Madness in the Age of Psychoanalysis," *Critical Inquiry* 20, no. 2 (Winter 1994): 227–66; Rodolphe Gasché, "La sorciére métapsychologique," *diagraphe* 4 (1974): 83–122.

My thanks, finally, to Peter Swales for sending me a copy of the Freud postcard to Lacan (8.1.1933), and to Tom Roberts and The Sigmund Freud Copyrights for allowing its reproduction here: © 1984, A.W. Freud et al, by arrangement with Mark Paterson & Associates.

—*Todd Dufresne, editor*

introduction

beyond the
french
freud

Todd Dufresne

The "French Freud," carefully erased in quotation marks, no longer belongs to France alone or to any one personality—assuming that it ever could have, or did. A term without referent, the "French Freud" has become a slippery piece of signification beyond the regulative fiction of circuitous return and reception. Consequently, despite its wide currency today, or perhaps because of it, it is difficult to demarcate where the "French Freud" begins and/or ends, or even to know what the phrase means anymore. Rigorously speaking, then, there can be no return to the "French Freud," but only multiple re-turns on a diversified investment in thinking psychoanalysis differently.

But however dramatic, necessary, clever, or banal these suggestions may be, we have not really dispensed with reading and writing about Jacques Lacan in relation to the "French Freud." It is not simply that people continue to identify Lacan with or as the French Freud, having deemed scare quotes superfluous. It is rather that the wild transmission and reception of Lacan's work, within France and around the world, has only helped ensure the continued significance of what passes as French psychoanalysis. For the spirit of both Freud and Lacan live on precisely to the extent that their work resists any final systematization or institutionalization. Similarly, the inevitable erasure of boundaries between the cultures of psychoanalysis, coupled with the so-called "death of psychoanalysis" in North America and elsewhere, has only enabled psychoanalysis to proliferate beyond the grip of any founding nation, school, or personality.

Returns of the "French Freud" was broadly conceived with this proliferation in mind and reflects a diversity of interests (or returns) that pass through the elusive theme of the "French Freud"; exported and commodified, today Lacan's thought pervades the intellectual and psychoanalytic worlds. Yet it cannot be easily introduced or thematized. To help situate the reader along this difficult and slippery terrain, I will nonetheless provide a cursory overview of the transmission and reception of psychoanalysis in France and America—if only to force a little sense into an irreducible biographical and theoretical scene. To this pedagogic end, I quickly explore some aspects of the "French Freud" in relation to Freud's work and its reception in America (or, as it were, in "America").

IN KEEPING WITH AN APOCALYPTIC TONE TYPICAL OF ANY *FIN-DE-SIÈCLE* (and no doubt exaggerated by the close of the millennium), it has become fashionable in all quarters to announce the failure or bankruptcy of psychoanalysis, if not its immanent death. After all, whether one takes such dire prophesies seriously or not, the "psychoanalytic century" is quickly drawing to a close. Of course, some critics announced the "death" of psychoanalysis even before its founder, Sigmund Freud, died in 1939. For them, psychoanalysis was always something of a con game, a stillborn science, the sublimated gift of Freud's own anality.[1]

Yet controversy has only fueled the fire, and by now more may have been written about Freud's life and work than about any other figure in Western history. At the very least, it is certainly remarkable that the autobiographical science of one man has made possible not only a vast body of secondary literature, but an enduring institutional body as well. Given this divisive history, it is not surprising that our picture of Freud and psychoanalysis has changed dramatically, especially over the last thirty years of revisionism. With the gradual release of previously restricted documents from the Library of Congress and the appearance of new, complete, uncensored editions of Freud's private correspondence, our view of psychoanalysis was bound to change. And no doubt it will continue to change, since, for instance, only about 6,000 of the estimated 35,000 letters Freud wrote have appeared in print. Incredibly enough, this fraction of the correspondence already fills twelve volumes. In this way and more, psychoanalysis has ensured itself a future, even if its status and direction remain uncertain.

If, moreover, the accumulation of new primary source material hasn't been enough to shake the old hagiographic picture of Freud, certainly the revisionist and pathographic research on the history of psychoanalysis has. Clearly the accumulation of psychoanalytic literature has not enforced our transference onto Freud and his theories; for many of us it has weakened this tie to its breaking point. As a result, we live in a time of critical reassessment, when many are taking a close second and third look at the legend(s) of Freud, the group psychology of his followers, the foundations of his "science," the therapeutic efficacy of analysis, and so on.

From a medical and therapeutic perspective, these are no longer the glory days that psychoanalysis enjoyed in urban America during the 1950s. But having unearthed, as Frederick Crews recently put it, "the unknown Freud" (1993), have we finally committed psychoanalysis to the grave? Echoing a 1966 cover story about the "death of God," *Time* captured this sentiment, recently asking: "Is Freud Dead?" This, however, was and remains an altogether audacious and ambivalent question. For when we pose the same question of God and Freud, we already pre-suppose that Freud's death will cast, as Nietzsche put it, a similarly long shadow. In this way, *Time* deferred and side-stepped at least one very important question about our transference onto Freud and his theories: namely, who among us still mistakes Freud for God?

While the Freudian corpus began to decompose in America during the 1970s, it gathered an afterlife in France. As Sherry Turkle (1992) suggests, the psycho-analytic "movement" became a genuine "culture" after the May 1968 student uprisings and throughout the 1970s. Disillusioned with the large questions of social reform, young radicals turned their attention to the individual and to psycho-analysis. As Mikkel Borch-Jacobsen has recently put it:

> In the wake of May '68 and its utopian dream, there weren't that many exciting intellectual projects around. May '68 had failed, you couldn't believe in Marxism anymore, and Structuralism was hopelessly removed from life. Psychoanalysis, with its transgressive and initiatory aspects, seemed to be the only theory left that could claim to effectively "change life"—*changer la vie*, as the May '68 slogan would have it. Remember, the May '68 movement wanted to revolutionize "everyday life" and, in retro-spect, it seems to me clear that my generation's interest in psychoanalysis was a way of pursuing this revolutionary project by other means. We all longed for that "high" that May '68 had provided, and that is how so many of us got hooked on psychoanalysis. Psychoanalysis was a substitute for the impossible revolution. (Unpublished interview with the author 1994)

Like other intellectual trends in France, psychoanalysis thrived as a cult of personality, one centered around the name and legend(s) of Jacques Lacan. As Stuart Schneiderman states: "Before Lacan, the history of psychoanalysis was a series of footnotes to Freud" (1983: 19). "Lacanism" quickly spread among intel-lectuals and, through the popular media, to everyone else; French psychoanalysis became synonymous with Lacan's name. In turn, psychoanalytic literature, or any-thing with an opportunistic dash of Freud in its title, became a large, profitable, "infinitely elastic" publishing industry in France (Turkle 1992: 195–96). After decades of apathy towards psychoanalysis, thoughts finally turned to a French Standard Edition of Freud's work. Unfortunately, as debates still rage over the proper translation of Freud's original German, the Edition has yet to appear in its entirety.[2]

In this atmosphere, exciting new ideas emerged about psychoanalysis, arguably for the first time since Freud and some of his more talented followers wrote and published. And while the majority of people hardly understood Lacan's baroque writings and free-associational seminars, everyone agreed that his work was timely and somehow significant. As Lacan himself put it: "We are confronted by this sin-gular contradiction—I don't know if it should be called dialectical—that the less you understand the better you listen. For I often say very difficult things and see you hanging on my every word, and I learn later that some of you didn't understand. On the other hand, when you're told things that are too simple, almost too familiar, you are less attentive" (1988a: 141, trans. modified). With this in mind, Lacan cer-tainly did his best to say "very difficult things."

With the acrimonious debate over "*la passe*" (from analysand to analyst) in the mid-1970s, the dissolution of the École Freudienne de Paris in 1980, and Lacan's death the following year, the once fertile climate for psychoanalysis in France began to change. The same media that propelled psychoanalysis into the public eye became the site of bitter and divisive feuds among traditionally silent analysts. If it hadn't already, Lacanian psychoanalysis took on a strangely surreal quality. This may not be altogether accidental, since—to Freud's great displeasure—it was the surrealists alone who embraced psychoanalysis in France during the 1920s (see Roudinesco 1990: ch. 1). In this regard, it is worth recalling that Lacan, with his eccentric and sometimes outrageous persona, was very much influenced by the early surrealists and published papers in their journals.

The contentious atmosphere of the late 1970s and early 1980s crystallized around the role that Lacan's son-in-law, the philosopher Jacques-Alain Miller, increasingly played in the institutional affairs of psychoanalysis. For Miller, at the time a non-analyst married to Lacan's daughter Judith, was the official editor of Lacan's seminars, the main power in the Department of Psychoanalysis at Vincennes (developed in the wake of May 1968), and the designated heir apparent to Lacan's name and considerable fortune (which consisted, among other things, of rare books, paintings, and gold bars). However, without delving too deeply into this family (and legal) romance, it is enough for us to note that many of Lacan's older, more established followers could never support Miller's *La Cause Freudienne* after the controversial dissolution of the *École Freudienne*. Consequently, although Miller may have successfully advanced one psychoanalytic movement among others in France, he has not managed to maintain the unique psychoanalytic "culture" that thrived under Lacan. To put it more bluntly, Miller has been unable to preserve and enhance Lacan's regal power in his own name. But, to be fair, who could?

While many mistook (and still mistake) Lacan for God, the transference onto his life and work has weakened considerably since his death. Recovering from their Lacanian hangovers, former analysts like François Roustang now plainly ask: "Why did we follow him for so long?" (1990: ch. 1). In turn, it may be almost impossible to avoid asking today whether or not Lacan, like Freud in America, has become a "dead" or purloined letter. For, on the one hand, the "French Freud" first associated with his name has begun to disappear as quickly as it appeared in France.

On the other hand, this turn of events may not be very important, since the French psychoanalytic plague has spread well beyond the geographical borders of France to encompass much of the world; it has become what James Clifford (following Edward Said) calls a "travelling culture" (1992). Consequently, the spirits of French psychoanalysis have successfully appropriated "outside" resistance into the Freudian field. This in fact was already an important part of the Lacanian program, for as Lacan once remarked: "Psychoanalysis currently has nothing better for ensuring its activities than the production of analysts" (in Borch-Jacobsen 1991: 165). Or as Roustang suggests, "If you want analytic knowledge to be generally recognized, it is both necessary and sufficient to produce analysts who will in turn produce others. . . . Once there is no longer anything *outside* psychoanalysis, its teachings will no longer meet with any objections and will be considered valid" (1990: 12). To this overtly proselytizing and political end, to which we must add (as usual) the financial one, many prominent Lacanians have relocated their practices to receptive romance-language countries with potentially large neurotic middle classes, such as Argentina. In fact, with the election of an Argentinean to the Presidency of the International Psychoanalytic Association, institutional power has taken a decisive shift away from traditional strongholds in either North America or France.

IT IS WELL KNOWN THAT LACAN'S "RETURN TO FREUD" WAS FUELED, at least in part, by his dislike of the more conformist, individualistic, and anti-intellectual aspects of Anglo-American ego psychology. Unlike most American analysts, Lacan's interests extended far beyond the traditional domain of medicine and included structural anthropology, linguistics, literature, mathematics, law, and philosophy. As Borch-Jacobsen convincingly argues, Lacan was an "autodidact" who "plagiarized" the works of great thinkers, including G.W. F. Hegel, Ferdinand de Saussure, Martin Heidegger, Claude Lévi-Strauss and, most of all, the Alexandre Kojève of *Introduction to the Reading of Hegel*. "Could it be," Borch-Jacobsen playfully taunts, "that Lacan did his analysis (the *real* one) with Alexandre Kojève?" (1991: 9). Though less critical of psychoanalysis than Borch-Jacobsen, historian Elizabeth Roudinesco agrees that Lacan "borrowed from the seductive master not only his concepts but a [flamboyant] teaching style. . . . For Kojève was, in his own way, a clinical observer, an artisan of the capital letter, a formalist of discourse, a mesmerizer of students, a legendary commentator on texts" (1990: 135).

Although Lacan was interested in the science of the unconscious, having dabbled with structural and mathematical models or "topologies" (e.g., borromean knots, Klein's bottle) he mostly effected ties between psychoanalysis and the less exact "human sciences" (or humanities, taken in the broadest sense)—especially literary studies (see Lacan 1977: 147). Meanwhile, on this side of the Atlantic, analysts like Harry Stack Sullivan tied psychoanalytic research to the mixed fortunes of the social and behavioral sciences. In turn, these disciplinary ties proved crucial for the specific transmission and reception of psychoanalysis in both countries. Among other things, they have meant that French analysts have been less effected (and affected) by the crisis in America over the uncertain medical, therapeutic, and scientific claims of psychoanalysis. In what is a typical French response, Serge Leclaire states: "What happened to Freudian psychoanalysis in America is the fault of Americans. They froze things into a doctrine, almost a religion, with its own dogma, instead of changing with the times" (in Gray 1993: 50).

With the exception of France (and perhaps the Netherlands), no nation has embraced psychoanalysis with the enthusiasm of America. But while Freud remains the singular reference point for all psychoanalytic movements, the reception and transmission of his work has always hinged on quite specific cultural conditions—a suggestion that may have troubled Freud. For although psychoanalysis was his own subjective creation, Freud hoped it would become an objectively true, universal science. As a result, he tended to overvalue the membership of gentiles like Carl Jung and Ernest Jones, not only as *Parade-Goy*, but as confirmation that psychoanalysis wasn't a product of his own, uniquely Jewish delusions.[3]

Reflecting upon his visit to Clark University in 1909, Freud wrote: "As I stepped on the platform at Worcester [Massachusetts] to deliver my *Five Lectures on*

Psychoanalysis it seemed like the realization of some incredible daydream: psycho-analysis was no longer a product of delusion, it had become a valuable part of real-ity" (*SE* 20: 52).[4] This event ended his so-called "splendid isolation," and was only the second time that Freud received official recognition from a university; after waiting five years, he was awarded the title of *Professor Extraordinarius* to the University of Vienna in 1902, and at Clark University the 53 year old Freud received (with Jung) an honorary Doctor of Laws degree. The rank of "Professor" gave Freud the added social standing needed for attracting new followers and, moreover, increasing his hourly rate.

Despite the importance of such recognition, personally and professionally, Freud disliked America and Americans. No doubt this is significant for our understanding of psychoanalysis as a specifically European invention. After all, America has long been a convenient scapegoat for Europeans seeking to protect their historical and cultural traditions from what Lacan called the "cultural ahistoricism peculiar to the United States of America" (1977: 115). To some extent, then, one can argue that Freud's negative reaction to America is instructive and puts the "spirit" of Lacan's own anti-American "return" in an interesting and often overlooked light.

To Ernest Jones, Freud once said that "America is a mistake; a gigantic mistake, it is true, but none the less a mistake" (Jones 1955: 60). Elsewhere he called America a *Missgeburt*—a miscarriage (Eastman 1962: 129). "These sentiments," Peter Gay admits, "run through Freud's correspondence like an unpleasant, monot-onous theme" (1988: 563). In addition, Freud wrote a "psychological study" of President Woodrow Wilson with American diplomat William Bullitt. Characteri-stically, Freud didn't keep his dislike of Wilson a secret; as he put it to Max Eastman in 1926, "Your Woodrow Wilson was the silliest fool of the century, if not all centuries" (Eastman 1962: 127). Not surprisingly, the analytic community reacted to the book's 1966 release with a mixture of denial, silence, and horror. It is no accident that this is the only work of Freud's that has been allowed to go out of print.

While Freud had many reasons for railing against America (including the rich food which, he implausibly claimed, was the cause of his intestinal troubles), he seemed to dislike America for the paradoxical reason that Americans *liked* psycho-analysis. Freud reasoned that anyone who accepted his views about childhood sex-uality without the accompanying resistance must have misunderstood the radical intent of psychoanalysis. He felt, in effect, that his findings merited the kind of seri-ous resistance missing in America. In fact he prophesied that the future of psycho-analysis was destined to unfold in the place of greatest resistance. In retrospect, this turned out to be France.

In general, Freud viewed America as a land of savagery, a wilderness that, by its very existence, might invalidate his universal findings. The myth of a wild America was irreconcilable with Freud's image of the Victorian bourgeoisie beset by uncon-scious conflict and neuroses. Like Dostoevsky and Nietzsche before him, Freud believed that the human capacity to endure suffering was an ennobling aspect of existence; greatness, on this view, was achieved through resignation or stoic endurance of hardship. Against the notion of a "psychoanalysis without tears" (Sachs 1945: 127), such as Alfred Adler's Individual Psychology, Freud liked to say that "One must learn to bear some portion of uncertainty" (145). But Freud's America was far too certain, optimistic, wild, simple, non-European—in a word, *healthy*—to appreciate the virtues of the psychoanalytic sickness. Consequently, when he wasn't too low on filthy lucre, Freud could afford to dismiss Americans—as when he refused to continue treatment of an American patient, ironically claiming that the patient had no unconscious!

According to Turkle, however, psychoanalysis thrived in America precisely because America lacked the sort of culture that produced someone like Freud. Unburdened by the weight of history on the one hand, but suffering an uncertain identity on the other, Americans easily turned psychoanalysis into a theology of liberal individualism and self-overcoming, into a kind of frontier analysis. Freudian psychoanalysis was received in America as a powerful new *therapy*, not as a grand metapsychological *theory*. Thus the speculative depths of psychoanalysis were dropped for the surface effects of everyday life. As French sociologist Jean Baudrillard remarks, "Here in America only what is produced or manifest has meaning; for us in Europe only what can be thought or concealed has meaning" (1988: 84).

Not surprisingly, then, the "American" Freud, which is by no means any more singular or homogeneous than the "French" version, has been famously distinguished by its optimistic streak. In America, for example, there has been little room for Freud's darker, pessimistic view of human existence—including his life/death dualism, announced in 1920. Against what is perceived as the "suicidal therapeutic pessimism" of Freud's late dualism, some American philosophers have proposed a more dialectical, *Christian* psychoanalysis. As Norman O. Brown argues, "our modification of Freud's [dualistic] ontology restores the possibility of salvation" (1959: 81). Similarly, and whether he knew it or not, Erik H. Erikson's dialectically prescriptive "Eight Ages of Man" maps fairly easily onto Hegel's *Phenomenology of Spirit* (see Erikson 1963: ch. 7). In these ways, Freud's Jewish science slowly became Christian, and dualism went "onto-theologic" in post-war America.

In contrast, war-torn Europe was more inclined to read Freud's pessimism in light of then current existential theory. For unlike America, which prospered after the war, Europe was ripe for Freud's darkest thoughts on death, aggression, war, civilization, and its multiple discontents—even for the spirit of German Romanticism. In a remarkable passage, Freud himself emphasized the enduring value of war against which he situated American superficiality:

> Life is impoverished, it loses interest, when the highest stake in the game of living, life itself, may not be risked. It becomes as shallow and empty as, let us say, an American flirtation, in which it is understood from the first that nothing is to happen, as contrasted with a Continental love-affair in which both partners must constantly bear its serious consequences in mind. (*SE* 14: 290).

It is in this feisty spirit that Lacan rejected ego psychology, which took its inspiration from Freud's later texts, and emphasized instead the early "id" psychology of Freud's *Interpretation of Dreams* (1900), *The Psychopathology of Everyday Life* (1901), and *Jokes and Their Relationship to the Unconscious* (1905). In this way,

Lacan returned psychoanalysis to the origins of a depth psychology proper, one uncontaminated by Freud's late, agency-driven, topographical model of super-ego, ego, id of the 1920s and 1930s.

To put it briefly, Lacan preferred the old model of "conscious, pre-conscious, unconscious" since it downplayed the role of agency and subjectivity. From this orientation he reasoned that American ego psychologists mistook the patient's ego for their therapeutic ally, unaware that "The core of our being does not coincide with the ego" (Lacan 1988a: 43). And thus Lacan challenged the flavor of Freud's 1933 announcement—"*Wo Es war, soll Ich werden,*" translated by James Strachey as "Where the id was, there ego shall be" (*SE* 22: 80)—that seemed to advocate ego reinforcement, and called instead for the dissolution of the ego in the murky depths of the chaotic id: "There where it was," Lacan re-translated Freud, "it is my duty that I should come into being" [*La où c'était . . . c'est mon devoir que je vienne à être*] (1977: 129). Lacan thereby launched a powerful critique of the modernist subject implicit within all metaphysical systems of thought.

"The fundamental fact which analysis reveals to us," Lacan wrote, "is that the *ego* is an imaginary function" (1988: 193). For Lacan, Freud's early (non)concept of the unconscious was best understood as an unknown something, an X which "abolishe[d] the subject presumed to know" (1968: 46). Or again, the unconscious undid the truth of the ego handed down through the rationalism of Cartesian "clear and distinct" ideas, the self-sufficient ground upon which Descartes sought to erect the modern subject, the *res cogitans*. The humanist conception of man, *zoon logon echon*, was thereby deconstructed by Lacan and left hanging over the proverbial abyss, mortally wounded if not dead.

With Lacan, the arrogant self-certainty of man, and with it the developmental history of (the philosophy of) consciousness that sustained that conception, was decentered, that is, placed under erasure by the unconscious. Freud's "Copernican revolution" thus suggested that "the very centre of the human being was no longer to be found in that place assigned to it by a whole humanist tradition" (Lacan 1977: 114). Consequently, some argue that Lacan brought "the discourse of psychoanalysis out of its modernist and into its post-modern phase" (Sussman 1990: 142).

It follows that the problem of an "introduction" in/to Lacan's life and work lies not in the *whole* of his corpus, as Jacques Derrida says of Hegel, but rather in the insatiable *hole* that informs it, the gap which opens the truth of the "subject presumed to know" to a yawning abyss. For truth is now conceived as a rift that can never be filled or, if you prefer, bridged by any finite subject. And thus death, or "being-toward-death," is recognized as a limit experience, the horizon which (un)structures human existence as alienation from one's self (or ego). Such are the repercussions of Kojève's influential lectures in France during the 1930s: namely, the inauguration of a philosophy based on the critical power of negation.

In fact, it is the stinking corpse of Man that Lacan drapes in psychoanalytic clothing. For while Freud spoke of analytic neutrality (only, mind you, to forget it immediately), Lacan spoke of the analytic *space of death*. According to Lacan, the silent analyst signifies to the patient an empty void, lack, death, the Real. And thus transference onto the analyst, or onto the fictitious ideal of a grounding super-ego, becomes logically impossible: there is no-body and no-thing to reflect or reinforce one's shattered, essentially false ego. "Any statement of authority," according to Lacan, "has no other guarantee than its very enunciation, and it is pointless for it to seek it in another signifier, which could not appear outside this locus in any way" (1977: 310). As a result, our modern Oedipus is less blinded by the rational light of day than deafened by the hollow fictions that are mastery, truth, closure, subjectivity, and so on. Or again, here in the twilight of the idols, the patient's transference (to Lacan, Freud, the history of philosophy, etc.) is broken and replaced with the fragmentary signifier finally set loose from its Father-Signified. It is precisely in this way that the proper name of "Jacques Lacan"—and with it, that of the "French Freud"—always announced the dead letters of a prescription that could never be filled. And thus we have finally "passed" from the false certainty of consciousness (typified by "American" thinking) to the unconquerable gap or hole in our infinitely circulating desires.

One begins to wonder whether we have also checked into what Georg Lukács once called the "Grand Hotel Abyss": "It is a hotel provided with every comfort, but resting on the edge of the abyss, of nothingness, of the absurd. The daily contemplation of the abyss, in between excellent meals or artistic entertainments, can only enhance the resident's enjoyment of this superlative comfort" (in Bottomore 1984: 34). For indeed, it remains to be seen whether the transference onto Freud and Lacan, onto the psychoanalytic family in general, can be broken, or if it really amounts to an exchange of one delusion for another. After all, having found the position of Truth empty in the deaths of God and Man, Lacan nonetheless continued to play the role of resurrected Father; like Freud, Lacan occupied a privileged reference point in the transmission of psychoanalytic knowledge. In other words, with the *example* of Lacan we are confronted with what Borch-Jacobsen calls "an I-the-autoanalyst-who-autoinstitutes-myself-as-me-the-analysis, me-the-psychoanalyst, as an I-who-leaves-my-ego-to-those-who-claim-to-descend-from-me, the-Freudian-cause" (1993: 7).[5] In other words, caught in the grip of an "infinite transference" that "never lets go" (Roustang 1983: 60), we risk staring into the (Hotel) abyss only to have Freud and Lacan stare back, the "footnotes" of the psychoanalytic horde having re-turned to the master hypnotists who, conveniently, counter-sign and authenticate the "truth" of the entire procedure. It can be no surprise, then,

> that people who had come to Lacan because of his critique of the "subject supposed to know" would turn into the most rigid, dogmatic, intolerant disciples; leftist radicals who had been attracted by Lacan's subversive aspects would become ultra-conformist bureaucrats of the Lacanian school; free spirits would start reading the *Ecrits* as if it was the Bible."
> (Borch-Jacobsen, unpublished interview with the author 1994).[6]

If the mirror has become a looking glass, the *Ecrits* a Bible, then perhaps Freud and Lacan served up no-thing but an authoritarian prescription which resolved, or dis-solved, all fragmented subjectivities in the group effect of the psychoanalytic cause. For finally, if you can't *be* your own subject, you can always become someone else's; as always, the price of admission is submission to an Other's mission.

CLEARLY PSYCHOANALYSIS, AT THE TURN OF THE CENTURY, remains confused and contested. This is true if only because it is difficult to keep track of when psychoanalysis is being "re-born," as in Russia, being "re-organized," as in France, or is "dead"
or dying, as in America; or, once again, what, where, and whose psychoanalysis is
being imported and exported, *fort/da*, from one time and location to the next. Certainly no one interested in psychoanalysis can avoid the turmoil of Freud's creation
limping into its 100 year anniversary. With this in mind, many of us have begun to
raise, implicitly or otherwise, a handful of timely and provocative questions. For
instance, is there a future for (or in) psychoanalysis outside the 20th Century? If so,
what will it look like? What is the state of psychoanalysis under siege, *coup d'etat*?
Are Freud and Lacan "dead"? Either way, does anyone care? What is, and who
cares for, the "French Freud"?

Without pretending to exhaust these sorts of questions, or to provide definitive
answers in the essays that follow, we have each taken a respectful stab at the fragmented corpus of psychoanalysis today. To this end, I have simply tried to outline
here in an introductory way the transmission and reception of the "French Freud"
in America, where the multiple deaths, wakes, and births continually make up and
break apart the psychoanalytic family. From Freud to Lacan and beyond, this is still
a history *sous rature,* that is in the (un)making . . .

NOTES

1. As the inimitable Karl Kraus once put it: "If mankind, with all its repulsive faults, is
   an organism, then the psychoanalyst is its excrement. Psychoanalysis is an occupa-
   tion in whose very name 'psycho' and 'anus' are united" (in Szasz 1976: 115).
2. Confronted with the same translation problems with Freud that others previously
   found with Martin Heidegger in France, new words are being invented to more
   faithfully approximate the German originals—a fetishistic practice that many argue
   muddies the water more often than not.
3. According to Paul Roazen, this "stemmed in part from Freud's own special kind of
   Anti-Semitism" (1991: 216).
4. All references to Freud are made to the *Standard Edition* here and in the essays that
   follow. See collected bibliography for complete reference.
5. The end of this string ["Moi-la-Cause-freudienne"] is a pointed reference to J.-A.
   Miller's controversial movement of that name, the "Freudian Cause," and not just to
   the general phenomena of Freudianism.
6. Similar sentiments are expressed by David James Fisher, who recalls meeting one of
   Lacan's former patients, now an analyst, in Paris 1987. Annoyed by the follower's
   "messianic enthusiasm," Fisher reminded him of Lacan's critique of the "subject
   supposed to know": "Without hesitation, the Lacanian replied to me with yet
   another epistemological question: 'What happens if your analyst *truly* knows?'"
   (1994: 377).

nietzsche,
freud,
and the history
of psychoanalysis

2

Paul Roazen

Editor's Note
Even though many scholars have pondered the complex relation between Nietzsche and Freud, the similarities and differences between the two have rarely been spelled out. Taking up this task, Paul Roazen demonstrates in this paper that Nietzsche and Freud shared an irreverent attitude towards traditional, notably Christian, values and ways of thinking. Part of this convergence, he argues, is attributable to their compatible psychological views on aggression, masochism, and conscience. Roazen suggests that both men applied these views in ways that were sometimes elitist, and explores the "horrifying" and "spooky" aspects of their works.

Unlike Nietzsche, Freud developed his ideas in accordance with scientific language and assumptions. As Roazen reminds us, Freud sometimes relied upon the rationality and optimism that, at other times, he eschewed. As a reader of the unconscious, Freud thus avoided philosophy and, in the same gesture, became the well-known founder of a transmittable science. Nietzsche, on the other hand, remained a staunch critic of rationality and was mostly unacknowledged during his own life.

Turning to Freud's followers, Roazen considers the different characters of French and American psychoanalysis. Unlike many commentators today, Roazen defends ego psychology as a just response to the negativism that is Freud's legacy at its most Nietzschean. Roazen's careful yet relaxed reading provides a welcome foothold for anyone interested in Nietzsche and Freud.

PAUL ROAZEN is a Professor Emeritus of Social and Political Science, York University, Toronto. His books include *Brother Animal: The Story of Freud and Tausk* (Knopf, 1969; Transaction, 1990), *Freud and His Followers* (Knopf, 1975; Da Capo, 1992),

Erik H. Erikson: The Power and Limits of a Vision (Free Press, 1976), *Helene Deutsch: A Psychoanalyst's Life* (Doubleday, 1985), *Meeting Freud's Family* (University of Massachusetts, 1993), *Heresy: Sandor Rado and the Psychoanalytic Movement* ([with Bluma Swerdloff] Jason Aronson, 1995), *How Freud Worked: First Hand Accounts of Patients* (Jason Aronson, 1995), and *Canada's King: An Essay in Political Psychology* (forthcoming).

T HE RELATIONSHIP BETWEEN NIETZSCHE AND FREUD is a complex one that has not received the detailed attention it deserves, especially among North American psychoanalysts. In France, though, the influence of Nietzsche in all areas of intellectual life, including psychoanalysis, has been well recognized (Assoun 1980). It is not my intention to unpack the role that Nietzsche has played in the creation of a "French Freud." I am rather more interested in those darker, Nietzschean aspects of Freud's own life and work that are still worrisome today and, moreover, relevant for an understanding of the current French situation. In turn, this approach might prove helpful for anyone interested in those aspects of Freud's legacy which informed, and still inform, the spirit of French psychoanalysis.

It is true that the relationship between Nietzsche and Freud has not been completely overlooked by intellectual historians (see Anderson 1980: 3–29; Mazlish 1968: 360–75). Yet just how disturbing a philosophy Nietzsche espoused, and the ways in which his spiritual subversiveness gets echoed throughout Freud's thinking, have rarely been spelled out. It is easy to show how some of Nietzsche's sayings, such as those on the sources of conscience, strikingly anticipate classical psychoanalytic doctrine; the resemblances are in fact so close as to be almost eerie. "Conscience is not," Nietzsche once wrote, "as is supposed, 'the voice of God in man'; it is the instinct of cruelty, turning in upon itself after it can no longer release itself outwardly" (Nietzsche 1927: 910). Freud himself rarely wrote about positive self-esteem, although some psychoanalysts after him have proposed its key importance; but he did suppose, just like Nietzsche, that moral convictions rest on the internalization of aggression.

Freud went beyond simply discussing the clinical significance of aggressive drives and how they can be deployed against the self. For in 1919, Freud postulated the existence of a death instinct, as disturbing as anything Nietzsche wrote, for instance, in praise of the inevitability of war (Pangle 1986: 140; Strong 1988: ix; see SE 14: 273–300; SE 18: 7–64). In Freud's view the aggression that we fail to turn against ourselves must be directed outward. As Erich Fromm once pointed out, Freud left us with the "tragic alternative" of destroying ourselves or destroying others. Freud could write: "holding back aggressiveness is in general unhealthy and leads to illness" (1973: 463–64); and further: "It really seems as though it is necessary for us to destroy some other thing or person in order not to destroy ourselves, in order to guard against the impulsion to self-destructiveness" (SE 22: 105).

Freud's view came to be that internalization of aggression was the instinctual source of ethics. In this connection, Nietzsche's account of the origins of morality and how we derive our values closely prefigure Freud's later notion of the super-ego. To quote Nietzsche again: "the content of our conscience is that which was, without any given reason, regularly demanded of us in our childhood by people we honoured or feared" (Hollingdale 1973: 150). Behind Nietzsche on the significance of early childhood can be found the thinking of Arthur Schopenhauer; but the curious collapse in our time of Schopenhauer's standing means that a comparison of his ideas and those of Freud is bound to seem an esoteric exercise (see Rieff 1959: 295).

Freud, like Nietzsche, had a prophetic side to him. He was sometimes intent on relentlessly denouncing religion, as in *The Future of an Illusion*. Unlike Nietzsche, however, Freud was willing to propose the tyranny of reason over instinct; religion was in Freud's view a wholly unnecessary institution, a collective superstition that could be abandoned. Freud assaulted religion based on the model of how the individual uses rational intelligence to overcome primal impulses and fears. Despite all of his reformist purposes (as in his criticisms of unnecessary sexual taboos), Freud wanted to go down in history as a scientist. He had, in his view, made certain "discoveries" based on the perception of "facts" which others found unpalatable. Part of Freud's moral fervor came from his conviction that he, unlike others (especially backsliding disciples), had been strong enough to bear distasteful truths. Science involves disciplined self-correction, and Freud was, in principle, willing to take whatever the future might bring in terms of validating his "findings."

In keeping with the scientific cap Freud often liked to wear, he could utter a belief in the self-evident facts of morality. He frequently expressed his dislike of philosophy. He wrote in a 1937 letter: "the moment a man questions the meaning and value of life, he is sick, since objectively neither has any existence: by asking this question one is merely admitting to a store of unsatisfied libido to which something else must have happened, a kind of fermentation leading to sadness and depression" (Freud 1960: 436). Jean-Paul Sartre was fascinated by Freud, even though the current French wave of concern with psychoanalysis ignores Sartre's interesting point of view on the subject. But the issues central to modern existentialism, involving the agonies of choice in the absence of traditional religious directives, were clearly not central to Freud himself. After all, Freud saw meaning everywhere; the death of God did not leave him with perplexing moral uncertainties.

As Freud aged he talked about his "indifference to the world." But this detachment of his also meant that he could write with a sometimes shocking air of seeming superiority: "In the depth of my heart I can't help being convinced that my dear fellowmen, with a few exceptions, are worthless." He was so disappointed in what he had seen of mankind that he maintained: "I have found little that is 'good' about human beings on the whole. In my experience most of them are trash." Freud thought of himself as a kind of superman: "I have never done anything mean or malicious and cannot trace any temptation to do so," but "other people are brutal and untrustworthy" (see Roazen 1969: 182).

In contrast to Nietzsche, Freud was lucky enough to be famous for much of his lifetime. Freud's fame added to Nietzsche's posthumous reputation, and yet also derived strength from it. Almost from the time that Freud had a following, students of his were pointing out analogies in his work to that of Nietzsche. The lines separating and joining Nietzsche and Freud were fully apparent even when Freud was in the midstream of his psychoanalytic career. Of the 1911 meeting of psychoanalysts at the Congress in Weimar, Ernest Jones recorded: "A few of us took the opportunity of paying our respects to Nietzsche's sister and biographer, who lived there, and she professed interest in various connections we had found between her famous brother's psychological insight and what psychoanalysts were now revealing in their daily work" (Jones 1959: 216; see 1955: 86).

Freud's disciples Otto Rank and Heinz Hartmann, and perhaps others as well, brought some of Nietzsche's aphorisms to his attention, and on one occasion Freud incorporated a bit of this material into one of his most famous case histories (*SE* 10: 184). In 1908 two meetings of the Vienna Psychoanalytic Society were devoted to discussing aspects of Nietzsche's work. Freud more than once tried to deny Nietzsche's impact on him, and also claimed that his fascination with Nietzsche was so overwhelming that it prevented him from reading this acknowledged philosophic master. Just before such a disclaimer, one of Freud's most loyal pupils publicly commented: "Nietzsche has come so close to our views that we can ask only, 'where has he not come close?' He intuitively knew a number of Freud's discoveries; he was the first to discover the significance of abreaction, of repression, of flight into illness, of the instincts—the normal sexual ones as well as the sadistic instincts."

It was after this follower's presentation that Freud chose to emphasize his independence, for he was concerned with his autonomy for the sake of establishing his scientific right to priority. The proceedings record Freud remarking on

> his own peculiar relationship to philosophy: its abstract nature is so unpleasant to him, that he has renounced the study of philosophy. He does not know Nietzsche's work; occasional attempts at reading it were smothered by an excess of interest. In spite of the similarities which many people have pointed out he can give the assurance that Nietzsche's ideas have had no influence whatsoever on his own work.

Freud must, however, have had some knowledge, since he was able to insist that "Nietzsche failed to recognize infantilism as well as the mechanism of displacement" (Nunberg and Federn 1962: 359–60).

A few months later we find Freud equally adamant about his alleged ignorance. "Prof. Freud would like to mention that he has never been able to study Nietzsche, partly because of the resemblance of Nietzsche's intuitive insights to our laborious investigations, and partly because of the wealth of his ideas, which has always prevented Freud from getting beyond the first half page whenever he tried to read him" (Nunberg and Federn 1967: 32). Walter Kaufmann, one of those who did the most to whitewash Nietzsche of charges of being a proto-fascist, comments credulously at this point about Freud: "I have never found him to be dishonest about anything" (1980: 268). But as one literary critic has observed, since the meetings of the Vienna Psychoanalytic Society had been specifically devoted to part of Nietzsche's *Genealogy of Morals* and his *Ecce Homo*, "it would scarcely be possible to discuss these works without having read them" (Rudnytsky 1987: 199).

Freud considered himself the expert on the phenomena of self-deception, a subject which Nietzsche prided himself on as well. In this light, Freud's special praise of Nietzsche could not have been more complimentary: "The degree of introspection achieved by Nietzsche had never been achieved by anyone, nor is it likely ever to be reached again." But Freud also had his reservations: "What disturbs us is that Nietzsche transformed 'is' into 'ought,' which is alien to science. In this he has remained, after all, the moralist: he could not free himself of the theologian" (Nunberg and Federn 1967: 31–32).

We now know, thanks to two sets of recently released Freud correspondences, that his debt to Nietzsche was far more direct than one might have ever guessed. At least two of his close friends from young adulthood knew Nietzsche personally. One historian comments: "Although Freud specifically denied reading Nietzsche until late in life, it seems quite probable that his philosophic friendships . . . brought him at least a general knowledge of Nietzsche's outlook much earlier" (McGrath 1986: 139). Another observer notes: "From the correspondence between Freud and his adolescent friend Eduard Silberstein, it is known that in 1873, during his first year at the University of Vienna, the seventeen-year-old Freud had read Nietzsche's published work, which at that date certainly included *The Birth of Tragedy* and probably also the first two *Untimely Meditations*" (Rudnytsky 1987: 198).

In 1900 Freud wrote to his intimate friend Wilhelm Fliess: "I have just acquired Nietzsche, in whom I hope to find words for much that remains mute in me, but have not opened him yet. Too lazy for the time being" (Freud and Fliess 1985: 398). It was no accident that in 1926, when Otto Rank was breaking with Freud, he sent as a seventieth birthday gift to Freud the collected works of Nietzsche; nor should we be surprised to hear that Freud is reported not to have appreciated this reminder from his former student of a spiritual teacher upon whom Freud himself was dependent (Roazen 1975: 412).

I AM NOT BRINGING UP THE ISSUE OF NIETZSCHE AND FREUD, on which much more might be said, only for the sake of tracing out any alleged influence. It is, however, worth noting that Lou Andreas-Salomé, Nietzsche's earliest popularizer and a woman that he supposedly proposed marriage to, was later a member of Freud's circle in Vienna and actually became a practicing psychoanalyst. (The complexities of Nietzsche's letters to her seem to me awesome; her own subtleties can be demonstrated in the diplomacy of her correspondence with Freud and the diary of her time in Vienna [Freud and Andreas-Salomé 1972; Andreas-Salomé 1964]). But nothing is more tricky, in the history of ideas, than trying to trace out the impact any one thinker has on another.

My main purpose in raising the Nietzsche-Freud problem has to do with contemporary political psychology. It is my conviction that theoretical inquiry in the field has been relatively neglected. Partly, this is a consequence of the past arrogance of political theorists within political science; the subject of social thought was considered to be an aristocratic preserve, above the hurly-burly of political life, and its study was pursued as the snob part of the academic discipline. When Harold Lasswell first proposed the significance of psychopathological thought for political science as a whole, he was understandably disdainful of the more traditional means of political knowledge and education. He was himself, of course, well educated in social philosophy, and his private family letters display a degree of artistry which now seems remarkable (Togerson 1987). In any case, a concern with the implications of modern psychology should lead, in the long run, to a rapprochement with social philosophy.

In addition to my general objective in bringing up the link between Nietzsche and Freud, I have a more specific one: to match the horrifying sides of Nietzsche, which were responsible for his reputation sinking to a low point during World War II, with spooky aspects in Freud. (Jones's account of analysts going to visit Nietzsche's sister was dissociated from the information that Hitler also paid a courtesy call.) Nietzsche and Freud both emerged from the underground of Western thought, and they each sought to challenge some key aspects of traditional morality. The most frightening parts of psychoanalysis, which were accurately perceived by some of Freud's earliest adherents, are harder to spot nowadays.

Even a thoroughly sophisticated analyst was so appalled by some aspects of the Freud–Jung correspondence when it finally appeared as to wonder publicly whether it should ever have been published (Rycroft 1974). Nietzsche was a favorite author of Jung's, and the two large volumes based on his 1934–1939 seminar on *Zarathustra* have now been published (Jung 1988). It is a tribute to Jung that he took the philosophic implications of psychoanalysis more seriously than Freud himself did. However, Jung's interest in Nietzsche reached its height precisely when Jung was collaborating with the Nazi regime in Germany.

For a variety of reasons, Freud's work since his death has been tamed and conventionalized, especially in North America. Psychoanalysis is now a profession with thousands of practitioners, and the field has had a powerful impact on how we think about ourselves; to be reminded of the most disquieting aspects of Freud's teachings is to threaten not only the professional status quo of analysis, but our sense of ourselves which has come, in part, to rest on acknowledging his seminal contribution divorced from its more alarming components.

Each time one of Freud's undiscovered texts emerges, establishment figures can be found to deplore the jolt to preconceived contemporary thinking. One should not underestimate the extent to which intellectuals have played a part in prettifying the historical Freud. This was true, for example, in connection with the 1966 publication of the Freud-Bullitt study of Woodrow Wilson, and also more recently with the publication of one of Freud's "lost" metapsychological essays. Loyal partisans wanted to minimize Freud's hand in the Wilson manuscript and in a similar spirit demoted Freud's own title—"Overview of the Transference Neuroses"—to a subtitle in the published version of the essay. Since the phylogenetic aspects of Freud's argument were so worrisome, the publication came out as *A Phylogenetic Fantasy* (Freud 1987). But Freud's most speculative sides, however much we may not want to go along with them now, were an intrinsic part of his creative achievement.

Fixing Freud up so that his public image will be good for the business of his profession in our time is one thing. But recently we have had the first indications that some of Freud's correspondence to his sister-in-law Minna from the historically most critical part of their emotional involvement with each other may have been destroyed. Although I have been skeptical for years now about the legend of an affair between Freud and Minna, I do not for a moment think that if it were in fact true this would lessen Freud's stature. On the contrary, their ability to function in the face of such unconventionality would be a tribute to their largeness of spirit. It would also be a sign that Freud considered himself entitled to go beyond accepted conventions of good and evil; after all, technically, his involvement with a sister-in-law would have been a form of incest.

Aside from exploring biographical questions, in the period since Freud's death many revisionists have sought to correct the harsh, negativistic imbalances in Freud's work. Outside of France, one cannot find any concrete traces of Nietzsche in current psychoanalytic periodicals. But from a clinical perspective, the concept of a death instinct, for instance, which almost none of Freud's followers endorsed and which seems a notion scarcely even remembered today among American analysts, can by itself lead to therapeutic despair and nihilism. A large block of disturbingly pessimistic thinking lay behind Freud's death instinct theory, and it is this side of Freud which has been widely but imperceptibly influential. This was of course an issue that Erich Fromm tried to bring up in the course of defending himself against Herbert Marcuse's famous critique of neo-Freudianism (Fromm 1958: 313–20).

Erik H. Erikson and others, most notably Donald W. Winnicott, tried to highlight the more positive aspects of psychotherapy, all the time maintaining their respective ties of continuity within the Freudian framework; no one who wants to influence how others think can enjoy the perils of being excommunicated from the ranks of the psychoanalytic faithful (Roazen 1976). Still, it is not a simple matter to inject healthy-mindedness into the heritage Freud bequeathed us. Unfortunately, analysts who have been writing in Freud's school, as well as those who have tried to set up alternative formulations, have not often had Freud's own philosophic sophistication, and well-meaning people have, with the best of intentions, committed themselves to some rather simple-minded notions about health and emotional "growth."

From the point of view of today's political thought, the most upsetting sides to Freud's thinking still have something important to teach. One could itemize, for example, all the occasions on which Freud quotes with approval Goethe's Mephistopheles, or consciously identifies himself with the devil. Freud wrote and said some absolutely shocking things, even if contemporary psychiatrists are apt for reasons of their own to downplay them.

Yet Freud flourished on controversy, and I would guess that he would have relished the central standing which even radical feminists seem to have accorded to his work. Freud has more often been attacked than ignored, and he thought such "resistances" were a sign of the secure, ultimate triumph of his message. For me at least, one of the chief attractions in Freud's whole outlook is the challenge he continues to pose to how we think about things, and the threat psychoanalysis poses for conventional political thought. Freud's concept of the unconscious does not readily suit the needs of North American social science. There was a mystical side to him, a disdain for the provable that his New World practitioners have chosen to try to forget—even as they sometimes canonized his writings. Freud was memorably telling us something about the limits of human rationality and what we cannot expect ever to know. Despite his occasional utopianism about the possibilities of scientific knowledge, on the whole Freud stood for the inevitability of suffering, the dark and tragic side of life.

One might go through the corpus of Freud's work and quote some of his letters and sayings in order to demonstrate his radical side. For instance, he did not mind speaking ill of the dead. Let me cite a sentence of his from a letter to Lou Andreas-Salomé written after the suicide of Victor Tausk. I got in trouble with many orthodox analysts, and especially Anna Freud, for daring to use this particular demonic passage, one which had originally been expurgated from Freud's published letters without even the benefit of the ellipses that indicate an omission. (After my work was in print, the cuts in the letter were abandoned and the words restored in the subsequent editions.) Tausk had been a devoted follower of Freud's for a decade; for a variety of reasons, professional and personal, Tausk sent Freud a touching suicide letter before tragically ending his own life. Freud then wrote a glowing, long obituary for Tausk. But Freud had privately come to view Tausk as a nuisance and a bother, and he wrote Lou, who had once been Tausk's lover: "I confess I do not really miss him; I had long taken him to be useless, indeed a threat to the future" (Roazen 1969: 140). Freud's comments to Arnold Zweig after Alfred Adler's death are equally arresting (Roazen 1975: 209).

It is clear to me that we must take the savage side of Freud along with the rest of him. For it was in Nietzsche's own spirit that Freud was determined to defy traditional proprieties. When in 1930 his mother, an old woman of ninety-five, finally died in Vienna, Freud chose not to attend the funeral and instead wrote that he had sent his daughter Anna to "represent" him. It seems scary that he could stay home and write a letter to a newborn American relative: "Welcome as a new output of life on the day great-grandmother was buried. Great uncle Sigmund" (Roazen 1985: 291).

To move from a biographical to a more theoretical level, Freud's assumption of the universality of bisexuality was intended to have a host of disturbing implications. Freud was proposing that human sexuality was at bottom incapable of gratification and that mankind was destined to self-torture. At the same time Freud's convictions about bisexuality gave him a powerful interpretive handle, a means of control; in fact, Otto Rank thought that Freud's concept of "unconscious homosexuality" was his way of tyrannizing over people in his circle of followers.

Freud thought up bold ideas but was apt also to faint at the sight of blood; his father had thought this trait boded ill for Sigmund's medical career. In his day-to-day life Freud was a conventional late-nineteenth-century physician; a barber came to his apartment every day to trim his beard, and he was surrounded by a large family— and six servants. The psychoanalytic movement became an extension of his own family. (It would be hard to think of a greater contrast to Nietzsche's own tortured, lonely existence.) Freud once said that he was so much "a petit bourgeois" that he could not approve of one of his sons getting a divorce or a daughter having an affair (Bertin 1982: 155). But however sexually conformist Freud made himself appear, in his thinking he dared to be outrageous—again, a side of him which is too often underestimated. He could be most arbitrary just when he was appearing the most cautious. It seems scarcely possible to untangle just what he was saying (besides being defiant) when he wrote: "I stand for an infinitely freer sexual life although I myself have made very little use of such freedom. Only so far as I considered myself entitled to" (Freud 1960: 308).

Freud saw himself, and those he cared most about, as exceptions; the title to his *Beyond the Pleasure Principle* was clearly meant to echo a Nietzsche text. Twice, in writing about his theory of dreams at the turn of the century, he put the phrase "transvaluation of all psychical values" in quotation marks, without having explicitly mentioned Nietzsche's name (*SE* 4: 330; *SE* 5: 655). Freud's notion of a compulsion to repeat almost sounds like a silent mockery of Nietzsche's view of perpetual recurrence of the same thing.

Although Jacques Lacan may have been expelled from the International Psychoanalytic Association with Freud's daughter Anna's approval, Lacan, like Wilhelm Reich and other so-called deviants before him, was building on a heretical streak within Freud himself. But we should probably not romanticize Lacan's heretical stance in the history of psychoanalysis. According to the usual story, Lacan was a hero because he refused to go along with the conformist thinking of the Anglo-American psychoanalysts. (Lacan, of course, made the term ego psychology into an uncontestably bad concept in Paris; Lacanianism was in some ways the equivalent to our own anti-psychiatric movement.) Yet if we follow Elizabeth Roudinesco in her encyclopedic *Jacques Lacan & Co.*, Lacan's life was consumed with his efforts to win recognition from the International Psychoanalytic Association. In effect, if Lacan failed to prevent his own excommunication, it was not for want of trying. Roudinesco provides an interesting but unconvincing rationalization for what she calls Lacan's "relentless pursuit of recognition by the IPA": supposedly he sought to avoid becoming a master in his own school. When one fully realizes what relative nonentities he was organizationally struggling against, then it does seem a poor show for him to have accused others of unnecessarily bowing to the weight of authority. Moreover, although Lacan was right to question the time restraints of the traditional analytic session, his experimentations with time were always in the direction of brevity. And this was not because he was wary of the impact of his personality being too great on his patients. For indeed, Lacan was as high-handed as anybody in the history of psychoanalysis has ever been.

Nonetheless, the liveliness of psychoanalysis in contemporary France owes a tremendous debt to the inspiration that Lacan provided. Indeed, by now there is no city in the world more abuzz with matters psychoanalytic than Paris. The bookstores there are full of fresh works about Freud and the history of his school. One society in Paris has the largest number of members in the world of any unit affiliated with the IPA. Controversies about psychoanalytic issues have become central to the Parisian life of the mind; readers of *Le Monde*, *L'Express*, and *Le Figaro* have been exposed to court battles between rival psychoanalytic factions. Nowhere has psychoanalysis secured itself so completely to university life as in France (although something not too dissimilar is taking place in Argentina today). And while Freud has taken a beating from North American feminists, in France Lacan's brand of psychoanalysis has been the vanguard of the movement for female emancipation. To the extent that these theorists have recognized something in Freud that challenges the preconceptions about the differences between femininity and masculinity, they can claim to have found the "real Freud." In my experience, at least, the French analysts have proven to be as interesting and intellectually stimulating as the group of followers that surrounded Freud.

WHEN IN *CIVILIZATION AND ITS DISCONTENTS* Freud took apart the maxim "love thy neighbour as thyself," he was doing so in Nietzsche's own anti-Christian spirit. With all the ritualistic quoting that takes place in technical psychoanalytic journals (almost always taken out of any historical context), the following example of Freud as a Nietzsche-like warrior of the spirit usually goes unmentioned. Freud had chosen to pick apart "one of the ideal demands" of "civilized" society: "It runs: 'Thou shalt love thy neighbour as thyself.' It is known throughout the world and is undoubtedly older than Christianity, which puts it forward as its proudest claim. Yet it is certainly not very old; even in historical times it was still strange to mankind." Freud then proposed to think philosophically about the Golden Rule:

> Let us adopt a naive attitude towards it, as though we were hearing it for the first time: we shall be unable then to suppress a feeling of surprise and bewilderment. Why should we do it? What good will it do us? But, above all, how shall we achieve it? How can it be possible? My love is something valuable to me which I ought not to throw away without reflection. It imposes duties on me for whose fulfilment I must be ready to make sacrifices. If I love someone, he must deserve it in some way. (I leave out of account the use he may be to me, and also his possible significance to me as a sexual object, for neither of these two kinds of relationship comes into question where the precept to love my neighbour is concerned.) (*SE* 21: 109)

The egocentricity of Freud's argument has gone almost unnoticed; yet even before World War I, Alfred Adler had pointed out the unacceptability of Freud's attack on altruistic love. (Adler came to believe that Freud's whole psychology, including the concept of the Oedipus Complex, reflected the thinking characteristic of a spoiled child.) Freud, however, was unremitting in his discussion of the proposed ideal to love one's neighbor. And the suspicious way Freud viewed other people played its role in his theorizing, as for example when he stated: "Not merely is this stranger in general unworthy of my love; I must honestly confess that he has more claim to my hostility and even my hatred." As if to put the last nail in the coffin of Christian altruism, Freud added the following footnote:

> A great imaginative writer may permit himself to give expression—jokingly, at all events—to psychological truths that are severely proscribed. Thus Heine confessed: 'Mine is a peaceable disposition. My wishes are: a humble cottage with a thatched roof, but a good bed, good food, the freshest milk and butter, flowers before my window, and a few fine trees before my door; and if God wants to make my happiness complete, he will grant me the joy of seeing some six or seven of my enemies hanging from those trees. Before their death I shall, moved in my heart, forgive them all the wrong they did me in their lifetime. One must, it is true, forgive one's enemies—but not before they have been hanged.' (*SE* 21: 109–10)

Freud was repelled by the pieties of Christian moralizing. Readers can be misled by his tendency to make use of Viennese schmaltz, as when he addresses Romain

Rolland in a 1926 letter: "Unforgettable man, to have soared to such heights of humanity through so much hardship and suffering! I revered you as an artist and as an apostle of love for mankind many years before I saw you. I myself always advocated the love of mankind . . . as indispensable for the preservation of the human species." A cynic might think that Freud was ingratiating himself to a Nobel-prize winning author, for in writing to Rolland, Freud approvingly refers to "the most precious of beautiful illusions, that of love extended to all mankind" (Homans 1988: 78).

Elsewhere, Freud sounds more characteristically himself. To his way of thinking, "most of our sentimentalists, friends of humanity, and protectors of animals have been evolved from little sadists and animal tormentors." In accounting for his choice of medicine as a career, he notes that he lacked "any craving in my early childhood to help suffering humanity"; he reasons by polar opposites, like Nietzsche: "My innate sadistic disposition was not a very strong one, so I had no need to develop this one of its derivatives." Dostoevsky gets termed by Freud a "sadist," by which Freud says he means "the mildest, kindliest, most helpful person possible." It is no wonder that an astute commentator finds Freud "capable of adopting a sardonic, levelling, almost Nietzschean tone" (Wallace 1986: 91). A 1924 *Time* magazine cover story about Freud quotes him as having called himself "the only rogue in a company of immaculate rascals."

As much as Freud could perplex and debunk, at the same time he sought to replace traditional ethics with a higher morality. (It will be remembered though that he had criticized Nietzsche for transforming "is" into "ought," and for having remained therefore a "moralist.") It was one of Freud's hopes and expectations that within the psychoanalytic clinical situation lay the potential source of a new ethical approach. In Freud's daily work, despite his many protestations about an analyst's scientific neutrality and his distancing himself from Nietzsche as a "theologian," Freud took for granted a fundamental distinction between "worthy" patients and those he deemed riff-raff, trash, or "worthless." In effect, psychoanalysis was intended by Freud as an ethic of self-overcoming; Nietzsche had likewise held that man had to conquer himself. Freud designed his treatment procedure for an elite; it was not suitable for everyone, even in theory. According to a well-established legend Freud once dismissed an American patient on the most devastating grounds—that "he had no unconscious." (Freud's theories, all of which have an autobiographical side to them, say that wit is a means for expressing hostility.)

If Freud had allowed himself to go further in Nietzsche's direction, he would have entertained more theoretical inquiry about the nature of human values. Freud would then have had to question the ideal nature of the whole concept of psychological normality. Freud's maxim "to love and to work" is a profound answer to the question of what a normal person can be expected to do. But a more philosophically minded observer would question the whole ethics of self-realization which is built into the psychoanalytic procedure. Nietzsche, too, tended to take for granted the morality of self-fulfilment, even as he criticized the prevalent moral beliefs of his era (especially Christianity), and explicitly proposed a different ethical outlook.

Analysts who talk in terms of a "higher" and "lower" self have moved well beyond what Freud himself wanted to consider. Yet even they would be hard pressed to explain on what grounds they justify that which they want to promote as "real." I am reminded of the convicted murderer who, on being released from prison, came for an analysis; the therapist tactfully explained to him that it had not been the "real you" who killed. But the murderer protested that that was the worst of it—for he had felt most like himself when he committed the crime. The analyst self-preservingly decided not to accept the patient for treatment.

As clear as Freud was about what constitutes a neurosis, he was shy indeed on the issue of what he might mean by the concept of psychological health. Opponents of psychoanalytic thinking like Hannah Arendt scorned the whole notion of "sanity"; Arendt sounds almost exultant when the psychiatrists, half a dozen of them whom she derides as "soul experts," certify Adolf Eichmann as "normal" (Arendt 1963: 22). Like Fromm, Arendt wanted to be able to denounce a whole culture; in this case she wanted all the ammunition she could use against Germany and its multiple war crimes. Freud's own reticence about getting involved in the philosophical issue of what is meant by psychological normality allowed for his teachings to be used for conformist purposes that I am convinced he would have disdained.

Even the standard of authenticity would have appeared to Freud, I believe, to be too readily used to be an excuse for human piggishness. Freud did sometimes think of his patients as swine, if not ninnies. (Jung once accused Freud, in a final parting letter, of hating the neurotics he treated.) Freud like Nietzsche did in some sense glorify human instincts; but both took for granted that they were writing for aristocrats of the spirit who could transmute and sublimate human conflicts. Both men had in mind the rare individual who is set apart from the "herd"; and for Freud, this justified all sorts of arbitrary conduct on his part. He did not even feel the need to defend analyzing his daughter Anna. Yet what, after all, did he think he was doing in violating all his own technical rules? Put simply, like Nietzsche, Freud proposed an ethic of transgression.

For Freud to have rejected so much of traditional Western ethical teachings does not mean, anymore than with Nietzsche, that the result has to be a repudiation of all moral values. But when Freud got invited to testify at the Leopold and Loeb trial in Chicago, he ought to have been aware of the dangers of some of his teachings— and of those of Nietzsche. Psychoanalysis was an implied invitation to normlessness, and the dangers of being a "free spirit" were a legitimate concern to skeptics of this new psychology. Norman Mailer once argued that had he not attacked his wife with a knife he would have turned his aggression inward and gotten cancer (Wallace 1986: 130). But whatever the implications of some of Freud's thinking, I am convinced that he was not personally advocating "anything goes." On the contrary, he took for granted a secure set of internalized controls.

In fact, Freud's inner security gave him the grounds for being suspicious of the ideal of altruism and for attacking the love of mankind; he saw humanitarianism as a sublimation of homosexuality, surely as debunking an insight as he ever proposed. (The notion that cooperation rests on a homosexual basis supposedly led a disaffected pupil of Freud's, Otto Rank, to declare: it is either psychoanalysis or humanity.) Like Nietzsche, Freud found in Christianity a corruption of human possibility. But by not doing enough philosophically on the matter of the implications of psychoanalysis for ethics, Freud left it for others after him to make the mistake of believing that the so-called science of psychology can automatically lead to moral values. Humanists like Fromm, Lasswell, and Erikson too readily thought that how we ought to behave could be derived from how we do in fact choose to live. To this extent, at least, Lacan and his followers have been a healthy tonic to some complacent thinking.

Still, although it goes unrecognized in Parisian intellectual circles today, ego psychology took root in America for legitimate therapeutic reasons. Freud's own practices as an analyst left much to be desired; after his death there was a problem of how to make teachable the arbitrary ways in which he had proceeded. Some of his concepts might sound intriguing, but at the same time be deadly from the point of view of successful therapy. For example, according to Freud, the so-called negative therapeutic reaction meant that patients supposedly got worse because of their own unconscious guilt feelings, rather than as a result of the mistakes of the analyst.

Finally, it is all well and good to admire how dazzling Lacan was capable of being, and doubtless that the "American Freud" has as many blind spots as the "French Freud"; but any one country can ill afford to dismiss in a wholesale way what has been accomplished elsewhere. For although psychoanalytic doctrine may look like a uniform system of thought, in fact different societies have taken up and magnified disparate strands in Freud's work that peculiarly suited their own national moods. For this reason, one certainly does not have to accept any of Lacan's technical recommendations to appreciate his criticism of North American analysis. On the other hand, Freud left a body of thought which conscientious followers found unduly negativistic, and American ego psychology was designed to breathe a more caring and optimistic component into Freud's legacy.

But wherever one stands on the uses and abuses of psychoanalysis in its varied incarnations, the figure of Nietzsche should remind us of a trend in psychoanalytic psychology that ought not to be forgotten, and that can valuably complement the human and social sciences today. Most importantly, Nietzsche's example can alert us to the ancient Socratic goal: philosophers should ask the most basic kinds of questions. For indeed, how we ought to live is a conundrum which both psychologists and philosophers need to keep posing. Thinking about how we think does not get enough attention in our kind of society, although it is the glory of that kind of speculative enterprise that I am trying to recall. If such an exercise takes us to the depths of intellectual history, even to its darker aspects, we have to accept that challenge as both the risk and the task of the critical historian.

sublimation: necessity and impossibility

3

François Roustang

translation by Sophie Thomas

Editor's Note

François Roustang takes up the challenge of understanding the psychoanalytic theory of "sublimation" in light of the "irritation" it once gave French analyst Jean Laplanche. As Roustang suggests, sublimation has always been difficult to define. For how can we account for the transition from sexuality to the "higher asexual aims" of, say, painting and poetry? But if, instead, we claim that the asexual is really independent of the sexual, then psychoanalysis as a theory fails.

Roustang turns directly to Freud's texts, and finds that he never justified his use of sublimation. On the contrary, Roustang argues that Freud adopted the term "sublimation" on the strength of its double association with "the sublime" of artistry, and the "sublimation" of chemistry. And thus it became in Freud's hands a "magic word" or "trick" that diverted critical attention away from its stunning ambiguity. Roustang further demonstrates that sublimation rests on the neurological assumptions of Freud's flawed, abandoned, pre-psychoanalytic *Project for a Scientific Psychology* (1895).

Consequently, Roustang reads Laplanche's efforts of explication as just another loyalist ploy to legitimize a theory that is wrong. For according to Roustang, one must either give in to the psychoanalytic sorcery or try something else. With his interesting consideration of "imagination," Roustang opts for the latter. Those interested in the creative process, the limits of psychoanalytic theory, and the vagaries of discipleship will find this essay fascinating.

FRANÇOIS ROUSTANG is a psychoanalyst in Paris, and a Visiting Professor at Johns Hopkins University, Baltimore, and at Emory University, Atlanta. His books have appeared in English as *Dire Mastery: Discipleship From Freud to Lacan* (Johns Hopkins, 1982), *Psychoanalysis Never Lets Go* (Johns Hopkins, 1983), *The Quadrille of Gender: Casanova's Memoirs* (Stanford, 1988), and *The Lacanian Delusion* (Oxford, 1990). His newest book is *Qu'est-ce que l'hypnose?* (Minuit, 1994).

A PPROACHING THE PROBLEM OF SUBLIMATION is an undertaking beset by difficulties. At the beginning of his course in 1976, Jean Laplanche, unquestionably the best interpreter of Freud's work, asked:

> Why sublimation? Because it's a particularly irritating problem. Previously, Pontalis and I had designated it as a basic need, as if sublimation didn't really have a theory—and in effect it hardly does in Freudianism. It is more, then, the measure of this irritating question: is there a non-sexual destiny for the sexual instinct, and yet a destiny not of the order of the symptom? (Laplanche 1980: 119)

Giving way to his irritation, Laplanche went on to ask increasingly serious questions. Either, he said, the non-sexual can be interpreted in the sexual, in which case sublimation doesn't exist, or else sublimation indeed exists and there is thus something of the non-sexual that escapes analysis, which is well known to be unsupportable from a theoretical point of view as well as from the point of view of the procedures of treatment. At this point, to avoid further difficulties, Laplanche wondered whether it wouldn't be better to simply get rid of the concept of sublimation. But since he was a professor who had to prepare a lecture, and since he remained Freudian and lucid, he had to pursue his interrogation and, believe me, it was worth the trouble. I quote:

> If one goes to the bottom of Freudian formulations and examples, one arrives at a far more disturbing paradox: it is not just a case of substituting one goal for another in an instinctual continuum which remains the same overall; in what is sublimated there is left neither the aim, nor the object, nor even the source of the instinct, so much so that we are only to discover, finally, 'sexual energy' itself—but a sexual energy . . . itself 'desexualized,' stripped of its defining qualities, and in the service of non-sexual activities. You see the enormity of the problem, simply, of knowing in what name to speak again of a conservation of energy. . . . What would this abstract energy be and why still characterize it as 'sexual' if it has lost all such characteristics? That which would characterize it, would this at least be its *origin*, its *history*? It would be necessary then to show the genesis of sublimating phenomena, the transmutation of energy, in the step-by-step process of analysis. This is in part what Freud attempts in his study of *Leonardo da Vinci*, but only to admit his failure to restore such a continuity which would, alone, be convincing: it is fully equipped, and very early in the life of the individual, that he sees sublimation emerging, most notably in the form of the painter's vocation.

After this explanation which says everything there is to say about Freudian sublimation, Laplanche threw in the face—or at the feet—of psychoanalysis the ultimate reason not only for his irritation but for his anxiety, which he called "the objection, or the problem of the new." Psychoanalysis is, he said, historically reductive because it is only concerned with the early years, after which it consigns human life to repetition. It is reductive on the level of values since it interprets the complex, the advanced, and the superior with a few impoverished elements such as "the gains of pleasure and intimidation." For psychoanalysis, there is thus nothing new—no invention—in civilization. But then, he exclaimed, "If there is nothing new anywhere, why expect anything new from treatment?"

We have not been listening to one of those delinquent psychoanalysts, traitors to the cause, denigrators of the breast that has fed them, but to a staunch defender, fostering the authority of Freudianism in academia as well as in print. We can thus rest easy as, in the case of this author, orthodoxy seems to co-exist with radical critique and the dismantling of doctrine. We are left with two possibilities: either we forget these radical questions and return to our tranquil beliefs, or we try to propose another vision which would allow us to work with a bit more clarity. It is the second solution that I have chosen, but beforehand, as I cannot content myself with taking for granted the conclusions that Laplanche arrived at, and must return to Freud's texts and re-examine all occurrences of "sublimation" in his work. This will necessitate numerous quotations (not all, rest assured; not those that are repetitive), lest I be accused of distorting or interpreting the texts to suit myself.

The term "sublimation" first appeared in his case history of Dora:

> We surely ought not to forget that the perversion which is the most repellent to us, the sensual love of a man for a man, was not only tolerated by a people so far our superiors in cultivation as were the Greeks, but was actually entrusted by them with important social functions. The sexual life of each one of us extends to a slight degree—now in this direction, now in that—beyond the narrow lines imposed as the standard of normality. The perversions are neither bestial nor degenerate in the emotional sense of the word. They are a development of germs all of which are contained in the undifferentiated sexual disposition of the child, and which, by being repressed [unterdrückung] or by being diverted to higher asexual aims—by being 'sublimated'—are destined to provide the energy for a great number of our cultural achievements. (SE 7: 50)[1]

Sublimation is thus defined as repression or as the diversion of sexually undifferentiated infantile perversions to non-sexual, cultural aims. One begins, then, in a state of perversion (the polymorphous perversion of the infant), and then in the course of development one sees either, by forcing back (here, repression), the appearance of neurosis, or, by diversion, sublimation. Nothing is said of the nature of this diversion, nor any more of the manner in which this passage from the sexual to the non-sexual might operate, nor, finally, of the reason why a part of the sexual instinct escapes repression. Freud simply affirms elsewhere that it varies with individuals, that it results from a particular, innate constitution, or even that it is a given from the beginning. But he always repeats that it is the sexual instinct itself that diverts its energy from the sexual and sublimates it. How the sexual, through its own development, transforms itself in the non-sexual is the enigma which provoked the irritation of Jean Laplanche. (Let us note right away that between 1901, the date of the first draft of Dora's case history, and the end of Freud's life, nothing appeared to illuminate this mystery.)

Here is a text from *Three Essays on the Theory of Sexuality* which offers us a different insight:

> The progressive concealment of the body which goes along with civilization keeps sexual curiosity awake. This curiosity seeks to complete the sexual object by revealing its hidden parts. It can, however, be diverted [*abgelenkt*] ('sublimated') in the direction of art, if its interest can be shifted away from the genitals on to the shape of the body as a whole. (*SE* 7: 156)

Thus, in the passage from the parts to the whole, we acquire access to art and to beauty. Here, no doubt, is a significant and potentially illuminating connection, but on the manner of this passage, which constitutes the whole question, no explanation is given or attempted. Now this amounts to a qualitative leap, which could not, it seems, result simply from sexual curiosity and the desire to know something about the functioning of sexuality. The interest in the shape of the body in its totality is of another order and appeals to an aesthetic dimension, the source of which remains to be named.

It is worrying that Freud does not address this question and that he regards it, henceforth, as settled, as future allusions to the problem of sublimation bear out. For example, again from *Three Essays*:

> Historians of civilization seem to be at one in assuming that powerful components are acquired for every kind of cultural achievement by this diversion of sexual instinctual forces from sexual aims and their direction to new ones—a process which deserves the name of 'sublimation.' To this we would add, accordingly, that the same process plays a part in the development of the individual and we would place its beginning in the period of sexual latency of childhood. (*SE* 7: 178)

There is no question here of linking sublimation with the repression of sexual instincts, as sublimation is defined only by their diversion. What happens in civilization applies equally to the individual. Development explains everything. It is, effectively, true that things happen in this way and, that in the course of development, an interest in civilization becomes apparent. But it is one thing to observe and another to interpret, that is, to attribute to sexual instincts a development that is no longer sexual. Development cannot be the cause of the transformation, for it would then be necessary that development be the cause of development. One sees then that it is the doctrine that is to be questioned, the doctrine that seeks the origin of everything in the sexual instinct. We cannot help but ask ourselves if we are not in the presence of a sleight of hand, of faulty reasoning, or of a lack of basic logic. For if the non-sexual appears in development, it cannot come from the sexual, but must be the product or the effect of a non-sexual force that must be identified.

Freud sometimes recognized the need to appeal to a non-sexual energy, but this is immediately to find in sublimation the *deus ex machina* that must explain everything without itself being explained. Again from *Three Essays*:

> At about the same time as the sexual life of children reaches its first peak, between the ages of three and five, they also begin to show signs of the activity which may be ascribed to the instinct for knowledge or research. *This instinct cannot be counted among the elementary instinctual components, nor can it be classed as exclusively belonging to sexuality*. Its activity corresponds on the one hand to a sublimated manner of obtaining mastery, while on the other it makes use of the energy of scopophilia. (*SE* 7: 194, Freud's emphasis)

Freud, in this passage, acknowledges our objection that the instinct for knowledge, an essential component of the development of civilization, doesn't arise from the sexual instinct. But from what does it arise? He gives us no indication and is satisfied that this instinct for knowledge corresponds to sublimation. Yet this is impossible: that which doesn't arise from the sexual instinct cannot, in any event, be diverted or sublimated from it. Therefore, sublimation doesn't exist. There is no other possible conclusion. There are no grounds for Laplanche's irritation. If he gets worked up, it must be because he wishes to remain loyal to Freud in the face of opposition, against logic and common sense. This concept of sublimation doesn't hold up. I could give you a whole series of written texts after *Three Essays*, but I will stop there, as all come to stumble over the same difficulty, the same enigma, and, when all is said and done, the same absurdity.

The following crucial question, then, arises: how was Freud able to trap himself on this point? How and why was the term "sublimation" taken up as the magic word that dispelled all objections? Quite simply, by the shrewdness inherent in the choice of word. *The Language of Psycho-Analysis* is illuminating on this subject: "Introduced into psycho-analysis by Freud, this term evokes the sense 'sublime' has when it is used, particularly in the fine arts, to qualify works that are grand or uplifting. It also evokes the sense 'sublimation' has for chemistry: the procedure whereby a body is caused to pass directly from a solid to a gaseous state" (Laplanche and Pontalis 1973: 432). With this word "sublimation," Freud wields a two-edged sword. If you hear "sublime" in "sublimation," you see how sexuality can beget the non-sexual; and if "sublimation" suggests chemistry, you have a continuity between the sexual and the non-sexual that is as scientific as that between a solid and a gas. This all seems rather like a magic trick, as even in physics such a transformation does not take place without the introduction of another energy—heat, for example. For the word "sublimation" to make the least sense, a solid would have to transform itself, by its own energy, into gas.

The authors of *The Language of Psycho-Analysis* unassumingly end their entry on "sublimation" with these words: "In the psycho-analytic literature the concept of sublimation is frequently called upon; the idea indeed answers a basic need of the

Freudian doctrine, and it is hard to see how it could be dispensed with. The lack of a coherent theory of sublimation remains one of the lacunae in psycho-analytic thought" (433). In other words, psychoanalysis needs the theory of sublimation, while that theory does not exist. But we must go further: the theory does not exist because it cannot exist, because it is impossible. I think that what we have said here adequately demonstrates this. Sublimation is needed to explain thought, art, and civilization, which would otherwise remain outside the domain of psychoanalysis; it is impossible because one will never be able to derive the non-sexual from the sexual, and never derive from an instinct that which arises from thought. If the non-sexual exists independently of the sexual, that is, if there is the sublime, then the theory of the sexual as the one and only origin collapses without remedy. One must chose. I fear that the deadly contradiction inherent in the necessary and impossible theory of sublimation implicates other territories of the Freudian empire. I've never understood why it was necessary to conclude, from the fact that sexuality penetrates all human activities, that everything comes from the sexual. Nor have I understood why one must confuse, with the Lacanians, the fact that language pervades man with the affirmation that everything is language. This impulse to reduce everything to one explanation must be essential for facilitating the transmission of doctrine, but it has little to do with the recognition and analysis of reality.

Faced with this necessity and impossibility of sublimation, what can we do? Laplanche attempted several times in his course on sublimation to mark out the way toward making the concept intelligible. Reflecting on the instincts, and picking up on a statement of Lagache's, he noted:

> [this concept of object-aim] means precisely that with regard to sexuality, the object cannot be taken separately from the phantasy where it places itself, the breast cannot be taken outside the process of incorporation-projection in which it functions. To come back to our object-source, the source is finally an object-aim-source, which is just another way of saying that it is the phantasy itself—which Freud's text on the phantasy "A Child is Being Beaten" clearly demonstrates. I refer you to the text (where Freud shows so well that *this phantasy is the source of sexuality*). (Laplanche 1980: 66, his emphasis; see *SE* 17: 177)

Certainly Laplanche would not want the phantasy to be autonomous, or else the source of sexuality would no longer be in sexuality. He makes use of the notion of "propping" (anaclisis) to show that phantasy and sexuality always go together.

Elsewhere he cites a passage from *Leonardo da Vinci and a Memory of his Childhood* in which Freud affirms that the libido escapes repression and is sublimated from the beginning, from the origin [*von Anfang an*]. "Sublimation," he comments,

> would not be a turning back, a second turning back with respect to the first stirrings of the sexual: propping and sublimation, in a way, would go together. 'From the origin' there is a sort of coupling when sublimation must take place. True sublimations are 'precocious' . . . I think one would

need to attempt to conceptualize sublimation as taking place at the same moment as the appearance of sexual excitation, [at] the time of the partial sexual instinct. But this term 'precocious' implies temporal, chronological significance, and risks imposing the idea that there can only be sublimation in the earliest years of life. Doesn't there exist the possibility, however rare, for late sublimation, and in particular, must we abandon the idea of sublimation taking place during analysis? (Laplanche 1980: 111)

In other words, Laplanche wants not only sublimation to have existed from the beginning, but also that it could be delayed—in short, that it always exists and has always existed. Isn't it odd that sublimation, initially defined as displacement during development, could be attributed the same duration as the sexual instinct itself?

What can we draw from these two quotes and commentaries? It is clear that Laplanche wishes to safeguard Freudian doctrine at all costs. He is thus obliged to state and to deceive at the same time, but he says enough to open up a fruitful path forward. In the first of the two passages quoted above, phantasy is given as the source of the instinct. Even if one then affirms that there is no anteriority of phantasy to instinct, one is still obliged to recognize, if this formula is to make sense, that phantasy is not a product of sexuality and is not diverted from it. It comes from elsewhere. But where? One must ask this question. It is to avoid it that the second passage no longer joins phantasy and instinct, but propping and sublimation—two terms already suffused with sexuality in the Freudian vocabulary. The problem is that these terms are at the heart of our questioning.

If sublimation exists from the beginning, one must conclude that the non-sexual exists from the beginning, and that if it did not, it would never exist. But to say that sublimation exists from the beginning is a contradiction in terms, since it has been defined as a diversion of the sexual instinct and as taking place in the course of an individual's development. It is phantasy, rather than sublimation, that is present with sexuality at the origin. Even if one admits that phantasy, at the time of its appearance (whether delayed or precocious), is indissociable from sexuality—and this is what is meant by propping—it cannot be made into a product of sexuality or else it would not be "the source of sexuality." You see that this is no longer a case of hoping to develop a theory of sublimation. The very fact of wanting to continue using the term engenders inextricable confusion. It is true that nothing prevents us—and we can't seem to help ourselves—from using terms any which way.

Having arrived at this point, it is necessary to take a leap. But by way of preparation, and before proposing a solution to the problem concerning us, I would again like to quote two texts. In "'Civilized' Sexual Morality and Modern Nervous Illness," Freud wrote: ". . . experience shows as well that women, who, as being the actual vehicle of the sexual interests of mankind, are only endowed in a small measure with the gift of sublimating [*die Gabe der Sublimierung*] their instincts . . ." etc. (*SE* 9: 179). It would be women, of course, who come to extract the truth of this question from the creator of psychoanalysis. Sublimation, the possibility of sublimation, is a gift, something that comes from elsewhere, that so resembles as to be mistaken for inspiration, since it is poets, painters, and sculptors—these pillars of civilization—who posed the crucial problem for Freud: how, from the sexual, can there emerge that which diverts and exceeds it? You have thus heard clearly that sublimation is a gift, something which falls to us without our being able to demand it.

The second text comes from the end of the postscript to the case history of Dora, and opens up the possibility of the new in treatment. Freud speaks of transference (a word, as you know, that he first used in the plural to designate representations which the analysand draws from the person of the analyst to tell his story):

> They are new editions or facsimiles of the impulses and phantasies which are aroused and made conscious during the progress of the analysis; but they have this peculiarity, which is characteristic for their species, that they replace some earlier person by the person of the physician. To put it another way: a whole series of psychological experiences are revived, not as belonging to the past, but as applying to the person of the physician at the present moment. Some of these transferences have a content which differs from that of their model in no respect whatever except for the substitution. These then—to keep to the same metaphor—are merely new impressions or reprints. Others are more ingeniously constructed; their content has been subjected to a moderating influence—to *sublimation* as I call it—and they may even become conscious, by cleverly taking advantage of some real peculiarity in the physician's person or circumstances and attaching themselves to that. These, then, will no longer be new impressions, but revised editions. (*SE* 7: 116)

We can now return to the question concerning us: where does this gift come from which allows for sublimation, in the sense of passing to the sublime, to something higher, to grandeur and elevation; and from where, once again, come these representations that will open treatment up to something new? Laplanche replied that it was phantasy. We have restricted the meaning of this word to that which traps the neurotic in his symptoms. Phantasy in Greek, from where Freud draws, refers simply to the image. We should also note that *fantasma*, in Aristotle's *Parva Naturalia* for example, is often translated as representation. What sets sexual energy in motion is nothing but the image or, to refer it to a faculty, nothing but the imagination.

When Freud sees one of the characteristic traits of sublimation in the passage from the parts to the form of the body in its totality, he refers to the essence of phantasy and the imagination or, simply, of thought. If the sexual instinct has a particular interest in the parts of the body most likely to satisfy it, the phantasy that excites it is already a function of the totality.

If Laplanche emphasizes that it is not possible to speak of the temporal anteriority of sexuality over phantasy, since this latter is present from the beginning, it is because phantasy refers to an anteriority of structure—*non tempore, sed natura*— as the image which doesn't precede in time is always anticipatory, since it connects and assembles. There are no representations which do not differentiate themselves by their relation to all other possible representations. This is the privilege of human thought, what Aristotle called the active imagination to distinguish it from the merely passive imagination with which animals are supplied.

I would like to take up again, in a few words, the reasoning I have attempted to follow. Since the sexual cannot be diverted to the non-sexual, one must appeal, for this diversion to take place, to another force: that of phantasy, which should not be restricted to its pathological sense, but which evokes the anticipatory power of the imagination for the human being—the imagination which, we know, not only manifests itself in waking life, but during the night through dreams.

Here we find ourselves back to Freud and, you will see, to sublimation. Where, in effect, does this term "diversion," which defines sublimation, come from if not from the psychic apparatus constructed to understand the nature of dreaming, an apparatus itself invented according to the neurological model proposed in Freud's "Project For a Scientific Psychology"? And what does this "Project" teach us? First of all, that neurons are reservoirs of energy, but that the source of that energy is external, that is, diverted. Then, that neurons are exclusively stimulating elements, and consequently, when the amount of energy becomes too great, it must be repressed or deflected. It follows that everything that happens in the brain comes from outside (either from the somatic or from the surrounding environment), and that the brain is weakened by this surplus of energy. Thus the deflection or diversion of sexual energy, which is assumed to make sense of sublimation, will come to Freud later as a scientific truth without any need of further justification. The theory of dreams will be established according to the same model; their cause must be sought out either in somatic stimuli, or in diurnal residues from the external world.

Yet contrary to what certain psychoanalysts still claim, neurophysiology has never supported these assumptions and even today runs in a diametrically opposed direction. In reality, neurons make use of their own energy sources. There is thus no grounds for appealing to a flow of energy passing from one neuron to another. Moreover, this energy has no need of being deflected or repressed because neurons have their own inhibiting systems. Cerebral energy is already located in the brain, and is endowed with its own autonomous activity and regulatory system. This, evidently, does not mean that diurnal residues and sexual themes do not make up part of the material of dreams, but rather that neither one nor the other is the cause of dream processes.

What Laplanche says of the presence—always and from the beginning—of phantasy accords well with the findings of modern neurophysiology. Phantasy, or more broadly, the imagination during waking and dreams during sleep, is given from the start by cerebral activity. The possibility of art and civilization exists as soon as there is a human brain. It is futile to wait until the age of sexual curiosity or the desire for knowledge for something sublime to appear. An infant already thinks, since he is able to note differences and to express his interests; he is eager for knowledge and establishes correspondences. His development, as there is certainly a development, finds its basis in all the characteristics of the human being as they are all, already, present. Each neuron is simultaneously active and passive; it transmits from a position of autonomy. If cerebral activity is essentially endogenous, it is already in relation to the exogenous: it is endogenous in order to be exogenous, it apprehends the world and the world allows itself to be apprehended by it. Everything is potentially given, and the action which is at the same time that of thought, of affectivity, of sensibility, partially achieves at each instant the potential totality which the future anticipates.

If things function in this way, and indeed they do, then we have no further need to irritate ourselves by seeing psychoanalysis twist itself toward regression, confine itself to reduction, or extenuate itself through repetition. Cerebral activity (or the imagination, or dreams) does not have its cause in the past history of an energy which must painfully accumulate, deflect, and divert itself—it is already the force of the future, which has so far only manifested itself, because of the limits and traumas of history, in a restrained manner. But it is possible to deploy it anew, to open it, as poets do, to new worlds. We must stop thinking that dreams are the guardians of sleep because they satisfy an infantile sexual desire, or that their cause is in the bygone days of infancy and that we have only to know it in order to be delivered of our troubles. The cause is rather in a "not yet," the efficacy of which resides in the fullness of the relation that we propose. It is the imagination and dreams that make humans grow, and we are left to demonstrate it.

NOTES

1. *Trans:* Roustang points out here that he has corrected the usual (French and English) translations of this passage, which read *Unterdrückung* as "suppression" rather than "repression," and which transform non-sexual into sexual aims.

fear of birth: freud's femininity

4

Kelly Oliver

Editor's Note

Freud has been both attacked and praised for his views on women and feminin-ity. To the extent that Freud, for example, emphasized the inevitability of female masochism, he seemed to play into the hand of patriarchy. But Freud also empha-sized the universality of human bisexuality and seemed to challenge the norms of patriarchy.

In this essay, Kelly Oliver demonstrates that Freud's view of femininity was ambiguous and even fetishistic. She argues that Freud may have taken certain steps toward a "feminine other," but in each case took those steps back. Thus Freud acknowledged the child's initial bond with the mother only to undermine that relation by postulating the mother's masculinity; similarly, Freud equated or reduced the clitoris to a (little) phallus. In other words, Oliver argues that the Freudian measure was never femininity, but always masculinity. Ultimately, then, she thinks Freud was less concerned with the "problem" of femininity than with the problem of how the masculine originates in the feminine. And although this, according to Oliver, has little to do with women, it has everything to do with Freud's "fear of birth."

Oliver makes a convincing and succinct case for her position and provides an excellent overview of, and introduction to, the important debate between Sarah Kofman and Luce Irigaray on Freud and femininity.

KELLY OLIVER is an Assistant Professor of Philosophy at the University of Texas at Austin. She is the author of *Reading Kristeva: Unraveling the Double-bind* (Indiana, 1993), *Womanizing Nietzsche* (Routledge, 1995), and editor of *Ethics, Politics and Difference in Julia Kristeva's Writing* (Routledge, 1993).

Throughout history people have knocked their heads against the riddle of the nature of femininity—"Heads in hieroglyphic bonnets, Heads in turbans and black birettas, Heads in wigs and thousand other Wretched, seating heads of humans" [Heine] . . . Nor will *you* have escaped worrying over this problem—those of you who are men; to those of you who are women this will not apply—you are yourselves the problem.

—Sigmund Freud, "Femininity"
in *New Introductory Lectures on Psychoanalyis*

MANY FEMINISTS HAVE WONDERED whose sweating heads have knocked against the riddle of femininity. To whom is Freud speaking? To whom is femininity a mystery? And who can we trust to solve this riddle? This riddle cannot be solved by contemporary science or psychoanalysis (*SE* 22: 114). Freud tells "us" all he can about femininity, but admits that it is "incomplete and fragmentary." Freud says that we will have to wait for the scientists or turn to the poets to solve the riddle of femininity (135). In other words, even if he cannot solve it, there are other men who might be able to. It seems clear that Freud addresses himself to other men about women. Women and femininity are his object, but not participants, in the discussion.

Sarah Kofman argues, however, that Freud did not want to "speak among men" and exclude women from his discussion of femininity. First, she argues that Freud explicitly addresses himself to a "mixed public": "Ladies and Gentlemen . . . " Second, she agues that Freud is trying to "establish complicity with the women analysts so as to clear himself of the suspicion of 'antifeminism'" (Kofman 1985: 104). Third, she argues that Freud cannot be excluding women because to do so he would have to assume that women are the opposite of men, which is what Freud is arguing against with his bisexuality thesis—Freud claims that all humans, especially women, are innately bisexual, both masculine and feminine.

I disagree. In spite of Freud's ironic "ladies and gentlemen" and his flirtation with the women analysts—I will come back to the bisexuality thesis—it seems undeniable that he makes women the objects of his investigation while men are the subjects: "Nor will you have escaped worrying over this problem—those of you who are men; to those of you who are women this will not apply—you yourselves are the problem" (*SE* 22: 113). Kofman admits that Freud makes women his accomplices in their own objectification, oppression, and silencing (Kofman 1985: 47, 222). And even though she defends Freud as addressing women as subjects, Kofman argues that Freud creates women as the type of object for psychoanalysis that he takes them to be: he/psychoanalysis makes women into hysterics. I maintain that Freud not only excludes the possibility of women subjects in his discussions of femininity, but also makes women into a particular kind of object of psychoanalysis, the hysteric.

One of Kofman's most powerful examples of how Freud turns women into hysterics is her interpretation of Freud's dream of Irma's injection. Freud interprets the dream to be a manifestation of his wish not to be responsible for Irma's continued pains. At one point in the dream, as Freud recounts it, Irma refuses to open her mouth and Freud attributes her reluctance to "female recalcitrance." Kofman argues that what Freud's dream tells him is that he has injected his female patients with a dirty solution, psychoanalysis, that makes their sexuality dirty and shameful:

> If Freud has such an urgent need to excuse himself, it is because he knows perfectly well that he himself is the criminal. Not only because he has not yet cured Irma, but, as another part of the dream indicates, because he himself (a transgression attributed in both the dream and the interpretation to his friend Otto) has infected her with his symbolic-spermatic "solution"—trimethylamin—injected with a dirty syringe. The term "trimethylamin" brings to mind the learned solutions he has thrown in his patient's faces: if Irma and all indomitable women refuse to open their mouths and their genitals, it is because Freud has already transformed each of these organs into a "cavity filled with pus," has closed women's mouths himself, has made them frigid, by injecting them with a learned, malignant, male solution. (47)

Kofman suggests that the dream of Irma's injection is another manifestation of Freud's fear of femininity and his fear of listening to women; he is afraid of the terrifying sight of open female genitals or their open mouths.

Many of his feminist critics argue that Freud fears feminine sexuality (for example, Cixous [1980: 245–64], Irigaray [1985], and Gallop [1982]). His bisexuality thesis might be further evidence of this fear. In "Female Sexuality" he argues that women are more bisexual than men because they have two erotic zones, one masculine and one feminine; they are hermaphrodites of a sort. Freud claims that the women in his audience who are intelligent enough to understand him are more masculine than feminine (*SE* 22: 116–17). But the bisexuality of men goes unanalyzed. What of the feminine in men? Freud protects himself against this radically other sexuality, feminine sexuality, this "Minoan-Mycenean civilization," as he calls it, by always comparing the situation of women to the situation of men, by turning women into men.

There are many ways in which Freud turns women into men, femininity into masculinity. He maintains that for boys and girls the first love object (with which they identify) is the phallic mother; this makes the mother masculine and it makes infants of both sexes masculine identified. In addition, Freud claims that there is only one libido, masculine libido. Also he defines all sexuality, both masculine and feminine, in terms of castration—having or not having the penis.[1] He reduces the clitoris to an inferior penis—never mind that this contradicts his claim that women are already castrated. In "Female Sexuality" he explicitly claims that "[i]t will help our exposition if, as we go along, we compare the state of things in women with that in men" (*SE* 21: 227).

It will be profitable at this point, in order to analyze Freud's troubled relation to the feminine, to enter a debate between Irigaray and Kofman over Freud's equation of phallus and *logos*. Luce Irigaray argues that by turning women into men and femininity into masculinity, Freud excludes women and the feminine from culture, from *logos* (Irigaray 1985: 14). In *The Enigma of Woman* Sarah Kofman, in the name of "intellectual honesty," defends Freud against Irigaray's powerful criticism of "Femininity." She maintains that:

> ... nothing in the text ["Femininity"] justifies Luce Irigaray's reading (according to which Freud, like Aristotle, deprives women of the right to the logos and phallus alike). We have seen that things are not that simple. And even supposing that Freud wished to speak "among men" of the enigma of femininity (which is not the case), that would not suffice to condemn him as a "metaphysician." (1985: 104)

While Kofman is right that Freud's text is fraught with ambiguities, there is plenty in Freud's "Femininity" to justify Irigaray's claim that his theory deprives women of the right to the *logos* and phallus. And Irigaray does not "condemn Freud as a metaphysician" because he speaks among men about women. Rather, Irigaray condemns Freud as a metaphysician because of the centrality of presence in his account of the evolution of subjectivity and sexual difference: for Freud everything hinges on the sight/presence of the male organ, and both masculine and feminine sexuality are defined in terms of its presence.

Irigaray's "condemnation" of Freud as metaphysician, however, is not unambiguous. She maintains that Freud makes a double move in relation to metaphysics:

> Thus Freud would strike at least two blows at the scene of representation. One, as it were, directly, when he destroys a certain conception of the present or presence, when he stresses secondary revision, over-determination, repetition compulsion, the death drive, etc., or when he indicates, in his practice, the impact of so-called unconscious mechanisms on the discourse of the "subject." The other blow, blinder and less direct, occurs when— himself a prisoner of a certain economy of the logos, of a certain logic, notably of "desire," whose link to classical philosophy he fails to see—he defines sexual difference as a function of the a priori of the same, having recourse, to support this demonstration, to the age-old processes: analogy, comparison, symmetry, dichotomic oppositions, and so on. When, as a card-carrying member of an "ideology" that he never questions, he insists that the sexual pleasure known as masculine is the paradigm for all sexual pleasure, to which all representations of pleasure can but defer in reference, support, and submission. (1985: 28)

So, while in one move Freud exposes a crisis in the metaphysics of presence, with a second move he closes off the possibility of acknowledging the impact of that crisis. The primary processes call into question the metaphysics of a fully present subject, but the identification of those primary processes with the masculine libido forces the question and closes off all possible discussion of difference. Irigaray argues that Freud leaves us with an economy of representation of the same, a homosexual economy. Kofman, on the other hand, takes issue with Irigaray's claim that Freud invokes science in the name of this masculine economy of the same. She argues that Freud does not invoke science to reassert sameness, as Irigaray claims, but rather to undermine popular opinions and stereotypes with regard to the sexes, especially the notion that the feminine is passive while the masculine is active (1985: 112, 115).

Yet, if we look at the passage in which Freud most insistently invokes science and denies the connections between femininity and passivity and masculinity and activity, it becomes clear that even while Freud sets up to break down popular prejudice, he reinforces it through his rhetoric. He points out that "[t]he male sex-cell is actively mobile and searches out the female one, and the latter, the ovum, is immobile and waits passively. This behaviour of the elementary sexual organisms is indeed a model for the conduct of sexual individuals during intercourse. The male pursues the female for the purpose of sexual union, seizes hold of her and penetrates into her" (*SE* 22: 114). Then he warns that this reduces masculinity to aggressiveness and that in some species the females are stronger than the males; so it is "inadequate . . . to make masculine behaviour coincide with activity and feminine with passivity" (115). Immediately after claiming that we should not associate masculinity with activity and femininity with passivity, Freud does so anyway. He argues that mothers exhibit activity but their activity is a sort of active passivity necessary to carry on the species. Next he makes a distinction between passivity and having passive aims. He suggests that the female has passive aims but that this does not make her passive. He qualifies this claim by pointing out that we should not underestimate social customs that condition women to have passive aims. But no sooner has he issued this warning than he says "[t]here is one particularly constant relation between femininity and instinctual life which we do not want to overlook"; this constant is masochism (116). So every time that Freud warns us against the prejudices of science, in the very next breath he reiterates them.

Although Kofman is right that Freud allows for women to enter society and have the right to the *logos* and the phallus, women do so only through the masculine. It is only Freud's bisexuality thesis that allows him to admit women into the order of the *logos* because for Freud the feminine is antithetical to the *logos* and the phallus. To feminist ears, Freud sounds outrageous when he says:

> For the ladies, whenever some comparison seemed to turn out unfavourable to their sex, were able to utter a suspicion that we, the male analysts, had been unable to overcome certain deeply-rooted prejudices against what was feminine, and that this was being paid for in the partiality of our researches. We, on the other hand, standing on the ground of bisexuality, had no difficulty in avoiding impoliteness. We had only to say: 'This doesn't apply to *you*. You're the exception; on this point you're more masculine than feminine.' (116–17)

Ultimately Kofman explains the ambiguities in Freud's writings on femininity as manifestations of his fear of death. In the following paragraphs, I will explain them as manifestations of Freud's fear of birth.

The riddle of femininity is really the riddle of masculinity. The question that is really at stake for Freud is how masculinity is possible—how can the male, who was once part of the female/mother, be masculine? It is necessary that Freud explain femininity in order to safe-guard masculinity. If he can't guarantee that the masculine is not identified with the feminine, one possible safe-guard is to make the feminine masculine after all. In this way, even if the masculine is identified with the feminine (or the mother), it is not threatened.

I maintain that Freud's solution to this problem is the fetishist's solution. He argues that little girls are in the beginning little men. That is, their sexuality is phallic and they are more masculine than feminine. In fact this is the mystery of femininity: how do masculine little girls, little men, become women? For Freud a little girl's erotic zone is masculine and her clitoris is a small penis: "Anatomy has recognized the clitoris within the female pudenda as being an organ that is homologous to the penis; and the physiology of the sexual processes has been able to add that this small penis which does not grow any bigger behaves in fact during childhood like a real and genuine penis" (*SE* 9: 217). The clitoris operates as a penis equivalent. Hers, however, as Freud tells us, is obviously inferior. Why is it inferior if it functions in the same way, brings the same phallic pleasure, and, as Freud says, "[f]requent erection of that organ make it possible for girls to form a correct judgment, even without any instruction, of the sexual manifestations of the other sex"? (*SE* 7: 219–20). As Kofman points out, it can only be the size of the girl's penis that makes her inferior. Sexual difference, then, is not a matter of kind or quality, but a matter of degree or quantity—unless at a small enough size the penis becomes feminine. Perhaps this is Freud's fear. He is afraid that the masculine is really feminine.

This is always the fear of players in what Irigaray calls the "game of castration" (1991: 80). Within the economy of castration there is no qualitative difference; everything is measured in terms of quantity. Irigaray criticizes the economy of castration because within it there can be no depth: "To simulate depth in the guise of the bigger or the smaller. To bring erection and limpness into the game of castration. And the other into the same: a comparison between the bigger and the smaller, the harder and the softer, etc., until it becomes impossible to evaluate anything except in terms of *less* and *more*" (80–81). Playing the game of castration, Freud reduces all sexual difference to a question of less and more.

Like the fetishist who cannot bear the mother's castration and substitutes another object for her missing penis in order to protect her from castration (and ultimately reassure himself that he is not castrated), Freud substitutes the clitoris for the missing penis. Oddly enough it is the impossible combination of women's castration and inferior penis that erects masculine sexuality. As Kofman says, "only the Freudian solution, that of granting woman an incomplete sexuality envious of man's penis, makes it possible at once to recognize woman's castration and to overcome one's own castration anxiety" (1985: 89). "Woman's genital organs arouse an inseparable blend of horror and pleasure; they at once awaken and appease castration anxiety" (85).

Like the fetishist, Freud has it both ways. The mother is both castrated and phallic. This ambiguity is necessary for Freud to imagine that masculinity is possible at all. The real problem for Freud is how it is that the male, once part of the woman's body, becomes masculine. His concerns for how the female performs the difficult task of changing both erogenous zones and love objects covers up the prior concern for the male's transition from literal identity with a female maternal body and a psychic identification with the mother to not only a separate body but also separate sexual identity. One way that Freud explains this transition is to invent the masculine mother, the mother who is either phallic or castrated, but never feminine. So Freud's conflicted theory of femininity and the phallic/castrated mother can be read as symptoms of the fetishist's logic. And these symptoms can be read as manifestations of a fear of birth; man fears his birth out of the body of a woman. For Freud there is nothing more frightening than the thought of being buried alive, which is the fear of internment in the maternal womb.

Freud turns all sexuality and all desire into masculine sexuality and desire. While he opens up the discussion of sexual difference, at the same time he closes off the possibility of sexual difference. In this way, as Irigaray suggests, Freud makes a double move to both challenge and protect a metaphysics of presence that favors the presence of the phallus. He resorts to the fetishist's logic in order to insure that the phallus is present in both sexes. So, while he opens up the discussion of an other to representation, the unconscious, repressed and over-determined, at the same time he closes off the possibility of a specifically feminine other. Freud's psychoanalytic theories invite attempts to represent the other but, like more traditional theories of representation, continue to exclude the feminine from representation.

NOTE

1. Both Elizabeth Grosz and Sarah Kofman argue in different ways that Freud's theory presupposes castration in order to set up castration in girls. Grosz maintains that "While it makes perfect sense for the young boy, before he understands the anatomical differences between the sexes, to see the other on a model derived from his own body morphology, it makes no sense at all to claim, as Freud and Lacan do, that the girl too sees the whole world on the model derived from the boy's experience ... [F]or the child herself to understand her [as lacking] requires her to accept castration long before the castration threat" (Grosz 1990a: 17).

can the phallus stand, or should it be stood up?

5

Tina Chanter

Editor's Note

Tina Chanter reconsiders the sex/gender distinction that has become so fundamental to feminist theory, and which she argues has important repercussions for the debate between feminists and psychoanalytic theorists. She suggests that, just as the relationship between sex and gender can be adequately construed neither as necessary nor as arbitrary, but only as contingent, so it is appropriate to see the relation between the penis and the "phallus" as contingent. Whether one belongs to the female or male sex is thus neither irrelevant to the power of the phallus nor determinative of it.

By exposing the Cartesian legacy informing both biological determinism and social constructionism, Chanter attempts to bridge the gap between feminism and Lacanianism. Gender acquisition can be reformulated so that femininity is no longer seen as constructed by society and imposed on a passive subject, but rather as a creative choice that is enacted against a background of specific cultural norms and options—and which is capable of subverting cultural expectations.

Focussing on work by Judith Butler, Moira Gatens, and Jacqueline Rose, Chanter suggests that if the body is not considered neutral or indifferent to gender formation, and if gender choice is not understood according to a simple causal model (biological or social), one can move beyond the impasse that has blocked dialogue between feminists (who seek to change gender configurations) and psychoanalytic theorists (who maintain that sexual difference cannot be reduced to the internalization of social roles). This essay continues the examination of essentialism that Chanter began in her recent book, and provides a formidable survey of and meditation upon issues of importance to anyone interested in feminism and its relation to psychoanalysis.

TINA CHANTER received her Ph.D. in philosophy from the State University of New York at Stony Brook, and currently teaches in the Department of Philosophy at the University of Memphis. She has published numerous articles on continental philosophy and feminism, focussing on the work of Derrida, Heidegger, Kristeva, and Levinas, and is the author of *Ethics of Eros: Irigaray's Rewriting of the Philosophers* (Routledge, 1995).

SECTION I: INTRODUCTORY REMARKS

THE STATUS OF THE PHALLUS HAS BECOME EMBLEMATIC of the extent to which feminists are prepared to tolerate, or engage with, psychoanalysis.[1] The degree to which the phallus as master-signifier is separable from the penis as its bodily referent provides an index of the legitimacy of Lacanian psychoanalytic discourse for feminists of divergent theoretical and political persuasions. The greater the distance that is assured between penis and phallus, it would seem, the more feminism can afford to entertain psychoanalytic hypotheses without fear that they will revert in the last analysis to biological determinism.

Debates between psychoanalytic and feminist theorists have largely been played out on grounds staked out by the same territorial claims that motivated the essentialism/anti-essentialism debate (see Schor 1994; Grosz 1990: 332–44). Both feminist criticisms of psychoanalysis and psychoanalytic defenses in the face of feminist critiques have, until recently, tended to read the relationship of the phallus to the penis according to a feminist grid that is orchestrated by the sex/gender distinction. Thus the penis is aligned with sex, bodies, and nature, while the phallus is associated with gender, society, and culture. A strong relation of dependence between the meaning of the phallus and the penis is taken to imply essentialism, whereas a weak and intangible relation appears to avoid essentialism. To equate the phallus with cultural meaning, or gender, and the penis with the body, or sex, is to reduce phallic signification to a series of assumptions about the sex/gender distinction that need to be questioned.

The explanatory force of appealing to the importance of gender, rather than sex, lies in the apparent flexibility of gender roles as opposed to the ostensible intransigence of bodies. Whereas sex seems to fix sexual identity, gender seems malleable, and therefore open to change. If gender roles are learned, they can also be unlearned or reformed—at least in principle. As Gatens says, the "'spot-lighting' of gender" has a "high explanatory" yield for feminists, "as opposed to the barren category of 'sex'" (Gatens 1991: 139).[2] The idea that "anatomy is destiny" (see *SE* 19: 173–79; Olivier 1989: 53–65), or that women's purpose lies in their reproductive function and all that this implies, is reversed in feminist denials that the body can be a fertile ground of inquiry—an irony that presumably is not lost on Gatens, given her description of sex as a "barren category" for feminists. The enthusiasm for privileging gender over sex arises from the fact that gender avoids, in Gatens' words, the "dangers of biological reductionism" (1991: 139).

It is far from clear that the forces to which explanations of gender variously appeal—under the headings of "culture," "history," or "society"—can be lumped together as if they were more or less identical, as if they carried the same ideological weight, and as if they functioned in similar ways.[3] Understood as the cause of gender roles, Society (or History, or Culture) is presumed to act on unsuspecting and passive agents, who respond to these grand forces with predictable, obedient, and simple acquiescence. In fact the processes by which cultural, social, and historical factors function vary widely, as do their impact on the subjects they are assumed to effects. The theoretical assumptions which are employed to explain these effects often go unstated, but sometimes, on conceptual delineation, prove mutually exclusive. To the extent that cultural, historical, or social considerations—amorphous "factors"—are taken to operate within a largely unquestioned framework of social constructionism that takes for granted a relatively unsophisticated causal model, both these factors and their opposites (equally vague categories such as nature, materiality, and biology) need to be adumbrated more precisely. If these categories are not to be taken as polar opposites that mutually exclude one another, and if the terms of the relationship between sex and gender are not to be reduced to a hierarchy in which one term is posited as the determining cause of the other, a more fluid conceptual framework is called for.

As influential and important as they have been, accounts of gender as imposed by socially prescribed norms leave unexplained several crucial considerations, and lend themselves to caricature. If biological determinism conceives of nature or biology as determinative of gender, feminists have responded by arguing that it is society or culture that shapes gender. In the name of gender, mowing down all who stand in its way, a huge, mythical, amorphous social body ploughs the natural land of sex, and sows the seeds of perfect, more or less identical, blonde, blue-eyed, white-skinned, barbie-doll look alikes.[4] Where the body proves uncooperative, fashion and technology ("cultural" innovations which have changed over time, and which are local to specific societies) provide help of multifarious kinds, including hair-dye, make-up, colored contact lenses, tokenism, and dietary or slimming instructions for those who can't quite make it on their own. Bolstering up this tank-like machine known as "society" we find the body-politic, an image which—as Moira Gatens shows—appeals to very specific bodies, bodies which, it will come as no surprise to learn, do not tend to be black, homosexual, or working class.[5] Implied by this incomplete list, of course, is the litany of minority views which is destined to remain forever unfinished.[6]

Neither will it be surprising to learn that at the root of the problem of defining sex and gender we find the omnipresent Cartesian legacy. Once again, mind-body dualism rears its loquacious gorgon head. Once we pare down the sex/gender distinction, as Gatens has also astutely shown, we are left with a core that is none other than a rehashed version of the rationalist conception of the mind as a "passive *tabula rasa*" (Gatens 1991: 140), and the body as conditioned automaton—a well-oiled machine that behaves (most of the time) as we tell it to. Only, instead of an infinite Cartesian God, it is society that constitutes a determining and all pervasive force, performing indelible lessons on our impressionistic minds, telling us what to do, how to behave, what to wear, how to work out—how to shape, and reshape our bodies—in order to approximate to gender ideals. Now it is culture writ large, rather than some perfect, omniscient, omnipotent, and ultimately incomprehensible deity, that makes us tick. How the body fits into this picture is unclear.

Is it conceived merely (and inadequately) as a kind of vessel or conduit, communicating sensory and social messages to an incarnate mind? Is it a passive material capable of receiving, and—as far as possible—conforming to, cultural norms? If culture tells us how to be, the task for feminists is that of reworking cultural norms. According to supporters of the backlash, feminists treat women as little more than cardboard cut-out figures, arranged with military precision by the sisterhood of politically correct thought-police, the imaginary agents of social conditioning: first the patriarchs, and then the feminists—at least if we are to believe Christine Hoff Sommers, who regards what she calls "gender feminists" as "gender wardens" (1994: 255–75). If feminists could just keep quiet, everything would be just fine. (Haven't we heard this somewhere before?)

While the idea that feminism in reality is orchestrated by vigilante groups is more than a little far-fetched, to the extent that feminism identifies itself with a botched Cartesian consciousness, we need to be prepared to rethink our assumptions. A new set of problems emerges if one accepts that the terms which are often invoked in accounts of gender formation are in need of careful scrutiny. One problem is the implicit appeal to a naive notion of subjectivity which presupposes, among other assumptions, that society affects individuals in the same way, that individuals react to social pressure in a uniform manner, and that the relation between social forces and individual responses can be adequately conceived along the lines of a quasi-behaviorist stimulus-response, or input-output model. The philosophical commitments underlying such a model hark back to Cartesian dualism, as Gatens (1991) has convincingly shown. The metaphysical and epistemological beliefs that support simplistic views about the efficacy of social conditioning are equally pervasive in the biological determinism which social constructionism is so keen to undermine.

Evelyn Fox-Keller suggests that "discussions of gender tend to lean towards one of two poles—either toward biological determinism, or toward infinite plasticity, a kind of generic anarchy." Either gender is "collapsed back onto sex, and science, back onto nature" or "gender and science run free, no longer grounded either by sex or by nature" (1989: 33–44). If we think of society simply as acting upon individuals, where the individual is conceived of as a passive residue of cultural sedimentation, all we seem to have gained by substituting gender for sex is a substitution of culture for nature as the overriding and overdetermining force. So long as the problem is posed in terms of these alternatives, the unspoken allegiance to several assumptions that I want to bring into question remains undisturbed. So long as feminists continue to allow their views to be governed by their rejection of biological determinism, and so long as we continue to employ fairly simplistic notions of the process by which society constructs gender roles, we are liable to fall into a number of traps, not the least of which is the tendency to construe society as a monolithic and unstoppable force, and to build into what we understand by "society" unstated and problematic assumptions. For example, social forces are assumed to affect all women, irrespective of geo-political location,[7] in more or less the same way, and yet at the same time—and in tension with this first assumption—they are also assumed to consist primarily of those pressures that characterize Western, capitalist, post-industrialist societies. The problems that may be more pressing in developing countries, such as controversies over whether women should wear the veil, and the ethics of clitoridectomy, are ignored, neglected, misunderstood and played down (see Ferguson 1989; Mernissi 1987).

How, then, do we account for changes in what counts as acceptable feminine and masculine behaviour? What is it that makes social expectations change? How do we explain, for example, the success of feminism (albeit limited) in challenging and transforming gender stereotypes? How do we account for differences among women? If the process of cultural construction is seen as responsible for creating gender roles, how do we explain individual variations—why aren't all women the same? Why aren't we all equally "successful" at embodying the feminine ideal? Why do we "fail" at our attempts to represent the perfect woman, and how are we able to reject the ideals that society and culture holds up for us to imitate in the form of cinematic, narrative, pictorial, artistic, and even pornographic representations? What accounts for the ability and desire of some women to reject these ideals as inadequate or inappropriate for them? The answers to these questions are various, but the first thing to note is that central to attempts to answer them is the recalcitrance of the body. The recent implosion, within feminist circles, of work on the body (Butler 1993; Grosz 1994; Braidotti 1994; Gatens 1996) is in response to the inadequacy with which feminist theories hitherto have explained bodies—female, or otherwise.

If the need to theorize the body is one of the problems that gender theory must confront, the socialization model of gender identity is found wanting on several other counts as well. It cannot account for variations among individuals, or for the fact that society does not merely produce gender roles to which individuals unhesitatingly conform. Whatever impact social construction has on gender identity, it certainly leaves room for subversion, rebellion, and rejection—which is not to deny its impact, since even if individuals react to stereotypical gender injunctions by refusing them, there is still a sense in which those injunctions govern individual reactions, albeit negatively or indirectly. If a woman prefers wearing black leather to pink flowery dresses, this choice is far from incidentally related to the ideal of femininity that culture holds up for her.

Before going on to address more directly the relation between psychoanalysis and feminism, I want to expand on some of the problems that I have identified with the notion of gender as a social construct that is imposed upon a passive subject. Although I will refer to various authors, I will be drawing, in particular, on the work of Butler (1986: 35–49; 1987: 128–42) and Gatens (1991). After sketching these problems under four headings, I will rehearse the politics of the debate around the phallus/penis distinction, and then go on to formulate some questions that need to be addressed if we are to make any progress beyond the stalemate that tends to characterize the relationship between feminists and the discourse of psychoanalysis.

SECTION II: BEYOND SOCIAL CONSTRUCTIONISM AND BIOLOGICAL DETERMINISM

The Arbitrary or Fictional Connection between Sex and Gender

The relation between sex and gender has been submitted to interrogation of late, so that some feminist theorists have suggested that the link between the two is not merely tenuous, but that it approaches the status of an arbitrary connection. The impetus for re-interpreting this connection as arbitrary, while emanating from various sources—some of which are indicated above—can be sketched briefly, by referring to a few representative theorists, texts, and problems. A key motivation for embracing the idea that gender is not determined by sex, but is rather independent of it, is the possibility for change that this shift opens up. Once it is conceded that there is no necessary relationship between sex and gender, stereotypical gender identifications are capable of being challenged. Not only does this mean that women need not be restricted to feminine roles, and men need not be constrained to masculinity, but also—and for some theorists this is the root of the issue—that fundamental normative assumptions about heterosexuality are brought into question. As Gayle Rubin pointed out in her important article "The Traffic in Women" (1975: 157–210), the heterosexual ethic is closely associated with, even integral to, sex/gender kinship systems. More recently, Monique Wittig (1992) and Judith Butler (1990) have emphasized how the meanings that gender and sex take on are far from innocent of heterosexual imperatives. Butler has also brought into focus the question of "whether gender need in any way be linked with sex, or whether this conventional linkage is itself culturally bound" (1986: 45). Butler says that "it appears that the female body is the arbitrary locus of the gender 'woman'" (35). Posing a question that she sees as implicit in de Beauvoir, Butler asks "whether sex was not gender all along" (46). The logical conclusion of de Beauvoir's position, suggests Butler, is to divorce gender entirely from sex, driving their conceptual differentiation to the point of "absolute difference" (46). It follows from this not only that "both gender and sex seem to be thoroughly cultural affairs," but also that "the natural body—and natural 'sex'—is a fiction" (Butler 1987: 134). As Butler is well aware, the fact that there is a sense in which both gender and sex are fictions does nothing to detract from their pervasive effects. To assert the fictional status of myths, far from defusing them, can be a way of acknowledging their power. Similarly, the suggestion that the phallus has a privileged position as a signifier is made in the context of a mythical discourse—but this need not in any way undercut its influence. I will return to the mythical status of the phallus at the end of the article.

To regard the connection between sex and gender, and the status of each category, as in some sense flexible and malleable, does not mitigate the regulative status of specific conceptions of sex and gender. The normative requirements of heterosexuality can make themselves felt in a variety of ways—and thus can be fluid and changeable within certain limits. Regulatory fictions of sex and gender can be productive, and do not exclude the very subversions that seem to put them into question—for example the existence of sado-masochistic lesbian relations.

The Body is Not Neutral,[8] and Gender is Not Arbitrary

To be identified as a member of the female sex does not necessarily lead to its usual corollary, femininity. Gender is not entailed by sex; femaleness does not necessarily lead to femininity; there is no necessary relation between being a woman and being feminine. But the fact that sex does not determine gender does not imply that their relation is arbitrary—that one's body type is irrelevant to one's gender identification. As a result of his research on transsexuals and transvestites, Robert Stoller

(1968) argued that, in Gatens' words, "The biological sex of a person has a tendency to augment, though not determine, the appropriate gender identity for that sex" (Gatens 1991: 141).

Gatens shows that feminists mistakenly found justification in Stoller's work for positing the relationship between sex and gender as arbitrary. They saw it as opening the way for what might be dubbed gender reprogramming, or degendering.[9] Stoller's work, although it did not in fact posit the relation between sex and gender as arbitrary, was invoked for feminist purposes as if it did. For Stoller, as Gatens says, "a person's gender identity is a result of post-natal psychological influences. These psychological influences on gender identity, he claims, can completely override the biological fact of a person's sex and result in, for example, the situation of the transsexual" (141–42). Gatens observes that Stoller's work "was generally heralded as a breakthrough in the area of sexuality and socialization. As such it was quickly taken up by feminist theorists as offering theoretical justification for the right to equality for all independently of sex" (142). In the euphoria of finding a way out of the "trap" of the body,[10] the temptation for feminists was to embrace what in retrospect look like theoretically naive assumptions about the ease with which gender could be moulded, as if at whim.

Gatens thinks that the relation between femininity and the female body (or masculinity and the male body) can helpfully be construed as contingent, but not as arbitrary (149), arguing that feminist celebrations of gender have resulted in a "neutralization of sexual difference and sexual politics" which can be "traced back to nineteenth century liberal environmentalism where 're-education' is the catchcry of radical social transformation. Much of contemporary radical politics is, perhaps unwittingly, enmeshed in this liberal tradition" (140). What needs to be brought under scrutiny according to Gatens is the "alleged *neutrality* of the body; the postulated *arbitrary* connection between femininity and the female body; masculinity and the male body; and the apparent simplicity of the ahistorical and theoretically naive solution, viz. resocialization" (140).

On the usual feminist account of gender as constructed, not only is the body seen as neutral and indifferent, but it is also posited as subject to consciousness—passive and malleable, rather than inscrutable and resistant. An ahistorical account of gender acquisition is provided (Gatens 1991: 143), and an a priori subject is assumed (Gatens 1991: 144). Cartesian ghosts lurk. Gatens argues, I think rightly, that: 1 a) The body is not "neutral and passive with regard to the formation of consciousness;" b) Consciousness is not primary and determining (the assumption that it is being an implicitly rationalist view); 2) Conscious efforts to change the material practices of culture do not suffice to definitively alter the "historical and cultural specificity of one's 'lived experience'" (1991: 143). While she does not mention Butler, Gatens' article, "A Critique of the Sex/Gender Distinction," can be read, in part, as a critical response to the position Butler endorses in her early accounts of gender (Butler 1986; 1987).[11]

The "degendering" view has difficulty accounting for, among other things, physical symptoms, which exhibit the defiance of the body. It has no way of explaining phenomena that require an understanding of how cultural norms play into our own relationships with our bodies. The anorexic subject, for example, has a complex relationship to her body that cannot be cashed out without taking into account the body image, or the "imaginary body."[12] The illusory gross distension of the stomach that the subject sees when she steps in front of the mirror can only be explained with the help of an account that sees that relation between cultural ideals of femininity on the one hand, and the empirical reality of the anorexic body on the other hand.

> Sixty-nine and a half pounds! I've gained a pound and a half in three days (not counting the five glasses of water I drank before being wheeled here: half a pound perhaps?) My belly feels tight to bursting and suddenly looks obscenely round; reflexively, I press it with my palm, resolving not to eat again today.
>
> I have a rule when I weigh myself: if I've gained weight, I starve for the rest of the day. But if I've lost weight, I starve too. (Shute 1992: 19)

The distorted and bloated image that confronts the anorexic after she has eaten only a few calories is real enough for her, but its incongruence with what an impartial observer would see—an emaciated and undernourished body—must be explained.

It is noteworthy that the ideal (and non-existent) body that the anorexic craves is culturally specific. The symbolic matrix and the imaginary register, in terms of which the anorexic desires to embody an impossible ideal of femininity, exhibit cultural norms that are fluid over time and subject to variation. Cultural expectations, the demands of fashion, and ideal body types are not fixed and static—and neither are the symbolic expressions or images in terms of which these are played out. Symbolic meanings are articulated precisely in terms of particular cultural norms, relative to time and place. Whatever universality the symbolic may claim for itself, it does not imply that the imaginary body is the same for everyone, everywhere, for all time. On the contrary, there are specific requirements that subjects will find imposed on them, and which will differ not only from culture to culture, but also within cultures, according to the demands of select communities that dictate local fashions.

Rejecting the Primacy of Cartesian Consciousness

The body has not quit the scene. It was never there in the first place. It was never what we thought. It was only ever gender—so we are told. We cannot see gender as a solitary deterministic, originating cause any more than we can invoke biology as a single origin. To construe gender as social construction is merely to substitute one oversimplification for another—what was previously explained by anatomy now gets shifted on to society. But in fact neither of these uniform and unassailable "causes" can do the work we ask of them. Both are thrown into instability from a number of directions (see Herdt 1994; 1980; Laqueur 1994).

Butler asks how we can be said to choose gender if we are already immersed in gender, always already gendered (Butler 1986: 37). If gender goes all the way down, as it were, how can we choose what we already are? "If we are mired in gender from the start, what sense can we make of gender as a kind of choice?" (40). We cannot stand back and choose a gender if we are already determined by our culture. But neither can we presuppose a Cartesian subject that is somehow prior to its chosen gender, and outside language and culture. We "become" our genders, but this process "does not follow a linear progression" (39); "gender is not originated at some point in time after which it is fixed in form" (39).

According to Butler, we need a more adequate view of the "specific mechanism" whereby gender takes effect (36). Following de Beauvoir, Butler says that "We become our genders, but become them from a place which, strictly speaking, cannot be said to exist (39)." Sex then becomes "fictional" in the sense that it is only ever lived through gender. As Butler points out, "Any effort to ascertain the 'natural' body before its entrance into culture is definitionally impossible, not only because the observer who seeks this phenomenon is him/herself entrenched in a specific cultural language, but because the body is as well" (46).

If the relationship between sex and gender is neither "causal" nor "mimetic," but rather "heteronomous" and "arbitrary" (35), if gender is not causally produced by sex, if identity is a postmodern fiction, if the subject position fluctuates and vacillates and can be transferred and passed on, then what sense can be made of the fact that "society" approves, condones, and encourages girls to be feminine but not boys? The meaning of a boy dressed in girls' clothes is very different from a girl dressed in girls' clothes. For a woman to act in a masculine way is at best to provoke comment, and at worst considered a travesty of tradition worthy of approbation; while a man is considered anything from slightly strange to completely aberrant if he does not confirm his desire and ability to conform to the stereotypes of masculinity. Bodies, then, male and female both, re-emerge as salient and specific sites of interrogation that cannot be adequately theorized by some aspiration for a gender-neutral world. Not that bodies ever really went away—they have been hiding under the mantle of culture, society, or history, as ostensible agents of change, just as the penis is hidden from sight but finds its meaning in the substitute phallus. Bodies have been veiled beneath the cloth, the high church of feminist chic, the omnipresence of gender. But the body never exited, never expired. Nevertheless, there is no naked, pure body, no body as such—it is not there as a stable empirical referent. Its permanence and stability are just as fictional as its apparently wayward and voluntaristic ability to don a gender as it dons its clothes.

Rejecting the Volitional or Voluntaristic Account of Gender
Butler resists the idea that gender operates as a single causal force by complicating the notion so that it is no longer seen as a simple matter of choosing. Drawing on the idea of a "project," she brings into question the notion of gender as a simple voluntaristic and volitional choice.[13] "Becoming a gender" is "a subtle and strategic project which only rarely becomes manifest to reflective understanding," says Butler. It is a "process of interpreting a cultural reality laden with sanctions, taboos, and prescriptions. To choose a gender is to interpret received gender norms in a way that organizes them anew." It is a "tacit project to renew one's cultural history in one's own terms" (Butler 1986: 40). One thing this means is that "oppressive gender norms persist only to the extent that human beings take them up and give them life again and again" (41).

Referring to Sartre's pre-reflective cogito (40), Butler builds an account of gender that avoids the assumption of volition, of gender being picked at will by a voluntaristic subject. Gender does not work like that. Instead, before you know it you are a girl or a boy, and acting like one. Gender is not always a consciously chosen project, but a process of imbibing cultural norms which are not chosen from a vacuum. Society presents certain options, and by adopting them we confirm them, and re-create ourselves—and them—in the process. By emphasizing "the idea of appropriation," says Butler, de Beauvoir eschews the idea that humans are merely "products of prior causes, culturally determined in a strict sense" (41), and thus provides a way of accounting for the rejection, and resignification, of gender. Its "emancipatory potential" is thereby envisaged. In a statement that echoes not just de Beauvoir, but also Foucault, Butler points out that "Oppression is not a self-contained system which either confronts individuals as a theoretical object or generates them as its cultural pawns" (41). Gender can be construed not only as oppressive and limiting but also as creative and productive: "To become a gender means both to submit to a cultural situation and to create one" (48). To see gender as a choice that is enacted against a cultural background that offers a number of options, some of which are culturally sanctioned, avoids the extremes of complete determinism or absolute freedom. It is rather "a dialectic of recovery and invention" which "grants the possibility of autonomy within corporeal life" (48). We act against a cultural background that informs us and is liable at the same time to be changed by our actions.

Let me close this section by recalling what I take to be its most pertinent points. Gatens and Butler, in different ways and by highlighting different issues, demonstrate clearly the need for feminists to overcome the legacy of Cartesian dualism. Gatens shows that it is appropriate to view the relation of sex and gender not as arbitrary, but as contingent. Butler shows that a viable account of gender must avoid the extremes of involuntarism and voluntarism—gender is neither completely determined, nor completely unconstrained.[14] Both show the need to develop a more sophisticated account of bodies in their interactions with the social and psychic dimensions of experience. The impact of bodies cannot necessarily be accounted for so long as we remain tied to the idea that everything happens at the level of logic and consciousness. It is at least arguable that the pre-reflective and the unconscious domains play important roles in gender formation and identities.

SECTION III: PSYCHOANALYSIS AND FEMINISM: THE DEBATE SO FAR

Jacqueline Rose's now classic introduction to *Feminine Sexuality* represents one of the earliest significant interventions in the debate between feminism and psychoanalysis, and conforms to the broad lines of the essentialism/anti-essentialism debate that was set up according to an underlying sex/gender grid (1983: 27–57). She consigns feminist arguments about psychoanalytic neglect—or denigration—of women to mistaken feminist assumptions about the stability of women's position within an allegedly inflexible psychoanalytic framework. Arguing against these assumptions, she underlines the fragility that psychoanalysis accords the position of women by its insistence on construing the precariousness of subjectivity as bound up with the question of sexuality.[15]

Rose defends the concept of the phallus with arguments that repeatedly characterize the position to which those who speak for feminism must appeal as stable and inflexible, while emphasizing that for Freud and Lacan both subjectivity and sexuality—and the position of subjectivity is inextricably implicated in the question of the feminine—are fraught with instability and ambiguity. She begins by making the point that the "concept of the phallus," which "exceeds any natural or biological division," is systematically opposed to "pre-given sexual difference" (28), and concludes by underlining how problematic it is to make a direct appeal to the body as empirically given:

> If the status of the phallus is to be challenged, it cannot, therefore, be directly from the feminine body but must be by means of a different symbolic term (in which case the relation to the body is immediately thrown into crisis), or else by an entirely different logic altogether (in which case one is no longer in the order of symbolisation at all). (56)

It seems to me that Irigaray's figure of the lips, and her strategy of mimicry, could be read as responses to these suggestive parenthetical remarks which Rose includes in this final rebuttal of feminists who want to appeal to the body as if it could be registered somehow prior to its symbolic meaning.[16]

For now, however, let me stay a little longer with Rose's argument, which replays the social constructionism versus biological determinism scenario with a significant new twist. Lacan's return to Freud's concept of the phallus, Rose suggests, marks Lacan's avoidance of the "trap" in which previous psychoanalytic attempts to resolve the problematic relationship between psychoanalysis and feminism remain caught. The trap that the phallus allows Lacan to avoid is that of "pre-given sexual difference," and the way that the phallus "exceeds any natural or biological division" is through the recognition that "sexual difference is constructed" (28). It is by complicating the mechanism of construction that Lacan, by Rose's account, goes beyond his predecessors—and let me add that Rose goes beyond the causality of social constructionism that was the popular basis of feminism.[17] For as Rose says, it was "Freud's sense"—the phrase is no doubt deliberately vague because Freud was distinctly ambivalent on this point—that sexual difference is constructed, but it "is constructed at a price" and "it involves subjection to a law" (28). This subjection—and not, the implication is, the penis—is what the phallus represents or stands in for. This, then, is the new twist: sexual identity is not merely constructed by some amorphous and unexplained social (or historical or cultural) force, but implies subjection to a law—a law which exacts a cost. We know that the subject must enter the symbolic, must take on the project of differentiating itself from others, must (the force from which these imperatives derive their strength is less than clear) subject itself to language—but we do not know precisely what the cost amounts to. The meaning of the "price" of sexual difference remains obscure. It is deferred, in Rose's text (and perhaps elsewhere too), at least for the moment. That there is a price to be paid, a "cost" (28) incurred by the normal ordering of sexuality, is not in doubt—but we have to wait to find out more about this enigmatic, economic pay-off.[18] What we are given to understand straight away, without further delay—economic or otherwise—is that the process of sexual differentiation, of attaining "normal" adult sexuality, is fraught with "constant difficulty, or even impossibility" (29).

While suspending the details of the cost to be exacted, Rose emphasizes the need to retain Lacan's revival of the central role of the unconscious and its pertinence for sexuality, stressing the "fictional" status of "the sexual category to which every human subject is none the less assigned. In Lacan's account, sexual identity operates as a law—it is something enjoined on the subject" (29). Rose asserts the importance of "the idea of a fiction" (30)—a fiction which, as we just saw, involves a "subjection" represented by the phallus, a fiction that "operates as a law" and is "enjoined on the subject." The fictional status that Rose attributes to subjectivity—which nonetheless functions as an imperative (a peculiar structure, and one which Butler's work has already alerted us to)—presents her with the occasion to turn to Lacan's well-known 1949 paper, "The Mirror Stage as Formative of the Function of the I as Revealed in the Psychoanalytic Experience," in which he re-visits the conception of the mirror image that he had first articulated in 1936.

Lacan opens his remarks on the mirror stage by emphasizing that this account of the formation of the I, as experienced in psychoanalysis, presents a challenge to the Cartesian idea of the subject: "It is an experience that leads us to oppose any philosophy directly issuing from the *Cogito*" (1966: 93; 1977: 1).[19] The discussion that follows brings into focus the challenge that Lacan issues to the Cartesian subject as a unified self that can, at least ideally, know itself, and as such be master and originator of its destiny. The anti-Cartesian aspect of Lacan's inheritance is not lost on Rose, who comments:

> For Lacan, the unconscious undermines the subject from any position of certainty, and from any relations of knowledge to his or her psychic processes and history, and *simultaneously* reveals the fictional nature of the sexual category to which every human subject is none the less assigned (1983: 29).

I want to pause to remark upon the fact that the fictional status of sexual difference is invoked as a corollary to the crucial importance of the unconscious—which, Rose is at pains to stress, cannot be separated from the question of sexuality.

For Lacan, the mirror stage concerns "identification" understood as "the transformation that takes place in the subject when he assumes an image" (1966: 94; 1977: 2).[20] If the child's recognition of its own image in the mirror and identification of the image with itself is marked by Lacan as a moment of jubilation, it is also fictional and alienating. Each of these three aspects—the "jubilant assumption of his specular image by the child at the *infans* stage" (1966: 94; 1977: 2), the fictive or illusory status of the child's recognition of itself, and the alienation inherent in the subject's anticipatory grasp of itself as a totality—is related to what Lacan means by the "*specific prematurity of birth* in man" (1966: 96; 1977: 4). Lacan is referring to the extreme dependency that young children exhibit in the early months of their lives (as compared with animals), in terms of what Jacqueline Rose calls the infant's "lack of motor co-ordination and the fragmentation of its drives" (Rose 1983: 30).[21]

About jubilation, Lacan says:

> Unable as yet to walk, or even to stand up, and held tightly as he is by some
> support, human or artificial (what, in France, we call a 'trotte-bébé'), he
> nevertheless overcomes, in a flutter of jubilant activity, the obstructions of
> his support and, fixing his attitude in a slightly leaning-forward position, in
> order to hold it in his gaze, brings back an instantaneous aspect of his
> image (1966: 94; 1977: 1–2; see also 1988: 169).

Despite the instability of the child's motor co-ordination, the child appears to
achieve stability and control in the mirror-image, which presents it with a reflection,
and "fixes it . . . in a symmetry that inverts it, in contrast with the turbulent movements that the subject feels are animating him" (1966: 95; 1977: 2). As Rose says,
the child's mirror image "is salutary for the child, since it gives it the first sense of
a coherent identity in which it can recognise itself" (1983: 30).[22] At the same time,
the image is based upon an illusion because, in Rose's words, "its apparent smooth-
ness and totality is a myth," and "because it conceals, or freezes, the infant's lack
of motor co-ordination" (30) so that, as Lee puts it, "the infant is basically taking
herself to be something other than herself" (1990: 18; see Bannet 1989: 15).

For Lacan then, the "fictional direction" according to which the "agency of the
ego" is situated in the mirror-stage ensures a fundamental "discordance" (1966: 94;
1977: 2), or a "certain dehiscence at the heart of the organism, a primordial Dis-
cord" (1966: 96; 1977: 4). There is an original lack of correspondence between the
uncoordinated and dependent infant and the chimerical unity of the mirror-image
that apparently confers on the infant "the total form of the body" (1966: 94; 1977:
2). The *Gestalt* that grants the infant "in a mirage the maturation of his power"
(1966: 94–95; 1977: 2) is in fact external to the infant, and as such it simultaneously undercuts the illusion it provides—namely the totality, unity, identity, autonomy, and self-mastery of the subject.

The illusion that the mirror-image sustains functions according to a split or division that becomes the ground for the future alienation of the subject, since the subject is based upon an always already illusory idea of itself as autonomous and
self-sufficient. Lacan says that the *Gestalt* symbolizes the mental permanence of the
I, at the same time as it prefigures its alienating destination.[23] Lacan states that "the
assumption of the armor of an alienating identity . . . will mark with its rigid structure the subject's entire mental development" (1966: 97; 1977: 4). This protective
"alienating identity" is the third moment of the "temporal dialectic" in terms of
which Lacan casts the development of the mirror stage.

These three moments—of insufficiency, anticipation, and alienation—allow
Lacan to thematize the lack of motor co-ordination of the infant, its jubilant identification with its own image, and the discordance or dehiscence—the fracturing or
fragmentation—on which this apparent (and therefore illusory) unity is based.
Before assuming an alienating identity, Lacan says the subject is "precipitated from
insufficiency to anticipation," which is experienced by the subject as "the succession of phantasies that extends from a fragmented body-image to a form of its totality" (1966: 97; 1977: 4). Thus Lacan concludes from his reflections on the mirror

stage that it is "the *function of méconnaissance* that characterizes the ego in all its structures" (1966: 99; 1977: 6). The wholeness, unity, and totality that the child is granted by the mirror-image operates at the level of phantasy—it is fundamentally a misrecognition (see Lacan 1988: 167), it is what the child is not.

Let me return to the cost of sexual identity, to which Rose constantly appeals, even including this cost in Lacan's "basic premise": for Lacan, "identity is constructed in language, but only at a cost. Identity shifts, and language speaks the loss which lay behind the first moment of symbolisation" (Rose 1983: 31–32). At this level, the symbolic rather than the imaginary, the subject's relation to language is also a relation to lack, to impossibility, to failure, to an unfulfillable demand, to a desire that cannot be satisfied, to a "remainder," to something "always left over" (32), to emptiness, to absence. Rose says "The other appears to hold the 'truth' of the subject and the power to make good its loss. But this is the ultimate fantasy. Language is the place where meaning circulates" (1989: 32). Proceeding to explain the arbitrary nature of the sign, with the obligatory references to Saussure, Rose thus establishes the inherent "instability" of sexuality (1983: 33), the need to understand the lack of satisfaction in the drive, a lack which is structurally analogous to the failed attempts at completion on the part of the subject in search of a sexual identity that she or he can be sure of (see Rose 1983: 35).

The phallus, it becomes clear, is a symbol not only of this lack of certainty on the part of subject, but also of the fact that there is no certainty: "the status of the phallus is a fraud" says Rose (1983: 40). The phallus signifies the "price of a loss" Rose tells us—and finally the nature of this loss, this cost, this price, begins to become clear. The loss consists of the impossibility of having and being the phallus at the same time—the necessity, in other words of becoming a woman or a man, a necessity that, as we have seen, is fraught with difficulty, impossibility, and failure.

The language of a failed economy continues to inform Rose's account, even as she turns to those who have persistently misunderstood Lacan through their failure to apprise themselves of the real problem, namely "the acquisition of sexual identity and its difficulty" (1983: 37, note 4). She says, "Only if this [the fact that 'having' only functions at the price of a loss and that 'being' is an effect of division] is dropped from the account can the phallus be taken to represent an unproblematic assertion of male privilege" (40). Feminist attempts to weigh up Freud and Lacan have gone astray, the implication is, precisely because they have lost sight in their calculations of the significance of the phallus. In overlooking the phallus, in neglecting its anchoring role in the symbolic function, they have evaded the difficulty of acquiring gender, and insisted instead on the importance of separating from the imaginary dyadic relation with the mother. Like those psychoanalytic failures to "grasp the concept of the symbolic" (37), some feminists have failed to see the importance of language. Feminists keep on returning to the imaginary. In short, they have tried to avoid castration.

Rose's account of Lacan, and her riposte to feminists, is brilliant and erudite, persuasive and tempting. For a long time I was vaguely persuaded and mildly tempted. I was attracted by the rigor of her arguments, and seduced to some extent by her defense of Lacan, even as I was not convinced by her critique of Irigaray. I did not know how to reconcile my conflicting responses, and did not have the language at my disposal to articulate a view that allowed me to say why it was that Irigaray's critique of Lacan could not be so easily dismissed. Rose's implied criticism—that Irigaray's challenge could be reduced to a challenge grounded in the "feminine body" (1983: 56)—struck me as wrong. But how and why was it wrong? I think that question can be addressed—if not resolved—by returning to the relationship between sex and gender in terms of the issues raised in the previous section: neutrality, arbitrariness, the role of consciousness, and the question of choice.

Rose says, "For Lacan, to say that difference is 'phallic' difference is to expose the symbolic and arbitrary nature of its division as such" (56). Recall Gatens' suggestion that the fact that the relationship between sex and gender is not one of necessity does not force us to concede its arbitrariness. This insight—that it might be more appropriate to conceive of the relationship between sex and gender as contingent rather than arbitrary—can be applied to the penis/phallus relationship. If we envisage the relationship between the penis and the phallus not as arbitrary, but as contingent, it looks as if Jane Gallop might be right when she suggests that:

> as long as psychoanalysts maintain the ideal separability of phallus from penis, they can hold on to their phallus in the belief that their phallocentric discourse need have no relation to sexual inequality, no relation to politics. (1988: 127)

The question seems to turn not on whether or not there is a necessary penile referent underlying the phallus,[24] but on just how insistent its "insistent referentiality" (99) is.[25]

I have rehearsed arguments that indicate that the body is not neutral with respect to how its gender is typically read. The femaleness of the body tends to significantly increase the expectation that it exhibit feminine behavior, even if it does not necessitate this connection, even if this expectation is not borne out, even if it is in fact fairly regularly subverted. Analogously, if the relationship between that sex which is indicated by the phallus—men, metonymically represented by the penis—is not arbitrarily indicated, if it is inappropriate to construe the referent of the phallus as neutral, or indifferent with respect to sex, then what does it mean to insist that the phallus is "neutral"?

Kaja Silverman begins her article, "The Lacanian Phallus" (1992: 84–115), by citing Jane Gallop's discussion of the ostensible neutrality of the phallus. I reproduce Silverman's citation of Gallop's *Reading Lacan* (1985) here, along with the lines that precede and follow it. "Jane Gallop," says Silverman,

> uses a misprint in the 1966 edition of *Ecrits* as the occasion for fantasizing about an "epicene" phallus:
> ... *the definite article preceding and modifying 'phallus' is feminine—* '*la*' *[in the first word of the first paragraph on p. 690] . . . If 'the phallic signifier is intrinsically neutral,' then the signifer 'phallus' . . . might be either feminine or masculine, epicene . . . A lovely fantasy, a wish-fulfilment . . .* ([Gallop] 137).

Jacqueline Rose might also be said to attribute a neutrality of sorts to the phallus; she characterizes it as a term which, having no value itself . . . can represent that to which value accrues" ([Rose 1983:] 43). (Silverman 1992: 84)

There are several things to notice about this quotation within a quotation. First, to employ a distinctly Gallopesque gesture, I would note the lack of punctuation to mark the separation between Silverman's words and Rose's words—a lack of separation that has the effect of running together Gallop, who is quoted first, with Rose, whose words should read: "having no value in itself . . . can represent that to which value *accrues*." Not only does Silverman's text elide the distance between Gallop and Rose, but it also misquotes Rose—who does not say that the phallus has "no value itself" but that it has "no value *in* itself," and who italicizes the word "accrues." These misprints and misrepresentations—no doubt mere oversights— nonetheless reflect Silverman's argument, making Gallop and Rose seem closer than they really are. This elision is particularly interesting given that, as I read it, Gallop's argument in fact sets her apart from Rose. Gallop, both in the text Silverman cites and elsewhere, emphasizes the difficulty of definitively separating the phallus from the penis, and the difficulty of keeping the distinction clear (Gallop 1988: 125–29; 1985: 132–37). Rose, on the other hand, has an interest in keeping the phallus and the penis apart, and in characterizing phallic difference as arbitrary (Rose 1983: 56).

Silverman substitutes ellipses for Gallop's words at several points and, while she does not provide the reference, she incorporates into her quotation of Gallop a line that Gallop cites from Ragland-Sullivan—a line that represents the position Gallop criticizes: that "the phallic signifier is intrinsically neutral."[26] Among the lines Silverman leaves out is another quotation from a different author—an author who is, as Gallop notes, "inspired by Irigaray" (against whom Ragland-Sullivan's complaint is launched). Mary Jacobus (1981: 219) is quoted thus: "In epicene language . . . gender is variable at will, a mere metaphor" (Gallop 1985: 137).

By supplying the context, and filling in the gaps of Silverman's quotation of Gallop, it can be seen that the voluntaristic language that Jacobus uses in describing gender acquisition (gender varies "at will")—presumably on the assumption that her authorization derives from Irigaray—is pitted against the neutrality of the phallus. Two equally misleading positions need to be negotiated here. It is no more accurate to claim that the status of the phallus is arbitrary, if what is meant by such a claim is that the relationship between the phallus and penis is an indifferent one, than it is to veer to the opposite extreme and claim that gender is a matter of unconstrained choice, "variable at will." Whether one defends psychoanalysis, as Rose does, by maintaining that the status of the phallus is arbitrary, or rejects psychoanalysis, as Jacobus does, on the ostensibly feminist grounds that gender is a matter of free choice, one avoids the question of the relationship between the penis and the phallus, or sex and gender. Both these positions miss the point that gender is neither necessarily and completely determined by sex, nor is it arbitrarily and incidentally related to sex. It is rather precisely contingent: given prevailing gender norms it is probable that members of the female sex will be encouraged to develop feminine gender characteristics, but it is neither necessary nor inevitable that this will be the case. Similarly, it is probable that the phallus will refer directly and positively to the penis, but is neither necessary nor inevitable. Women can and do identify with masculine positions, and men can and do identify with feminine positions. Since identification is no simple matter—it cannot be adequately thought as merely an adoption of a position, for example—the results of such identification are highly variable. The details of how and why certain gender identification develops for certain individuals are left open: how much society can be said to produce gender identification, how much family histories encourage oedipal identifications, to what extent the individual can be said to freely adopt socially prescribed gender norms, and in what ways individuals are capable of transforming, creating, subverting, and challenging the very familial roles that they in some sense accept as enabling—all these factors will vary from case to case, and in this sense they remain indeterminate. Similarly, it is an open question as to whether power structures can be significantly altered through substituting women's sex for men's, substituting, perhaps, Irigaray's lips for Freud's phallus, or—for that matter, Irigaray's mimicry for Lacan's mastery.

Once the developments in feminist theory sketched above, in section two of this paper, are taken into account, Rose's critique of feminism has to be significantly tempered, or even withdrawn. This is not surprising, given that the terms of feminism have undergone significant alterations since Rose wrote her introduction to *Feminine Sexuality*. What is surprising is that more recent interventions have not moved the debate decisively beyond the framework that is played out in Rose's text, as we can see by a brief look at Teresa Brennan's introduction to *Between Feminism and Psychoanalysis* (1989). My point here is not to criticize Brennan—her introduction to that representative volume is helpful, concise, and clear. Indeed it is her very clarity about the issues that helps me make my point: the desire for change is one of the motivating factors in feminist espousals of social constructionism, which are aimed at combatting biological determinism, but attempts to conceive of the mechanism of change remain inadequate. An underlying grid—society versus biology—still governs the debate between feminism and psychoanalysis to a significant extent; but what these terms mean, what their opposition amounts to, and their status as ostensible causes remain undeveloped.

Beyond dispute however, as Jane Gallop expresses it in her inimitable way, is that "feminists find that central, transcendental phallus particularly hard to swallow" (Gallop 1988: 125). Brennan puts the problem that feminists have had with the phallus succinctly when she says: "Outside the symbolic law, there is psychosis" (1989: 2). Insofar as the symbolic privileges men, it puts women outside its law, and insofar as it excludes women from language, it seems to affirm the most reactionary epistemic assumptions about women's relationship to culture. Most problematic of all is the appearance of inevitability that patriarchy takes on (see Brennan 1989: 3). At issue is how the subject can successfully effect a process of psychic differentiation, or undergo a separation from the mother that does not result in psychosis—and whether feminism can intervene to interrupt, put off, or bring into question the patriarchal structures that remain unquestioned so long as the law of the father which effects the subject's entry into language remains unassailable. Brennan raises the question—only to push it aside to make way for other more pressing issues—of what would happen if the symbolic third term that effects a separation from imaginary unity, reconfiguring the mother-child dyad as differentiated, were not associated with the father. Of special interest here is the way this question is posed in relation to the category of sex. Brennan says:

> How changing the sex of either the intervening third party or the primary care-giver, or the actual father's social position, would affect the process of differentiation is another matter; but real changes in either parenting patterns or the social position of women and men must have consequences for the symbolic (3).

What does the phrase "changing the sex" of the parenting function mean here? What would constitute "real changes" in the "social" position of the sexes? Precisely what effects social changes in parenting practices have on the apparent inevitability of the patriarchal scenario for psychoanalysis cannot be assessed without at the same time articulating the discrepancy between women's experience of motherhood and various aspects of their official roles—the conflicting cultural, ideological, or symbolic meanings that are attached to their social roles. Acknowledging and theorizing these contradictory meanings shed light on how it is possible for women to be at once denigrated and deified—how women can both be effectively put outside the law, excluded from the symbolic, and at the same time guarantee the meaning of the phallus.

In *The Second Sex* Simone de Beauvoir observes the irreconcilable and polarized positions that women are imagined to occupy—as both goddess and whore, both mysterious other and object of subjugation. Influenced by de Beauvoir, Sherry Ortner points to the *intermediary* role of women, as between culture and nature (1993: 59–72). What is interesting about Ortner's article is that in confronting complex demands made on women, and the resultant conflicting images and representations of women, it exhibits the influence of diverse sources. Presented as an anthropological enquiry and written in the early 1970s, it also employs psychoanalytic insights, while at the same time Marxism clearly informs the argument. By bringing together psychoanalysis and a Marxist orientation, Ortner's text can be situated in the shift—to which Brennan draws attention (1989: 6)—away from Marxist humanism and towards structuralist reinterpretations of Marx that informed a good deal of socialist feminism in the 1970s.[27] In the tradition of anti-humanism, feminists, persuaded by a structuralist reading of Marx, were also suspicious of any talk of human nature which implied an unchanging essence. Informed by this legacy, Ortner provides a fairly sophisticated analysis of the "sadly efficient feedback system" whereby the "various aspects of woman's situation (physical, social, psychological) contribute to her being seen as closer to nature, while the view of her as closer to nature [than men] is in turn embodied in institutional forms that reproduce her situation" (Ortner 1993: 71). Ortner's account of the ways in which women appear to be on the cusp of the nature/culture distinction allows her to explain how the faulty equation of women with nature also subordinates them to culture, and why women are seen as that which is to be ruled over, contained, and controlled—in much the same way as nature is to be tamed by man. Ortner's account also accommodates the fact that even if women are often construed as on a par with or as part of nature, they also escape, contradict, and transcend their association with nature, resisting easy categorization in terms of the nature/culture dichotomy. Both symbolically (as chaste, decorous, and virtuous wife, for example, or as divine and higher being), and materially or actually (from the point of view of their social products, in particular the moral well-being of their children) women defy attempts to exclude them from social production and intervention, or to deny them the right to partake in the political sphere.

If Ortner avoids the discourse of essentialism in one way—eschewing the idea of an innate human nature—her project still aspires to a universalism that has become unfashionable of late.[28] Haraway echoes the ambiguous status that Ortner attributes to women, but she does not couch her enquiry as an attempt to discover "pan-cultural" facts about women. When Haraway says that "women, as well as 'tribal' peoples, existed unstably at the boundary of the natural and social," she is following up her earlier suggestion that in order to appreciate the complexity of the sex/gender distinction we need to be aware of the resonance terms such as *Geschlecht* have not merely with sex, but also with stock, class, and race (Haraway 1991: 127–48, esp. 131). Rather than joining Ortner in her pretensions to universality, Haraway reminds us to take account of the variegated history that the term "gender" carries with it in its various translations, pointing to the Latin verb *generare* (to beget) as the root of the English term "gender," the French *genre* and the Spanish *género* (130). Despite this, as she says, "It has seemed very rare for feminist theory to hold race, sex/gender, and class analytically together—all the best intentions, hues of authors, and remarks in prefaces notwithstanding" (129).

SECTION IV: THE RETURN OF THE PHALLUS

If a certain resistance is discernible on my part—in the fact that I found myself talking about the mirror-stage, the scene of the imaginary, rather than scene of language, castration, and the entry into the symbolic—no doubt this is not accidental. I would nevertheless insist that the absence of any direct discussion of the phallus does nothing to indicate that it is dispensable. I am aware of the fact that I keep on putting off any direct discussion of the phallus. Keeping it at bay, warding it off, pushing it further and further to the end of the text—until there is a danger that it will be cut out altogether. I have not even mentioned what one would think was a pivotal essay by Lacan, "The Meaning of the Phallus" (1983: 74–85). This was not something that I had intended.

Of course the phallus never really disappeared—because it never really appeared. The cult of the phallus was just that—worship of and devotion to an absent, non-existent thing, an occult object, a sign that has no materiality in itself, but which serves a symbolic function. It stands in for the penis in its own absence, representing in an ideal way what is far from ideal. The penis does not behave at all like the phallus. Precisely its deficiencies, its failure to stand up for itself, on its own, all alone without any support are, perhaps, what make it necessary to represent it as if it were autochthonous. It is "fabulous," a "fabrication" (Goux 1992: 40–41)—its meaning derives from a fable, and not from an accurate description of a fact, anatomical or otherwise. "It is a constructed model. It is an artifact that simulates what is missing, at the same time rendering it sacred and larger than life to make it a cult object" (43). The phallus returns, not in the sense that it was ever really absent—for it never really existed at all, at least not as a mere existent or being[29]—but insofar as its presence haunts even the most critical interrogation of psychoanalysis. As Butler shows in her discussion of the lesbian phallus, none of us can do without the phallus, even if we want to.[30] We can't just get rid of it, or pretend we don't know about it. For the phallus is not simply a matter of choice. And choice itself is not a simple matter. It is not just a matter of one object-choice among others, it is what guarantees the meaning of any choice, and even of our refusal to choose.

Without psychoanalysis, the phallus would be absent—psychoanalysis constantly presents the phallus, but it presents it as forever absent, as impossible, like a dream. You can't have it, you can't do without it.[31] One might even say (as Irigaray does) that it is in the interests of psychoanalysis to keep the phallus under wraps, to surround it with subterfuge, to constantly displace it, to maintain it by constantly removing it, according to the logic of veiling and unveiling. Psychoanalysis "operates an unveiling," says Goux, in his remarkable essay "The Phallus: Masculine Identity and the 'Exchange of Women'"—an essay from which I learned a great deal, I might add (in a deferential gesture which is, perhaps, only proper in the context) before I proceed to question the privilege it accords to unveiling. Goux suggests that psychoanalysis "is a double revelation, first of the phallus and secondly of the reasons for its revelation" (1992: 43). I want to suggest that the discourse of psychoanalysis is just as interested in the veiling of the phallus as it is in its unveiling. Psychoanalysis has a vested interest—and we saw this rather precisely in the deferral of its meaning that marks Rose's defense of it—in maintaining the difficulty of understanding the relationship between the phallus and the penis. Jane Gallop says:

> The Lacanians' desire clearly to separate *phallus* from *penis*, to control the meaning of the signifier *phallus*, is precisely symptomatic of their desire to have the phallus, that is their desire to be at the center of language, at its origin. And their inability to control the meaning of the word *phallus* is evidence of what Lacan calls symbolic castration (1988: 126).

Feminists cannot have and be the phallus at the same time. And yet they can, and they are—that is one of the contradictions that we must learn, if not to live with, then, at least to think through and transform.

NOTES

1. I am grateful to Charles Shepherdson for discussing this paper with me, and for his helpful comments and suggestions.
2. A revised version is the first chapter of Moira Gatens, *Imaginary Bodies* (1996).
3. The work of Judith Butler has gone a long way towards interrogating oversimplifications of these and related terms.

4. In Toni Morrison's *The Bluest Eye* (1994), Pecola Breedlove presents Elihue Michah Whitcomb, who is regarded by the women of the town as having supernatural powers (171), with a request to change the color of her eyes: "I want them blue" she tells him (174)—"Like she was buying shoes" (180). Summing up the situation, the narrator observes, "A little black girl yearns for the blue eyes of a little white girl, and the horror at the heart of her yearning is exceeded only by the evil of fulfilment" (204). See also Barbara Kingsolver, *Pigs in Heaven* (1993), in which a waitress, who has had her name legally changed to Barbie (139), owns "probably the largest personal collection of Barbie-related items in the entire world" (134), knows every Barbie model on the market (141), and dresses in Barbie doll look-alike ensembles. She is also wanted for counterfeiting money and robbing a casino (204).

5. See Moira Gatens (1996) discussion of the metaphorical and metonymical slippage at play in the idea of the body politic that has been so central to social contract theorists. Her discussion focuses in particular of Hobbes and Locke, and specifies that the notion of the body politic appeals to an exclusive type of body—the male body-type. See also Carol Pateman (1988), a text that Gatens reads in an appreciative yet critical way.

6. Following Judith Butler, we might call feminist attempts to include its infinite "others," whose identity we could never fully enumerate in terms of class, race, sexual preference, able-bodiedness or any number of other qualifiers, the "illimitable *et cetera*" (1990: 143). Teresa de Lauretis refers to the same phenomenon as "various axes of difference" which "are usually seen as parallel or coequal, although with varying 'priorities' for particular women." She goes on,

> For some women, the racial may have priority over the sexual in defining subjectivity and ground identity; for others still it may be the ethnic/cultural that has priority at a given moment—hence the phrase one hears so often now in feminist contexts: "gender, race, and class," or its local variant, "gender, race, and class, and sexual preference." But what this string of seemingly coequal terms, conveying the notion of layers of oppression along parallel axes of "difference," does not grasp is their constant intersection and mutual implication or how each one may affect the others—for example, how gender affects racial oppression in its subjective effects." (1990: 133–4)

7. On the politics of location see Rosi Braidotti's important book (1994), which betrays the influence of Deleuze's nomadism, as well as numerous feminists ranging from artist Martha Rosler and film producer Laurie Anderson, to poet Adrienne Rich and theorist Luce Irigaray.

8. Jacques Derrida has emphasized the need for a re-sexualizing of philosophical or theoretical discourse that he sees as too neutralizing in a number of different contexts (see Derrida, 1988: 163–85; 1987a: 189–203; 1983: 65–83).

9. Degendering implies the elimination of differences between femininity and masculinity.

10. As Hannah Arendt says in the opening pages of *The Human Condition*, "philosophers have looked upon their body as a kind of prison of mind or soul" (1971: 2). See also Elizabeth Spelman (1982: 109–131), who shows how the derogatory equation of women with their bodies has carried over from the Greeks—she traces it

back to Plato—and that somatophobia is still prevalent in some contemporary feminist work.

11. Gatens first published "A Critique of the Sex/Gender Distinction" in 1983, so I am not suggesting that she conceived it as a response to Butler, only that it can be read as a corrective to the kind of position Butler espouses, at least at times, in 1986 and 1987. By 1990, with the publication of *Gender Trouble*, there is more room for Gatens' view within Butler's discussion, and by the time *Bodies that Matter* appears, their positions converge, it seems to me, still more.

12. Gatens uses this term, and her analysis is influenced by M. Merleau-Ponty's (1962) account of the phantom limb.

13. The notion of project, elaborated by Heidegger, and taken up by Sartre, is of course central to de Beauvoir's (1952) analysis of the need to transcend immanence.

14. I have referred largely to Butler's earlier work. Let me add that, in my view, a significant shift takes place that marks a difference between *Gender Trouble* and *Bodies that Matter*. Butler's account of gender as performative—not to be confused with gender as performance (see Butler 1994: 32–9)—becomes increasingly nuanced. If, at least at times, *Gender Trouble* construes the relation between gender and sex as arbitrary, *Bodies that Matter* develops an insight already implicit in *Gender Trouble*, but perhaps not elaborated fully: namely, that bodies are significant sites of resistance, that bodies *matter*, i.e., they signify, but they also intervene and interrupt, insistently breaking up and rearranging cultural attempts to code their meanings. Bodies cannot be easily contained. They erupt from the categories we prescribe for and invent to describe them. In this sense, even if there is some validity to the suggestion that both gender and sex are cultural, it must be emphasized that they are cultural in very different ways for both—and it is important that these differences between sex and gender be articulated. I take it that one of the projects of *Bodies that Matter* is to do precisely that.

15. Teresa Brennan remarks on the fact that "commentaries on Lacan" emphasize that "the subject's construction and identity alike rest on a fragile basis" and that "the subject's identity and the subject's 'meaning' are precarious" (1991: 114–38, esp. 125).

16. For indications as to how this suggestion might be developed see Chisholm (1994: 263–83), and Schwab (1994: 351–78).

17. Also see Rose's later comment that "a rigid determinism by either biology or culture . . . simply will not do" (1989: 25–39, esp. 31–32).

18. Informing my discussion here is Derrida's (1987) discussion of the economy of the repetition compulsion in Freud's *Beyond the Pleasure Principle*. In the background there are also a number of texts on the economy of the gift, including Derrida's (1991a: 11–48) discussion of Levinas.

19. See Lee (1990: 22) on Lacan's undermining of the Cartesian subject.

20. Although the idea of the mirror seems to emphasize the visual image, Rose points out that "Lacan is careful to stress, however, that his point is not restricted to the field of the visible alone: 'the idea of the mirror should be understood as an object which reflects—not just the visible, but also what is heard, touched and willed by the child' (Lacan, 1949, p. 567) [Rose 1983: 30]."

21. Lacan also refers to the inability of the infant to fend for itself: "still sunk in his motor incapacity and nursling dependence" (1966: 94; 1977: 2).

22. Rose adds that this sense of coherent identity is "already a fantasy—the very image which places the child divides its identity into two. Furthermore, that moment only has meaning in relation to the presence and the look of the mother who guarantees its reality for the child. The mother does not (as in D. W. Winnicott's account . . . mirror the child to itself; she grants an image *to* the child, which her presence instantly deflects. Holding the child is, therefore, to be understood not only as a containing, but as a process of referring, which fractures the unity it seems to offer" (Rose 1983: 30). The parentheses are unclosed in Rose's text, and the reference is to a 1967 paper by D. W. Winnicott, "Mirror-role of Mother and Family in Child Development" (1971: 111–18).

23. Lee explains:

> The *moi* [ego] is hurled into a largely alien environment by forces outside its control . . . This precipitated *moi* is . . . in an important sense illusory, and the *béance* between this illusory identity and the infant's lived experience of the body provides the basis for a more or less permanent alienation of the subject from herself. Moreover, the Cartesian confidence that knowledge of the external world finds its ultimate justification in the subject's certain knowledge of its self is replaced in Lacan's essay by the haunting image of the *moi's* alienating identity as an armor. (1990: 22–23)

24. It is correct, in my opinion, to suggest, as Charles Bernheimer does, that "penile reference" is not necessarily "essentializing" (1992: 116–32, esp. 117).

25. Here I borrow Gallop's phrase, importing it from another context—her discussion of Irigaray's figure of the lips—which is perhaps not, in the end, so distant from the referentiality of phallus to penis.

26. The line is itself employed in a critique of Irigaray's failure to see the neutrality of the phallus, and is quoted from Ragland-Sullivan (1982: 10).

27. It would be interesting to trace the impact of Althusser's conception of ideology on feminism in Britain. As Callinicos notes, "The greatest influence on British Marxists has been the work of Louis Althusser, while the Frankfurt school appears to have had more impact in the United States" (1985: 4). See, for example, Althusser (1969), and Althusser and Balibar (1979).

28. See Butler's discussion however, which can be read as a cautionary corrective to the fear of essentialism that has driven some feminists too far in the other direction (1995: 127–43, esp. 130).

29. I am thinking of Heidegger's distinction between *Seiendes* (being) and *Sein* (Being), and Levinas's reworking of the ontological distinction as separation of the existent from its existing. See Heidegger (1980), Emmanuel Levinas (1987: esp. 44).

30. Butler observes at the beginning of her important paper, "The Lesbian Phallus and the Morphological Imaginary" (later revised as a chapter in *Bodies That Matter*): "It may not seem that the lesbian phallus has much to do with what you are about to read, but I assure you (promise you?) that it could not have been done without it" (1993: 57).

31. I am thinking of the sentiment expressed in Tarantino's *Pulp Fiction*: women, you can't live with them, you can't shoot them.

lacan's debt to freud: how the ratman paid off his debt

6

John Forrester

Editor's Note

In his re-reading of Freudian theory, Lacan located the origins of psychoanalysis in the decline of the family in general, and of the paternal imago in particular. Lacan's psychoanalysis was thus consumed with the problem of narcissism, that is, with the problem of how the male child becomes a man in the absence (or decline) of the father.

John Forrester traces the steps that made possible Lacan's mature theory of full speech which was, he argues, based on the same sort of "unconditional obliga-tion" that framed Lacan's strategy for reading Freud: namely, that we must put our "faith" and "trust" in the founder. Like paper money, Freud's texts were to be treated as "promissory notes" which needed no additional guarantee. At the same time, Lacan recognized an opportunity for revisionism wherever Freud seemed too doctrinaire in his thinking. With this in mind, Forrester outlines how Lacan began in the 1930s to revise Freud's Oedipus Complex, a task that hinged on the explication and modification of "debt" (taken from Mauss and Lévi-Strauss). Forrester then demonstrates in detail how debt harmonized Lacan's later theories of lack, speech, exchange, and death.

To these multiple ends, Forrester provides a compelling account of Lacan's reading of Freud's famous "Ratman" case study of 1909. He shows how Lacan could both capture and misconstrue the spirit and letter of Freud's meaning in his "return to Freud." This essay reviews much of Lacan's theory by focussing upon a single text, and is a clear and valued addition to the most complex discussions on psychoanalysis.

JOHN FORRESTER is a Professor in the Department of History and Philosophy of Science, Cambridge. His is the author of *The Language and Origins of Psychoanalysis* (Columbia, 1980), *The Seductions of Psychoanalysis: Freud, Lacan, and Derrida* (Cambridge, 1990), and *The Dream of Psychoanalysis* (forthcoming). He is also the translator of Jacques Lacan's *The Seminar: Book I, Freud's Papers on Technique 1953–54* (Norton/Cambridge, 1988).

> Therefore the proud man can afford to wait, because he has no doubt of the strength of his capital, and can also live, by anticipation, on that fame which he has persuaded himself that he deserves. He often draws indeed too largely on posterity, but even here he is safe; for should the bills be dishonoured, this cannot happen until *that debt* which cancels all others, shall have been paid.
>
> Charles Colton, *Lacon, or many things in few words; addressed to those who think*[1]

FOR SOMEONE WHO ADVOCATED A RETURN TO FREUD, Lacan was little prone to quoting him. "Quoting," he is quoted as saying—though I can't exactly remember when and where—"is for imbeciles." So, if we find the name Freud in Lacan's work, it is very rarely followed by the words invoked by Marie Bonaparte so frequently that they became her nickname: "Freud-a-dit." In this respect—and I am only saying the obvious, so we are clear about it—Lacan quoted Freud far less often than other psychoanalysts do and did, and certainly far less than, say, Lacanians cite Lacan.[2]

So the famous return to Freud is *not* a return to the letter, if only because what is commonly regarded as the letter of Freud, the text itself, is missing from Lacan's work. It thus can only have been, and palpably was, a return to the spirit of Freud. And, perhaps, Lacan's own practice implied that those who return to the letter of the text are imbeciles, if that is where they think they will discover its spirit.

Yet Lacan exhorted others to return to Freud, to those very texts he himself eschewed citing. To take an example, from the last page of "La chose freudienne":

> One has only to turn the pages of his works for it to become abundantly clear that Freud regarded a study of languages and institutions, of the resonances, whether attested or not in memory, of literature and of the significations involved in works of art as necessary to an understanding of the text of our experience. Indeed, Freud himself is a striking instance of his own belief: he derived his inspiration, his ways of thinking and his technical weapons from just such a study. (1966: 435; 1977: 144)

Even if you flick through Freud's pages, not bothering to read, you will see that Lacan's reading of Freud is correct. This is typical of one important mode of citation in Lacan's work.

The implication is that anyone can understand what Freud is saying, since it is written down in black and white, in plain French for all to see; yet no one before

Lacan has managed to do this simple thing. For example, he writes in "The Freudian Thing": "Freud's intention, which is so legible to anyone who is not content simply to stumble through this text . . ." (1977: 142). Yet the most extended piece of analysis and commentary on any text of Freud's to be found in Lacan's *Ecrits* is in an Appendix: "Commentaire parlé sur la *Verneinung* de Freud." The author is Jean Hyppolite.

So Lacan's reading of Freud is always something different from commentary, from the traditional art of *explication de texte*. To speculate somewhat: the diffidence and reluctance Lacan betrayed in relation to the telling of case histories may be of the same sort, may have the same source, as his reluctance to quote Freud. And, we should remember, this reluctance to confront the text of his analyses when discussing the technique of analysis with others is a distinctive feature of the theorist who proposed the transmission of the experience of analysis with others in "*la passé*" as one of the analyst's fundamental tasks. Speculatively, then, we surmise that this analyst, whose textual indirection was so prominent a part of his relation to his colleagues and students, also felt the pressure to find some theory of how textual directness was possible—of how the experience of analysis, or of reading Freud, could be transmitted to others.

However, this is not altogether true or just. One knows that Lacan did succeed both in transmitting his own experience of reading Freud to others and in giving a clear sense of analytic practice as he conceived and executed it. How did he do this, being so firmly committed to indirection?

THE FUNDAMENTAL PREREQUISITE FOR READING FREUD IS, according to Lacan, the principle of faith: one must place one's faith in Freud's writing, otherwise one won't know where to start. In one of the principle texts I will be commenting upon, "Le mythe individuel du névrosé, ou 'Poésie et Vérité' dans la névrosé" (1953),[3] Lacan recognizes that all of Freud's case histories are "incomplete," that they seem to many analysts to be "analyses broken off midway," and that they are only "fragments of analysis." But this, he goes on, "must all the same stimulate us to reflect, to ask ourselves why the author has made this choice, *and of course to place our trust in Freud*" (1953: 6; 1979: 408, emphasis added, trans. modified).

This register of *trust*—of faith not only in the other's good intentions but in his intelligence—must precede and organize any reading of Freud which will do justice to his work. In other words, in order to read Freud, one must place Freud in one's debt *before the reading starts*. So, in order to be a psychoanalyst who can read Freud, one must first place Freud in one's debt.

"*Trust*," "*have faith*": this register is not only the register of the necessary cement of social life in general, not only in the register of a non-relational relation to God, it is also the register of financial exchange. When Lacan refers to symbolic exchange, or to symbolic debt, we must not neglect to enquire into the economics of this system—to the point where the principles which govern the Symbolic system might well be called an "economics of the symbol."

So let us return to the question of reading Freud and the trust we must place in him. In order to read Freud, one must postulate that he has, in effect, issued a currency, a psychoanalytic currency, and that in holding the text, we are holding the notes of credit of this economic system. Placing trust in Freud is thus like placing trust in the institution that issues notes of credit or bank notes. Freud's texts thus *must* be treated as promissory notes, if one is going to read them properly.

The analogy with the banking system is revealing. In financial reality, when we place money in savings, it is the Bank that is in *our* debt. The confidence we have in the Bank is a way of saying we actually believe the Bank when it promises that it will honour the debt represented by the bank note and will never foreclose on that debt. The banking system works in large part because the social roles of creditor and debtor have been refined to the point where "the debtor has become perfectly specific (in the guise of the state) and the creditor, completely general (in the guise of any one who happens to have had the debt assigned to him). No one can be substituted for the debtor; anyone can be substituted for the creditor" (Crump 1981: 82).

We often catch such overtones in Lacan's conception of the relationship between Freud and his readers: as we have seen, the reader is anyone who can read, anyone who can turn a page. Indeed, Lacan sometimes appears willing to speak only so as to help other potential readers of Freud free themselves from what is blinding them, from what is preventing them from reading Freud: "I would take this opportunity of reminding those who cannot be persuaded to seek in Freud's texts an extension of the enlightenment that their pedagogues dispense to them" (1977: 199).

Lacan's "reminder" is only necessary, is perhaps only *defensible*, he implies, because it is obliged to function as a substitute, a *semblant* (counterpart), of Freud's texts. It is as if some readers, some analysts, find Freud's texts to be in need of something additional, something that, accompanying the text, makes it trustworthy, a proper currency. In Britain, we have pieces of plastic called cheque guarantee cards. Lacan is, in effect, implying that readers and analysts treat Freud's texts as if they were cheques issued by any private citizen, in need of a cheque guarantee card. If only they could recognize, through placing the appropriate trust in Freud's texts, that these are not cheques but bank notes issued by the National Bank, they would give up requiring supplemental guarantees from others (such as Lacan), just as nobody requires a respected National Bank to issue a guarantee card with each bank note. The note is its own guarantee; one need look no further. Freud's text is its own guarantee; one need look no further.

However, having placed such trust in the text, Lacan then points to one condition of this trust. Freud's case histories are trustworthy only to the extent that they are free of doctrinal constriction, so free that they appear to the trained psychoanalytic eye as running contrary to the basic technical procedures of psychoanalysis:

> The successes obtained by Freud, because of the heedlessness about matters
> of doctrine from which they seem to proceed, are now a matter of aston-
> ishment, and the display so evident in the cases of Dora, the Rat Man, and
> the Wolf Man seems to us to be little short of scandalous. (1977: 77)

These texts are trustworthy precisely because they are, each and every one, unique deviants. They do not obey their own rules. And therefore they can be used to correct the rules, to reach down to the fundamental doctrines the texts embody and sink new doctrinal foundations upon which they may rest. In "Le mythe individuel du névrosé, ou 'Poésie et Vérité' dans la névrosé," Lacan used the case of the Rat-man, Freud's own clinical evidence, to show the limitations of Freud's own Oedipal schema. Freud's case history is shown to be a resource that embodies its own cur-tailment and correction. This necessary deviation from Freud's text is sanctioned by the refusal of slavish imitation. Lacan is the last person who would recommend being a slave to another master: "it is not a question of imitating him. In order to rediscover the effects of Freud's speech, it is not to its terms that we shall have recourse, but to the principles that govern it" (1977: 79). And it is also not clear the extent to which Freud was a sleepwalker, that is, if he made his discoveries and acted in accordance with these principles despite himself or in full and deliberate knowledge. Certainly now, after Freud's death, when psychoanalytic doctrine has taken over from those principles, if one wishes to recover those principles one can-not repeat these texts. Lacan's discourse of a Freudian golden age forever lost to us moderns entails that we can only recover the essence of that age by re-inventing it in an alternative, mythical guise. So Lacan will not quote, will not follow Freud, but will give something at once simpler and more subtle: he gives us a *compte rendu*.

Lacan's gifts as a story teller have not been widely advertised. As quasi-epi-gramist, spinner of semantic spider's webs, as tortuous and complex edifier of the-ories, he is well known. But Lacan simple story-teller? Yet he opens *Ecrit* with a seminar on a story by Poe, and much of the exhilarating novelty of his reading is imbedded in a retelling of the story. *Lacan reconte le conte.* He was immensely gifted in this art of retelling, and with each of Freud's case histories, as well as Poe's story and Sophocles's *Antigone*, not to mention the case histories he selects and dis-sects from the psychoanalytic literature, he retells the story in such a way that the Lacanian point is imbedded in the process of recounting. This is a gift.

Thus Lacan had the gift of making his *compte rendu* of Freud's cases or papers in the form of a story. In this way he paid off the debt he owed to Freud for this material. "Le mythe individuel du névrosé" is also the theory of the debt which is enacted in the reading. Its ethos is tragic: the debt is *impayable*—there is no settling of accounts possible without death.

I WANT TO CONSIDER LACAN'S VARIOUS READINGS OF FREUD'S CASE HISTORY of the Rat-man. His discussions focus on two main themes: the first a doctrinal element, the second a question of analytic technique. The doctrine is that of *debt*; the technical point arises out of a consideration of Freud's errors. However, as we will see, the two are intimately linked together. "I pointed out to him that this attempt to deny the reality of his father's death is the basis of his whole neurosis" (*SE* 10: 300).[4] This interpretation that Freud offered the Ratman some two months into his treat-ment was not available to Lacan when he gave his 1953 lecture, yet it sums up very well the heart of Lacan's reading of Freud's published case history. The Ratman's attempt to deny the reality of his father's death explains why he is pursued by his father in his imagination: that is, he is pursued by an imaginary father. To begin with, we should recognize how Lacan's reading of Freud's text isolates the precipi-tating cause as the original scene of the analysis, and links it closely with its repeti-tion, the scene of the payment of the debt—the *delire* of repayment of the 3.80 *kronen* the Ratman owes to someone for the safe delivery of his pince-nez.

The organization of the account, the way it is told, is very similar to that more famous compte-rendu, "Seminar on *The Purloined Letter.*" In the analysis of *The Purloined Letter*, the letter structurally organizes the two scenes, and also provides continuity between them. In the compte-rendu of the Ratman, it is debt that organizes the two separate scene, making the recent scene the repetition of the two others, the scenes of his father's premarital indebtedness and that of marriage. *The Purloined Letter* has the triangle of King, Queen, and Minister, repeated in the guise of the police, the Minister, and Dupin. For the Ratman, however, there is no one simple scene that is repeated once; rather, we find these two primary scenes, each of which is then repeated.

First, there is the scene of the patient's father's debt to the mysterious friend, which is repeated with Lieutenant A, the lady at the post office, and Lieutenant B. Second, there is the Ratman's father and the two women: the rich girl and the poor girl. The scene of the father and the rich/poor girls is repeated with his son, both in the debt repayment drama involving the lady at the post office and the inn-keeper's daughter and in the structure that precipitates the neurosis in the first place: the scene of the Ratman, the cousin whom it is proposed he should marry, and his lady. Lacan characteristically sums this up:

> You cannot fail to recognize in this scenario—which includes the passing of a certain sum of money from Lieutenant A to the generous lady at the post office who met the payment, then from the lady to another masculine figure—a schema which, complementary in certain points and supplementary in others, parallel in one way and inverted in another, is the equivalent of the original situation. (1953: 12–13; 1979: 413)

According to Freud, and following him Lacan, the Ratman's neurosis began when his mother told him of her plan for him to follow in his dead father's footsteps and marry a young, rich, beautiful member of her family:

> This family plan stirred up in him a conflict as to whether he should remain faithful to the lady he loved in spite of her poverty, or whether he should follow in his father's footsteps and marry the lovely, rich and well-connected girl who had been assigned to him. And he resolved this conflict, which was in fact between his love and the persisting influence of his father's wishes, by falling ill; or, to put it more correctly, by falling ill he avoided the task of resolving it in real life. (*SE* 10: 195–99)

His father had also confronted the choice that the Ratman's mother was now presenting her son with: the choice between marrying a rich or a poor girl. In his father's case, the poor girl had been a butcher's daughter (*SE* 10: 293) and the rich girl the Ratman's mother, who brought to the uneducated father the security of the family business.

Lacan follows Freud's account closely both in seeing this family "constellation" as the pathogenic cause of the patient's neurosis, and in seeing that it had become pathogenic through its being a repetition of the father's own early experiences, of what Freud, in his case notes, called "his regression to the story of his father's marriage" (292). But, whereas Freud attributes crucial elements of this story to "chance," adding that "chance may play a part in the formation of a symptom, just as the wording may help in the making of a joke" (210–11), Lacan makes these specific chance elements effects of a structure whose existence he will put forward as being more fundamental than Freud's explanation, in terms of the conflict between the father's prohibition and the son's libidinal desire. The two chance elements that are focussed on are the debt and the choice between the rich and the "poor, but pretty" girls.

> His father, in his capacity as non-commissioned officer, had control over a small sum of money and had on occasion lost it at cards. (Thus he had been a *'Spielratte'*.) He would have found himself in a serious position if one of his comrades had not advanced him the amount. After he had left the army and become well-off, he had tried to find this friend in need so as to pay him back the money, but had not managed to trace him. The patient was uncertain whether he had ever succeeded in returning the money. The recollection of this sin of his father's youth was painful to him, for, in spite of appearances, his unconscious was filled with hostile strictures upon his father's character. The captain's words, 'You must pay back the 3.80 *kronen* to Lieutenant A.', had sounded to his ears like an allusion to this unpaid debt of his father's. (*SE* 10: 210–11)

Lacan's account places greater emphasis on this friend, and highlights—by forgetting to mention it earlier—the fact that the debt was never repaid:

> On the one hand, we have originally the father's debt to the friend; I failed to mention that he never found the friend again (this is what remains mysterious in the original story) and that he never succeeded in repaying his debt. (1953: 14; 1979: 414)

Lacan displays his acute "intuition" here, since Freud himself, in his unpublished case notes, had focussed on exactly this question, in an urgent note to himself:

> He lost some of it in a game of cards with some other men, let himself be tempted to go on playing and lost the whole of it. 'By all means shoot yourself,' said the other, 'a man who does a thing like this ought to shoot himself,' but then lent him the money. After ending his military service, his father tried to find the man, but failed. (Did he ever pay him back?) (*SE* 10: 290)

Yet in a recapitulatory account of this incident, Lacan introduces a new note, one of the mysterious stranger, "the mysterious friend who is never found and who plays such an essential role in the family legend" (1953: 28; 1979: 425)—one almost sees the black coat, the shadowy profile. Such Hoffmannesque tones would not be out of keeping with Freud's focus, again only in the case notes unavailable to Lacan, given the recommendation to suicide this stranger-friend had so firmly enounced to the father. So Lacan's tracking of the original moment of the debt to this gambling debt of the Ratman's father's youth is entirely in keeping with the way in which Freud himself had sewn the Oedipus Complex into the lining of the Ratman's family romance.

Freud and Lacan both agree, then, that the military manoeuvres of the Ratman, with the loss of the pince-nez and the compulsion to pay 3.80 kronen to Lt. A. is a repetition of the primal scene of the Ratman's father's marriage, in which he was saved from dishonor, prison, and worse by a mysterious friend, to whom he remained for the rest of his life in debt. The question of the debt is also present in the other primal scene that is repeated: the choice between the poor but pretty girl (taking over the role of the father's butcher's daughter) and the rich heiress who promises professional security. In marrying the Ratman's mother, the father placed himself in debt to her ("status comes from the mother's side" [Lacan 1953: 9]).

Yet Lacan wishes to place the accent elsewhere: instead of conflict between the father's wishes and the patient's love for the poor lady, Lacan wishes to accent the narcissistic rivalry with the father and the consequent dissolution and splitting of an object relationship. In this sense, Lacan makes the mysterious creditor friend a structural feature of the "parental imago." The general principle Lacan invokes is the following: "In this very special form of narcissistic splitting lies the drama of the neurotic" (1953: 18; 1979: 417). To back up this point, Lacan gives an account of the three terms of each scene as follows:

```
                 ┌------ Idealized woman
                 ┊
       Subject---┊------┤
                        ┊
                        └-----Debased woman


               ┌----Alienated subject
               ┊
      Woman┊--┬-----┊
             ┊ ┊
             ┊ └- Social representative, friend
```

The splitting of the function of the male subject has as its correlative the complementary splitting of the function of the female object. Lacan insists that these are two versions of one structure; it is this conviction that underpins his rejection of the triangular Oedipal structure in favor of a quaternary structure:

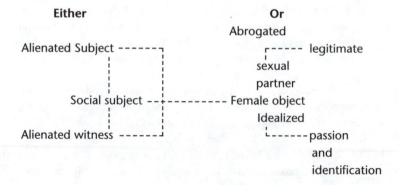

This is the account Lacan gives of the articulation of the different characters in terms of the debt:

> In order to understand thoroughly, one must see that in the original situation, as I described it to you, there is a double debt. There is, on the one hand, the frustration, indeed a kind of castration of the father. On the other hand, there is the never resolved social debt implied in the relationship to the figure of the friend in the background. We have here something quite different from the triangular relation considered to be the typical source of neurotic development. The situation presents a kind of ambiguity, of diplopia—the element of the debt is placed on two levels at once, and is precisely in the light of the impossibility of bringing these two levels together that the drama of the neurotic is played out. By trying to make one coincide with the other, he makes a perennially unsatisfying turning manoeuvre and never succeeds in closing the loop. (1953: 15; 1979: 415)

Yet in a text from the same year, Lacan began to repudiate, or at least question, the element of castration in this account of debt, and to concentrate instead on the notion of the "social debt." The means by which he achieves this is striking, since it involves accusing Freud's text of claiming something that is difficult to find in that text:

> Freud even goes so far as to take liberties with factual accuracy when it is a question of attaining to the truth of the subject. At one moment he perceives the determining role played by the proposal of marriage brought to the subject by his mother at the origin of the present phase of his neurosis. In any case, as I have shown in my seminar, Freud had had a lightning intuition of it as a result of personal experience. Nevertheless, he does not hesitate to interpret its effect to the subject as that of his dead father's prohibition against his liaison with the lady of his thoughts.
>
>   This interpretation is not only factually inaccurate. It is also psychologically inaccurate, for the castrating action of the father, which Freud affirms here with an insistence that might be considered systematic, played only a secondary role in this case. But the apperception of the dialectical relationship is so apt that Freud's act of interpretation at that moment sets off the decisive lifting of the death-bearing symbols that bind the subject narcissistically both to his dead father and to the idealized lady. (1966: 303; 1977: 88)

As I have pointed out, Freud claimed that it was a conflict between the "persistence of his father's wishes" and the Ratman's love for his lady that led to his neurosis. This "persistence" is not necessarily, not even primarily, restricted to a prohibition. But it is also clear that Freud sought to discover the source of the Ratman's fears about his father's death, and that he interpreted these fears, and the obsessional defenses against them, as evidence of *wishes* for that death.

> At this point I told him I thought he had now produced the answer we were waiting for ... The source from which hostility to his father derived its

indestructibility was evidently something in the nature of *sensual desires*, and in that connection he must have felt his father as in some way or other an *interference*. (*SE* 10: 182)

But in accusing him of factual inaccuracy, Lacan was imputing to Freud something beyond this insistence that the patient's fear of his dead father stems from early memories of interference with sensual desires. Clearly Lacan is perturbed by the fact that it is the mother's plan, not the father's, which constitutes the implicit prohibition on his marrying his lady. Lacan states that Freud sees the father's speech as prohibiting the marriage with his poor lady love:

> the turning-point came when Freud understood the resentment provoked in the subject by the calculation his mother suggested to him concerning his choice of a spouse. That Freud links the fact that such advice implied for the subject the interdiction of his engagement to the woman he loved to certain words of his father, when this linkage is in conflict with the basic facts of the matter, notably the prize fact of all that his father is dead, does surprise one, but it is justified in terms of a deeper truth, which he appears to have come upon within himself and which is revealed by the chain of associations which the subject then adds. Its justification is to be found in nothing other that what we call here the "chain of speech," which, while making itself heard in the neurosis and in the fate of the subject, extends well beyond the individual: namely that a similar lack of faith had presided over his father's marriage, and that this ambiguity itself conceals an abuse of trust in a money matter which, in driving the father out of the army, decided his marriage. . .
>
> But if Freud's interpretation, so as to untie this chain, with all its latent significance, will end up dissolving the imaginary web of the neurosis, that is because, in terms of the symbolic debt which is promulgated by the subject's tribunal, this chain renders him comparable less to his legatee than to his living witness. (1966: 353–55)

Some clarifications may help here. Lacan conflates the father's opposition to the poor girl with the mother's promotion of the rich girl. Now, Freud sees that for the Ratman this conflation also takes place: from the Ratman's point of view the choice 'rich girl vs poor girl' lines up his own desire against those of his family, particularly against the disapproval his father expresses of the lady ("his father, shortly before his death, had directly opposed what later became our patient's dominating passion. He had noticed that his son was always in the lady's company, and had advised him to keep away from her, saying that it was imprudent of him and that he would make a fool of himself" [*SE* 10: 201]). Yet at no point in his compte-rendu does Freud impute to the father an *active* prohibition of the marriage to the poor lady. Lacan is, we might say, textually incorrect, but, one must immediately add, true to the entire thrust of Freud's reconstruction. Because behind the mother's plan to marry her son into her family and its business is, for the Ratman, the coincidence of this plan with the choice his father made, marrying (his mother) for

money, not love. The Ratman's conflict about his father is not so much the prohibition, as the identification that is being required of him. And, we might say, Freud's
careful term "persistent influence of his father's wishes [*fortwickenden Willen des
Vaters*]," interpreted too readily by Lacan as "prohibition," covers both cases.

The background to this flurry of imputed factual inaccuracies and textual impre-
cisions is the long-term strategy of Lacan's reading of the Ratman. This reading will
lead to two fundamental revisions of the Freudian account. The first is the need "to
make certain structural modifications in the oedipal myth, inasmuch as it is at the
heart of the analytic experience" (Lacan 1979: 407). This modification will require
Lacan to introduce the concept of the moral master, the Absolute Master, we might
say, the antecedent of the concepts of the Other and the Master in Lacan's later
writings. In the case histories we perceive the "fundamental conflict which, through
the mediation of rivalry with the father, binds the subject to an essential symbolic
value" (407). This binding occurs in relation to an actual debasement of the figure
of the father; analysis takes place in the space, or the gap, or the ambiguity, between
the debased and this other, masterly figure of the father:

> the analyst nevertheless assumes almost surreptitiously, in the symbolic
> relationship with the subject, the position of this figure dimmed in the
> course of history, that of the master—the moral master, the master who ini-
> tiates the one still in ignorance into the dimension of fundamental human
> relationships and who opens for him what one might call the way to moral
> consciousness, even to wisdom, in assuming the human condition. (407–8)

Whereas Derrida, in his reading of *The Purloined Letter*, accuses Lacan of an
unwarranted superposition of the triangular Oedipal scenario on the scene of the
theft of the letter (Minister, King, Queen—where is the observer/narrator of this
scene? Derrida asks), in the case history of the Ratman it is Lacan who, in effect,
accuses Freud of superimposing an Oedipal triangle (prohibiting father, object
mother, desiring subject). The discovery that there are four, not three, elements
involved in the neurotic's individual myth requires a revision of the founding myth
of psychoanalysis:

> The quaternary system so fundamental to the impasses, the insolubilities in
> the life situation of neurotics, has a structure quite different from the one
> traditionally given—the incestuous desire for the mother, the father's pro-
> hibition, its obstructive effects, and, around all that, the more or less luxu-
> riant proliferation of symptoms. I think that this difference ought to lead us
> to question the general anthropology derived from analytic doctrine as it
> has been taught up to the present. In short, the whole oedipal schema needs
> to be re-examined. (1953: 25; 1979: 422)

The splitting of one of the three figures in the Oedipus myth is what makes this revision necessary, and Lacan gives, as I have already noted, an account of how each of
the three terms of the Oedipal triangle may be split: the subject (social subject and
alienated witness), object, the woman (rich vs. poor; legitimate vs. passionate

object) and the mediating third term, the father (debased, symbolic). However, the scene of splitting, although prone to being duplicated in a variety of ways, stems from a single fundamental moment—the specular moment of narcissism, imbued with aggressivity and idealization. This is the second of Lacan's fundamental revisions of the Freudian account: "The narcissistic relation to a fellow being is the fundamental experience in the development of the imaginary sphere in human beings" (1979: 423). Yet this discovery of the fundamental character of narcissism, usually summed up in accounts of Lacan's work under the rubric of the mirror-phase, was always linked with the question of the position of the father in the symptomatology, the mythology of the neurotic. More than any other analyst, more even than Freud, I suggest, Lacan was concerned with the destiny of the father. The question of the father emerges in an anthropological, even culturalist register in Lacan's writings of the 1930s, already juxtaposed with, contrasted with, and correcting the myth of the primal father found in Freud's *Totem and Taboo*:

> Our experience leads us to discern the principal determinant [of the major contemporary neurosis] in the father's personality, which is always lacking in some respect: absent, humiliated, divided against himself or a sham. (1938: 8.40–16)

On the basis of this phenomenology of the neuroses, Lacan suggests an explanation for the very existence of psychoanalysis:

> a great number of psychological phenomena appear to stem from the decline in society of the paternal imago . . . Perhaps the very emergence of psychoanalysis should be linked to this crisis. The sublime chance of genius does not, perhaps, by itself explain that it was in Vienna—then the centre of a State which was the melting pot [in English] of extremely diverse familial forms, from the most primitive to the most sophisticated, from the last agnatic groupings of Slav peasants to the most simplified petit-bourgeois households and the most decadent of unstable family menages, by way of feudal and mercantile paternalisms—that a son of the Jewish patriarchy came up with the Oedipus complex. (8.40–16)

In this culturalist account of the origins of psychoanalysis, Freud's discovery of the Oedipus complex is linked to his prior investigation of the anomie whose two principal causes are the incomplete repression of desire for the mother, and the "narcissistic degeneration of the idealization of the father, which highlights, in the Oedipal identification, the aggressive ambivalence immanent in the primitive relation to one's counterpart" (8.42–5).

At the center of the Oedipus complex, for Lacan in 1938, stands "the father, in so far as he represents authority and in so far as he is the centre of sexual revelation; we have linked to the inherent ambiguity of his imago, the incarnation of repression and catalyst of an essential access to reality, the twofold development, typical of our culture, of a certain character of the super-ego and a particularly evolutive orientation of the personality" (8.42–6–7).

We should not forget that in the 1930s the attention of most psychoanalysts was turned to the question of the mother, and away from the father. Lacan's early work reflects these researches, in particular those of Melanie Klein, and the importance of what he called the "separation complex," which included what other analysts would have called oral and anal sexualities. Yet however modified and central the figure of the mother became in his work, he insisted on the pivotal role played by the father—even, in 1949, in the culturalist dialect of the absent, wounded or unemployed father:

> The maternal imago is far more castrating than the paternal imago. At the end of each of my analyses, I have seen appear the fantasy of dismembering, the myth of Osiris. It is when the father is lacking in some way (dead, absent, blind even), that the most severe neuroses develop. (1949: 317)

Lacan's reflections expressed a nostalgia for a society where familial structures would, "at each stage in life, become enriched by a growing complexity of hierarchical relations" (1966: 133). The themes continued into the 1960s, when he described the obligation of the small boy confronted with the symbolic burden of the phallus as the continuation of "Daddy's rules, and as everyone knows, for some time now Daddy hasn't had any rules at all, and that's where all the problems start" (1961–62: 9). On many occasions we are reminded of this grandiose figure of the father whose decline we have participated in, indeed inherited. Yet we are inclined to forget that the tragic cast of this now ancient story—if in keeping both with Freud's vision of the murdered father at the beginning of history, and with Lacan's invocation of the "stone guest who comes, in symptoms, to disturb the banquet of one's desires" (1977: 143)[5]—is equally invoked in the comic mode of Count Almaviva, condemned to be forgiven by his spouse instead of exercising his *droit, ou dette, de seigneur.*

So, BY THE 1930S (AND THROUGH TO THE EARLY 1950S), Lacan had established the doctrinal foundation of the decline of the father imago and its relation to imaginary narcissistic rivalry; he made it clear that the Oedipus complex was itself a culturally relative structure, linked to the familial and marital structures of modern society, and to the decline of the father. With his examination of the Ratman case history he found, in the very symptom the patient presented, a term which would allow him to take one more step towards elaborating the system of the Symbolic, Imaginary, and Real with which he would be able to replace, or at least reinterpret, the Oedipus complex. That term was "debt." As the clear doctrinal exposition of the "Discours de Rome" put it:

> the paternal function concentrates in itself both imaginary and real relations, always more or less inadequate to the symbolic relation that essentially constitutes it. It is in the *name of the father* that we must recognize the support of the symbolic function which, from the dawn of history, has identified his person with the figure of the law. This conception enables us to distinguish clearly, in the analysis of a case, the unconscious effects of

this function from the narcissistic relations . . . Thus it is the virtue of the Word that perpetuates the movement of the Great Debt whose economy Rabelais, in a famous metaphor, extended to the stars themselves. (1966: 278; 1977: 67)

The English translator of the *Ecrits* helpfully provides the reference from Rabelais. Debt, says Panurge, is "the connecting link between Earth and Heaven, the unique mainstay of the human race; one, I believe, without which all mankind would speedily perish." Debts, he continues, are "the great soul of the universe" (1977: 109).

This passage confirms the way in which Lacan conceives of his androcentric psychoanalytic revision: one will not be able to understand or intervene effectively in the Oedipus complex if one does not recognize the "interference" of narcissistic rivalry and fascination which one finds in the figure of the imaginary father; the surest way to secure this recognition is to remain aware of the fundamental symbolic function of the father. As the Rabelais reference indicates, the universe that the symbolic father inhabits is the universe of the Grande Dette.

Let us remind ourselves that for the Ratman, the debt in question was purely imaginary. By the time he came to Freud, the real debt had already been paid off. What was left of his *delire* were occasional impulses to find Lieutenant A. and pay the debt. And these impulses were redirected toward a search for a doctor who would help him pay off his debt:

> His determination to consult a doctor was woven into his delirium in the following ingenious manner. He thought he would get a doctor to give him a certificate to the effect that it was necessary for him, in order to recover his health, to perform some such action as he had planned in connection with Lieutenant A.; and the lieutenant would no doubt let himself be persuaded by the certificate into accepting the 3.80 crowns from him. The chance that one of my books happened to fall into his hands at that moment directed his choice to me. There was no question of getting a certificate from me, however, [*Bei mir war aber jenem Zeugnis nicht die Rede*] all that he asked of me was, very reasonably, to be freed of his obsessions. (*SE* 10: 173)

But Freud is quite certain that he will not help this deluded patient to pay off any debt whatsoever. Freud will offer him freedom. He will not help him pay his debt.

Yet this debt will, for Lacan, become something magnificent, the mark of individual destiny, and the signifier of the social order itself. Perhaps it is significant that Lacan overlooked this passage in Freud's case history and, in one reading distorted the chronology of the case history so that Freud emerges as the friend who did help him pay his debt: "once the treatment is begun, he is content quite simply to send a money order to the lady at the post office" (1953: 13; 1979: 414). Lacan con-certinas the chronology here: the Ratman had paid the generous lady at the post office well before coming to analysis with Freud. In so doing, Lacan elides the presence of the sensible friend, and coalesces the action of the sensible friend and Freud, who had had nothing to do with the repayment of the debt to the lady at the post office:

> His friend had held up his hands in amazement to think that he could still be in doubt whether he was suffering from an obsession, and had calmed him down for the night, so that he had slept excellently. Next morning they had gone together to the post office, to dispatch the 3.80 *kronen* to the post office [Z——] at which the packet containing the pince-nez had arrived. (*SE* 10: 172)

In this elision, we glimpse the long-term strategy of Lacan's revision of psychoanalytic theory. Through his reading of the Ratman case history, he will install the notion of debt as a crucial element of the quaternary structure that replaces the Oedipus complex. This debt is no longer imaginary; it will be called "symbolic debt." The fact that Lacan makes Freud, in his analytic role, the best possible representative of the symbolic function, actively involved (despite the phrase "tout bonnement") in the repayment of the debt, in the place of the friend, shows how Lacan will shift the Ratman's debt from the register of the imaginary to that of the symbolic. This elision of the friend and the analyst in the course of the interpretation which leads him to the centrality of the symbolic debt is associated with another curious amalgamation we find in his commentaries on this case: the rapprochement of the analyst and the patient.

On two different occasions, with respect to two different elements, Lacan amalgamates the unconscious of the analyst and that of the patient. The first concerns Freud's own arranged marriage. Twice, Lacan points out that Freud was able to perceive the determining role of the mother's marriage plan in the Ratman's neurosis as a result of a personal experience (1966: 302). On the second of these occasions, in "Variantes de la cure-type," he specifies the incident to which he is referring:

> Now it appears that Freud's gaining access to the crucial point of the meaning, in which the subject can literally decipher his destiny, was made possible by the fact of having himself been the object of a similar suggestion stemming from prudential family considerations—which we know about through a portion of his self-analysis to be found in his writings, unmasked by Bernfeld—and if, on that occasion, he hadn't responded with opposition, that might have been enough for him to have missed the moment, in treatment, of recognizing it. (1966: 354–55)

Lacan is alluding here to the paper "Screen memories," in which Freud showed how his earliest memory—of playing in the field near Freiburg with his two playmates, John and Pauline—was a product of the repression of two later events: his calf-love for Gisela Fluss at the age of sixteen, and his father's and brother's plan to marry him to his cousin Pauline and settle them in Manchester (*SE* 3: 314).[6] Lacan is surmising that in order to be able to recognize the determining effect of the Ratman's mother's proposed marriage on the neurosis, Freud must himself have reacted, when nineteen, with opposition to the plan his family had cooked up; if he had not, if he had acquiesced in the plan, he would not have been able to recognize this incident as the cause of the neurosis. A strong claim, couched in a characteristically oblique fashion. It proposes, in effect, that the neurotic formation of Freud's that corresponds to the Ratman's obsessional neurosis was his screen memory, and it was through the similarity of structure of these two neurotic formations that Freud was able to isolate the precipitating cause, the fundamental determinant, of the recent phase of the Ratman's neurosis. What Lacan does not point out is that Freud had already *analyzed* this particular neurotic symptom, his screen memory, and that rather than having been in a position to identify with the unconscious structure, he had benefited from some knowledge of the structure that was organized around the marriage proposal.

We might also add another element which brought Freud's and the Ratman's personal experiences together: the analysis of Freud's own dream of *Company at table or table d'hôte*, which centered on the idea of what has to be paid for love, and the debts we necessarily incur in our friendships and family relations (see *SE 5*: 636–9; Anzieu 1986). The desire was expressed in the dream through the theme of "beautiful eyes." Freud's crowning interpretation was, as it would be in the key transferential dream of the Ratman, that he wished to be loved for his *beaux yeux* only, he wished to be loved for love that was not *countable*, not rendered in the register of gratitude and debt—love beyond the debt principle. However, where Freud's dream registered a protest against love's always having to be paid for, the Ratman's dream eagerly forced love into the framework of a marriage with Freud's daughter which was for her money, not her beauty. Whereas Freud already inhabited the register of marriage, yet regretted the curtailments that implied, the Ratman refused to recognize the register itself, save in his dreams and symptoms, since marriage meant for him the identification with his (dead) father and the renunciation of love in favour of money (rats).

That such rapprochements between Freud and his patient can be drawn is clear. Yet the second of Lacan's rapprochements is far more curious, because so obscure as to be almost undetectable. It occurs in the rhetorically baroque and esoteric penultimate section of "La chose freudienne," the section entitled "La dette symbolique." The title indicates that, for my reading of Lacan's reading of Freud, this is a key passage:

> Will our action go as far, then, as to repress the very truth that it bears in its exercise? Will it send this truth back to sleep, a truth that Freud in the passion of the Rat Man would maintain presented for ever to our recognition, even if we must increasingly divert our vigilance away from it: namely, that it is out of the forfeits and vain oaths, lapses in speech and unconsidered words, the constellation of which presides at the putting into the world of a man, that is moulded the stone guest who comes, in symptoms, to disturb the banquet of one's desires?
>
> For the unripe grape of speech by which the child receives too early from a father the authentification of the nothingness of existence, and the bunch of wrath that replies to the words of this false hope with which the mother

has baited him in feeding him with the milk of her true despair, set his teeth
on edge more than having been weaned on/from an imaginary *jouissance* or
even having been deprived of such real attentions. (1977: 143)[7]

The mention of the Ratman's passion leads one to believe that the two allusions
that follow are to his experience; far from it. The two references of the second paragraph are, I deduce, taken not from the Ratman's childhood, but from Freud's own
catalogue of childhood experiences. The first refers to the judgement passed by his
father on the son who had urinated in his parents's bedroom: "The boy will come
to nothing"—a judgement which pursued Freud in his dreams for the rest of his life,
obliging him to enumerate constantly for his imaginary father the substantiality of
his existence (*SE* 4: 216).

There is, it is true, an episode in the Ratman's childhood which has some similarities with Freud's memory: when the father declares that his son's elemental fury
indicates he will be either a great man or a great criminal (*SE* 10: 205). Freud adds
in a note, as if wanting to confirm the importance of such prophecies, that the
father overlooked the most likely outcome of such premature passions: a neurosis.
But this incident from the Ratman's childhood could not be, despite the obliquity
of Lacan's prose, what is referred to with the phrase "the authentification of the
nothingness of existence"; at most, it provided Lacan with a switchword to the
Freudian allusion.

The second allusion, to the mother's despair, is, I suspect, to the vivid demonstration of mortality that Freud's mother once gave him:

> When I was six years old and was given my first lessons by my mother, I
> was expected to believe that we were all made of earth and must therefore
> return to earth. This did not suit me and I expressed doubts of the doctrine.
> My mother thereupon rubbed the palms of her hands together—just as she
> did in making dumplings, except that there was no dough between them—
> and showed me the blackish scales of *epidermis* produced by the friction as
> a proof that we were made of earth. (*SE* 4: 205)

And, Freud continues, "I acquiesced in the belief which I was later to hear
expressed in the words: 'Du bist der Natur einen Tod schuldig' ['Thou owest
Nature a death']."[8]

With this passage, we have stumbled upon the strangest, most allusive sub-text
to Lacan's commentary on the Ratman: passing via an elision between the Ratman's
and Freud's childhood experiences, we come upon the unpayable debt of each
speaking being, which Lacan, in a less Shakespearian, less directly religious mode,
will call, a page later, "the symbolic debt for which the subject as subject of speech
is responsible" (1977: 143).[9] Passing from the Ratman, via a circuitous reading of
Freud, we arrive at the final doctrinal end-point: the symbolic debt of the subject
insofar as he is speaking, the debt he owes to the Other.

Debt as a fundamental property of the Symbolic is the mature Lacanian axiom.
The notion of symbolic debt is indissolubly linked to the notion of the symbolic
father, whose genesis from the 1930s on we have followed:

the attribute of procreation to the father can only be the effect of a pure signifier, of a recognition, not of a real father, but of what religion has taught us to refer to as the Name-of-the-Father.

Of course, there is no need of a signifier to be a father, any more than to be dead, but without a signifier, no one would ever know anything about either state of being.

I would take this opportunity of reminding those who cannot be persuaded to seek in Freud's texts an extension of the enlightenment that their pedagogues dispense to them how insistently Freud stresses the affinity of the two signifying relations that I have just referred to, whenever the neurotic subject (especially the obsessional) manifests this affinity through the conjunction of the themes of the father and death.

How, indeed, could Freud fail to recognize such an affinity, when the necessity of his reflexion led him to link the appearance of the signifier of the Father, as the author of the Law, with death, even to the murder of the Father—this showing that if this murder is the fruitful moment of debt through which the subject binds himself for life to the Law, the symbolic Father is, in so far as he signifies this Law, the dead Father. (1977: 199)

The debt is now Lacan's manner of purifying the notion of guilt and of morality at its "instinctual" sources. The ambiguity of the Ratman's debt—the imaginary debt to the friend as separate from the symbolic debt to his father, which can only be recognized once he ceases, as Freud put it, to deny the death of his father—is now the means by which Lacan can articulate the junction of the symbolic and the imaginary. And with the register of debt, Lacan can fuse the notion of exchange, borrowed from the anthropology of Marcel Mauss (*le don*) and Claude Lévi-Strauss, with the exchange of words, the pure symbols that constitute the articulation of the Symbolic, and, most intriguingly, with the register of money. For can we forget that debt is first and foremost a financial term? It certainly was for the Ratman, and for Freud, who talked of the regular rat currency his patient had created, in which even the psychoanalyst was paid in those countable rats, florins.

WE MUST NOW ASK: WITH WHAT THEORY OF MONEY does Lacan propose to underpin his concept of debt? The most obvious feature of the theory of money is that it appears to be subsumed within a general theory of exchange, that of Mauss, in which the act of giving imposes an obligation upon the recipient. Money, in this theory, is simply the objective measure of obligation, the measure of debt. Certain features of this theory can then be applied across to whatever else is exchangeable. Lacan's axiom is that the Symbolic will be more deeply grounded in the gift of one specific human property, that of speech: "it is by way of this gift [of speech] that all reality has come to man and it is by his continued act that he maintains it" (1977: 106). Hence all symbolic elements can be exchanged, via the universal medium of speech; speech itself is both medium and element transmitted. Thus, for instance, the function of symbolic love can be deduced from the theory of potlatch in Mauss: love is the gift of what one hasn't, just as one accumulates debts to the destroyers of pigs through being present at the potlatch feast, in which the objects of symbolic exchange—"pots made to remain empty, shields too heavy to be carried, sheaves of wheat that wither, lances stuck in the ground" (1977: 61–2)—are "the signifiers of the pact that they constitute as signified" (61).

The register of symbolic debt also allows Lacan to recast many of the difficulties in Freudian theory. If "what does a woman want?" is the enigmatic question that haunts Freud's theory of sexuality—he had begun with the intention of dispensing with the question altogether but found himself obliged to return to it once his attention has been turned to the maternal function—then the correspondingly persistent Lacanian enigma is: "What is a father?" Where Freud conceives of the passage from girl to woman as being complex, delicate, and beset with difficulties, for Lacan becoming a man is the psychoanalytic problem. The boy's trajectory becomes complex because of the necessity of his identification with the parent of the same sex who also functions as the bearer of the object of the mother's desire; according to the fundamental formula of desire, desire is the desire of the other, and following the child's recognition of the mother's desire being the desire of the other, the girl simply locates the lack of mother's phallus as being the child. For her, there is the simple chain, the simple system of exchanges, from gift to penis. The boy's destiny raises the question of *being* the father, and the confusion of having the penis and having the phallus. To which Lacan provides the answer: "What the boy has, as an appurtenance, he must take it as from another; this is what we have called the *symbolic debt*." (1956–57: 851).

Lacan thus used the Ratman's debt to put together his revision of "the general anthropology derived from analytic doctrine" (1953: 25; 1979: 422). With the concept of debt, Lacan had found something that would harmonize equally well with both the theory of the lack, whether in its existential version (*manque-à-être*) or in its erotic version (the lack of the phallus), and the theory of speech, exchange and death which underpinned the revision of the psychoanalytic anthropology. The reading of Freud he gave that underpinned this new anthropology was certainly idiosyncratic, one might even say retroactively effective:

> in establishing, in *The interpretation of dreams*, the Oedipus complex as the central motivation of the unconscious, he recognized this unconscious as the agency of the laws on which marriage alliance and kinship are based. . . it is essentially on sexual relations—by ordering them according to the laws of preferential marriage alliances and forbidden relations—that the first combinatory for the exchanges of women between nominal lineages is based, in order to develop in an exchange of gifts and in an exchange of master-words the fundamental commerce and concrete discourse on which human societies are based. (1977: 172)

This combinatory of exchanges—of gifts, women, and words—is a fundamental departure from Freud's theory. And in the 1930s Lacan had explicitly recognized it as such: the model of one primal horde, transformed into a society through the inner logic of the murder of the primal father had, Lacan sensed, included the key (neo-Hegelian, neo-Kojèvian) intuition that the father becomes a human father insofar as he is dead; however, *Totem and Taboo*'s model of social relations was not

only historically but also conceptually implausible (see Borch-Jacobsen 1991).
Replacing the anthropology of the father's murder, the key term in Lacan's anthropology became exchange. There are elementary structures of lineages, secured by
the dynamic reality of renewed and repeated exchange—of women, gifts and
words. And "the exchange that characterizes such a society has other foundations
than the needs even to satisfy them, what has been called the gift 'as total social
fact'" (1977: 127).

The metaphysics of speech eventually came to underpin this system of exchange,
which embodied the overly formal Maussian theory of the gift as expressing an
algebra of obligation and reciprocity. To found a more generalized anthropology
for psychoanalysis, Lacan turned to a theory of full speech, of the unconditional
obligation and unconscious effects of every act of speech (see Forrester 1990:
141–67). And in this theory of speech, we come back to our starting-point, the pre-
requisites of trust and of faith: the Good Faith of the Other invoked in the act of
speech (Lacan 1966: 454). The concept of debt also finds a natural home here. It is
a means by which Lacan brings into the circle of mediations the concept of death.
As the quote at the head of this paper indicates, and as Freud's Shakespearean
"Thou owest Nature a death" implies, the debt that over-trumps all others, the debt
that Lacan suggests all other debts reduce to, is the debt of death. We owe our lives
to the dead father.

Yet this attempt to find the unit of currency of symbolic debt in death is not
entirely convincing. Take a step back in the argument. To talk of debt, we must be
in the realm of the countable. We must always be able to ask: "How *much* is
owed?" We can take our cue from the Ratman: he knew *exactly* how much he owed
to Lieutenant A., and Freud's text repeats the figure frequently: 3.80 *kronen*. But,
as Freud and Lacan are both aware, this is his imaginary debt. His symbolic debt
may well have been, may have had to have been, countable in a different currency.
But in order to be in any sense related to our ordinary sense of what debt is, we
should take our argument from another Hegelian, Karl Marx:

> this commodity [exchange value] is the commodity as money, and, to be
> more precise, not as money in general, but as a *certain definite sum of
> money*, for, in order to represent exchange value in all its variety, money
> has to be countable, quantitatively divisible. Money—the common form
> into which all commodities as exchange values are transformed, i.e. the
> universal commodity—must itself exist as a *particular* commodity along-
> side the others, since what is required is not only that they can be measured
> against it in the head, but that they can be changed and exchanged for it in
> the actual exchange process. (Marx 1973: 165)

So what is the currency of Lacan's symbolic debt?

Lacan's social theory vacillates on this point. Is he committed to the view that
debt is measured in terms of a substance, like coins or paper? Or does he view debt
as an accounting procedure, a system of writing which records the transactions of
the parties? His espousal of the Maussian exchange theory implicitly commits him
to the concept of money as a unit of account, of its fundamental relation to oblig-

ation and debt. And we might view his later explorations of number theory as one way to render this assumption more plausible and more rational.

Equally apposite is the question of whether money is a measure of exchange or whether it is a representative of debt (see Macleod 1872). Lacan appears to conflate exchange and debt. The debt theory has the advantage of linking money closely to the theory of contract and thus to the creditors and debtors linked together by contracts. It does have one paradoxical feature, though, that Lacan would have appreciated: because one cannot be in debt to oneself, the Central Bank finds itself in a self-contradictory position. It lists notes it holds as assets, whereas in fact these are debts to the Issuing Department of the Bank. The bank solves the paradox as follows: it publishes how many notes it possesses as assets, but in fact they are counted in order to show *how few* it has, not how many. The number of notes it possesses is a guarantee of the *limits* of the Bank's printing capacity. Again, the Bank's assets amount to being a measure of the confidence, the trust, and the sense of its good faith that it is instilling in its customers.

This aspect of so many theories of money may help us address Lacan's problem. There does seem to be some kind of centralized agency in Lacan's theory, corresponding to the function of the Bank. It is sometimes given attributes appropriate to a Bank, when it is called the "treasury of signifiers." This is Lacan's concept of the Other. The notorious indefiniteness of Lacan's concept of the Other includes, amongst many others, this financial function of upholding the system of debt that the symbolic father creates, of keeping it from folding in a crisis of confidence. And we also know the element that functions as some kind of guarantee of the system: it is known as the phallus, the gold standard of the system of symbolic debt. This is one of the bridges to the psychoanalytic theory of sexuality: the phallus is the key term by which the notion of symbolic debt is rendered workable in clinical accounts of sexuality. The phallus very neatly conforms to another of the properties of money that Marx noted (1973: 163), that of allowing "the equation of the incompatible," as Shakespeare nicely defined money in *Timons of Athens*:

> ' . . . Thou visible God!
> That solder'st close impossibilities,
> And mak'st them kiss!' (Act 4, Scene 3)

After all, the phallus acts, as a famously controversial passage from Lacan asserts, by joining "la part du logos" to "l'avènement du désir":

> It can be said that this signifier is chosen because it is the most tangible element in the real of sexual copulation, and also the most symbolic in the literal (typographical) sense of the term, since it is equivalent to the (logical) copula. It might also be said that, by virtue of its turgidity, it is the image of the vital flow as it is transmitted in generation. (1966: 692; 1977: 287)

Lacan also sensed that a system of exchange, of money, may not be an entirely stable self-regulating system; it may require something outside of itself to maintain it. Money often attaches itself to other social institutions (e.g., the State as guaranteed by its military power) for this stabilizing function. Here again, like the Bank, Lacan may have felt that the reference to the good faith, the confidence, of the creditors suffices.

Yet we have not found the means by which to measure debt. We have two plausible answers in Lacan's work: the phallus (as the gold standard issued by the treasury of signifiers) and the order of the signifier itself. Perhaps we might conclude that the currency in which the symbolic debt is counted will be unique to each and every analytic subject. The rat currency of the Ratman will have to remain our model, by which to look beyond his imaginary commerce to the symbolic debt he owed his father, which can only be recognized through the mediation of his death. Certainly the Ratman and Lacan would have appreciated the description of paradise of the Tangu of New Guinea, summed up in the word *mngwotngwotiki*, which means "a particular field of relations in which the individuals concerned are temporarily unobliged to each other" (Burridge 1969: 8).

There is, moreover, a lesson in psychoanalytic technique to be drawn from the question of the countability of the symbolic debt. We have seen how Freud was quite clear that he would not get drawn into the system of imaginary debts the Ratman was caught in, and I have drawn attention to the fact that Lacan, mistakenly, implicated Freud more closely in that system than did Freud's own account. Freud does not respond to the Ratman's demand for a medical certificate to aid his payment of the debt which still haunts him. There is, however, the by no means simple question of extricating oneself from the transference. As Lacan put it in his allegory of psychoanalysis (which uses the same model as his analysis of the Ratman): "If symbolic efficacy stops there [with the finding and the return of the purloined letter to the Prefect], is that because the symbolic debt is also extinguished there?" (1966: 36) Lacan shows that it is not so easy for Dupin to extract himself from the letter's symbolic circuit. Two incidents demonstrate this. First, the infernal trap Dupin leaves for the Minister, with the deadly lines from Crébillon. This, as Lacan indicates, and as Derrida underlines in his commentary "Le facteur de la vérité," shows how Dupin does not extract himself successfully. Does the other incident prove the termination of the system of obligations and debts of analysis any the more likely?

> Does this mean that this Dupin, who up until then was an admirable, almost excessively lucid character, has all of a sudden become a small time wheeler and dealer? I don't hesitate to see in this action the re-purchasing of what one could call the bad *mana* attached to the letter. And indeed, from the moment he receives his fee, he has pulled out of the game. It isn't only because he has handed the letter over to another, but because his motives are clear to everyone—he got his money, it's no longer of any concern to him. I don't mean to insist on it, but you might gently point out to me that we, who spend our time being the bearers of all the purloined letters of the patient, also get paid somewhat dearly. Think about this with some care—were we not to be paid, we would get involved in the drama of Atreus and Thyestes, the drama in which all the subjects who come to confide the truth in us are involved. They tell us their damned [*sacré*] stories,

and because of that we are not at all within the domain of the sacred and of sacrifice. Everyone knows that money doesn't just buy things, but that the prices which, in our culture, are calculated at rock-bottom, have the function of neutralising something infinitely more dangerous than paying in money, namely owing somebody something. (1978: 239; 1988a: 204)

In truth, this does not seem a very reliable method for extracting oneself from the system of symbolic debt. And this dangerous situation of owing something to somebody reminds us that, in the end, it is not clear if Lacan as a reader of Freud owes more to Freud than Freud owes to Lacan, to posterity and any given reader whatsoever. After all, if symbolic debt is countable and commutative, then the dead are in credit to posterity.

NOTES

This study was commissioned by Conrad Stein for a conference on "Lacan lecteur de Freud," organized by Association d'Etudes Freudiennes, 20-22 September 1991, in Paris.

1. The word "Lacon" is derived from the ascetic habits of the Laconians, or Spartans (see Colton 1882: 49).
2. There are moments, however, in the *Ecrits*, where there is a flurry of page references to Freud's texts (e.g., "Intervention sur le transfert"); but even when he is closely following a text, and directing his reader's attention to that text, Lacan does not directly quote that text.
3. The French version of this text that I am using is the unpublished 1953 mimeo. version issued by the Centre de la Documentation Universitaire, a copy is deposited in the Bibliothèque Nationale. The published French version does not differ significantly from the 1953 version.
4. Freud to the Ratman, 21 December, 1907. Note that this volume of the *Standard Edition* (*SE* 10), in which the Ratman's case notes first appeared, was first published in 1956, some time after most of Lacan's discussions of the Ratman; hence the original case notes were not available to him.
5. See Muller and Richardson (1982: 159) for a correction of the translation of this passage.
6. See McGrath (1986: 129–31); Swales (1983: 33–7); and Appignanesi and Forrester (1992: 23–7).
7. See Muller and Richardson (1982: 158) for a correction of the translation of this passage.
8. A version of the Shakespearian 'Thou owest God a death.'
9. See Muller and Richardson (1982: 159) for a correction of the translation of this passage.

lacan, sure — and then what?

Daniel Bougnoux

translation by
John Caruana and Charles Dudas

Editor's Note

Freud was always unclear about the relationship between the analysand's speech and the (repressed) truth, since he never devised a theory of language. According to Daniel Bougnoux, Lacan solved this problem by theorizing a "speech divested of its referential element." In other words, Lacan directed psychoanalysis away from the patient's memory of an actual event and towards the self-referentiality of his or her own speech within the analytic setting. Bougnoux thus argues that Lacan's view of referentiality made psychoanalysis "non-criticizable."

To this end, Bougnoux critically explores Lacan's structuralist re-reading of psychoanalysis. He argues that Lacan adopted exchange theory (through Lévi-Strauss) the better to disable Saussure's correspondence theory of truth. In its place, Lacan invoked the "omni-signifier" without grounding in the *point de capiton* of a signified. Bougnoux examines the four "proofs" Lacan offered to substantiate his views: dream distortion, metaphor, metonymy, and rhetoric in psychoanalysis.

Railing against the "stupefying project" that reduces everything to language, the signifier, self-referentiality, and finally, the Symbolic, Bougnoux prefers the "dynamism" of the Freudian unconscious. For it is with Freud that psychoanalysis at least recognized the vital concerns that Lacan left behind with his structuralist "calculus"—concerns of affect, history, cure, suffering, and so on. Throughout this essay, Bougnoux provides a well argued and unflinching assessment of Lacan that should attract a wide audience of readers, including those with a special interest in speech act theory.

DANIEL BOUGNOUX is Professor of Sciences de la communication, Université Stendhal, Grenoble. His books include *Vices et vertus des cercles: l'autoréférence en poétique et pragmatique* (La Découverte, 1989), *La Communication par la bande: introduction aux sciences de l'information et de la communication* (La Decouverte, 1991), *Le Fantôme de la psychanalyse: critique de l'archéologie freudienne* (Ombres/du Mirail, 1991), and *Sciences de l'information et de la communication* (Larousse, 1993). His newest work, *La Communication contre l'information*, is forthcoming.

THE THREAD THAT HELD TOGETHER THE LACAN LEGEND—a romantic fiction which Lacan's character certainly helped to nourish from 1960 to 1980—is presently unravelling. Ten years after his death, Lacan's daughter edits an album of photographs in which piety blends with the comical (as when he strikes a saintly pose for the camera); the *Collège International de Philosophie* organizes an important symposium; former patients publish their wonder-filled recollections of their time spent on his couch (recently sold at an auction for just under one hundred thousand francs); and Minister Jack Lang[1] is urged to make *5, rue de Lille* into a museum, and gives a speech to that effect. While canonization of Lacan proceeds as well as can be expected, the search for patients hardens in a market that is, henceforth, bitterly contested. Will new openings—yesterday, Latin America, tomorrow, Eastern Europe or Russia—compensate for the evident shortage of patients that threatens psychoanalysts in Paris? Satirical pamphlets, along with pirated editions of Lacan's famous seminars, appear. Meanwhile, the official editions, authorized by Lacan's editor, Jacques-Alain Miller, are passed on to the publisher, Seuil, with a slowness that the poor editing does not justify.

And still, a reference to Lacan continues to carry authority. In a recent address that constitutes a surprising reassessment, Derrida now sees in Lacan's work a bulwark against the "insipid restoration [of the subject that] is presently in progress." For other philosophers, no doubt, Lacan offers today, after the misadventures of the Heidegger affair, an inexhaustible reservoir of commentaries and the best of any alternative metaphysics. For the clinicians, the Lacanian citation, clinging to discourse like a pin, as always yields its added value of dandyism. It also serves to attest to a kind of eccentric originality or imagination; a touch of folly which, since Clérambault, still manifests itself amongst the physicians making the rounds of the (mental) hospital. Others, the piece-workers of Lacanism, have succeeded, not without due pain and effort, in acquiring this marvellous *article de Paris*; they cling to it, and cannot allow themselves to leave it again. We have all come across these virgins or chaste women who, in the dimmer recesses of their hearts, conceived and parsimoniously nourished the sacred words: *Signifier, big Other, objet petit a*, and many others. They played with the "knots" and, in this grand effort, ruined their health. The procession of Lacan's followers is a march to the whistle. They travel and timidly pay to hear their gurus and, should they happen to write, churn out annoying literature. The world might change, but these people take no notice. Don't they ever get it? In this respect, the contrast is sharp between Lacan's sparkling intellect—his incredible cultural receptivity to the intellectual innovations of his time—and the mental restriction or lack of curiosity of his followers, which verges on stupidity. Lacan, himself, certainly lamented this fact. He regretted having drawn attention to a connection in French between "school" and "glue" [*École et colle*]—all the while hammering students into the role of followers. Today, Panurge will teach his sheep the *Ecrits*.

It is indeed difficult to draw an impartial assessment of Lacanism and to engage with its representatives, as knowledge in this field has turned into an apparatus of power and intimidation. Despite the reflux of ideologies, or perhaps because of it, Lacanism is one of the last bastions of arrogance, and few domains today remain so jealously guarded.

> But this manner of philosophizing is very convenient for those with only mediocre minds, for the obscurity of the distinctions and principles they use makes it possible for them to speak about everything as confidently as if they knew it, and to defend all they say against the most subtle and clever thinkers without anyone having the means to convince them that they are wrong. In this they seem to resemble a blind man who, in order to fight without disadvantage against someone who can see, lures him into the depths of a very dark cellar. (Descartes 1985: 147)

The essence of a great thought, if it is not to fall into religion, is that it remain debatable or falsifiable. In homage to one of the finest intellectual efforts marking our epoch, we will attempt to discuss some of its tenets, and to open the windows that would admit "daylight into the cellar where they have gone down to fight" (147).

TRUTH OF THE STATEMENT OR OF THE ENUNCIATION?

One of Lacan's merits is to have put forward the position that the enunciation on the couch always takes precedence over the statement. "What am I after if not to convince you that the unconscious is the subject of our inquiry, the law that does not allow that an enunciation be reduced to the statement of any discourse?" (Lacan 1966: 892). No doubt. But why summon the unconscious to establish this incontestable "law" of pragmatics? As shown by Austin's pioneer work on speech acts, the enunciation or utterance always benefits from an irreducible superiority, prescribed in the hierarchical position of speaking over the said, of speech [*parole*] over language, of the event or illocutionary act over the code. Thanks to current theories of enunciation we have a better understanding of the strange intention of communication in psychoanalysis—wherein the reference seems less oriented towards the object or the reality (of a past history) than towards the subject itself, that is, towards the intersubjectivity of the transference. Exterior reality and psychic reality are tightly interwoven into analytic speech. Consider, for instance, the truth value of a proposition such as: "I assert that the earth is flat." Do we regard such a proposition in terms of the falseness of the statement or the truthfulness of the enunciation? That the earth should be flat is false. That I assert it, however, is incontestable. The prefix, "I assert that," renders my proposition self-validating (or "primary performative," as Austin might say).

This banal example reminds us that in psychoanalysis such a sentence would in fact be a basic given and, as, such worthy of examination. Analytic listening pays less attention to the content of statements than to the here and now of their enunciation. What is dismissed in science, for instance, idiolect, lies, semblance, and nonsense, becomes in analysis the *thing itself*. The same holds for myths. Regarded as false on the referential level, myths are said to be automatically true the moment we attempt to find in them the expression of fantasy and the truth of a twisted desire. They are, therefore, like dreams, the royal road to the unconscious. If the *meta* perspective entertained by psychoanalysis consists (contrary to that of the exact sciences) in occupying itself only with the hazards and values of the enunciation, the analytic meaning will consequently always weave together the three senses of "meaning" [*sens*]: signification [*signification*], strictly speaking, is overlaid with the sense of meaning as the sensuousness or flavor of words, that is, their sensible meaning [*sens sensible*] and, above all, with the sense of meaning as the direction [*direction*] of words. The speech of the analysand is violently addressed; to speak, in such a setting, always signifies a demand, a desire to be understood and recognized. This interpretation of the analysand's speech, therefore, cares little for the truth of elucidation.

The setting of the analytic session was hardly suspected or questioned as to its usefulness. Freud and his successors (though not Lacan, not even Ferenczi) saw in the apparatus of the *talking cure* a mirror that was, more or less, transparent; a neutral or neutralizing medium. The couch would remove obstacles without interposing any itself; its role would be purely negative, that is, facilitating. According to this liberal deontology, the appeal to speech sufficed as a way to come to terms with violence—without the medium itself being subjected to theoretical scrutiny. The study of language is hardly advanced in Freud. He put forward the *Witz* "in its relations with the unconscious," without really deepening our understanding of these relations. Is language constitutive or only expressive of the unconscious phenomena that it brings to light? It was left to Lacan to problematize the effects of the analytic setting, not only in manipulating the duration of the so-called variable session (that is to say, invariably shortened), but in devoting the essence of his theory to a reflection on the effects of speech and on the entrance into the symbolic. This, however, could not be accomplished without twisting the notion of truth, investing it entirely in the speech act or the enunciation.

FULL SPEECH: ARCHAEOLOGICAL REFERENCE OR PERFORMATIVE SELF-REFERENCE?

As mentioned earlier, the content of a statement, which expresses the facts, can be true or false, but the enunciation which itself constitutes a fact escapes this alternative; act or event, it is sufficient for it to have taken place. The *truth* of a proposition will always distinguish itself from the reality of its enunciation, that is, from its self-reference. This is so because the falsest enunciation continues to designate something, namely, itself and its pretension of being authenticated as speech. In 1953, Lacan writes:

> The ambiguity of the hysterical revelation of the past is due not so much to
> the vacillation of its contents between the imaginary and the real, for it is
> situated in both. Nor is it because it is made up of lies. The reason is that it

presents us with the birth of truth in speech and thereby brings us up against the reality of what is neither true nor false. At any rate, that is the most disquieting aspect of the problem. (1966: 47; 1977: 255–56)

Proceeding in a delicate manner, little by little, Lacan manages to substitute analysis conceived of as recollection, or as an archaeological search for a more or less repressed past (that is, as constative or referential statement, in which truth is judged on the basis of a correspondence between speech and fact), with a self-referential speech wagered on intersubjectivity which, in turn, becomes a self-fulfilling prophecy pushed to the point of identifying itself with truth:

> I might as well be categorical: in psychoanalytic anamnesis, it is not a question of reality, but of truth, because the effect of full speech is to reorder past contingencies by conferring on them the sense of necessities to come, such as they are constituted by the little freedom through which the subject makes present. (1966: 48; 1977: 256)

Analysis, from that moment on, changes *direction*. A speech oriented retrospectively is made prospective. And this "full speech" does not owe its fullness to a verifiable correspondence of the statement with some extra-linguistic reality, but solely to the pragmatics of its enunciation with reference to an intersubjective relation: "It is certainly this assumption of his history by the subject, insofar as it is constituted by the speech addressed to the other, that constitutes the ground of the new method ... " (1966: 48; 1977: 257). It is not, if we understand these cryptic sentences well, the history of the subject that engenders such speech. On the contrary, it is the speech addressed to the other that "constitutes" or *causes [la cause]* this history on the basis of a play on words that organizes this entire reversal, and which Lacan dubs as the "revision of the process of causality" (1966: 127; 1977: 416).

Full speech is due to its reorganizing and self-validating aspect. The authentication of an enunciation depends only on its being heard by the other. The truth-effect, or rather, the effect of validation, no longer passes through the object but through the relation and the intersubjective agreement. Hence the following rigorous conclusion: "speech as such appears all the more true if its truth is based less on what we would call its correspondence to the thing" (1966: 351). "Full speech therefore is defined by its (taken on) identity of which it speaks" (351). With these elliptic remarks Lacan returns speech to itself, *bei sich*, to the nearest or shortest enunciative circuit. This route aims at nothing less than a self-assured truth of the thing/cause in the theological circle of the *causa sui* where speech binds only with itself, performatively, poetically. And it says "I, the truth, I speak" in a self-reference or identification (identity of which it speaks), and attains a self-induced climax which is also the climax of presence or the belonging to oneself. In short: "the thing speaks of itself" (1966: 121; 1977: 408).

With the Lacanian variation of the typical treatment, therefore, we see a setting stripped of all non-linguistic components and guided towards a speech divested of its referential dimension. When all is said and done, what counts is the illocutionary force or the self-referential loop through which the enunciation closes on the pure punctuation of the relation, for example, in the admission that "You are my master" (1966: 351). This understanding of speech as self-centered is fraught with religious or shamanistic elements. Lacan's own prophetic speech is at once commentary, indexical expression, and proof-by-style. This pulling away from the treatment, introduced by Lacan, revealed and intensified an ambiguity or equivocation already latent in Freud's work: neither true nor false, analytic speech is "transitional," oriented from the beginning towards the construction of a relation. Analytic speech expresses intersubjectivity up-front in the treatment, and is the advent of an enunciation or a retrieved communication.

This conception of the analytic setting was not in itself criticizable. In opposition to Freud, who had drawn speech towards its referential-constative effects, Lacan rightly insists on its self-referential and performative dimension. But it is surprising that this distinction, which is the basis around 1960 for the discovery of speech acts by Austin and the rapid development of pragmatics, does not divert Lacan away from the Saussurian framework to which he obstinately clings (to my knowledge there is no mention of Austin in Lacan's writing). For pragmatics is incompatible with this framework, and it has not ceased, since Austin and some others, to gnaw at the structuralist paradigm, and at logocentrism in general.

THE UNCONSCIOUS STRUCTURED LIKE A LANGUAGE?

Freud wanted to broaden the scientific method and to open up the domain of positive knowledge to unruly objects. In confronting dreams, as well as hysteria, affect, art images, the unconscious, transference, and the psychopathology or impulses of everyday life, Freud launched a project of scientific inquiry into domains of subjectivity that had traditionally eluded theoretical investigation.

Judged against this ambition, the Lacanian *reaction*—adorned with the slogan "return to Freud"—appears highly ambiguous. Lacanism would actually like to formalize (and to know in the guise of an algebra) those objects that Freudian rationality searches for at the antipodes of discourse or of so-called secondary processes. With a flamboyant style, of which it would be petty to deny artistic accomplishment and seductive appeal, Lacan's thought returns to a reason of the most limited kind, that is, to the hard kernel of science: the combinative and matheme. In spite of being saddled with a scientific, even positivist, style, Freud practiced an *open rationality* which Lacan, under the pretences of an extravagant imagination and unbridled genius, manages to restrict. Lacan, for instance, wishes to know nothing of affect or of the affective: "I believe that is a term which one must completely expunge from our papers" (1975: 304; 1988: 275). A brief discussion of Lacan's classic, though by now abused, thesis, "the unconscious is structured like a language," will allow us to determine in which conceptual orbit psychoanalysis is made to revolve.

Lacan's wording manages the following equivocation: a comparison does not hold for an identity. How are we to understand the indeterminacy of the article in "a language"? A number of converging statements will serve to clarify.

As my title ["The Agency of the Letter in the Unconscious or Reason Since Freud"] suggests, beyond this 'speech,' what the psychoanalytic experience discovers in the unconscious is the whole structure of language. Thus from the outset I have alerted informed minds to the extent to which the notion that the unconscious is merely the seat of the instincts will have to be rethought. (1966: 147; 1977: 495)

Or, "[t]he unconscious is neither primordial nor instinctual; what it knows about the elementary is no more than the elements of the signifier" (1966: 170; 1977: 522). Or, on the cover of the 1966 edition of the *Ecrits*: "[w]hat will be demonstrated to the reader is that the unconscious is a matter for pure logic; in other words, for the signifier." These provocative statements seem to be at variance with a fundamental tenet of Freudian analysis: namely, that representations of words are the prerogative of the preconscious-conscious system, whereas the unconscious knows only the "representation of things." Quite removed from the order of language, the unconscious, according to Freud, appears to be structured more like cotton candy. The unconscious is a reservoir of drives, in the form of affects. It is a jumble of preverbal traces that are less symbolic than analogical or indexical.

Lacan anticipates this objection, and a number of justifications are presented that lend his thesis an appearance of soundness. Let us group them together:

1. *The subject, whatever it may do, is held by the signifier; a language envelopes and precedes the individual down to his slightest activities.* Lacan here generalizes the communicative imperative which Lévi-Strauss formulates from the start of *The Elementary Structures of Kinship*—a book which reinterprets the universal prohibition against incest in terms of the law of exchange and of the combinative enrichment of the group. The subject belongs to the community down to his unconscious, defined by Lacan as "the discourse of the Other." By this it must be understood that the subject inserts himself, even before his birth, in the signifying chain that fashions his identity (the famous *Nom-du-Père*). The interpretation of *The Purloined Letter*, initially put forward in the "cybernetic" context of the 1955 seminar, gives to this signifying chain its mechanical character. It also reminds us that the signifier—or letter, according to Lacan—expresses itself always in the imperative: it is that which assigns to us difference and a place. This distance or gap to himself, wherein the whole subject is distributed by the signifier, enables Lacan, fortified by this same cybernetics, to envisage a combinative deduction of the subject. If the big Other "is nothing but the pure subject of the modern strategy of games" (1966: 809), then we can calculate the subject. "This game theory, or rather strategy, provides an example of where one can profit of an entirely calculable character of a subject strictly reduced to the formula of a matrix of signifying combinations" (860). This calculus is particularly operative once an entirely linguistic dimension of the treatment is enforced, which amounts to a deduction of the respective places. To accede to the subject, *Ich werden*, is to acknowledge or recognize and play into the hands of the signifier.

2. But how are we to understand this omnipresent signifier in the Lacanian literature? In its ability or capacity to divide or assign, the signifier—or letter, strictly speaking—holds no monopoly over language. "Language," moreover, is not immaterial: "it is a subtle body, but body it is. Words are trapped in all the corporeal images that captivate the subject" (1966: 87; 1977: 301)—for example, in the struc-

turing image of the mirror, or in the articulation of the imaginary with the symbolic. Upon this aperture of the subtle body, the signifier, according to Lacan, could comfortably extend itself to the images or representations of things in general. But the restrictive interpretation of the "letter," as well as the connotations of this term, despite the gracious definitions given by Lacan and his followers (in particular, Leclaire), did not move analysis to a consideration of icons and indexes. Instead, Lacanian analysis veered towards a logic of the signifier as always more "pure"— mesmerized and fascinated by the riddle, the anagram, the play on words, as well as by the algorithm and the mathematical combinative (topological figures, Borromean knots, Miller's "sutures," etc.).

It is important to recognize, at the heart of these games, the nature of the criticism that had been brought against the very notion of the sign, namely, the departure from Saussurian linguistics (which Lacan embraced in order to stifle it more effectively). This doctrine of the omni-signifier hinges in fact on the refusal of the referential dimension of the sign. This refusal was prescribed in the Saussurian pair, signifier and signified, that is, in the material aspect of the sign and the concept or idea that corresponds to it. To his credit, Lacan uses this refusal to repudiate the traditional correspondence theory of truth. But Lacan continues in dissociating the signifier from the signified: every signifier enters into a contrastive chain of differences and oppositions. With reference to St. Augustine, Lacan makes the point that no "signification can be sustained other than by reference to another signification" (1966: 150; 1977: 498). And finally, that "each [signifier] is sustained only by the principle of its opposition to each of the others" (1966: 304; 1977: 806). It would not be difficult to offer other citations that work to reinforce the bar which in Saussure separates the signifier from the signified, so as to affirm and to follow a circular logic that would credit the signifier with autonomy. This explains the proliferation in Lacan's style of "*signifiance*,"[2] metaphor and play of connotations where the signified slides freely under the signifier with no "*point de capiton*" between the two domains. This explains Lacan's taste for literature as opposed to clinical case studies, which are remarkably absent from the *Ecrits*. Above all, this accounts for his prophetic conception of a self-verifying truth, of a language freed from any reference to the real, and which does not—to use Lacanian verbs—authorize or sustain itself outside its own enunciation.

3. The work of "the letter"—that is to say, the differential element, for example, the 0/1 binary (the sole states known of the synaptic relations) from which today attempts are being made in artificial intelligence to understand the mind— insists, therefore, on the web of the unconscious. In his own way, Lacan makes a contribution to this new epistemology:

> Of course, as it is said, the letter killeth while the spirit giveth life. We can't help but agree . . . but we should also like to know how the spirit could live without the letter. Even so, the pretensions of the spirit would remain unassailable if the letter had not shown [*fait la preuve*] us that it produces all the effects of truth in man without involving the spirit at all. It is none other than Freud who had this revelation, and he called his discovery the unconscious. (1966: 158–9; 1977: 509)

Lacan thinks he has found this "proof" [*preuve*] by demonstrating, in the activity of the dream-work or the Freudian primary-processes, the work of the letter itself. He shows this in the following formulations: *Enstellung* (distorted transpositions of the dream) must be interpreted as the incessant sliding of the signified under the signifier; *Verdichtung* (condensation) refers to metaphor; *Verschiebung* (displacement) refers to metonymy (later discussed, in comparatively similar ways, by Ricoeur, Benveniste, Lyotard, Jakobson); *Rücksicht auf Darstellbarkeit* ("consideration of the means of representation") relates to figurative expression only in the rhetorical sense of that term, as "a form of writing rather than of mime"; finally, secondary elaboration obeys, in any case, symbolic thought (already presented in the *Traumgedanke* or dream thought) (see 1966: 160–1; 1977: 511–12).

At the end of this trajectory, we can see to what extent Lacanism tends towards a logico-linguistic unification. By incorporating the indexical-iconic into the symbolic, and the symbolic into the numeric, Lacan wanted to make psychoanalysis enter the world of calculation or modern communication. He wanted to model psychoanalysis after paradigms that imitate those of a cybernetic epistemology whose blossoming popularity fascinated the author of the *Ecrits*. Against this inordinate and, moreover, stupefying, project, we will level the following objections:

1. Lacan renders certain experiences homogeneous which are clearly lived as disparate at the phenomenological level. His unifying desire leads him to align psychoanalysis with the number crunching of the exact sciences (for whom indeed an image, an idea, or a sound can indeed be transcribed and calculated according to the sequence of "letters"). He also desires that psychoanalysis could, like these sciences, superimpose its entire domain of observations and experiences upon that of the system of language [*langage*] in the form of a logical algebra. In the specific field of psychoanalysis, such reduction entails a certain amount of violence that verges on the absurd. It suffices to have dreamed at least once to know what immense and insurmountable distance separates the dream from its narrative. It is the distance of the affect or of the image (its colour, its vividness) from the word. Very few analysts are aware of the *colour* of a dream (this quite particular nuance that certain surrealist texts desire to grasp), and that it does not allow itself to be translated into words. A Lacanian prefers to search for it in the *Witz* or in the word-puzzle, which is actually more suited to the analytic instrument, as in the unverifiable "dream of the unicorn" that served as a gold mine for Leclaire. But seen from this angle, man appears like the models painted by De Chirico; the mathematical bric-à-brac, employed to represent the body, supports a face that is too smooth.

"There is no other master apart from the signifier," says the introduction of the pocket edition of the *Ecrits*. One would, with Freud, think it more natural to put the suffering body—for example, Irma's tortured throat in the founding dream of the *Traumdeutung*—in the place of the signifier. But since flesh is animal, Lacan wants to know nothing of this abyss. Especially when it suffers, it does not *sustain* itself (to state it in Lacanian fashion). One would think that the unconscious is not the discourse of the Other but rather that it stands up to all discourse as its other. One would also think that the unconscious, weaving together affects, indices, and representations of things, would be of very little import for semiology. Lacan's wager was to consider this other of language as still being part of language, as though the emergence of the logico-linguistic had reorganized under its law, and reoriented in man, all former layers (of his animality). According to Lacan, if the superior explains the inferior in human beings, then the subject, defined as the speaking-being [*parlêtre*], is alienated only in the absolute power of words. And as an aside to this great gain: all that our unconscious-language—structured some-what like the mouth of a shadow—desires, is to speak through the intervention of a wise man. Lacan would have been the high priest of a remarkable ceremony, where all would gather to listen to the unconscious, which usually plays dead or mute, come to life in speech through ventriloquism.

2. To make metonymy of displacement and metaphor of condensation is to punctuate the wrong way around: rhetoric cannot account for the work of the dream. On the contrary, it is the tropes, the figures of speech, and all the "follies" of the *Witz* or of poetry that show, in the secondary order of language, the inces-sant movement or stealth advance of the primary processes. The dream or poem "speaks more than one dialect," as Freud used to say of the unconscious. Its orga-nization exhibits a compromise attained by the primary and secondary processes, a line where index, icon, and symbolic are mutually stabilized.

3. That analysis borrows from the symbolic streams of language does not in the least imply that the unconscious amounts to an ordering of signifiers. To claim that we know affect, immediate experience, drive, and dream only insofar as they are spoken of seems quite questionable. Does it follow that these objects of analysis might in the last instance be linguistic? The doctrine confounds the object with the method; in this respect the stars which we can only know with a telescope would themselves be the aggregates of crushed glass (see Roustang 1986). This reduction is idealist (it skirts the object), and returns full circle. But this circle panders to intel-lectual narcissism, where one reassures oneself: *"Oh yes, I know the unconscious."* This postulate, especially, confirms Lacan in his rivalry with Lévi-Strauss. Does he not in 1953, at the moment of the "Rome Discourse," dream of reproducing the glorious feat that was Lévi-Strauss's 1950 "Introduction to Mauss" (manifesto of the structuralist method), and direct that success to establishing psychoanalysis on a more scientific basis than linguistics—the latter being in its pilot phase at the time? His fascination with algorithms and the formalism of the sciences reminds one of the dadaists and their fascination with the "bachelor machines." Of course the difference being that the machines Picabia and Duchamp tinkered with were artificial and designed for the purpose of exhibition.

This confusion around object and method has deeper roots. Beyond Lévi-Strauss, it is to Hegel and to the founders of logic that Lacan would have likened himself. This is evident in his allusions to Gödel and Frege. It is particularly evident in his thesis that *there is no metalanguage,* or, in other words, that it is futile to search for the meaning of meaning (because language is, in any case, in itself and definitively *meta*, there is *only* metalanguage for Lacan). In the self-exposition of Hegelian logic (made known to Lacan through Kojève's lectures), as in the subse-quent logical and mathematical formalisms, logic and its epistemology necessarily merge [*se confondent*], that is to say, they co-found [*se co-fondent*] and rest on themselves. It is quite apparent that this self-validation obsesses Lacan. It accounts for his already mentioned doctrine of truth, for his dream of a scientific analysis of the letter, an analysis which would be—in immanence, self-reference, the *mise en abyme*, or the most confined proximity of a mind expressing itself—*its own object*. On this Hegelian slope of absolute knowledge, theory becomes the very reality of which it sets out to analyze, namely, the enunciation. Amongst other consequences of this short-circuited logicist sliding we note that Lacanian analysis does not have therapy as its object (something as bagatelle as the cure), but rather, the formation of other analysts. What mission, therefore, is assigned to the École freudienne? The recruitment of new members and the expansion of the École. "Psychoanalysis at present has nothing better for ensuring its activity than the production of psycho-analysts" (1964).

4. Under the pretext that the entirety of the symbolic is real [*réel*] for the psychotic, Lacan rushed to proclaim the antithesis: *the real is the impossible* (to symbolize). What runs through Lacan's fiercely structural style is a passionate dislike for nuance and mediating images: it is all or nothing. Though this costly separation of the real and the symbolic, which runs through his entire "science," bears the stamp of cynicism, it still flatters philosophical minds. The theory of the ostensible autonomy of the signifier offered the philosophically minded some enticing benefits: no need for verification, no reason to be concerned with clinical work and all its inevitable pitfalls, no need for basic ground work, and so forth. After such a stint as conjurer, it remained for Lacanian analysts to pass the signifier to one another as in a game of tennis. This verbal tennis match engendered a set of publications (recall Lacan's word-play, *poubellications*)[3] recognizable by many but, certainly, hastily read; the dadaism revived in the epistemological rehash of the later Seminars is just as annoying and tedious as these other publications. While the real was initially conceived as the object to know, it was, here, sacredly positioned as a counter or foil to knowledge. As a result of this reversal, the unconscious became the condition of linguistics or *linguisterie*, and psychoanalysis the condition of the sciences (compare, for example, amongst other symptoms, the appearance beginning in 1966 of *Cahiers pour l'analyse* of the "*Cercle d'Epistémologie de l'Ecole Normale Supérieure*"). This doctrine satisfied the philosophers of l'Ecole Normale Supérieure, who celebrated Lacanism as the best form of metaphysics available—heralding it as the science of sciences. With this kind of psychoanalysis they could continue to philosophize, that is to say, to "suspect" and undermine other forms of knowledge from the position of a meta-science that was meticulously muddled and opaque to the point of vulgarity—all the while upholding the Socratic dictum that knowledge is a lure, that one must never give in to one's desire, and that the master appeals to no authority other than himself.

Alongside this foreclosure of the imaginary (again this Lacanian promotion of the adjective to an absolute or self-sufficient noun), the *imaginary* found itself devalued as a "specular," simplistic reflection. Lacan envisages the imaginary neither as Winnicott's transitional space of creativity, nor Castoriadis's opening of the possible and radical institution.

In brief, the assertion that language [*le langage*] or logical structures comprise the sole object of psychoanalysis—and, therefore, the condemnation of all that is nonverbal—returns consciousness to *itself* (as decentered and ex-centric under the sway of "the" signifier). Lacan reduced "reason since Freud" to language encountering language. "You would not look for me if you hadn't already found me." This circle is theological. It reminds us of the story of the man searching for his keys at night under the street lamp—in a place where he has no chance of finding them, yet where, at least, *one has some light to look*. In other words, in a place where one is perceived as a brilliantly enlightened seeker (of truth). A number of fickle people, unlike butterflies, have darted directly into the lamp in order to be seen dancing in its light—people who we would not exactly qualify as "enlightened seekers." By ignoring all that was inadmissible to his project, Lacan reinforced the closure surrounding it. It is rare that self-reference should dominate a discipline to such an extreme, and push its followers to mimic the same. In many respects Lacanism functions like the mirror-stage of psychoanalysis.

THE EQUIVOCATION OR AMBIGUITY OF THE SYMBOLIC

All scientific procedure tends towards eliminating from the cone of light that which proves resistant to its processing. And just as Procrustes trimmed the bodies of travellers to fit his bed, the psychoanalyst is inclined to foreclose the reality of phenomena that escape him. Lacanism would hardly favor the *knowledge of knowledge*, nor the necessary self-critique of the seeker. The more brilliant the speech of the master, the more unknowable will the objects remain that he casts into outer darkness. In concluding this brief inventory, let us focus on some equivocations or ambiguities relating to this access to the symbolic as theorized by Lacan.

The term *symbolic*, depending on the thinker, designates the two extremes of the semiotic spectrum. Hegel and Freud place it on the side of confusion in the sign (ambiguity, sensible) and the thing. Peirce and Lacan place it at the other extreme. By connoting "the symbolic" via algebra and the combinatives of arbitrary and discrete units, their approach shields the analyst from the threats of a speech of relation. Interpreting the conversation of Oedipus with the Sphinx, Freud, likewise, had already privileged theoretical speech by effacing sensible inflexion or corporal contacts—as well as the bewitchment of moaning and singing (see Schneider 1980). The ritual celebration of language in psychoanalysis ties the treatment to a direction that is avowedly intellectual in nature. Whereas the *efficacy of symbols* studied by Lévi-Strauss hinged on the mysterious continuity of a suffering body inscribed with the words of the tribe (this continuity establishes the procedures of the sacraments, of shamanism, of poetry, of magic, and so forth), the rigidly structural conception advocated by Lacan from the other end of the signifying chain no doubt serves as a barrier against the encroachments of a primary oral seduction. Which would lead to what? To state it bluntly: the *autonomy of the signifier* induces the cut or castration. In "the" symbolic as such, submerged in algebra, nothing will ever explain either the origin or the history of a subject.

"The symbolic world is the world of the machine" (1978: 63; 1988a: 247). Now, as is recognized in the next seminar,

> there is always something that eludes or escapes the web of the symbolic, which is procreation ... It sustains something that radically refuses to be assimilated into the signifier. This is simply the singular existence of the subject. Why is he here? Where does he come from? What is he doing here?

Why is he going to disappear? The signifier is unable to provide him with answers, for the simple reason that it places or situates him beyond death. The signifier already perceives him as dead and, in essence, renders him immortal. (1981: 202)

The capital letter is essential to this celebration of the symbolic order. The nominalization of the adjective, common in philosophy, finds in Lacanian analysis its finest effects. If we were to forbid any kind of reference to *an* unconscious, *the* imaginary, *the* real, or *the* symbolic as entities endowed with autonomous functions, what would remain of Freudianism and of Lacanism? Lacan squared, mathematically speaking, this anasemia and raised non-meaning to its second degree by crowning his whole edifice with THE symbolic conceived as the order of orders, as the separator (as well as the agent of separation). Lacan thereby abandoned the immense field of the preverbal, of images, of the visual, tactile, olfactory representations, of affect, of the drive and of everything that lent dynamism to the Freudian unconscious. But an autonomous symbolic no longer means anything. Lacan rejoined the symbolic to theology and reintroduced "God behind a mask," nuanced it by the God of Schreber who, like Lacan's symbolic, only deals with cadavers. If structuralism has to consider the subject as dead in order to understand it, it is certainly a bad sign when the field of the life sciences, in turn, appeals to this structuralism.

Lacan wants *the* symbolic to confront the tribulations of an impure subject with the ideal of a calculus or calculation, and thinks he has found proof for it in the famous course of the *purloined letter*. This metaphysics of the signifier had at the same time condemned itself to remain in the dark with regards to individual accident. Birth, affects, suffering, development, history, cure, subject—all subjected to the logic of calculus—would have no theoretical import. By contrast, the greatness of the Freudian paradigm lay in its sustained interest in these details rejected by the combinative. It would be much better to drop this highly ambiguous term, "symbolic." This term, which initially designated the token, or even a certain pass word that might *save life*, has come to be identified with conventions associated with calculus—a domain in which all references to subjective existence are banished.

And yet Lacan's style more than makes up for the reductionism of his ideas. In the Seminars as well as in the *Ecrits*, by playing the role of rhetorician and incomparable artist, he makes thorough use of the shimmer of a symbolic that is closer to Hegel's than to Peirce's. In searching for neither truth nor evidence, but rather seduction and illumination, Lacan's poetic language selects its addressee in a carefully sustained darkness and gloom. Each person is allowed to seize on what interests him, and to find in this polyphony something to satisfy a nostalgic yearning. One of the paradoxes of Lacanism was that it opened the valves to this erotically charged enunciation while promoting statements to the opposite effect and underwriting the autonomy and closure of the signifier.

This speech-mirror catered to and delighted the minds of an easily impressed and even fascinated intelligentsia; it was expressed in the name of science, yet ambiguous and prophetic enough to evade all discussion and debate. In this sense, was Lacan's discourse not teaching, through its style, self-referentially and directly, the *thing itself*—namely, the rhetoric of the unconscious, the relation of the transference, the authority and ridicule of the master, the undecidedness and infinite arabesques of desire? His enunciation nonetheless undermined his theory. By bringing incantation to its peak, his speech no longer referred to the calling or vocation of a symbolic conceived as a procession of numbers, but to the more impure ceremonies of hypnosis and *psychology of the masses*. This communicational strategy to stereophonic presentation (the living word of the Seminars, the book of *Ecrits*) deserves a merit and comment of excellence: what better way to flatter the narcissism of the addressees? By advocating itself as incomprehensible, revolutionary or categorically *meta*—and who can be more *meta* than Lacan!?—this discourse contained something to please everyone.

SOME TASKS THAT LIE AHEAD

We are making a plea here for the mutual exchange of information between psychoanalysis and the themes and concepts belonging to the disciplines of communication, semiotics, pragmatism, and some rudiments of cybernetics. One of the present tasks concerns an examination of the *relation*—beginning with the relation of the utterance with which pragmatics occupies itself, and whose introduction necessarily desexualizes psychoanalysis. Lacan amply cleared this path by showing, thanks notably to Hegel, how the relation of being [*d'être*] or of the drama of intersubjectivity, tied to the infinite specularity of desire (always "desire of the other's desire"), infinitely precedes the relation of having [*d'avoir*] some object. And though we readily welcome this move on Lacan's part, which is also that of Girard's "mimetic rivalry," at the same time we realize how unfathomable this move is for a psychoanalysis wanting to establish itself as a science. The ground of the psychoanalytic edifice is giving way, confronting us with identification, transference, or hypnosis (against which Freud established his method). In other words, we are left stranded before a specularity or interminable imaginary that cannot be subsumed under "the symbolic," nor under any kind of objectivity.

It is the relation of the transference that thoroughly pervades this speech that we call transitional; that is, the first degree of the trance. There is no *I* without *you*: "*Ich*" cannot come about except in a full address or speech, in neither an erring nor a neutral manner with regards to the addressee, but resolutely addressed. We have to note that this barely objective speech, moving from the depths of anamnesis towards the surface of therapy, cannot lead back to the same past, as claimed by analysts. Passing from "one analyst to the another,"[4] the analysand will draw quite different scenes from the narrative of his life, even different versions of the same scene. The unverifiable historical truth counts less than the capacity of the *I* to secure its speech and to assign itself responsibility in relation to a particular addressee. The truth effect here is not referential, but, as Lacan emphatically points out, always depends on the act of enunciation. *Myself/the truth/I speak*.

This necessary overflowing of the enunciation onto the statement (of the relation onto the content of the communication, according to the school of Palo Alto) displaces the dynamic of the treatment from an improbable personal history onto the act of capturing speech. Now that the recognition of one's past would be of less significance than acquiring the recognition of the other through interaction, interpretation slides into second place, as it becomes the means of punctuating and guaranteeing the patient's desire to save face and thereby place himself in the presence of the cure. As well, the so-called fissured subject owes its split less to the bar of the signifier than to the effects of a system set up in a particular manner and into which the point of entry is not exclusively symbolic (this "fissure," obvious in cybernetics, is everywhere observed by a systematic approach).

Furthermore, to the extent that we privilege the contents of our representations, the component aspects of our relations escape us. The unconscious is not simply buried like an archaeological object, but is spread out onto the surface and played out, for example, in the *agieren* of affect. Let us not search for it solely in some "repressed" well. The sprawling middle space lingering between us, in the present of our relations, remains as invisible to our representation as the purloined letter.

This immediacy of affect in action, present in every enunciation—and by and large remaining unconscious in the act—would give added weight to the critique raised against logocentrism by pragmatism and semiotics. The affect, inseparable from the assertion [*du dire*], is no doubt not the object of diction, hence of re-presentation: it is either present, or it is not. Indexical or expressive, it cannot help but elude the "representation of words," and the symbolic order in general. Of course we know, thanks to Lacan and the study of the enunciation, that there is no absolute metalanguage. We also know, despite him, that not everything is language, and that the indexes that surround or precede even the least significant speech cannot be articulated, but only "shown." For the index [*indice*] is unspeakable [*indicible*]. Or, to paraphrase, while at the same time revising, a famous proposition made by Wittgenstein: that of which we cannot speak, we need not so much be silent about as to *show* it. The index and the shown (which are certainly not "structured like a language") filter through every segment of our statements without allowing themselves to be verbalized or linearized.

Having recognized the role played by affect, the critique of representation—and, consequently, of logocentrism—could be renewed. Conversely, we mutilate semiotics by stripping it of its iconic and indexical dimensions. Lacan promised to free up communication (via cybernetics and Lévi-Strauss). Instead, he actually closed communication down by way of its gross reduction to a one and only symbolic. We will henceforth have to ask the Lacanian who speaks of the signifier to specify: the index, the icon, or the symbol? Their functions are quite different. So much depends on their distinction at the heart of semiotics and pragmatics, both keenly attentive to the entire domain of the perceptible and the institutional in which the enunciation acts. Through these distinctions we will also explain how the symbolic emerges from the imaginary, instead of separating these two realms, or how three is begotten from two, and how order is generated from noise, as argued by a contemporary paradigm.

LAST BUT NOT LEAST, and included among our reasons for questioning Lacanism, we will comment on the gloominess that surrounds the Lacanian.

Lacan's teaching—initially invigorating, and attracting the cream of the intelligentsia in the 1960s—ended up with arguments which, by dint of justifying all the failings (from the so-called sexual relation to thought itself), also became the gospel—of failures. We can read about this particular point and some others in a book by Jean-Guy Godin. This book serves as both symptom of and testimony to what is wrong with Lacanism. It is doubly damning. First, as concerns the actual practices of Lacan the analyst, we learn that during his (very short) sessions Lacan might leave the door of his office open, forget his patients at the back of the library, or even physically attack some "bad debtor." Secondly, Godin's book is damning because of the justifications this determined believer offers, despite all evidence, in order to conceal the fault of the Father with Noah's cloak. Should one laugh or be indignant before such a display of humiliation and complicity in this perverse game? Like so many others, Godin left 5 rue de Lille deceived and fleeced—and yet proud to be so. His fortune was to have produced a book, and one that would sell. There you go, at least he has been reimbursed—not to mention that he is now also a psychoanalyst. But one still wonders: should the Minister read this book, would he still be willing to convert Lacan's premises into a museum?

NOTES

1. *Trans:* Former minister of culture.
2. *Trans:* Lacan uses this neologism in "The Agency of the Letter" to translate Freud's term *Traumdeutung* as *la signifiance du rêve*. Sheridan translates the term as "significance."
3. *Trans:* This neologism is constructed on the basis of two words: *poubelle* (trash can) and *publication* (publishing or publication).
4. *Trans:* "*De tranche en tranche*" refers to the Lacanian practice of going to a different analyst.

"mac"   8

Gary Genosko

Editor's Note

Although Jacques Lacan and Marshall McLuhan never met one another, neither on the television screen nor anywhere else, Gary Genosko sets the stage for their meeting with the help of a little "a": Lacan's obscure theory of the "*objet petit a.*" In this essay, Genosko uncovers the desire of McLuhan's French followers in the slippage of another, perhaps not unconnected, little "a." This, he suggests, is the "a" that interposed itself into McLuhan's name during the 1960s with the creation of a French "*Mac*Luhan."

Genosko argues that these French followers, caught in the grip of popular "*macluhanisme*," found the ideal medium for promoting themselves and media studies in the academy. For unlike Lacanianism, *macluhanisme* was always a movement from "below." Given the impossible position of the idealized master, it is no surprise that MacLuhan could not live up to his followers' expectations. And thus Genosko explores "*l'affaire McLuhan*" that tried to expose "Mac" as a surreal fraud in France during the 1970s.

Since Lacan, on the strength of his tele-genetic personality, was once referred to as "The psychoanalyst for the Age of McLuhan," it is appropriate that Genosko attends to their similarities and differences. For at the intersection of their names lie the interesting encounter of two famous personalities, tongues, prophets, and Catholics, and their acceptance and rejection at the hands of their respective French followers and detractors. Anyone interested in cultural and social studies with a psychoanalytic slant will find this essay entertaining and informative.   .

GARY GENOSKO received his Ph.D. in Social and Political Thought from York University, and is currently an independent researcher in many fields, including the history of psychoanalysis. He is the author of *Baudrillard and Signs: Signification Ablaze* (Routledge, 1994), *Undisciplined Theory* (Sage, forthcoming), is editor of *The Guattari Reader* (Basil Blackwell, 1996), and author of a new Introduction to Marie Bonaparte's *Topsy* (Transaction, 1994). Genosko is currently preparing a manuscript on the French reception of Marshall McLuhan.

THERE WAS A MOMENT, OR MOMENTS, in the French reception of the writings of Marshall McLuhan, in which his views were revealed to be a *trompe l'oeil* splashed across the mediascape. After an initial wide-eyed fixation, the gaze of his admirers' shifted, and they noticed that McLuhan's views did not move with their own. These views appeared as something other than they seemed, or rather, they now seemed to be something else, to paraphrase Lacan (1977a: 112). This other thing was the *objet petit a*.

We have just imagined the moment(s) in which McLuhan became MacLuhan for his French readers with the help of an extra little *a*. If this imagining is too hard to swallow, it is all for the better since the *objet petit a* is, Lacan noted, hard to swallow. As the loving stares of MacLuhan's French readers broke away from their precious object, I would like to think they did so in terms similar to those Lacan used in describing the relation between analysand and analyst: the love transference hung on something more than the analyst had, and the analysand's gift of love turned out to be a load of shit (Lacan 1977a: 268). There is very little difference between the *objet petit a* and the *objet petit tas*, as Lacan once punned. The Lacanian concept of the *objet petit a* will help us to understand the meaning MacLuhan had for his French readers, especially those who insisted on spelling his name in this manner—a phenomenon that took place in France but not in Québec. The word "reader" is already problematic, since one of the things Lacan and McLuhan had in common was television.

Both Lacan and McLuhan appeared on "primal-time television" (Rickels 1990) broadcasts in France in the early 1970s. While Lacan's appearance may have alarmed certain bookish Lacanians who feared that by massaging the masses psychoanalysis said nothing at all, Lacan himself spoke in the name of "non-idiots" (analysts) and, presumably, "idiots" (non-analysts) as well. If it didn't make a difference to Lacan if he spoke in the name of the public before the blackboard in his seminar or the couch potatoes glued to their television screens it was because he addressed neither of their gazes, which he claimed were really only one. But this is just the sort of difference upon which McLuhan's theory of media rested. To be fair to Lacan, he recognized that the mass media had psychical effects linked to technological developments, a lesson he adapted brilliantly through appeals to a variety of media and learned, not from McLuhan, but from "Freud's analogical hook-up of technology and the unconscious" (Rickels 1990: 43). For Lacan, McLuhan's mediatic extensions of man could not account for what was more than themselves.

MACSPELL

McLuhan's great-grandfather William McLughan arrived in Essa Township in the Province of Ontario, Canada from Country Down, Ireland in 1849 and began his life in Canada with a new, shortened name: McLuhan (1987: 1). Such changes of family name were not uncommon in the 19th or even 20th centuries; Canadian immigration officers have, with every new wave of immigrants, indulged in the disfiguration of names, not to mention families. Having lost a letter from his family name, McLuhan would ultimately gain another, albeit a different one, from many of his French readers for whom a certain "MacLuhan" appeared, at least at first and in certain circles, as a prophet of sorts. This re-spelling was not an overt attempt at some kind of Franco-Scots-Irish amalgamation, according to which the little imported *a* would signify an international family affair. Taken on its face value, the little *a* filled a perceived gap between *M* and *c* for the delicate French ear for which a little thing, already worming its way into pronunciation, would smooth over a ragged, foreign construction uncommon in French. For this reason, then, "MacLuhan" is in a way a Gallicized version of "McLuhan," even if the very gesture makes it foreign. But it is not without its confusions since, on the one hand, "Mac" means "son" while, on the other hand, in France a person called "Mac" may attract notice in polite academic and analytic circles since this is the abbreviated form of *maquereau* (pimp). Although the two Macs are unrelated, they cannot be kept apart. Of course, not all of McLuhan's French readers participated in this renaming game or, for that matter, name-calling game. McLuhan and MacLuhan would appear alongside one another in contributions to learned journals and newspapers; French translations of books written by McLuhan became, under review, books by MacLuhan.

There were readers and commentators, however, whose desire had an object and appeared to them in this object: the little *a* of Mac. The *a* really depends upon desire. In this *a* certain readers could identify themselves, even though this little sliver of a broken mirror might very well disappear in the next version of McLuhan's name. For a reader whose desire is tied to this object and whose subjecthood is constituted by it, this instability is doubly significant, since it indicates the fragility of this constitution and the division of the desiring subject which accomplishes it. In other words, McLuhan needs to be constantly rewritten as MacLuhan so as to embody the object of phantasy of the desiring subject. Yet no amount of constitutive respelling can change the significance of the little *a* as an image in which the subject's lack appears to him.

I am supposing that the little *a* is akin to an *objet petit a[utre]*. There are limits to this Lacanian supposition as a strategy of making sense of a cultural phenomenon since, as Mikkel Borch-Jacobsen (1991: 230–31) reminds us, the *objet a* is a part of oneself which one separates from oneself, a quite literal—that is, real—matter of giving up or sacrificing a bodily substance or organ, the loss of which is irrecuperable. The little *a* of Mac is not a real body part. Bertolt Brecht's (1979) gangster Macheath—"Mac the Knife" from *The Threepenny Opera*—has turned his blade neither on himself nor on the other, although in principle he handles a knife as well as, or better than, Macbeth. Still, the little *a* of Mac is an alphabetic morsel dropped into the gap between *M* and *c*, a gap which it moreover manifests as it drops into place, as one would expect of an *objet petit a* since it is a "symbol of the lack ... in so far as it is lacking" (Lacan 1977a: 103). It does not so much resist "significantization," as Borch-Jacobsen puts it, as allude, by its very instability across the pages of French readings of the words of their erstwhile prophet, to the structural interdependency of the signifier and thus to its condition as an element whose identity depends on what it is not. I am not chasing after spittle, sperm, faeces, the maternal breast, Van Gogh's ear, etc.—these real objects which a body separates from itself or "sacrifices," as it were. This language is not wholly adequate to the diversity of such objects as they require a typology distinguishing, for example, those that are cut from those from which one is weaned; Lacan's "unthinkable list" (1977: 315) indicates just how hard it is to put one's finger on the *objet petit a*; another list, no less thinkable, includes breasts, faeces, the gaze, and the voice (Lacan 1977a: 242). All the same, the little *a* is figurally a "little pile," a loop with a tail, a curled dropping evacuated from a pen. Our little *a* is a simulacrum of a semblance that is a pile as such.

What's in a name? The *a* of Mac circulates in and out of a family name. It is a fiction that embodies desire. This *objet petit a* slips in and out of signification through the passageway between *M* and *c* despite the claim that it "falls outside of signification" by "evading the signifier" (Grigg 1991: 112). It plays the game of presence/absence as well as any other signifier and, in addition, it comes and goes as the reader/writer pleases. The little *a* holds the prophet and his disciples together, and it is a letter that has had and continues to have a hold on the French imagination. In Alfred Jarry's (1972) "neoscientific novel" *Gestes et opinions du Docteur Faustroll*, the doctor's assistant Bosse-de-Nage utters two French words at opportune moments throughout the text: "Ha Ha." Jean Baudrillard (1976) understands this laughter in terms of the formula "A = A," the operational and tautological perfection of a system grown as obese as a *gidouille*, and therefore ready to be pushed over the edge by means of the revolutionary pataphysical principle of "more A than A." A string of identical little mathemes (aaaaa . . .) is a laughable object.

MACK

McLuhan began his correspondence with the British painter, writer, and polemicist (less kindly, for many, a Fascist) Wyndham Lewis in the early 1940s from his post at St. Louis University. During this period Lewis was teaching at Assumption College in Windsor, Ontario. McLuhan vigorously promoted Lewis as a portrait artist and had some success in opening the "big pocket-books," as he called them, of St. Louis. McLuhan also arranged lectures for Lewis. The nickname "Mac" was adopted by McLuhan himself as a short form in a letter to Lewis in 1944 (McLuhan 1987: 142–43). For years thereafter McLuhan signed his letters to Lewis with "Mac." According to the editors of McLuhan's published *Letters*, Lewis remarked upon this nickname to the effect that "Mack is not too matey, but it is too generic. I have known so many "Macks"—it blurs the image. Shall think up a less dignified abbreviation of my *Feldherr*" (McLuhan 1987: 142, n. 1). This "Mac attack" did not in the end deter McLuhan, although Lewis appears to have used it sparingly. Meanwhile, McLuhan adopted it as his moniker with several other correspondents. Lewis himself blurred the image with the addition of the final *k*, suggesting another big American object, a truck. The nickname or *Surnommant* of Lewis's *Feldherr* opens onto the matter of the remainder central to the *objet a*. By overnaming his *Feldherr* Mac, a diminished name actually and ironically accomplished the production of a surplus.

McLuhan ultimately admitted in a letter of January 1944 that "'McLuhan' suits me and is preferable to 'Mac'" (1987: 146). Indeed, for a field marshall patrolling the promotional front, "Mac" was simply and sardonically too dignified and indistinct for Lewis's taste. Despite this, Lewis never came up with a new name. And while he had doubts about his little name, McLuhan continued to use it in his correspondence with one of his former graduate students in St. Louis, Walter J. Ong, as well as with his colleague Felix Giovanelli. Ezra Pound put his own twist on McLuhan with "Mc L," a subtle architectural arrangement which had little of the chuminess of Lewis's remarks, but sufficient ideographic peculiarity to amuse them both (McLuhan 1987: 232, n. 3, 4). This is, then, the story of Mac before it was taken up by McLuhan's French readers in the 1960s, having long since disappeared from view in McLuhan's correspondence with Lewis. In the manner of Lewis's (1981 and 1981a) Vorticist journals *BLAST* 1 (orig. June 1914) and *BLAST* 2 (orig. July 1915), whose influence on McLuhan would be decisive in the areas of book design and rhetorical posturing, one might say: "Blast Mack for its British chuminess; Bless Mac for its Gallic mannerism."

Lacan and McLuhan come together through the letter-object *a* rather than under the glare of the video's light that records, for some, the meetings of great men. Lacan was a master of the media—not the absolute master, of course, since this position was reserved for McLuhan. Consider Sherry Turkle's description of Lacan with reference to the broadcast of an interview with him called *Psychoanalysis* in January 1973 (published as *Télévision* the following year) by the ORTF (Office de la Radio-diffusion- Télévision Française):

> Lacan established himself as the undisputed master of the media, or as one analyst, who has always been hostile to Lacan but who said he was "overwhelmed by a virtuoso performance," described him: "The psychoanalyst for the Age of McLuhan." Like a neurotic's symptom, Lacan's *Télévision* was a program that people loved to hate. (Turkle 1992: 201–2)

French television viewers had already entered *la galaxie MacLuhan* during his appearance *au petit écran* on July 5 1972, as part of the program "Dossiers de l'écran" (one needs to keep in mind that this was before Bernard Pivot and "Apostrophes" [see Heath 1989]). McLuhan's appearance was organized by the telecommunications engineer and music professor Pierre Schaeffer, long-serving Chef du service de la RTF (and later ORTF). In the early 1970s, Schaeffer was one of McLuhan's promoters in French media circles. Later in the decade, however, Schaeffer's criticisms of McLuhan's work became severe (1978–79: 104ff). His charges included professional and political irresponsibility, conceptual confusion, and above all else, deception. For Schaeffer, McLuhan was the first university professor to draw positive attention to the media. McLuhan made the media a legitimate object of intellectual concern, and in doing so presented Schaeffer with the opportunity to elevate his own work and position in the eyes of the French professors whose lofty gazes the media had hitherto remained below. Yet, in what Schaeffer regarded as often brilliant texts, McLuhan failed to live up to his promise of bringing the study of media into the academy, adhering instead to jokes, bad journalistic practices, and sensationalism. In short, Schaeffer claimed that McLuhan's texts were unfortunately surrealistic and they distracted French researchers from developing their own lines of inquiry into the mediascape. Schaeffer did not take any blame for what he called, with as much cliché as prescience, *l'affaire McLuhan* (bringing to mind the more recent print media event, *l'affaire Derrida*), although he helped to stage McLuhan's entry into French televisual consciousness.

Despite the poignancy of Schaeffer's predicament, media workers found themselves making similar statements again and again during the course of McLuhan's French revolution.

McLuhan was not particularly pleased with his performance(s) on French television. He wrote to his friends Tom and Dorothy Easterbrook that they "were complicated by my inadequate French." Still, Paris provided Mac with the pleasing diversion of Eugene Ionesco's (1973) play *Macbett*, performed for the first time at Le Théâtre Rive-Gauche in 1972. For its part, television provided McLuhan with a low definition rendezvous with the French public, a doubly cool (owing to the medium and the messenger) point of contact deepened by his awkward oral skills which would have necessitated, for those who cared to listen, a high level of involvement in the completion and perhaps correction of his remarks. McLuhan had mastered the media before he had mastered French. A perfectly fluent McLuhan may have been too hot for French audiences and, by the same token, a transparent and straightforwardly descriptive Lacan would not have "mastered" television. Lacan was never cooler than on television—except, perhaps, when he was thought to be addressing a dog during a talk at Vincennes (Lacan 1990: 117).

It is evident from the letters he wrote to his family from Cambridge in the 1930s that the French language and culture had entered McLuhan's consciousness in an enthusiastic but incomplete manner. These letters radiate youthful exuberance and his belief that the mastery of French opens one to "the mind of the greatest European people" (1987: 28). While McLuhan did become a competent reader of French, he later lamented that he read only this language in addition to his own. Unlike his friend Lewis (1981: 13), McLuhan would not "Blast Parisian Parochialism" and "Sentimental Gallic Gush."

MA—MA—MA—MA

The journalist Guy Dumur reported on his meeting with McLuhan at the ORTF and the prophet's television appearance(s) for readers of *La nouvel observateur* shortly after "Dossiers de l'écran" was aired. McLuhan was a media personality and therefore newsworthy in the eyes of the media, turned as they are towards themselves. Dumur claimed ignorance when it came to evaluating McLuhan's intellectual contributions. Despite what McLuhan admirers like Schaeffer, Morin, Jean Duvignaud, and Alain Bourdin have claimed in the name of an "open" sociology, Dumur simply could not understand McLuhan because "he is too anglo-saxon" (an odd thing to say of a Celt) (1972: 36–7). Indeed, it was already commonplace in journalistic reports on McLuhan to claim that his work was contrary to the French spirit of Cartesian thought. Figured as an "anti-Descartes," McLuhan challenged the methods of separation, dissection and causal explanation by stringing together apparently unrelated ideas; this practice made his texts surrealistic, and surrealism had long since passed out of fashion. But for many French journalists, several pieces of the puzzle of McLuhan always seemed to be missing. More to the point, Daniel Garric and others specified that while English is direct, and permits the formation of neologisms and explosive links between disparate ideas, French is at the pole opposite *la pensée McLuhanienne* because it is intimately neo-classical in construction (Garric 1967; Marcotte 1974). This made him difficult to understand in translation.

These vague contrasts set the stage for more bizarre pronouncements, themselves worthy of the label surreal. For example, Dominique Desanti referred mistakenly to McLuhan as "un pur WASP!" (1974: 40–1). White—yes—but anglo-saxon and protestant—no; well, at least not after his conversion to Catholicism. Moreover, a mantra was being chanted in Parisian circles courtesy, among others, of the journalist associated with *Le figaro littéraire*, André Brincourt (1972): "Ma—Ma—Ma—Ma: Marx, Mao, Marshall McLuhan." The last syllable of the chant indicated what it was in the prophet and so-called revolutionary that was more than himself, an *objet petit a* that did not in this instance find its way into his name, but nonetheless transfixed those like Brincourt, sunk in their chanting; it may as well have been Macheath, Macbett, Macbeth, MacLuhan (whom, it is rumored, enjoyed more than a few Big Macs in his time). One needn't go further than Yves Knockaert's (1988) *Third Interlude* for piano to find a soundtrack suitable for Big Mac's Mac Attack; after all, he composed this piece for the ballet aptly titled *MacLuhan at MacDonalds*. What is also more than itself or the residue of the residue of the name? It is the further remainder that reminds us of a cry for mother: mama, mama. The pain of this cry is real enough because it wants satisfaction from an object from which one will soon enough be weaned. This *objet petit a* belongs to the (m)other or ma-ma.

In the introduction to Jean Marabini's book *Marcuse & McLuhan et la nouvelle révolution mondiale*, Armand Lanoux (1973) refers to "les deux grands M: M. et M," whose respective revolutionary ideas are like thermometers since it is absurd to blame them for the heat they register. Lanoux's activities in the French media included the presidency of the Comité de la télévision française in the late 1950s, as well as the directorship of the review *A la page* from 1964–70. Today, the very notion that Marx, Mao, Marcuse, and MacLuhan could be brought together in a consciousness-raising chant about youth and revolution indicates the brilliant superficiality of mediatic representations of the political field and the abuses of "Eastern" practices prevalent in the 1960s. Several years before Marabini's book, writing in Montreál, Renault Gariépy had observed in the heady atmosphere of Expo '67 that "on our little French screen . . . the presence of MM (these initials no longer translate the reality of Marilyn Monroe or Mickey Mantle) has begun to make itself felt" (1967). A Canadian "MM" had replaced several American standards. Let's not forget that years after "MM" disappeared from the French scene, another MM (Mickey Mouse), a further American standard, would make his presence felt among the francophones.

The little *a* is the remainder, the surplus of the prophet's message. This message was a sublime object of fascination, inspiring an impressive range of responses. McLuhan's flaws (awkward French, alleged journalistic excesses, flippancy, political irresponsibility in the eyes of the Left) helped to solidify his position as prophet rather than diminish his status. As Slavoj Žižek explains in the case of the body of the king, his ordinary features undergo a transubstantiation as he becomes an object of fascination (1991: 254–55). To debase the king is not to diminish his status, since the accentuation of his flaws reinforces his position by arousing compassion and fascination. This holds equally true in the case of the prophet MacLuhan, especially in his heyday. The more his work was subject to critical debate, the more fascinating he became. A sublime object is a difficult target to hit, for the *objet petit a* is a second order semblance framed by a television screen. Having smashed the set, the medium may reassert itself through the adjoining wall of a neighbor's apartment, in a bar, in a picture window, etc. Standing over the wreck of a television set or, to use Žižek's example, over the body of Ceausescu, one asks oneself: is it/he really dead? The *objet petit a* cannot be destroyed—unlike one of the sign vehicles by means of which it is delivered—and this is brought home by the image of Ceausescu's body broadcast televisually around the world, persisting not only in the memory of Romanians but in the international image banks. The lost *objet a* needs a medium to clothe it; even a name will suffice. Of course, McLuhan was not subject to the regicidal intentions of his televisual audience. This did not make him any easier to hit. For the paradox of striking McLuhan was this: it put one in the strange position of being seen as a counter-revolutionary, for one was thought to be on the side of mechanical reason and rationality, of Western values—on the wrong side of the "generation gap," anti-youth, a proponent of explication over exploration. In short, because McLuhan aligned himself with youth culture and counter-cultural revolution against the academy, to attack him as a counter-revolutionary was paradoxically to become one oneself (see Dommergues 1969). Ultimately, however, McLuhan's own corporatist assumptions, homophobia, and "right to life" politics were read as the signs of a deeply conservative Catholic thinker. No paradox could, in the end, erase or obscure these beliefs.

The little *a* embodies the impossible *jouissance* of certain members of the French media community, such as Schaeffer. The realization that their prophet was also an impostor caught them in a painful paradox. Mac could not provide "it"; that is, he could not satisfy the desire of media workers for legitimation in relation to the French intellectuals. As he continued not to provide "it," Mac still embodied the *objet a* of the legitimation phantasy by showing those such as Schaeffer what they were: little twisted semblances of shit. Even the message of the medium, critically battered, taught a painful lesson about exclusion from intellectual discourse, while at the same time it filled page after page of reviews: yes, it's all over with Mac, isn't it? It was his success that destroyed him, wasn't it? We technicians must have been wrong. It needs to be said again, doesn't it? This was the rather lengthy lesson taught by the little *a* of Mac. But Mac was not an analyst who could teach his followers how to give up the *objet petit a* and readjust themselves to French intellectual life in the wake of another failed revolution; to give his name back its quasi-original spelling, leaving a gap between *M* and *c* which would really show the technicians where they belonged and what they were made of.

One of the most important features of McLuhan's reception in France is precisely the issue of who read and promoted him and the sites from which they worked. While those in the mass media, artists of all stripes (especially graphic artists), and pedagogues eager to introduce new audio-visual tools into the classroom found inspiration in his theories, this led to claims that it was his success that destroyed him, that his prestige did not originate from a site where prestige could be afforded to a thinker.

With the advent of the concept of *macluhanisme* there emerged the figure of a prophet who might have provided satisfaction for the "men of images," the professionals of the communications industries (advertisers, media technicians, printers, designers, and teachers). But the prophet failed to do so for, as we have seen, several reasons; and with this disappointment came a barrage of criticism against him. The very inseparability of the desire of the "men of images" and the object-cause of their desire, led to very public suffering and loss of potential prestige and glory.

François Mariet correctly diagnosed this situation in recognizing that *macluhanisme* "is inseparable from the public whose expectations it fulfils and for whom McLuhan becomes ... a prophet" (1978–79: 108–9). Occupying a position subordinate to the theoretical disciplines of the academy from which concepts are borrowed, and less well known than philosophers, writers, and filmmakers, the media workers, represented by Mariet as a "fan club," entered the public sphere of intellectual debate only to have their own subordinate position displayed to them in the media in which they worked. Moreover, in his study of the recognition factor of *macluhanisme* among teachers in France, Mariet catalogued the diverse effects of hearsay and found that McLuhan's French readers in the pedagogical milieu needed no specific competence in order to tune into his messages. Mariet attributes the success of *macluhanisme* among teachers to the "conjunction of this diffuse expectation of a philosophy of the media and to an unusual oeuvre in which no scientific method of demonstration limits the access of the hurried or untrained reader, and against which no critical text forewarns" (1977: 51). Mariet situates himself on the side of the critical, unhurried pedagogue, the trained reader who specializes in identifying the follies of interpretation of a servile class.

On the other hand of this rhetoric of speed, the hurried McReader has no time to reflect, Mariet suggests. But among such typographically-minded groups as the Association des Campagnons de Lure, for example, points of resistance against just this sort of professional pronouncement had been established in the course of a seminar (attended by McLuhan in August 1969) devoted to "M.McL." In his introduction to the seminar, Gilles Gheerbrand presents a reading of three categories of French articles on McLuhan (reviews, those which purport to reveal the fraud of *macluhanisme*, and serious and honest reflections), the second of which briefly describes some of the errors made by the intellectuals in their attempts to discredit McLuhan, while hinting at the similarity of some their ideas to those of McLuhan (1969: 10). Even distinguished university professor François Châtelet (1967), Gheerbrand remarks, read McLuhan hurriedly, pointing out his error in thinking that the telephone was a hot medium. The speed of one's reading was the shit which was slung back and forth over of course of the public debates on the merits of McLuhan.[1]

Into the gap between desire and fulfilment went the little *a* of Mac, and the prophet was taken as the cause of his subjects' desires. *Le mac*, or the pimp, didn't and couldn't deliver—or rather, he delivered his followers into servitude. This does not mean that they went without a struggle. Žižek would have us believe that such servitude is voluntary since the other name, the sublime Mac, hypnotized his readers because they conferred upon it the power to do so. They were glued to their sets, if you will; and, after smashing them, they were glued to the idea of the set that Mac preached. To be called *un petit mac* carries a further meaning. *Un mac* is a person who invites a guest to dinner and, when the time comes to settle the bill, notices that he is short of money, and asks his guest to loan him some. Mac's followers suffered the indignity of having to pay the price of accepting an invitation to bring their work to the intellectual table, a table set for them in the name of their host, but for which they had to pay.

Both "le pape du pop," as Garric dubbed McLuhan in a catholic gesture (in this name alone one senses why the dictates of the prophet were followed to the letter by certain believers), and Lacan renounced personal brilliance in the name of orders greater than themselves; for Lacan, it was sainthood. The saintly psychoanalyst, too, embodies the *objet petit a* and it is one of the "oddities of the acts of saints," Lacan noted (1990: 15–16), to make those whose ears were glued to their television sets aware of this and to unstick them. It was only after the program was over, after the screen had absorbed its blue glow and Lacan was silent—as mum as a saint— that one could really hear what one is in the sound of sight. The important displacement hinted at by Lacan is that of sight by sound, eye by ear, even before the television set. Recall, however, that we are in the "Age of McLuhan." This displacement was, McLuhan claimed, at the center of the Gutenberg civilization's deafening of the tribal ear for the sake of the biases of literacy and visual culture. This made one ill-equipped to experience the auditory-tactile world of the new electronic technologies. For McLuhan, tuning in meant keeping one's ears glued to the set. Unlike the saintly analyst, and despite his renunciation of personal brilliance, McLuhan didn't stop producing euphoria. He simply could not be mum in the oral-aural electronic village even if, in French, he occasionally stumbled. Watching television made *théorie à la conne*—that is, lousy theory.

NOTE

1. How did McLuhan himself read? He was not a slow and careful hermeneut by any stretch of the imagination. His reading habits were, as Philip Marchand explains, selective:

   > To determine whether a book was worth reading, he usually looked at page 69 of the work, plus the adjacent page and the table of contents. If the author gave no promise of insight or worthwhile information on page 69, McLuhan reasoned, the book was probably not worth reading. If he decided the book did merit his attention, he started by reading only the left hand pages. (1989: 129)

   The charge of unreflective speed reading could not be used effectively against McLuhan's followers on the grounds of its inadequacy to the master's habits and the texts they informed. One may claim against his detractors that the errors of their readings were the result of slow reading against the grain.

freud and his followers, or how psychoanalysis brings out the worst in everyone

9

Todd Dufresne

Editor's Note

In some circles biography is disparaged as naive and irrelevant with respect to theory. In turn, biographers may be quick to dismiss theory as unconnected to real life. Taking his cue from the works of Roazen and Derrida in these different fields, Todd Dufresne grafts biography to theory in the exploration and production of a "wild" biography/analysis of Freud and his followers. To this end he explores the "unforeseen collision of interests" that unfold in the space between the biographical subject and studied object of psychoanalysis: Freud himself.

Dufresne argues that Freud spun the web that is psychoanalysis from out of his own delusions—his self-analysis or autobiography—and that his followers remain to this day his proof by (or as) repetition. For it is with Freud's followers that the subjective nature of psychoanalysis becomes concrete, objective, "real," transferred, and transmissible. It becomes, that is, an institution: scientific, political, religious, and so on. Arguing that the position of follower is an impossible one, Dufresne suggests, echoing Freud, that psychoanalysis invariably "brings out the worst in everyone."

Even as Dufresne makes a broad theoretical case for a "Freud" that is self-deconstructive, he covers much of the anecdotal, biographical and historical literature on psychoanalysis. His essay may be a good guide for readers lost on either side of the biographical/theoretical divide, including those with an interest in deconstruction.

TODD DUFRESNE is a doctoral candidate in Social and Political Thought, York University, Toronto, where he is preparing *Beyond Beyond: Tales from the Freudian Crypt* and *Margins of Psychoanalysis, For Example.* His work has appeared in *The International Journal of Psychoanalysis, The Psychoanalytic Review, Psychoanalytic Books, Werkblatt,* and elsewhere.

> You are not neurotic, but you can be in time.
>
> —Freud

IN A LECTURE FOR THE COLLÈGE INTERNATIONALE DE PHILOSOPHIE entitled "What's Wrong With French Psychoanalysis?," renowned historian of psychoanalysis Paul Roazen argued that proponents of the French Freud have "forgotten" Freud. And thus he bluntly asked, Where's Freud?[1] Without by any means taking on the mantle of the "French Freud," we will try in what follows to appease Roazen by recalling (or, as it were, conjuring) the historico-biographical image of Sigmund Freud. On the one hand, located as we are within the closure of the "psychoanalytic century," if only for a few more years, this should be a fairly simple affair. Indeed, it may be that Freud is precisely the ghost we cannot exorcise, despite our best efforts. However, and on the other hand, while Roazen makes an interesting and no doubt timely point, his question is still tied to matters of essence, presence, truth, and so on. Suffice to say that Roazen's subject—the science of psychoanalysis, Freud himself—is no longer the self-evident or common-sense subject of modernity. In fact, we are increasingly skeptical today that there is or ever was a privileged access to the "truth of Freud"—*wherever* he might have been or may still remain.

In what follows, then, we attempt to both answer and problematize Roazen's question, in part by addressing the subject of psychoanalysis through a timely question of our own: namely, *Who's* Freud? At the same time, we explore the structural role that institutionalization and discipleship play in the invention, adjudication, and transmission of Freud's science, effectively asking: *Whose* Freud? Between the who's/whose of these questions, we hope to reveal a Freud that is irreducible to any biographical or institutional closure, one that is, in effect, radically self-deconstructive. To this end we attempt to locate Roazen's own work, the "Where's Roazen?" implicit within his question, alongside some current theoretical trends in psychoanalysis.

1.

Since it is biography that is in question here, even the truth of biography and its contested utility, we might begin by citing a fairly well-known passage from Freud. "Alarmed by the threat" that Arnold Zweig is thinking of becoming his biographer, Freud writes:

> No, I am far too fond of you to permit such a thing. Anyone who writes a
> biography is committed to lies, concealments, hypocrisy, flattery, and even

to hiding his own lack of understanding, for biographical truth does not
exist, and if it did we could not use it.

    Truth is unobtainable, mankind does not deserve it, and in any case is
not our Prince Hamlet right when he asks who would escape a whipping if
he got what he deserved? (Freud and Zweig 1970: 127; see also Freud
1960: 430)

Freud not only feared the inevitable distortion that results from the "furor bio-
graphicus" (Sachs 1945: 108) but, more importantly, the possibility that his science
might be reduced to a piece of his own subjective phantasying—less a dream-work
than a nightmare.[2]

    In his "elementary" introduction to psychoanalysis, Freud evoked the case of
historical research, against which he situated psychoanalysis. He claimed that the
analyst, unlike the historian, "does at least report things in which he himself played
a part" (*SE* 15: 18). However, Freud begs the question as to whether the "report"
in question has more to tell us about the analyst than about an event from someone's repressed past. And of course the same problematic plagues historical
research, at least insofar as historians attempt to transcend the limitations of a
purely descriptive accounting of events—what R. G. Collingwood disparagingly
called "scissor and paste" history (1956)—to the unspoken motivation lying behind
some past action. Thus both psychoanalyst and historian are caught up in the questionable reconstruction of events to which they are by necessity outsiders.

    Still, Freud had good reasons for distinguishing psychoanalysis from the histo-
rian's uncritical depth or psycho-history. After all, a psycho-history always risks
mistaking phantasy for reality in precisely the same way that Freud did before privately dropping the seduction theory in 1897. To Wilhelm Fliess, Freud wrote of
"the certain insight that there are no indications of reality in the unconscious, so
that one cannot distinguish between truth and [affective] fiction" (1985: 264). In
striking contrast, the scientific historian has always been committed to the literal
(realist) truth of the subject, since without it history would be reduced to the production of fictions; from this perspective, scientific method is never just another tall-
tale, but the privileged medium through which interpretations claim objective truth.

    To put it quickly, we are thus confronted with two difficulties. First, we are no
longer certain that the distinction between contemporary historian and past object
can be bridged; that, for instance, the gap Collingwood (dis)solves or leaps by pen-
etrating from the "outside" of an event to its motivational "inside" ever occurs.
Second, we cannot be certain that there ever was or is an accessible "inside," an
essential object or kernel of truth that becomes subject in the historian's mind (and
objectified in his text, a subject for his readers). For as François Roustang argues:
"Historical truth exists no more than do the origins of the Indo-European languages. What exists are delusions founded upon the supposition of its existence"
(1983: 37). Thus confronted with the "invention" of culture and history (see Wagner 1975), the fact of interpretation probably tells us more about the analyst than
about his object. As Nietzsche first guessed, system-building is always "the personal
confession of its author and a kind of involuntary or unconscious memoir" (1989:
13).

Consequently, the "truth" of the subject, of the cogito itself, is revealed as the invisible ghost which propels the historian's imaginary time machine.

2.

Though we will return to these problematics, they are not new suspicions and we won't dwell upon them too closely here. Instead we might profitably turn to John Forrester's consideration of the "four ways of breaching the membrane" that forms between analyst and analysand: namely, scientific communications, acting-out, gossip, and telepathy (1990: 253). In each case the contractual relationship upon which therapy is grounded is violated; in effect, representation as "wild transference" leaks outside the office, beyond the couch. While Freud accounts for the first two breaches in security—the first being "permitted," the second being "expected"—he never comes to grips with the last two, which remain as non-theorized contaminants in the Freudian corpus. Forrester thus suggests that "Gossip is the underbelly of analysis, telepathy its shadow."

It is arguably for the same reasons that Freud never came to grips with biography: as a discourse outside the analytic fold, biography breaches the space or bond between analyst and patient and produces a public or wild transference. In fact, as a kind of *voluntary whispering*—in contrast to "involuntary whispering," which is tied to issues in telepathy (Hacking 1988: 442)—biography is not unconnected with "hearsay," as Freud likened it, or even gossip (*SE* 15: 18). But as Roazen rightly suggests in his introduction to *Brother Animal*, "what seems gossip to one generation may be history to the next" (1969: xiv). Or again, as Kurt Eissler put it to Wilhelm Reich: "I think gossip—for the historian, gossip is extremely important" (in Reich 1973: 447).

Indeed, by reducing the already shaky foundations of biography to the level of gossip, the more orthodox followers of Freud have often done their best to silence dissenters and limit the breach that is biography. Steven Marcus thus rails against the "idle gossip and chatter" in Roazen's early, controversial work, preferring instead those "differences [that] have meaning for the history of the movement" (1984: 213). Of course, we might reasonably ask what these so-called differences amount to and, more critically, who is in a position to judge them. That supposed differences are reducible to an orthodox "archaeology" of psychoanalysis surely doesn't make them any more favorable (see Vichyn 1993: 134–38).

If Freud and his followers often reject biography as theoretically impossible or, at least, as a show of bad taste (often "American"[3]), it may only indicate the extent to which they have something to hide, minimize, or sweep under the analytic rug (see Dufresne 1994). Yet we have to wonder: if biographical truth, the truth of the subject, cannot be had (even supposing for a moment, against Freud, that we deserve it) or verified objectively by historians of psychoanalysis, to what extent was or is the science of psychoanalysis possible?

For finally, the same questions we ask of psycho-history can be asked of psychoanalysis: Can the analyst-patient duo join forces and bridge the gap between (screen) memory and objective fact? And when they (think they) do, is the re-membered product any less invented that the historian's? In his *An Outline of Psycho-Analysis* and elsewhere Freud certainly admits that:

we fill in what is omitted by making plausible inferences and translating it to conscious material. In this way we construct, as it were, a sequence of conscious events complementary to the unconscious psychical processes. The relative certainty of our psychical science is based on the binding force of those inferences. (*SE* 23: 159)

Leaving aside Freud's tireless assertion that anyone who disagrees with these constructions is lacking a deep enough understanding of psychoanalysis—as the inimitable Karl Kraus puts it, "If I tell the analyst to kiss my ass, they tell me I have an anal fixation" (in Szasz 1976: 119)—or is really committed to its repressed underbelly, we are at least beginning to appreciate that Freud was dealing with highly dubious representations in his practice. Could it be that the "relative certainty" of psychoanalysis was based not on the "binding force of those inferences," but upon the transference which bound the patient's recovery to the analyst's suggestions? For as Fliess quite properly suspected of Freud in late 1901, "the reader of thoughts merely reads his own thoughts into other people" (1985: 447).

Actually, as Mikkel Borch-Jacobsen demonstrates, in his attempt to break with hypnosis Freud confused the repetition of "acting out" in the transference with remembering (1993: 46–7); theatre is not history. What, then, does the analyst-patient construction re-present? Freud of course always maintained that "we never fail to make a strict distinction between *our* knowledge and *his* knowledge" (*SE* 23: 178). But if the patient's transference onto the analyst is indistinguishable from good-old-suggestion and hypnosis—if, in other words, "hypnotic suggestion had returned *into* psychoanalysis, *as* psychoanalysis" (Borch-Jacobsen 1988: 150; see 1993: 58–9)—then analytic construction does not necessarily (or even likely) represent an actual (original) event at all. "One could say," Roustang therefore argues, "that analyst and patient finally enter into the same cultural mini-universe ... [T]hat is, their delusions, which are based on the same supposed historical truth, have become similar enough to communicate and found a mini-society" (1983: 38).

In this respect, it was no accident that Freud recommended to Ernest Jones that "the simplest way of learning psychoanalysis was to believe that all he wrote was true and then, after understanding it, one could criticize it any way one wished" (Jones 1959: 204). But confronted with such "Catholicism," as Joseph Wortis recently put it (Dufresne 1995), there was always the danger that Freud's student-patients would never emerge from the "hypnotransferential tie" (Borch-Jacobsen 1993: 59) that bound, and still binds, this delusional mini-society together (see Roazen 1975: 354).

And no doubt Jacques Lacan only pushed this mad logic to its extreme when he declared that the goal of psychoanalysis was the creation of more psychoanalysts. As Stuart Schneiderman puts it, "someone chooses to practice psychoanalysis because he cannot see himself doing anything else, because he cannot think of any other way to deploy his desire in terms of work" (1983: 86). Or as Marie Bonaparte remarks in a letter of 1927: "How wonderful analysis is! One cannot embrace another profession after savouring this one" (in Bertin 1982: 171).With these sentiments psychoanalysis truly became "an elegant solution to the problem of madness, since it amounted to dissolving that problem in the establishment of a society that was itself delirious" (Borch-Jacobsen 1991: 166).[4] When recovery becomes synonymous with the directives of a cause, sickness gains in meaning what it loses in substance. This unbeatable strategy is nicely captured in a humorous story told by Abram Kardiner, who once claimed to get "nothing" out of his analysis with Horace Frink. In response to this news Freud ironically said: "You did get something out of it ... A little neurosis" (1977: 17). He might not have *been* neurotic, but psychoanalysis made all the difference (see Wortis 1984: 57).

Hence the troublesome question: given psychoanalysis, "Is there an end to analysis, after all?" (Borch-Jacobsen 1993: 57). Similarly, is there an "outside" of the transference? (see Lacan 1966: 591). And if there is, who is in a position to end the analysis, to introduce the break that Jacques Derrida calls the "*tranche*-fer-ence"? (1987: 510).

3.

A Spatially Enlarged, Solitary Solitariness: Psychoanalysis was inaugurated into the 20th Century with Freud's autobiographical and self-analytical *Interpretation of Dreams.* There Freud admitted that he had "to reveal to the public gaze more of the intimacies of my mental life than I liked, or that is normally necessary for any writer who is a man of science and not a poet" (*SE* 4: xxiii–xxiv).

But why then should Freud's "auto" be considered any less delusional, gossipy, or different than the biographer's tall-tale? As Roazen was among the first to insist, "The psychological system Freud created closely fit his personal peculiarities—demonstrating that the rise of psychoanalysis was far from a coldly neutral scientific advance" (1975: 87). Consequently, and as Freud once admitted, "It remains for the future to decide whether there is more delusion in my theory than I should like to admit" (*SE* 12: 79). To be sure, Freud "very much needed a 'yes' from the outside world" (Roazen 1969: 47), "someone who would confirm him, comfort him, encourage him, listen to him and even feed him" (Fromm 1959: 47). And thus, as Roustang brilliantly formulates it:

> In these circumstances, how can he who either invents a new theory or ren-
> ovates a theory prevent himself from wanting to share his findings, that is,
> to find a public who will applaud his sayings, which would no longer be
> delirious because others would share them? Delirium is the theory of the one,
> while theory is the delirium of several, which is transmissible. (1982: 34)

Or again, as Nietzsche succinctly argued long ago: "*Multiplication Table.*—One is always wrong, but with two, truth begins.—*One* cannot prove his case, but two are irrefutable" (1974: 218). Following Freud in *Civilization and Its Discontents*, we need only add that the delirium "of the one," of Freud's defiant "hermit" turned fool or madman, often becomes transmissible in the "mass-delusions" of a religion; in this case, the psychoanalytic religion. Unfortunately, and as Freud realized, "No one who shares a delusion ever recognizes it as such" (*SE* 21: 81).

This was certainly the fate for Freud's pupils for whom psychoanalysis became a way of life—and a way of making a living. For although psychoanalysis may have found outside recognition, Freud's own solitary role, his unparalleled position as mythic hero, hardly changed; as Deutsch suggests, it merely lent itself to "a spatially enlarged, socialized solitariness" (1973: 173). One of the most forgotten critics, Maurice Natenberg, thus rightly concludes that Freud's followers were entranced by "the same influences which had driven men through endless time to create religions, cults, systems of authority, bizarre ideologies and even fraudulent enterprises. All these have one common factor—they are based on inducing belief in the unknown, the undemonstrable, the illogical and occult" (1955: 239–40).

Grounded as it is upon the subjectivity (or autobiography) of Sigmund Freud, the objectivity (or science) of psychoanalysis is, from (or at) the very beginning, severely compromised, split in two. At the same time, since Freud "could not separate his creation, the theory of psychoanalysis, from himself" (Grosskurth 1991: 53), and since it "would be impossible to overestimate how much of himself Freud put into his work" (Roazen 1975: 86), we are quite unable to determine *where* exactly that split takes place—assuming it does or should take place at all. In other words, and perhaps this is the crux of the matter, we are unable without considerable interpretive violence to distinguish once and for all the auto from the biography, the man from the science, the flesh from the word, the dream from its manifestation or, if you prefer, the self, psyche, or psycho from the analysis.

Consequently, Where's Freud? And furthermore, Who is (and isn't) Freud? Whose Freud is it anyway?

4.

Stemming, no doubt, from the French preoccupation with the abyss (in all its poststructural guises), many critics today emphasize the structure of this uncertain, split, double origin; and this, it occasionally seems, at the expense of the "true" biographical Freud and his ernest biographers. This abyss betrays an altogether different kind of madness than that which we usually confront, especially in North America. In the first place, it does not necessarily entail just another excursion into existentialism, which always remained a humanism. Rather, the abyssal madness of poststructuralist thought typically refers to a contamination or mixing of boundaries that mark the outer limits of an inner dehiscence; a "*double chiasmatic invagination of edges,*" as Derrida colorfully puts it (1992: 238, Derrida's emphasis), which undoes the purity of our scientific model, our logical law of non-contradiction, even as it points towards the impossible, the beyond, the mad as instituted *within* our rational categories of thought, "inside" the dream of a synchronic, essentialized truth.

Despite, then, what appears to be the taming, normalization, or institutionalization of psychoanalysis—its freezing in time, its timely death—we should not be too surprised if we now find at the heart of Freud's science a logic of madness, a madness of logic; a lively (de)logic that disrupts the singular subject of psychoanalysis and, with it, the possibility of its simple transmission from Freud to his attentive followers. If so, and here Roazen & Co. would have to agree, it is no longer possible to simply and naturally—that is, without pre-judgement and prejudice—foreclose in advance the choice between subject and object, Freud and analysis. For in what is not by any means a new formula, psychoanalysis *is* Sigmund Freud. By insisting upon this "convergence" or "mutual interference," not just of the unconscious and conscious forces in the production of manifest symptoms

(*SE* 15: 42, 60) but also of subject and object, of autobiography and biography, psychoanalysis reveals itself as its own symptom or accident, a veritable slip of the old man's tongue. Kraus of course knew this and more when he coined the famously witty line in *Die Fackel*: "Psychoanalysis is the disease of which it claims to be the cure" (in Szasz 1976: 24).

In this way, we stumble upon a radical undecidability that exists both at the origins of psychoanalysis and in its multiple after-effects—an undecidability that exists along the borderline between its autobiographical "inside" (subject as object) and scientific "outside" (object as subject) and, at the heart of that coupling, in the irreducible monster *subjectobject*. Consequently, the invention or construction of psychoanalysis already implies its inevitable de-construction, its circular logic exploded and transformed by the structure of the "chiasmus."

5.

Usually in the most vague and clumsy way, this sort of troublesome complexity makes some think, no doubt a bit too quickly, that Freud was never much of a philosopher and, in any case, was more than a little neurotic himself. Indeed, that Freud was never properly analyzed by a fellow analyst, that psychoanalysis originates in his incomplete self-analysis—what Ellis calls, with a chuckle, "a simple and economical method!" (in Wortis 1954: 13)—has been for some of his followers an uncomfortable, regrettable, and even forgettable detail. But let's not forget that on November 14, 1897, Freud sent a letter to Fliess, writing: "True self-analysis is impossible, else there would be no [neurotic] illness" (1985: 281). Actually, this rather pessimistic sentiment is not an abberation in Freud's thinking, and forty years later in his important "Analysis Terminable and Interminable" he concluded that psychoanalysis itself, along with education and government, was an "impossible" profession (*SE* 23: 248).

Part of what is so unnerving about Freud's inaugural and interminable self-analysis is captured by Peter Gay when he rightly asks: "How could Freud, no matter how bold or original, become his own Other?" (1988: 97). How could Freud, in other words, create the distance of an Other through which psychoanalysis (and its mediating transference) was made possible? Or again, more simply, how did psychoanalysis happen (to Freud) before it was founded (by Freud)? This leads Alberto Ceiman, a Lacanian analyst from Mexico City, to propose the following paradox:

> Transference was discovered when the analytical setting had already been invented. Transference got there late. We have here a funny paradox: psychoanalysis only makes sense in terms of transference, however it was discovered after it was invented; at least this was the case for Freud and the Freudians. (1992 unpublished)

Transference, the emotional bond between analyst and patient, missed its appointment with itself; we might even say, in Derridean jargon, that it differed and deferred from itself, from the possibility of an original self-same. Ceiman, however, is far too comfortable with the idea that this inaugural paradox can be restricted to "Freud and the freudians," as though the aporia shrinks rather than expands over time and space. After all, Lacan and his followers never resolved the paradox, but were only its most uncanny embodiment and (re)incarnation. Passing through Lacan, they were always just another link "in a historical chain of training analyses that can be traced back, through a kind of apostolic succession, to the personal analytical inter-actions of Freud and his first disciples" (Jay 1993: 167). As Lacan put it near the end of his life, shortly after the dissolution of the École Freudienne: "C'est à vous d'être lacanien, si vous voulez. Moi, je suis freudien" (in Schneiderman 1983: 91).

As embarrassing as it may sound, we are beginning to grapple here with the pos-sibility that psychoanalysis is a science that has yet to happen—even to itself—and is still being invented from out of the rupture of a "non-origin which is originary." And thus Derrida argues:

> If one wished to simplify the question, it would become, for example: how can an autobiographical writing, in the abyss of an unterminated self-analysis, give to a worldwide institution *its* birth? The birth of whom? of what? and how does the interruption or the limit of self-analysis. . . repro-duce its mark in the institutional movement, the possibility of this remark from then on never ceasing to make little ones, multiplying the progeniture with its cleavages, conflicts, divisions, alliances, marriages, and regroup-ings? (1987: 305)

Once again, conditioned by its own certain uncertainty, how did psychoanalysis happen—if it did in fact happen?

Like some others before him (see Rieff 1959: 71), Lacan felt that psychoanalysis only became a method, a happening, for Freud's followers: "Freud, for his part, did not apply a method. If we overlook the unique and inaugural character of his endeavor, we will be committing a serious error" (1988: 21). For this very reason, though, Havelock Ellis wisely cautioned a young Joseph Wortis against a "didactic analysis" with Freud in a letter of September 14, 1934. Ellis wrote:

> About being psychoanalysed, my own feeling most decidedly is that it would be better to follow his *example* than his precept. *He* did not begin by being psychoanalysed (never was!) or attaching himself to any sect or school, but . . . always retained his own independence. If he had himself fol-lowed the advice he gives you, he would have attached himself to Charcot with whom he was working, and became a disciple, like Gilles de la Tourette, an able man now forgotten. If you are psychoanalysed you either become a Freudian or you don't. If you don't, you remain pretty much where you are now; if you do—you are done for!—unless you break away . . . To every great leader one may apply the saying of Nietzsche about Jesus:—There has only been one Christian and he died on the cross. There has only been one Freudian! (in Wortis 1984: 11–2)

At the very least, we can no longer avoid asking what psychoanalysis means and for whom, since what we call Freud's creation has always been tied up with factors other than those of "science" and "objectivity."

6.

Situated within its historico-political context, Freud's refusal to submit to an official psychoanalysis is perhaps less scandalous than it might otherwise seem. For, in the first place, and despite protests to the contrary, we can argue that Freud never *needed* to submit to an analysis. It is not only that he was his own analyst and best patient—as he put it, "the most important patient for me was my own person" (Freud to Fliess 1985: 279)—or that he was and remains the father of psychoanalysis. Of course, all of this is true and we can hardly overestimate its importance. More generally, though, Freud was able to escape institutional psychoanalysis because he was always "something of a scientific wildman," as Marcus admits (1984: 12), his own heretic, the first and only orthodox but wild analyst.

But, lest we forget, the training (or didactic) analysis was meant to screen, police, or exclude such heretical thoughts from the theory, practice, transmission, and reception of psychoanalysis. It is a great unappreciated irony in the history of psychoanalysis that Carl Jung, of all people, was the first to suggest to Freud that all future analysts be analyzed (Roazen 1991: 213–14; 1992: 11–12)—that is, trained in accordance with the rules and regulations of a new and expanding institution. As Freud himself put it later, "There should be some headquarters whose business it is to declare: 'All this nonsense is nothing to do with analysis; this is not psycho-analysis'" (*SE* 14: 43). Hanns Sachs thus noted that "It can be seen that analysis needs something corresponding to the novitiate of the Church" (in Roazen 1975: 323). Or as Jones more romantically suggested, psychoanalysis required something along the lines of Plato's ideal Republic, with Freud as uncontested Philosopher King (1955: 69).

A few years after Jung's fateful suggestion, Jones recommended to Freud's great delight that they form a "secret" committee as a way of protecting the Freudian cause—only now from the immediate threat posed by Jung's desertion! (see Jones 1955: 153–54; Paskauskas 1985; Grosskurth 1991). As you might expect, the newly trained analysts generally proved more committed and domesticated—that is *paranoid*—than Freud's earliest band of followers. For if anything the training analyses were less concerned with the objective truth of psychoanalysis—whatever that means—than with the truth of Freud and his interminable self-analysis. Or more exactly, the new institution was concerned with simultaneously maintaining *and* eliding the tenuous link or difference between these two realms. And this because Freud himself always walked that thin borderline, careful not to upset the balance in favor of the one or the Other, the self or the science.

Freud's role as an orthodox but wild analyst is echoed throughout the literature. For instance, he once told self-proclaimed "wild analyst" Georg Groddeck that "I myself am a heretic who has not yet turned into a fanatic" (in Grossman 1965: 102). This sort of admission is worth keeping in mind when we hear our "orthodox" colleagues—those more orthodox than orthodoxy it(him)self—bemoan some idiosyncracy of Freud's life and work, or when they dryly claim that Freud, alas, was beset by unresolved conflict. At the same time, we are not trying to make a large claim on behalf of Freud's conscious life or freedom from neurotic conflict. To the contrary. Our claim is much more mundane: namely, that only Freud could get away with being Freud, that only Freud could transgress the rules of psychoanalysis with absolute impunity. For this reason, some of Freud's followers would say (or complain) that "What was permitted to Jove is not permitted to an ox" [*Quod licet Jovi, non licet bovi*] (in Sterba 1982: 124).

The law it(him)self, Freud was above all exempt from his own regulations concerning proper conduct and technique. For example, and in no particular order: we know that Freud adorned his office with personal items, especially antiquities, sometimes allowed patients to live in his house during short analyses, lent patient's books and money, accepted money for institutional affairs, told jokes and "chattered," rapped on the head of the couch when irritated, gossiped about colleagues, nodded off to sleep, let his chows into the office, shook hands before and after each session, offered photos of himself, complimented patients on their clothing, invited some for supper, left the office to urinate and, of course, habitually smoked cigars during sessions. Such imprudent violations of technique enforced the transference and made a great "mausoleum" of Berggasse 19 (see Roustang 1983: 62).

We should also recall that Freud as a clinician could be idiosyncratic, judgemental, and aristocratic; never a fan of the "furor therapeuticus" (Reik 1956: 6), at times he considered people unworthy of analysis. To his friend and colleague Sándor Ferenczi, Freud wrote that "Patients are a rabble" (Ferenczi 1988: 93); and to Sachs he once referred aloud to patients as "the fools" [*die Narren*] (Sachs 1945: 105). Elsewhere he simply remarked that "In the depth of my heart I can't help being convinced that my dear fellowmen, with a few exceptions, are worthless" (in Roazen 1991: 329). Or again, as Freud told Victor von Weizsaecker, "You surely agree that most people are stupid" (Weizsaecker 1957: 62). Erich Fromm thus concluded that "Freud had little love for people in general" (1959: 37). (Arguably though, and this is revealing, it is this side of Freud that intellectuals still find so compelling and attractive.)

But in what Roazen first disclosed and recently describes as Freud's most "wild" piece of analysis, Freud actually analyzed his own daughter Anna between 1918 and 1921, and between 1924 and 1925. "If it was a matter of heresy to treat a patient sitting up, instead of lying on the couch," Roazen writes, "what did it mean to analyze one's own child" (1992: 10; see Weiss 1991: 81). Interestingly enough, in later years some of Freud's followers—including A. A. Brill, Melanie Klein, Marianne and Ernst Kris, and Anna Freud—would repeat this heresy of analyzing family members. Against the fact of such wild analyses, Roazen rightly suggests that "all these squabbles about what constitutes proper psychoanalytic technique . . . are reduced to trivia" (Roazen 1975: 439).

Julius Tandler put it this way in a private memorandum of November 29, 1931: "[Freud] is a person who is only accountable to his own law, who lives according to its direction and cannot subordinate himself to rules" (in Freud 1992: 284). As Freud once remarked, "I discovered analysis; that is enough to excuse me (in Wortis 1984:17).

7.

To Be the Law Itself: let's try and be more clear about this law (which is also an excuse). Freud's attempt to be his own law was always tied up with his audacious bid, his wager, to *be* the borderline between subject and object, an orthodox but wild analyst, the founding father who operates as the liminal condition making possible and impossible the circle of exchange that begins *and* ends with the Father analyst. At the same time and in the same movement this was also Freud's bid to escape the reciprocity of that very exchange, the *counter*, by making it impossible to identify his position with either term in the opposition father/son, analyst/patient, sender/receiver. At least, it cannot be identified as such in any simple or unequivocal way.

We should probably be careful here, since this is not really, as Michel Foucault most dramatically put it, a "wager that man would be erased, like a face drawn in sand at the edge of the sea" (1973: 387). For on the contrary, what Freud points to (this time in a letter to Paul Schilder on November 26, 1935) is his "right to an exceptional position" (in Gay 1988: 97) as the father of analysis.

But what is, and who occupies, this exceptional position? Parroting Roazen again, Where's Freud? Outside the exchange of transference/counter-transference, a position that is, rigorously understood, non-positional, Freud-the-subject is not erased exactly,[5] but is from the outset *generalized as the fractured structure of psychoanalysis itself,* a sort of ghost in the influencing machine. To be the law, then, is to be this irreducible structure, the chiasmatic container of conflict, two in one; the simultaneous condition, in other words, of reason and madness beyond the confines of our law of non-contradiction. In turn, from out of this inaugural incompleteness is fashioned the grounds upon which all institutional and therapeutic successes sit—and inevitably slip.

As the method it(him)self, the very figure (or complex) of Sigmund Freud defies capture and cannot be tamed or unified into a singular method, concept, word, or name. And thus we are never encountering Freud, the subject (or victim) of some unobtainable or gossipy biography, but always "Freud," or a multiplicity of little "Freuds"; a differentiated and deferred X, a liminal something *sous rature*. Or again, between the original subject and studied object of Sigmund Freud lies a "Freud" as *differance*, which is to say, a "Freud" that is radically self-deconstructive.

8.

The Crapule that Surrounds Me: Defined from within the snare of a double bind, it is perhaps no accident that the politics of psychoanalysis have been both tragic and comic, suicidal and surreal.[6] For how could the father *be* a heretic, a bastard, and still keep the family peace? Or what is the same thing, how could a disciple *be* like the father, a heretic, and still keep the family peace? "For a man to be like Freud," Roazen writes, "meant finally for him to be original. Yet originality ended his usefulness to Freud" (1969: 48). Such was, according to Thomas Szasz, "Freud's overweening selfishness and vanity. His world [was] divided into two kinds of persons: those who are useful to the 'cause' and those that are not" (1976: 35; see Fromm 1959: 67; Natenberg 1955: 166; Deutsch 1973: 170–79). Roustang similarly suggests "that only two solutions were available: either to stay within the mainstream, which implies accepting a permanent allegiance to Freud, or to acting independently and find oneself rejected from psychoanalysis, to cease to count for it" (1982: 7). Of course, Freud understood this dilemma well, once stating to a patient in the late 1920s that "the goody-goodys are no good, and the naughty ones go away" (in Roazen 1975: 303). "The truth is," Edoardo Weiss writes, "no one felt completely free to express ideas very divergent from Freud's basic concepts" (1991: 12). Jung, who finally had enough of this bind, told Freud plainly: "your technique of treating your pupils like patients is a *blunder*." More to the point, he asked Freud "*Who's* got the neurosis?" (Freud and Jung 1974: 534–35).

With the institutionalization of psychoanalysis, it is at last no wonder that Freud looked upon his disciples, following Jung, as "slavish sons and impudent puppies." For Freud was always the pack-leader: "They take a bone from the table, and chew it independently in a corner. But it is my bone!" (in Roazen 1969: 163). Freud demanded that his psychanalytic "bestiary," not unlike his dogs Jo-Fi, Lün, Wolfi, and Jumbo, demonstrate "both obedience and innovation within certain boundaries" (Genosko 1993: 629). But once faced with his grow(l)ing creation, his primal horde, Freud had "to ask what has become of the ennobling influence of psychoanalysis on its followers" (in Jones 1955: 71; see Weisaecker 1957: 66). As it happened, the psychoanalytic Republic was hardly the refuge he had envisioned. For even here, perhaps especially here, "*Homo homini lupus*"—"man is a wolf to man" (*SE* 21: 111).

In fact, around this time Freud was beginning to realize a central, horrible truth of psychoanalysis. "I had learnt," he writes, "that psycho-analysis brings out the worst in everyone" (*SE* 14: 39). Such were, according to Freud, "the crapule that surrounds me" (in Natenberg 1955: 189).

9.

Moi, je ne suis pas une Freudiste: Never much of a disciple himself, Freud once declared (only to cut it out in later editions) that "there is scarcely any group of ideas to which I feel so antagonistic as that of being someone's protege" (*SE* 6: 149; see Jones 1953: 188-89). Instead, Freud the father was devoured in the totem feast he prepared for his disciples, a willing sacrifice to the science he embodied. For in his followers he might live on, paradoxically, as their unforgettable father-ghost, the signified space of death, the spirit of guilt, finally, the only-analyst-that-matters.

But like many innovators, Freud never wanted to be his own follower, an all too common "Freudian." On the contrary, as he once told Theodor Reik: "Moi, je ne suis pas un Freudiste" (Reik 1954: 513).[7] Neither son nor father to himself, Freud revealed through his life and work a most precious (though entirely open) secret: *Me, Sigmund Freud, I don't follow him/me*. Alienated from himself in this way, from the self-same, Freud was always his own impossible condition of psychoanalysis, his own Other (recalling Gay), what we used to call the abyss itself. Positioned in (or as) this unrepresentable space between, Freud therefore remains father *and* son, everywhere *and* nowhere, no one *and* everyone. As a result, we have been quite unable to answer Roazen's timely though inherently logocentric question— Where's Freud?—except through a strategy of deconstruction, one whereby the proper name of Sigmund Freud is deferred and displaced as yet another in a list of undecidables. Here in this non-place—(w)here?!—we both can and cannot submit to Freud's audacious wager to live on through his science.

At least *I* can't; for if you haven't already guessed, this subject is not a *Freudiste*. But, then again, who among us really is—or isn't?

10.

Ce sont les mort qu'il faut qu'on tue. Finally, then, our modest act of parricide, this wild and hyperbolic analysis, has been unavoidable and only reflects a kind of faithfulness to the irreducible legends of Freud and his followers. As Ellis advised, ours is a faithfulness to Freud's (ambivalent, dangerous, wild) example but hardly his precepts. To this end we have given Freud and his followers, our charming Prince Hamlets, the whippings they demand and deserve. For as Borch-Jacobsen submits, "Sometimes you have to kill your father to preserve his heritage. Sometimes you have to throw away the doctrine to find its 'meaning'" (1994: 267). Or as Nietzsche's Zarathustra says, "One repays a teacher badly if one always remains nothing but a pupil" (1954: 190). With this in mind, even if psychoanalysis, like biography, has all along been committed to lies, concealments, hypocrisy, flattery, and even to hiding its own lack of understanding, even if psychoanalytic truth doesn't exist, it has in any case been good for *something*.

IN THIS ESSAY WE HAVE TRIED TO MAKE POSSIBLE a hitherto unforeseen collision of interests between the revisionist work in the history of psychoanalysis and aspects of poststructuralist theory. Our most general aim has been to demonstrate that historico-biographical work is not foreign to abstract theoretical concerns, even when the modernist "subject" has seemingly disappeared without a trace. In turn, the encounter between Roazen's important contribution to psychoanalysis and the field of deconstruction has helped displace some of our more established positions on either side of the Atlantic, while at the same time placing Freud and his followers in an interesting light.

NOTES

1. On September 17, 1992, at the invitation of Dr. René Major. A round-table followed with W. Granoff, P. Guyomar, R. Major, and E. Roudinesco.
2. Of course, such fears hardly interfered with his own enthusiastic works of psychobiography (see de Mijolla 1993).
3. In print, Anna Freud refers to Roazen in particular as "a malicious American author," referring to his *Brother Animal*. In a private letter she dramatically suggests that Roazen "is a menace whatever he writes" (see Roazen 1993: 201).
4. Near the end of his life, Lacan could no longer receive patients. Apparently, though, his patients continued to gather in his waiting room and, incredibly, paid fees for that privilege.
5. One can argue that Foucault's subject is not erased or "liquidated" either, as Derrida does, but that is not my concern here (see Derrida 1991: 96–119).
6. The following list of suicides in the history of psychoanalysis may help balance our books in this regard. In addition to Victor Tausk, whose life and death Roazen first discussed in 1969, the following *analysts* have taken their own lives: Edward Bibring, Paul Federn, Johann Honegger, Max Kahane, Karl Landauer, Monroe Meyer, Sophie Morgenstern, Martin Peck, Tatiana Rosenthal, Karl Schrötter, Herbert Silberer, Eugenia Sokolnicka, Karin Stephen, and Wilhelm Stekel (Roazen 1992a: 243).

7. It is probably no accident that Freud said this to Reik. For according to Kardiner, Reik was once jokingly referred to within Freud's inner circle as "the imitation Freud" (1977: 84; see also Roazen 1975: 327). In passing, it is worth recalling that many of Freud's followers engaged in such imitative behavior. Tausk, for example, wore his hair like Freud's (Weiss 1991: 10), while others adopted Freud's love for cigars (Sachs 1945: 82), collected antiquities, and so on.

"to do justice to freud": the history of madness in the age of psychoanalysis

Jacques Derrida

*translation by
Pascale-Anne Brault
and Michael Naas*

Editor's Note

Broadly conceived, in this essay Jacques Derrida explores the site that framed
French psychoanalysis in terms of the "subject": Lacan's critique of Cartesian
rationalism in the 1960s. While Derrida once attended to the description of madness in Foucault's celebrated book, *Folie et déraison: Histoire de la folie à l'âge classique* (abridged as *Madness and Civilization*), he now attends to "the time and
historical conditions" within which Foucault's book on madness was written. Derrida thus supplements his early, well-known analysis of Foucault and Descartes
with a consideration of Foucault and Freud.

According to Derrida, Freud acts as "doorman" and "door" in Foucault's
book—that is, as an opening to and a closing against the history of madness that
Foucault described. Consequently, Derrida argues, Foucault tried to "do justice to
Freud" in two different ways: on the one hand, by placing Freud in a line of figures that includes Nietzsche and an ongoing dialogue with madness and, on the
other hand, by placing Freud in a line of figures that includes Pinel and a history
of Law, Order, Morality, etc. Either way, Freud is "always [placed] on the side of
the Evil Genius." For Derrida, the performativity of this irreducible reference to
Freud demonstrates that Foucault's book "does and does not" belong to the
"age of psychoanalysis."

Derrida further explores Foucault's treatments of Freud through, for example,
deliberations on finitude and on power in *The Order of Things* and *The History of*

Sexuality respectively. Here (as elsewhere) Derrida is keenly interested in underscoring the speculative Freud of *Beyond the Pleasure Principle* (1920). Anyone interested in Derrida's work, especially as it intersects with Foucault on the topic of psychoanalysis, will find this rich essay mandatory reading.

JACQUES DERRIDA is Directeur d'Études at the École des Hautes Études en Sciences Sociales, Paris. His books include *Writing and Difference* (Chicago, 1978), *Dissemination* (Chicago, 1981), *Glas* (Nebraska, 1986), *The Post Card: From Socrates to Freud and Beyond* (Chicago, 1987), *Of Spirit: Heidegger and the Question* (Chicago, 1989), *Given Time: I. Counterfeit Money* (Chicago, 1992), *Specters of Marx* (Routledge, 1994), and *The Gift of Death* (Chicago, 1995).

WHEN ELISABETH ROUDINESCO AND RENÉ MAJOR did me the honor and kindness of inviting me to a commemoration that would also be a reflection, to one of these genuine tributes where thought is plied to fidelity and fidelity honed by thought, I did not hesitate for one moment.

First of all, because I love memory. This is nothing original, of course, and yet how else can one love? Indeed, thirty years ago, this great book of Foucault's was an event whose repercussions were so intense and multiple that I will not even try to identify much less measure them deep down inside me. Next, because I love friendship, and the trusting affection that Foucault showed me thirty years ago, which was to last for many years, was all the more precious in that, being shared, it corresponded to my professed admiration. Then, after 1972, what came to obscure this friendship, without, however, affecting my admiration, was not, in fact, alien to this book and to a certain debate that ensued—or at least to its distant, delayed, and indirect effects. There was in all of this a sort of dramatic chain of events, a compulsive and repeated precipitation that I do not wish to describe here because I do not wish to be alone, to be the only one to speak of this after the death of Michel Foucault—except to say that this shadow that made us invisible to one another, that made us not associate with one another for close to ten years (until 1 January 1982, when I returned from a Czech prison)[1] is still part of a story that I also love like life itself. It is part of a story or history that is related, and that thus relates me by the same token, to the book whose great event we are commemorating here, to something like its postface, one of its postfaces, since the drama I just alluded to also arose out of a certain postface, and even out of a sort of postscript added by Foucault to a postface in 1972.

While accepting wholeheartedly this generous invitation, I nonetheless declined the suggestion that came along with it to return to the discussion that began some twenty-eight years ago. I declined for numerous reasons, the first being the one I just mentioned: one does not carry on a stormy discussion after the other has departed. Second, because this whole thing is more than just overdetermined (so many difficult and intersecting texts—Descartes's, Foucault's; so many objections and responses—from me but also from all those, in France and elsewhere, who later came to act as arbiters); it has become too distant from me, and perhaps because of the drama just alluded to I no longer wish to return to it. In the end, the debate is archived and those who might be interested in it can analyze as much as they want and decide for themselves. By rereading all the texts of this discussion, right up to the last word, and especially the last word, one will be better able to understand, I imagine, why I prefer not to give it a new impetus today. There is no privileged witness for such a situation—which, moreover, only ever has the chance of forming, and this from the very origin, with the possible disappearance of the witness. This is perhaps one of the meanings of any history of madness, one of the problems for any project or discourse concerning a history of madness, or even a history of sexuality: Is there any witnessing to madness? Who can witness? Does witnessing mean seeing? Is it to provide a reason [*rendre raison*]? Does it have an object? Is there any object? Is there a possible third that might provide a reason without objectifying, or even identifying, that is to say, without examining [*arraisoner*]?

Though I have decided not to return to what was debated close to thirty years ago, it would nevertheless be absurd, obsessional to the point of pathological, to say nothing of impossible, to give in to a sort of fetishistic denial and to think that I can protect myself from any contact with the place or meaning of this discussion. Although I intend to speak today of something else altogether, starting from a very recent rereading of *The History of Madness in the Classical Age*, I am not surprised, and you will probably not be either, to see the silhouette of certain questions reemerge: not their content, of course, to which I will in no way return, but their abstract type, the schema or spectre of an analogous problematic. For example, if I speak not of Descartes but of Freud, if I thus avoid a figure who seems central to this book and who—because he is decisive as far as its center or centering of perspective is concerned—emerges right from the early pages on, right from the first border or approach (see Foucault 1961: 53–57),[2] if I thus avoid this Cartesian reference in order to move toward another (psychoanalysis, Freudian, or some other) that is evoked only on the edges of the book and is named only right near the end, or ends, on the other border, this will perhaps be once again in order to pose a question that will resemble the one that imposed itself upon me thirty years ago, namely, that of the very possibility of a history of madness. The question will be, in the end, just about the same, though it will be posed from another border, and it still imposes itself upon me as the first tribute owed such a book. If this book was possible, if it had from the beginning and retains today a certain monumental value, the presence and undeniable necessity of a *monument*, that is, of what imposes itself by recalling and cautioning, it must tell us, teach us, or ask us something about its own possibility.

About its own possibility *today*: yes, we are saying *today*, a certain today. Whatever else one may think of this book, whatever questions or reservations it might inspire in those who come at it from some other point of view, its pathbreaking force seems incontestable. Just as incontestable, in fact, as the law according to which all pathbreaking opens the way only at a certain price, that is, by bolting shut other passages, by ligaturing, stitching up, or compressing—indeed repressing—at least provisionally, other veins. And so today, like yesterday (I mean in March of 1963), it is this question of the *today* that is important to me, the question such as I had tried to formulate it yesterday. I ask you to pardon me this once, then, since I will not make a habit of it, for citing a few lines that then defined, in its general form, a task that seems to me still necessary, on the side of [*du côté de*] Freud this time rather than on the side of Descartes. By saying "on the side of Freud" rather than "on the side of Descartes," let us not give in too quickly to the naivete that would precipitate us into believing that we are closer to a today with Freud than with Descartes, though this is the opinion of most historians.

Here, then, is the question of yesterday, of the today of yesterday, such as I would like to translate it today, on the side of Freud, transporting it in this way into the today of today:

> Therefore, if Foucault's book, despite all the acknowledged impossibilities and difficulties [acknowledged by him, of course],[3] was capable of being written, we have the right to ask what, in the last resort, supports this language without recourse or support ["without recourse" and "without support" are expressions of Foucault that I had just cited]: who enunciates the possibility of nonrecourse? Who wrote and who is to understand, in what language and from what historical situation of logos, who wrote and who is to understand this history of madness? For it is not by chance that such a project could take shape today. Without forgetting, *quite to the contrary*, the audacity of Foucault's act in the *History of Madness*, we must assume that a certain liberation of madness has gotten underway, that psychiatry has opened itself up, however minimally [and, in the end, I would be tempted simply to replace *psychiatry* by *psychoanalysis* in order to translate the today of yesterday into the today of my question of today], and that the concept of madness as unreason, if it ever had a unity, has been dislocated. And that a project such as Foucault's can find its historical origin and passageway in the opening produced by this dislocation.
>
> If Foucault, more than anyone else, is attentive and sensitive to these kinds of questions, it nevertheless appears that he does not acknowledge their quality of being prerequisite methodological or philosophical considerations. (Derrida 1967: 61; 1978: 38)

If this type of question made any sense or had any legitimacy, if the point was then to question that which, today, in this time that is ours, this time in which Foucault's *History of Madness* was written, made possible the event of such a discourse, it would have been more appropriate for me to elaborate this problematic on the side of modernity, *a parte subjecti*, in some sense, on the side where the book was written, and thus on the side, for example, of what must have happened to the modern psychiatry mentioned in the passage I just read. To modern psychiatry or, indeed, to psychoanalysis, or rather to psychoanalyses or psychoanalysts, since the passage to the plural will be precisely what is at stake in this discussion. It would have thus been more imperative to insist on modern psychiatry or psychoanalysis than to direct the same question toward Descartes. To study the place and role of psychoanalysis in the Foucauldian project of a history of madness, as I am now going to try to do, might thus consist in correcting an oversight or in confronting more directly a problematic that I had left in a preliminary stage, as a general, programmatic frame, in the introduction to my lecture of 1963. That lecture made only one allusion to psychoanalysis. It is true, however, that it inscribed it from the very opening. In a protocol that laid out certain reading positions, I spoke of the way in which philosophical language is rooted in nonphilosophical language, and I recalled a rule of hermeneutical method that still seems to me valid for the historian of philosophy as well as for the psychanalyst: namely, the necessity of first ascertaining a surface or manifest meaning and thus of speaking the language of the patient to whom one is listening—the necessity of gaining a good understanding, in a quasi-scholastic way, philologically and grammatically, by taking into account the dominant and stable conventions, of what Descartes *meant* on the already so difficult surface of his text, such as it is interpretable according to classical norms of reading; the necessity of gaining this understanding *before* submitting the first reading to a symptomatic and historical interpretation regulated by other axioms or protocols, *before and in order to* destabilize, wherever this is possible and if it is necessary, the authority of canonical interpretations. Whatever one ends up doing with it, one must begin by listening to the canon. It is in this context that I recalled Ferenczi's remark cited by Freud in *The Interpretation of Dreams* ("Every language has its own dream language") and Lagache's observations concerning polyglotism in analysis (Derrida 1967: 53; 1978: 307).

In its general and historical form, my question concerned the *site* that *today* gives rise to a history of madness and thereby makes it possible. Such a question should have led me, it is true, toward the situation of psychiatry and psychoanalysis rather than toward a questioning of a reading of Descartes. This logic would have seemed more natural and the consequence more immediate. But if, in so strictly delimiting the field, I substituted Descartes for Freud, it was perhaps not only because of the significant and strategic place that Foucault confers upon the Cartesian moment in his interpretations of the *Great Confinement* and of the *Classical Age*, that is to say, in the layout of the very object of the book; it was already, at least implicitly, because of the role that the reference to a certain Descartes played in the thought of that time (in the early sixties), as close as possible to psychoanalysis, in the very element, in truth, of a certain psychoanalysis and Lacanian theory. This theory developed around the question of the subject and the subject of science. Whether it was a question of anticipated certainty and logical time (1945, in *Ecrits*) or, some years later (1965–66), of the role of the cogito and—precisely—of the deceitful God in "La Science et la vérité," Lacan returned time and again to a certain unsurpassability of Descartes.[4] In 1945, Lacan associated Descartes with Freud in his "Propos sur la causalité psychique" and concluded by saying that "neither Socrates, nor Descartes, nor Marx, nor Freud, can be 'surpassed' insofar as they led their research with this passion for unveiling whose object is the truth" (1966: 193).

The title I have proposed for the few reflections I will risk today, "The History of Madness in the Age of Psychoanalysis," clearly indicates a change—a change in tense, in mode or in voice. It is no longer a question of the age *described* by a *History of Madness*. It is no longer a question of an epoch or period, such as the classical age, that would, inasmuch as it is its very object, stand before the history of madness such as Foucault writes it. It is a question today of the age to which the book itself belongs, the age from out of which it takes place, the age that provides it with its situation; it is a question of the age that is *describing* rather than the age that is *described*. In my title, it would be necessary to put "the history of madness" in quotation marks since the title designates the age of the book, *The History (historia rerum gestarum) of Madness*—as a book—in the age of psychoanalysis and not the history (*res gestae*) of madness, of madness itself, in the age of psychoanalysis, even though, as we will see, Foucault regularly attempts to objectify psychoanalysis and to reduce it to that of which he speaks rather than to that from out of which he speaks. What will interest me will thus be rather the time and historical conditions in which the book is rooted, those that it takes as its point of departure, and not so much the time or historical conditions that it recounts and tries in a certain sense to objectify. Were one to trust too readily the opposition between subject and object, as well as the category of objectification (something that I here believe to be neither possible nor just, and hardly faithful to Foucault's own intention), one would say for the sake of convenience that it is a question of considering the history of madness *a parte subjecti*, that is, from the side where it is written or inscribed and not from the side of what it describes.

Now, from the side where this history is written, there is, of course, a certain state of psychiatry—as well as psychoanalysis. Would Foucault's project have been possible without psychoanalysis, with which it is contemporary and of which it speaks little and in such an equivocal or ambivalent manner in the book? Does the project owe psychoanalysis anything? What? Would the debt, if it had been contracted, be essential? Or would it, on the contrary, define the very thing from which the project had to detach itself, and in a critical fashion, in order to take shape? In a word, what is the situation of psychoanalysis at the moment of, and with respect to, Foucault's book? And how does this book situate its project with respect to psychoanalysis?

Let us put our trust for a moment in this common name, psychoanalysis. And let us delay a bit the arrival of proper names, for example Freud or Lacan, and provisionally assume that there is indeed a psychoanalysis that is a single whole; as if it were not, already in Freud, sufficiently divided to make its localization and identification more than problematic. Yet the very thing whose coming due we are here trying to delay will no doubt form the very horizon, in any case the provisional conclusion, of this talk.

As you well know, Foucault speaks rather little of Freud in this book. This may seem justified, on the whole, by the very delimitation that a historian of madness in the classical age must impose upon himself. If one accepts the great caesura of this layout (even though this raises a question, or swarm of questions, that I prudently, and by economy, decide not to approach in order to get a better grasp on what Foucault *means* by Freud, thereby situating therefore, within the thesis or hypothesis of the partition between a classical and a postclassical age), then Freud does not have to be treated. He can and must be located at the very most on the borderline. The borderline is never a secure place, it never forms an indivisible line, and it is always on the border that the most disconcerting problems of topology get posed. Where, in fact, would a problem of topology get posed if not *on the border*? Would one ever have to worry about the border if it formed an indivisible line? A borderline is, moreover, not a place per se. It is always risky, particularly for the historian, to assign to whatever happens on the borderline, to whatever happens between sites, the taking-place of a determinable event.

Now, Foucault *does and does not want* to situate Freud in a historical place that is stabilizable, identifiable, and open to a univocal understanding. The interpretation or topography of the Freudian moment that he presents to us is always uncertain, divided, mobile, some would say ambiguous, others ambivalent, confused, or contradictory. Sometimes he wants to credit Freud, sometimes discredit him, unless he is actually doing both indiscernibly and at the same time. One will always have the choice of attributing this ambivalence to either Foucault or Freud; it can characterize a motivation, the gesture of the interpreter and a certain state of his work. But it can also (or in the first place) refer simply to the interpreter or historian's taking account of a structural duplicity that his work reflects from the thing itself, namely, from the event of psychoanalysis. The motivation would thus be *justly* motivated, it would be *just that*—motivated; it would be called for and justified by the very thing that is in question. For the ambiguity of which we are going to speak could indeed be on the side of psychoanalysis, on the side of the event of this invention named psychoanalysis.

To begin, let us indicate a few telling signs. If most of the explicit references to Freud are grouped in the conclusions of the book (at the end of "The Birth of the Asylum" and in the beginning of "The Anthropological Circle"),[5] what I would here call a *charnière*, a *hinge*, comes earlier on, right in the middle of the volume, to divide at once the book and the book's relation to Freud.

Why a *charnière*? This word can be taken in the technical or anatomical sense of a central or cardinal articulation, a hinge pin (*cardo*) or pivot. A *charnière* or hinge is an axial device that enables the circuit, the trope, or the movement of rotation. But one might also dream a bit in the vicinity of its homonym, that is, in line with this other *artifact* that the code of falconry also calls a *charnière*, the place where the hunter attracts the bird by laying out the flesh of a lure.

This double articulation, this double movement or alternation between opening and closing that is assured by the workings of a hinge, this coming and going, indeed this *fort/da* of a pendulum [*pendule*] or balance [*balancier*]—this is what Freud means to Foucault. And this technico-historical hinge also remains the place of a possible simulacrum or lure—for both the body and the flesh. Taken at this level of generality, things will never change for Foucault. There will always be this interminable alternating movement that successively opens and closes, draws near and distances, rejects and accepts, excludes and includes, disqualifies and legitimates, masters and liberates. The Freudian place is not only the technico-historical apparatus, the *artifact* called *charnière* or hinge. Freud himself will in fact take on the ambiguous figure of a doorman or doorkeeper [*huissier*]. Ushering in a new epoch of madness, our epoch, the one out of which is written *The History of Madness* (the book bearing this title), Freud also represents the best guardian of an epoch that comes to a close with him, the history of madness such as it is recounted by the book bearing this title.

Freud as the doorman of the today, the holder of the keys—of those that open as well as those that close the door, that is, the *huis*: onto the today [*l'aujourd'hui*] or onto madness. He [*Lui*], Freud, is the double figure of the door and the doorkeeper. He stands guard and ushers in. Alternatively or simultaneously, he closes one epoch and opens another. And as we will see, this double possibility is not alien to an institution, to what is called the analytic situation as a scene behind closed doors [*huis clos*]. That is why—and this would be the paradox of a serial law—Freud does and does not belong to the different series in which Foucault inscribes him. What is outstanding, outside the series [*hors-série*], turns out to be regularly reinscribed within different series. I am not now going to get involved in formal questions concerning a quasi-transcendental law of seriality that could be illustrated in an analogous way by so many other examples, each time, in fact, that the transcendental condition of a series is also, paradoxically, a part of that series, creating aporias for the constitution of any set or whole [*ensemble*], particularly, of any historical configuration (age, *episteme*, paradigm, *themata*, epoch, and so on). These aporias are anything but accidental impasses that one should try to force at all costs into received theoretical models. The putting to the test of these aporias is also the chance of thinking.

To keep to the contract of this conference, I will restrict myself to a single example.

The first sign comes right in the middle of the book (Foucault 1961: 410–11; 1965: 197–98). It comes at the end of the second part, in the chapter entitled "Doctors and Patients." We have there a sort of epilogue, less than a page and a half long. Separated from the conclusion by asterisks,[6] the epilogue also signals the truth of a transition and the meaning of a passage. It seems to be firmly structured by two unequivocal statements:

1. Psychology does not exist in the classical age. It does *not yet* exist. Foucault says this without hesitation right at the beginning of the epilogue: "In the classical age, it is futile to try to distinguish physical therapeutics from psychological medications, for the simple reason that psychology did not exist."

2. But as for the psychology that was to be born after the classical age, psychoanalysis would not be a part, it would *no longer* be a part. Foucault writes: "It is not psychology that is involved in psychoanalysis."

In other words, if in the classical age there is *not yet* psychology, there is in psychoanalysis *already no more* psychology. But in order to affirm this, it is necessary, *on the one hand*, to resist a prejudice or a temptation, to resist that which continues to urge so many interpreters of good sense (and sometimes, in part, Foucault among them) to take psychoanalysis for a psychology (however original or new it may be). Foucault is going to show signs of this resistance, as we will see. But it is also necessary, *on the other hand*, to accept, within this historical schema, the hypothesis of a return: not the *return to Freud* but the *return of Freud* to—.

What return? Return to what? *Return* is Foucault's word, an underscored word. If psychoanalysis is already *no longer* a psychology, does it not, at least in this respect, seem to suggest a certain return to the time when psychology was *not yet*? Beyond eighteenth-century psychology and, very broadly, beyond the psychologistic modernity of the nineteenth century, beyond the positivist institution of psychology, does it not seem as if Freud were joining back up with a certain classical age or, at least, with whatever in this age does not determine madness as a psychical illness but as unreason, that is, as something that has to do with reason? In the classical age, if such a thing exists (a hypothesis of Foucault's that I take here, in this context, as such, as if it were not debatable), unreason is no doubt reduced to silence; one does not speak with it. One interrupts or forbids dialogue; and this suspension or interdiction would have received from the Cartesian cogito the violent form of a sentence. For Freud, *too*, madness would be unreason (and in this sense, at least, there would be a neo-Cartesian logic at work in psychoanalysis). But this time one should resume speaking with it: one would reestablish a dialogue with unreason and lift the Cartesian interdiction. Like the word *return*, the expression "dialogue with unreason" is a quotation. The two expressions scan a final paragraph of this epilogue, in the middle of the book, that begins with the phrase with which I entitled this talk: "We must do justice to Freud" (1961: 411; 1965: 198).

When one says, "one must do justice," "one has to be fair" [*"il faut être juste"*], it is often with the intention of correcting an impulse or reversing the direction of a tendency; one is also recommending resisting a temptation. Foucault had to have felt this temptation, the temptation to do an injustice to Freud, to be unfair to him, that is, in this case, to write him into the age of the psychopathological institution (which we will define in a moment). He must have felt it outside or within himself. Indeed, such a temptation must still be threatening and liable to reemerge since it is still necessary to call for vigilance and greater justice.

Here, then, is the paragraph, which I read in extenso, since its internal tension determines, it seems to me, the matrix of all future statements about psychoanalysis; it determines them in the very oscillation of their movement back and forth. It is like scales of justice [*la balance d'une justice*] that not even the death sentence [*arrêt de mort*] would ever be able to stop [*arrêterait*] in their even or just [*juste*] stability. It is as if justice were to remain its own movement:

> This is why we must do justice to Freud. Between Freud's *Five Case Histories* and Janet's scrupulous investigations of *Psychological Healing*, there is more than the density of a *discovery*; there is the sovereign violence of a *return*. Janet enumerated the elements of a division, drew up his inventory, annexed here and there, perhaps conquered. Freud went back to madness at the level of its *language*, reconstituted one of the essential elements of an experience reduced to silence by positivism; he did not make a major addition to the list of psychological treatments for madness; he restored, in medical thought, the possibility of a dialogue with unreason. Let us not be surprised that the most "psychological" of medications has so quickly encountered its converse and its organic confirmations. It is not psychology that is involved in psychoanalysis: but precisely an experience of unreason that it has been psychology's meaning, in the modern world, to mask. (1961: 411; 1965: 198)[7]

"To mask": positivist psychology would thus have masked the experience of unreason: an imposition of the mask, a violent dissimulation of the face, of truth or of visibility. Such violence would have consisted in disrupting a certain unity, that which corresponded precisely [*justement*] to the presumed unity of the classical age: from then on there would be, on the one hand, illness of an organic nature and, on the other, unreason, an unreason often tempered by this modernity under its "epithetic" form: the *unreasonable*, whose discursive manifestations will become the object of a psychology (see Foucault 1961: 195). This psychology then loses all relation to a certain truth of madness, that is, to a certain truth of unreason. Psychoanalysis, on the contrary, breaks with psychology *by speaking with the Unreason* that speaks within madness and, thus, by returning through this exchange of words not to the classical age itself—which also determined madness as unreason, but, unlike psychology, did so only in order to exclude or confine it—but toward this eve of the classical age that still haunted it.

While this schema is firmly established by the page just cited, I was struck in rereading *The History of Madness* by a paradox in the form of a chiasm. I had not, in my first reading, given it the attention it deserves. What is the schema of this paradox? By reason of what we have just heard, in order to do "justice" to Freud we ought to give him credit—and this is what happens—for finding a place in the gallery of all those who, from one end of the book to the other, announce, like heralds of good tidings, the very possibility of the book: Nietzsche above all and, most frequently, Nietzsche and Artaud, who are often associated in the same sentence, Nietzsche, Artaud, Van Gogh, sometimes Nerval, and Hölderlin from time to time. Their excess, "the madness in which the work of art is engulfed," is the gulf or abyss out of which opens "the space of our enterprise" (1961: 643; 1965: 288).

It is *before* this madness, in the fleeting moment when it is joined to the work, that we are *responsible*. We are far from being able to arraign it or make it appear, for it is we who must appear *before* it. Let us recognize, then, that we are responsible before it rather than being authorized to examine it [*arraisonner*], to objectify and demand an explanation from it. At the end of the last page, after having spent a good deal of time speaking of Nietzsche and after having mentioned Van Gogh, Foucault writes: "The moment when, together, the work of art and madness are born and fulfilled is the beginning of the time when the world finds itself arraigned by that work of art and responsible before it for what it is" (1961: 643; 1965: 289). This is what *The History of Madness*, in responding to the summons, takes note of and assumes responsibility for. It assumes responsibility before that which is named by the names of Nietzsche and all these others who, as everyone knows, were deemed crazy by society (Artaud, and before him Van Gogh, and before him Nerval, and before him Hölderlin).

But what about Freud? Why is he, in the same book, sometimes associated with and sometimes opposed to these great witnesses of madness and excess, these great witnesses who are also great judges, our judges, those who judge us? Must we be arraigned before Freud? And why do things then get complicated?

I would see the chiasm of which I just spoke appearing in a place where Freud is in fact found near Nietzsche, on the same side as he, that is, on our side, on the side of what Foucault calls "contemporary man": this enigmatic "we" for whom a history of madness opens today, for whom the door of today [*l'huis d'aujourd'hui*] is cracked open so that its possibility may be glimpsed. Foucault has just described the loss of unreason, the background against which the classical age determined madness. It is the moment when unreason degenerates or disappears into the unreasonable; it is the tendency to pathologize, so to speak, madness. And there again, it is through a return to unreason, this time without exclusion, that Nietzsche and Freud reopen the dialogue with madness *itself* (assuming, along with Foucault, that one can here say "itself"). This dialogue had, in a sense, been *broken off* twice, and in two different ways: the second time, by a psychological positivism that no longer conceived of madness as unreason, and the first time, already by the classical age, which, while excluding madness and breaking off the dialogue with it, still determined it as unreason, and excluded it precisely because of this—but excluded it as close as possible to itself, as its other and its adversary: this is the Cartesian moment, such as it is determined, at least, in the three pages that were the object of our debate nearly thirty years ago.

I will underscore everything that marks the today, the present, the now, the contemporary, this time that is proper and common to us, the time of this fragile and divided "we" from which is decided the possibility of a book like *The History of Madness*—decided while scarcely being sketched out, while promising itself, in short, rather than giving itself over. Nietzsche *and* Freud are here conjoined, conjugated, like a couple, Nietzsche *and* Freud, and the conjunction of their coupling is also the copula-hinge or, if you prefer, the middle term of the modern proposition:

> If *contemporary* man, since Nietzsche and Freud, finds deep within himself the site for contesting all truth, being able to read, in what he *now* knows of himself, the signs of fragility through which unreason threatens, seventeenth-century man, on the contrary, discovers, in the immediate presence of his thought to itself, the certainty in which reason in its pure form is announced. (1961: 195–96)

Why did I speak of a chiasm? And why would we be fascinated by the multiple chiasm that organizes this entire interpretative scene?

It is because, in the three pages devoted to Descartes at the beginning of the second chapter "The Great Confinement," Foucault spoke of an *exclusion*. He described it, posed it, declared it unequivocally and firmly ("madness is excluded by the subject who doubts"). This exclusion was the result of a "decision," the result (and these are all his words) of a "strange act of force" that was going to "reduce to silence" the excluded madness and trace a very strict "line of division." In the part of the *Meditations* that he cited and focused on, Foucault left out all mention of the Evil Genius. It was thus in recalling the hyperbolic raising of the stakes in the fiction of the Evil Genius that I had then confessed my perplexity and proposed other questions. When Foucault responds to me nine years later in the afterward to the 1972 Gallimard edition of *The History of Madness*, he still firmly contests the way that I used this Cartesian fiction of the Evil Genius and this hyperbolic moment of doubt. He accuses me of erasing "everything that shows that the episode of the evil genius is an exercise that is voluntary, controlled, mastered and carried out from start to finish by a meditating subject who never lets himself be surprised" (1979, 26, trans. modified; see Foucault 1961: 601).[8] (Such a reproach was indeed unfair, unjust, since I had stressed that this methodical mastery of the voluntary subject is "almost always" at work and that Foucault, therefore, like Descartes, is "almost always right [*a . . . raison*]," and almost always wins out over [*a raison de*] the Evil Genius [Derrida 1967: 91; 1978: 58]. But that is not what is at issue here, and I said that I would not reopen the debate.) And by accusing me of erasing this methodical neutralization of the Evil Genius, Foucault—once again in his response of 1972—confirms the claims of the three pages in question and maintains that "if the evil genius again takes on the powers of *madness*, this is only after the exercise of meditation has excluded the risk of *being mad*" (1979: 26). One might be tempted to respond that if the Evil Genius can *again take on* these powers of madness, if he once "again takes them on" afterwards, after the fact, it is because the exclusion of the risk of being mad makes way for an *after*. The narrative is thus not interrupted during the exclusion alleged by Foucault, an exclusion that is, up to a certain point at least, attested to and incontestable (and I never in fact contested this exclusion in this regard, quite the contrary); neither the narrative nor the exercise of the meditation that it retraces are any more interrupted than the order of reasons is definitively stopped by this same exclusion. But let us move on. As I said earlier, I am not invoking this difficulty in order to return to an old discussion. I am doing it because Freud is going to be, as I will try to show, doubly situated, *twice* implicated in the chiasm that interests me: *on the one hand*, in the sentence that I cited a moment ago (where Freud was immediately associated with Nietzsche, the only one to be associated with him, on the "good" side, so to speak, on the side where "we" contemporaries reopen the dialogue with unreason that was twice interrupted); this sentence is followed by a few references to the Evil Genius that complicate, as I myself had tried to do, the reading of the scene of Cartesian doubt as the moment of the great confinement; but also, and *on the other hand*, since I will later try, in a more indirect way—and this would be in the end the essence of my talk today—to recall the necessity of taking into account a certain Evil Genius *of* Freud, namely, the presence of the demonic, the devil, the devil's advocate, the limping devil, and so on in *Beyond the Pleasure Principle*, where psychoanalysis finds, it seems to me, its greatest speculative power but also the place of greatest resistance to psychoanalysis (death drive, repetition compulsion, and so on, and *fort/da!*).

Thus, just after having spoken of "contemporary man, since Nietzsche and Freud," Foucault offers a development *on the subject of the Evil Genius*. The logic of this sequence seems to me guided by a "One must not forget" that I would be tempted to relate to the "One must do justice" of a moment ago. What must one not forget? The Evil Genius, of course [*justement*]. And especially, I emphasize, the fact that the Evil Genius is *anterior* to the cogito, such that its threat remains *perpetual*.

This might contradict (as I had attempted to do) the thesis argued 150 pages earlier on the subject of the Cartesian cogito as the simple exclusion of madness. This could have, as a result, indeed this should have, spared us a long and dramatic debate. But it is too late now. Foucault reaffirms all the same, despite the recognized anteriority of the Evil Genius, that the cogito is the absolute beginning, even if, in this absolute beginning, "one must not forget" what has, in short, been forgotten or omitted in the discourse on the exclusion of madness by the cogito. The question thus still remains what a methodically absolute beginning would be that does not let us forget this anterior—and, moreover, perpetual—threat, nor the haunting backdrop that first lets it appear. As always, I prefer to cite, even though it is a long passage. Here is what Foucault says immediately after having evoked the "contemporary man" who, "since Nietzsche and Freud," meets in "what he now knows of himself" that "through which unreason threatens." He says, in effect, that what is called contemporary had already begun in the classical age and with the Evil Genius, which clearly, to my eyes at least, cannot leave intact the historical categories of reference and the presumed identity of something like the classical age (for example).

> But this does not mean that classical man was, in his experience of the truth, more distanced from unreason than we ourselves might be. It is true that the cogito is the absolute beginning [this statement thus confirms the thesis of 1961: 54–57] *but one must not forget* [my emphasis] that the evil genius is anterior to it. And the evil genius is not the symbol in which are summed up and systematized all the dangers of such psychological events as dream images and sensory errors. Between God and man, the evil genius has an absolute meaning: he is in all his rigor the possibility of unreason and the totality of its powers. He is more than the refraction of human finitude; well beyond man, he signals the danger that could prevent man once and for all from gaining access to the truth: he is the main obstacle, not of such a spirit but of such reason. And it is not because the truth that gets illuminated in the cogito ends up entirely masking the shadow of the evil genius that one *ought to forget* its perpetually threatening power [my emphasis: Foucault had earlier said that *one must not forget* that the evil genius is anterior to the cogito, and he now says that *one must not forget* its perpetually threatening power, even after the passage, the moment, the experience, the certainty of the cogito, and the exclusion of madness that this brings about]: this danger will hover over Descartes' reflections right up until the establishment of the existence and truth of the external world. (1961: 196)

One would have to ask, though we will not have the time and this is not the place, about the effects that the category of the "perpetual threat" (and this is Foucault's term) can have on indications of presence, positive markings, the determinations made by means of signs or statements, in short, the whole criteriology and symptomatology that can give assurance to a historical knowledge concerning a figure, an *episteme*, an age, an epoch, a paradigm, once all these determinations are found to be in effect [*justement*] threatened by a perpetual haunting. For, in principle, all these determinations are, for the historian, either presences or absences; as such, they exclude haunting; they allow themselves to be located by means of signs, one would almost say on a table of absences and presences; they come out of the logic of opposition, in this case, the logic of inclusion *or* exclusion, of the alternative between the inside and the outside, and so on. The perpetual threat, that is, the shadow of haunting (and haunting is, like the phantom or fiction of an Evil Genius, neither present nor absent, neither positive nor negative, neither inside nor outside) does not challenge only one thing or another; it threatens the logic that distinguishes between one thing and another, the very logic of exclusion or foreclosure, as well as the history that is founded upon this logic and its alternatives. What is excluded is, of course, never simply excluded, not by the cogito nor by anything else, without this eventually returning—and that is what a certain psychoanalysis will have also helped us to understand. Let me leave undeveloped this general problem, however, in order to return to a certain regulated functioning in the references to psychoanalysis and to the name of Freud in *The History of Madness in the Classical Age*.

Let us consider the couple Nietzsche/Freud, this *odd couple* about which there is so much else to say (I have attempted this elsewhere, especially in *The Post Card* and precisely [*justement*] in relationship to *Beyond the Pleasure Principle*). The affiliation of filiation of this couple reappears elsewhere. It is again at a filial limit, in the introduction to the third and final part, when the "delirium" of *Rameau's Nephew* sets the tone or gives the key, just as the Cartesian cogito had, for a new arrangement or division [*partition*]. For the "delirium" of *Rameau's Nephew* "announces Freud and Nietzsche." Let us set aside all the questions that the concept of "announcing" might pose for the historian. It is not by accident that they resemble those raised a moment ago by the concept of *haunting*. As soon as that which *announces* already no longer completely belongs to a present configuration and already belongs to the future of another, its place, the taking-place of its events, calls for another logic; it disrupts, in any case, the axiomatics of a history that places too much trust in the opposition between absence and presence, outside and inside, inclusion and exclusion. Let us read, then, this sentence and note the recurring and thus all the more striking association of this *announcement* with the figure of the Evil Genius, but, this time, with the figure of "another evil genius":

> The delirium of Rameau's Nephew is a tragic confrontation of need and illusion in an oneiric mode, one that announces Freud and Nietzsche [the order of names is this time reversed]; it is also the ironic repetition of the world, its destructive reconstitution in the theatre of illusion. (1961: 422)

An Evil Genius then immediately reappears. And who will see this inevitable repetition as a coincidence? But it is not the same Evil Genius. It is another figure of the evil genius. There would thus be a recurring function of the Evil Genius, a function that, in making reference to a Platonic *hyperbole*, I had called hyperbolic in "Cogito and the History of Madness." This function had been fulfilled by the Evil Genius, under the guise as well as under the name that it takes on in Descartes. But another Evil Genius, which is also the same one, can reappear without this name and under a different guise, for example, in the vicinity or lineage of Rameau's Nephew: a different Evil Genius, certainly, but bearing enough of a resemblance because of its recurring function that the historian, here Foucault, allows himself a metonymy that is legitimate enough in his eyes to continue calling it Evil Genius. This reappearance occurs after the second passage of Freud-and-Nietzsche, as they are furtively announced by *Rameau's Nephew*, whose laugh "prefigures in advance and reduces the whole movement of nineteenth-century anthropology" (1961: 424). This time of prefiguration and announcement, this delay between the anticipatory lightning flash and the event of what is foreseen, is explained by the very structure of an experience of unreason, if there is any—namely, an experience in which one cannot maintain oneself and out of which one cannot but fall after having approached it. All this thus forbids us from making this history into a properly successive and sequential history of events. This is formulated in Foucault's question: "Why is it not possible to maintain oneself in the difference of unreason?" (1961: 425).

> But in this vertigo where the truth of the world is maintained only on the inside of an absolute void, man also encounters the ironic perversion of his own truth, at the moment when it moves from the dreams of interiority to the forms of exchange. Unreason then takes on the figure of *another evil genius* [my emphasis]—no longer the one who exiles man from the truth of the world, but the one who at once mystifies and demystifies, enchants to the point of extreme disenchantment, this truth of man that man had entrusted to his hands, to his face, to his speech; an evil genius who no longer operates when man wants to accede to the truth but when he wants to restitute to the world a truth that is his own, when, thrown into the intoxication of the sensible realm where he is lost, he finally remains "immobile, stupid, astonished." It is no longer in *perception* that the possibility of the evil genius resides [that is, as in Descartes] but in *expression*. (1961: 423)

But immediately after this appearance or arraignment of Freud next to Nietzsche and all the Evil Geniuses, the pendulum of the *fort/da* is put back in motion; from this point on, it will not cease to convoke and dismiss Freud from the two sides of the dividing line, both inside and outside of the series from out of which the history of madness is signed. For it is here, in the following pages, that we find Freud separated from the lineage in which are gathered all those worthy heirs of Rameau's Nephew. The name of the one who was not crazy (not crazy enough in any case), the name of Freud, is dissociated from that of Nietzsche. It is regularly passed over in silence when, according to another filiation, Hölderlin, Nerval, Nietzsche, Van Gogh, Roussel, and Artaud are at several reprieves named and renamed— renowned—within the same "family."

From this point on, things are going to deteriorate. "To do justice to Freud" will more and more come to mean putting on trial a psychoanalysis that will have participated, in its own way, however original that may be, in the order of the immemorial figures of the Father and the Judge, of Family and Law, in the order of Order, of Authority and Punishment; whose immemorial figures must, as Philippe Pinel had noted, be brought into play by the doctor in order to cure (see 1961: 607; 1965: 272). There was already a disturbing sign of this long before the chapter on "The Birth of the Asylum," a chapter which will strictly inscribe psychoanalysis into the tradition of Tuke and Pinel and will go so far as to say that "all nineteenth-century psychiatry really converges on Freud" (1961: 611; 1965: 277). For the latter had already appeared in another chain—the chain of those who, since the nineteenth century, know that madness, like its counterpart reason, has a history. These will have been led astray by a sort of historicism of reason and madness, a risk that is avoided by those who, "from Sade to Hölderlin, to Nerval and to Nietzsche," are given over to a "repeated poetic and philosophical experience" and plunge into a language "that abolishes history." As a cultural historian of madness, like others are of reason, Freud thus appears between Janet and Brunschvicg (1961: 456).

While accumulating the two errors, the rationalist historian of this cultural phenomenon called madness nonetheless continues to pay tribute to myth, magic, and thaumaturgy. Indeed *thaumaturgy* will be the word chosen by Foucault himself for the verdict. There is nothing surprising in this collusion of reason and a certain occultism. Montaigne and Pascal would have perhaps called it mystical authority; the history of reason and reason within history would exercise essentially the same violence, the same obscure, irrational, dictatorial violence, serving the same interests in the name of the same fictional allegation, as psychoanalysis does when it confers all powers to the doctor's speech. Freud would free the patient interned in the asylum only in order to reconstitute him "in his essential character" at the heart of the analytic situation. There is a continuity from Pinel and Tuke to psychoanalysis. There is an inevitable movement, right up to Freud, a persistence of what Foucault calls "the myth of Pinel, like that of Tuke" (1961: 577). This same insistence is always concentrated in the figure of the doctor; it is, in the eyes of the patient who is always an accomplice, the becoming-thaumaturge of the doctor, of a doctor who is not even supposed to know. *Homo medicus* does not exercise his authority in the name of science but, as Pinel himself seems to recognize and to claim, in the name of order, law, and morality, specifically, by "relying upon that prestige that envelops the *secrets* of the Family, of Authority, of Punishment, and of Love; . . . by wearing the mask of Father and of Judge" (1961: 607–8; 1965: 273, my emphasis).

And when the walls of the asylum give way to psychoanalysis, it is in effect a certain concept of the *secret* that assures the tradition from Pinel to Freud. It would be necessary to follow throughout these pages all the ins and outs of the value—itself barely visible—of a secret, of a certain secrecy value. This value would come down, in the end, to a *technique* of the secret, and of the secret without knowledge. Wherever knowledge can only be supposed, wherever, as a result, one knows that supposition cannot give rise to knowledge, wherever no knowledge could ever be disputed, there is the production of a *secrecy effect*, of what we might be able to call a *speculation on the capital secret or on the capital of the secret*. The calculated and yet finally incalculable production of this secrecy effect relies on a simulacrum. This simulacrum recalls, from another point of view, the situation described at the opening of *Raymond Roussel*: the risk of "being deceived less by a secret than by the awareness that there is a secret" (Foucault 1963a: 10; 1986a: 3).

What persists from Pinel to Freud, in spite of all the differences, is the figure of the doctor as a man not of knowledge but of order. In this figure all *secret, magic, esoteric, thaumaturgical* powers are brought together—and these are all Foucault's words. The scientific objectivity that is claimed by this tradition is only a magical reification:

> If we wanted to analyze the profound structures of objectivity in the knowledge and practice of nineteenth-century psychiatry from Pinel to Freud [this is the definitive divorce between Nietzsche and Freud, the second coupling for the latter], we should have to show in fact that such objectivity was from the start a reification of a magical nature which could only be accomplished with the complicity of the patient himself, and beginning

from a transparent and clear moral practice, gradually forgotten as positivism imposed its myths of scientific objectivity. (1961: 610; 1965: 276)

In the name of Freud, one can read the call for a note. At the bottom of the page Foucault persists, dates, and signs, but the note introduces a slight precaution. It is indeed a note of prudence, but Foucault insists nonetheless and speaks of persistence: "These structures still persist in non-psychoanalytic psychiatry, and in many aspects or on many sides [*par bien des côtés*] of psychoanalysis itself" (1961: 610; 1965: 299).

Though too discretely marked, there is indeed a limit to what persists "on many sides." The always divisible line of this limit situates, in its form, the totality of the stakes. More precisely, the stakes are nothing other than those of totality, and of the procedures of totalization: what does it mean to say psychoanalysis "itself"? What does one thereby identify in such a global way? Is it psychoanalysis *"itself,"* as Foucault says, that inherits from Pinel? What is psychoanalysis *itself*? And are the aspects or sides, through which it inherits, the essential and irreducible aspects or sides of psychoanalysis itself, or the residual "asides" that it can win out over [*avoir raison de*]? or even, that it must, that it should, win out over?

If the answer to this last question still seems up in the air in this note, it is soon going to come in a more determined and less equivocal form: no, psychoanalysis will never free itself of the psychiatric heritage. Its essential historical situation is linked to what is called the "*analytic situation*," that is, to the thaumaturgical mystification of the couple doctor-patient, regulated this time by institutional protocols. Before citing word for word a conclusion that will remain, I believe, without appeal not only in *The History of Madness* but in Foucault's entire oeuvre—and right up to its awful interruption—I will once again risk wearing out your patience in order to look for a moment at the way in which Foucault describes the thaumaturgical play whose *techne* Pinel would have passed down to Freud—a *techne* that would be at once art and technique, the secret, the secret of the secret, the secret that consists in knowing how to make one suppose knowledge and believe in the secret. It is worth pausing here in order to point out another paradoxical effect of the chiasm—one of the most significant for what concerns us here, namely, a certain diabolical repetition and the recurrence of the various figures of the Evil Genius. What does Foucault say? That in the couple doctor-patient "the doctor becomes a thaumaturge" (1961: 609; 1965: 275). Now, to describe this thaumaturgy, Foucault does not hesitate to speak of the demonic and satanic, as if the Evil Genius resided this time not on the side of unreason, of absolute disorder and madness (to say it quickly and with a bit of a smile, using all the necessary quotation marks, "on the good side"), but on the side of order, on the side of a subtly authoritative violence, the side of the Father, the Judge, the Law, and so on:

It was thought, and by the patient first of all, that it was in the esotericism of his knowledge, in some *almost* daemonic secret of knowledge [I emphasize "almost": Foucault will later say—his relation to Freud surely being anything but simple—that the philistine representation of mental illness in the nineteenth century would last "right up to Freud—or almost"] that the doctor had found the power to unravel insanity; and increasingly the patient would accept this self-surrender to a doctor both divine and satanic, beyond human measure in any case. (1961: 609; 1965: 275)

Two pages later, it is said that Freud "amplified the thaumaturgical virtues" of the "medical personage," "preparing for his omnipotence a quasi-divine status." And Foucault continues:

> He focussed upon this single presence—concealed behind the patient and above him, in an absence that is also a total presence—all the powers that had been distributed in the collective existence of the asylum; he transformed this into an absolute Observation, a pure and circumspect Silence, a Judge who punishes and rewards in a judgment that does not even condescend to language; he made it the mirror in which madness, in an almost motionless movement, clings to and casts off itself.
> To the doctor, Freud transferred all the structures Pinel and Tuke had set up within confinement. (1961: 611; 1965: 277–78)

Fictive omnipotence and a divine, or rather "quasi-divine," power, divine by simulacrum, at once divine and satanic—these are the very traits of an Evil Genius that are now being attributed to the figure of the doctor. The doctor suddenly begins to resemble in a troubling way the figure of unreason that continued to haunt what is called the classical age after the *act of force* [*coup de force*] of the *cogito*. And like the authority of the laws whose "mystical foundation" is recalled by Montaigne and Pascal,[9] the authority of the psychoanalyst-doctor is the result of a fiction; it is the result, by transfer, of the credit given to a fiction; and this fiction appears analogous to that which provisionally confers all powers—and even more than knowledge—to the Evil Genius.

At the conclusion of "The Birth of the Asylum," Foucault is going to dismiss without appeal this bad genius of the thaumaturgical doctor in the figure of the psychoanalyst; he is going to do this—I believe one can say without stretching the paradox—*against Descartes*, against a certain Cartesian subject still represented in the filiation that runs from Descartes to Pinel to Freud. But he is also going to do this, more or less willingly, *as Descartes* or, at least, as the Descartes whom he had accused of excluding madness by excluding, mastering, or dismissing—since these all come down to the same thing—the powers of the Evil Genius. Against Freud, this descendant of Descartes, against Descartes, it is still the Cartesian exclusion that is repeated in a deadly and devilish way, like a heritage inscribed within a diabolical and almost all-powerful program that one should admit one never gets rid of or frees oneself from without remainder.

To substantiate what I have just said, I will cite the conclusion of this chapter. It describes the transfer from Pinel to Freud (stroke of genius, "masterful short-circuit"—it is a question of Freud's genius, the good like the bad, the good as bad)— and it implacably judges psychoanalysis *in the past, in the present, and even in the future*. For psychoanalysis is condemned in advance. No future is promised that might allow it to escape its destiny once it has been determined both within the institutional (and supposedly inflexible) structure of what is called the *analytic situation* and in the figure of the doctor as *subject*:

> To the doctor, Freud transferred all the structures Pinel and Tuke had set up within confinement. He did deliver the patient from the existence of the asylum within which his "liberators" had alienated him; but he did not deliver him from what was essential in this existence; he regrouped its powers, extended them to the maximum by uniting them in the doctor's hands; he created the psychoanalytical situation where, by a masterful short-circuit [*court-circuit génial*; I underscore this allusion to the stroke of genius (*coup de génie*), which, as soon as it confirms the evil of confinement and of the interior asylum, is diabolical and properly evil (*malin*); and as we will see, for more than twenty years Foucault never stopped seeing in Freud— and quite literally so—sometimes a good and sometimes a bad or evil (*mauvais*) genius], alienation becomes disalienating because, in the doctor, it becomes a subject.
>
> The doctor, as an alienating figure, remains the key to psychoanalysis. It is perhaps because it did not suppress this ultimate structure, and because it referred all the others to it, that psychoanalysis has not been able, *will not be able* [I thus emphasize this future; it announces the invariability of this verdict in Foucault's subsequent work], to hear the voices of unreason, nor to decipher in themselves the signs of the madman. Psychoanalysis can unravel some of the forms of madness; it remains a stranger to the sovereign enterprise of unreason. It can neither liberate nor transcribe, nor most certainly explain, what is essential in this enterprise. (1961: 611–12; 1965: 278)

And here, just after, are the very last lines of the chapter; we are far from the couple Nietzsche/Freud. They are now separated on both sides of what Foucault calls "moral imprisonment," and it will be difficult to say, in certain situations, who is to be found on the *inside* and who on the *outside*—and sometimes outside but inside. As opposed to Nietzsche and a few other great madmen, Freud no longer belongs to the space *from out of* which *The History of Madness* could be written. He belongs, rather, to this history of madness that the book in turn makes its *object*:

> Since the end of the eighteenth century, the life of unreason no longer manifests itself except in the lightning-flash of works such as those of Hölderlin, of Nerval, of Nietzsche, or of Artaud—forever irreducible to those alienations that can be cured, resisting by their own strength that gigantic moral imprisonment which we are in the habit of calling, doubtless by antiphrasis, the liberation of the insane [*aliénés*] by Pinel and Tuke. (1961: 612; 1965: 278)

This diagnosis, which is also a verdict, is confirmed in the last chapter of the book, "The Anthropological Circle." This chapter fixes the new distribution of names and places into the great series that form the grid of the book. When it is a question of showing that since the end of the eighteenth century the liberation of the mad has been replaced by an objectification of the concept of their freedom (within such categories as desire and will, determinism and responsibility, the automatic and the spontaneous), and that "one will now untiringly recount the trials and tribulations of freedom," which is also to say, of a certain humanization as anthropologization, Freud is then regularly included among the exemplary figures of this anthropologism of freedom. Foucault says, page after page: "From Esquirol to Janet, as from Reil to Freud or from Tuke to Jackson" (1961: 616), or again, "From Esquirol to Freud" (1961: 617), or again "since Esquirol and Broussais right up to Janet, Bleuler, and Freud" (1961: 624). A slight yet troubling reservation comes just after to mitigate all these regroupings. Concerning general paralysis and neurosyphilis, philistinism is everywhere, "right up to Freud—or almost" (1961: 626).

The chiasmatic effects multiply. Some two hundred pages earlier, what had inscribed both Freud *and* Nietzsche, like two accomplices of the same age, was the reopening of the dialogue with unreason, the lifting of the interdiction against *language*, the *return* to a proximity with madness. Yet it is precisely this or, rather, the silent double and hypocritical simulacrum of this, the mask of this language, the same freedom now objectified, that separates Freud from Nietzsche. It is this that now makes them unable to associate or to be associated with one another from the two sides of a wall that is all the more unsurmountable insofar as it consists of an asylum's partition—an invisible, interior, but eloquent partition, that of truth itself as the truth of man and his alienation. Foucault was able, much earlier, to say that Freudian psychoanalysis, to which one must be fair or "do justice," ceases to be a psychology as soon as it takes language into account. Now it is language itself that brings psychoanalysis back down to the status of a psycho-anthropology of alienation, "this language wherein man appears in madness as being other than himself," this "alterity," "a dialectic that is always begun anew between the *Same* and the *Other*," revealing to man his truth "in the babbling movement of *alienation* or *madness*" (1961: 631).

Concerning dialectic and alienation or madness—concerning everything, in fact, that happens in the circulation of this "anthropological circle" wherein psychoanalysis is caught up or held—one should, and I myself would have liked to have done this given more time, pause a bit longer than Foucault did on a passage from Hegel's *Encyclopedia*. I am referring to the Remark of §408 in which Hegel situates and deduces madness as a contraction of the subject between the particular determination of self-feeling and the network of mediations that is called consciousness. Hegel makes in passing a spirited praise of Pinel (I do not understand why Foucault, in quickly citing this passage, replaces this praise for Pinel by an ellipsis). More important, perhaps, is the fact that Hegel also interprets madness as the taking control of a certain Evil Genius (*der böse Genius*) in man. Foucault elliptically cites a short phrase in translation ("méchant génie") without remarking on it and without linking these few extraordinary pages of Hegel to the great dramaturgy of the Evil Genius that concerns us here.

Let me be absolutely clear about this: my intention here is not at all to accuse or criticize Foucault, to say, for example, that he was wrong to confine *Freud himself* (*in general*) or *psychoanalysis itself* (*in general*) to this role and place; on the subject of Freud or psychoanalysis *themselves and in general*, I have in this form and place almost nothing to say or think, except perhaps that Foucault has some good arguments and that others would have some pretty good ones as well to oppose to his. It is also not my intention, in spite of what it may look like, to suggest that Foucault contradicts himself when he so firmly places the same Freud (in general) or the same psychoanalysis (in general) sometimes on one side and sometimes on the other of the dividing line, *and always on the side of the Evil Genius*—who is found sometimes on the side of madness, sometimes on the side of its exclusion-reappropriation, on the side of its confinement to the outside or the inside, with or without asylum walls. The contradiction is no doubt in the things themselves, so to speak. And we are in a region where the wrong (the *being-wrong* or the *doing-someone-wrong*) would want to be more than ever on the side of a certain reason, on the side of what is called *raison garder*—that is, on the side of keeping one's cool, keeping one's head—on the side, precisely, where one is right [*a raison*], and where *being right* [*avoir raison*] is to *win out over* or *prove someone wrong* [*avoir raison de*], with a violence whose subtlety, whose hyperdialectic and hyperchiasmatic resources, cannot be completely formalized, that is, can no longer be dominated by a metalanguage. Which means that we are always caught in the knots that are woven, before us and beyond us, by this powerful—all too powerful—logic. The history of reason embedded in all these turbulent idioms (*to prove someone wrong* [*donner tort*] or *to prove them right* [*donner raison*], *to be right* [*avoir raison*], *to be wrong* [*avoir tort*], *to win out over* [*avoir raison de*], *to do someone wrong* [*faire tort*], and so on) is also the history of madness that Foucault wished to recount to us. The fact that he was caught up, caught up even before setting out, in the snares of this logic—which he sometimes thematizes as having to do with a "system of contractions" and "antinomies" whose "coherence" remains "hidden"—cannot be reduced to a fault or wrong on his part (1961: 624). This does not mean, however, that we, without ever finding him to be radically wrong or at fault, have to subscribe a priori to all his statements. One would be able to master this entire problematic, assuming this were possible, only after having satisfactorily answered a few questions, questions as innocent—or as hardly innocent—as, What is reason? for example, or more narrowly, What is the principle of reason? What does it mean to be right [*avoir raison*]? What does it mean to be right or to prove someone right [*avoir ou donner raison*]? To be wrong, to prove someone wrong, or to do them wrong [*avoir, donner ou faire tort*]? You will forgive me here, I hope, for leaving these enigmas as they are.

I will restrict myself to a modest and more accessible question. The distribution of statements, such as it appears to be set out before us, should lead us to think two apparently incompatible things: the book entitled *The History of Madness*, as the history of madness itself, is and is not the same age as Freudian psychoanalysis. The project of this book thus does and does not belong to the age of psychoanalysis; it already belongs to it and already no longer belongs to it. This division without division would put us back on the track of another logic of division, one that would urge us to think the internal partitions of wholes, partitions that would make such things as madness, reason, history, and age—especially the whole we call age—but also psychoanalysis, Freud, and so on, into rather dubious identities, sufficiently divided from within to threaten in advance all our statements and all our reference with parasitism: it would be a bit as if a virus were introduced into the matrix of language, the way such things are today introduced into computer software, the difference being that we are—and for a very good reason—very far from having at our disposal any of these diagnostic and remedial antiviral programs that are available on the market today, even though these same programs—and for a very good reason—have a hard time keeping pace with the industrial production of these viruses, which are themselves sometimes produced by those who produce the intercepting programs. A maddening situation for any discourse, certainly, but a certain mad panic is not necessarily the worst thing that can happen to a discourse on madness as soon as it does not go all out to confine or exclude its object, that is, in the sense Foucault gives to this word, to *objectify* it.

Does one have the right to stop here and be content with this as an internal reading of Foucault's great book? Is an *internal* reading possible? Is it legitimate to privilege to this extent its relation to something like an "age" of psychoanalysis "itself"? The reservations that such presumptions of identity might arouse (the unity of an "age, the indivisibility of psychoanalysis "itself," and so on)—and I've made more than one allusion to them—would be enough to make us question this.

One would be able to justify a response to this question, in any case, only by continuing to read and to analyze, by continuing to take into account particularly Foucault's corpus, his archive, what this archive says on the subject of the archive. Without limiting ourselves to this, think in particular of the problems posed some five to eight years later: (1) by *The Order of Things* concerning something that has always seemed enigmatic to me and that Foucault calls for a time *episteme* (there where it is said, "We think in that place" [1966: 396; 1973: 384]); a place that, and I will return to this in a moment, encompasses or comprehends the psychoanalysis that does not comprehend it or, more precisely, that comprehends it without comprehending it and without acceding to it; (2) by *The Archaeology of Knowledge* concerning "The Historical *a priori* and the Archive" (this is the title of the central chapter) and archaeology in its relation to the history of ideas.

It is out of the question to get involved here, in so short a time, in such difficult readings. I will thus be content to conclude, if you will still allow me, with a few indications (two at the most) along one of the paths I would have wanted to follow on the basis of these readings.

1. On the one hand, I would have tried to identify the signs of an imperturbable constancy in this movement of the pendulum or balance. The oscillation *regularly* leads from one topological assignation to the other: as if psychoanalysis had *two places* or took place *two times*. Yet it seems to me that the law of this displacement operates without the structural possibility of an event or a place being analyzed for itself, and without the consequences being drawn with regard to the identity of all the concepts at work in this history that does not want to be a history of ideas and representations.

This constancy in the oscillation of the pendulum is first marked, of course, in books that are more or less contemporary with *The History of Madness*. *Maladie mentale et psychologie [Mental Illness and Psychology]* (1962) intersects and coincides at many points with *The History of Madness*. In the history of mental illness,

Freud appears as "the first to open up once again the possibility for reason and unreason to communicate in the danger of a common language, ever ready to break down and disintegrate into the inaccessible" (1962: 82; 1987: 69). In truth, though profoundly in accord with the movement and logic of *The History of Madness*, this book of 1962 is, in the end, a bit more precise and differentiated in its references to Freud, although *Beyond the Pleasure Principle* is never mentioned. Foucault speaks both of Freud's "stroke of genius" (and this is indeed his word) and of the dividing line that runs down his work. Freud's "stroke of genius" was to have escaped the evolutionist horizon of John Hughlings Jackson (1962: 37; 1987: 31), whose model can nevertheless be found in the description of the evolutive forms of neurosis and the history of libidinal stages,[10] the libido being mythological (a myth to destroy, often a biopsychological myth that is abandoned, Foucault then thinks, by psychoanalysts), just as mythological as Janet's "psychic force," with which Foucault associates it more than once (1962: 29; 1987: 24).[11]

If the assignation of Freud is thus double, it is because his work is divided: "In psychoanalysis, it is always possible," says Foucault, "to separate that which pertains to a psychology of evolution (as in *Three Essays on the Theory of Sexuality*) and that which belongs to a psychology of individual history (as in *Five Psychoanalyses* and the accompanying texts)" (1962: 37; 1987: 31).

Despite this consideration for the "stroke of genius," Foucault is indeed speaking here of an analytic psychology. This is what he calls it. Insofar as it remains a psychology, it remains speechless before the language of madness. Indeed, "there is a very good reason why psychology can never master madness; it is because psychology became possible in our world only when madness had already been mastered and excluded from the drama" (1962: 104; 1987: 87—a few lines before the end of the book).

In other words, the logic at work in this conclusion, the consequences—the ruinous consequences—of which one would ceaselessly have to take account, is that what has already been mastered can no longer be mastered, and that too much mastery (in the form of exclusion, but also of objectification) deprives one of mastery (in the form of access, knowledge, competence). The concept of mastery is an impossible concept to manipulate, as we know: the more there is, the less there is, and vice versa. The conclusion drawn in the few lines I just cited thus excludes *both* Freud's "stroke of genius" *and* psychology, be it analytic or some other. Freudian man remains a *homo psychologicus*. Freud is once again passed over in silence, cut out of both the lineage and the work of mad geniuses. He is given over to a forgetfulness where one can then accuse him of silence and forgetting.

> And when, in lightning flashes and cries, madness reappears, as in Nerval or Artaud, Nietzsche, or Roussel, it is psychology that remains silent, *speechless*, before this language that borrows a meaning of its own from that *tragic split* [I emphasize this phrase; this is a tragic and romantic discourse on the essence of madness and the birth of tragedy, a discourse just as close, literally, to that of a certain Novalis as to that of Hölderlin], from that freedom, that, for contemporary man, only the existence of "psychologists" allows him to forget. (1962: 104; 1987: 87–88)[12]

And yet. Still according to the interminable and inexhaustible *fort/da* that we have been following for some time now, the same *Freudian man* is reinscribed into the noble lineage at the end of *Naissance de la clinique* [*The Birth of the Clinic*] (a book published in 1963 but clearly written during the same creative period). Why single out this occurrence of the reinscription rather than another? Because it might give us (and this is, in fact, the hypothesis that interests me) a rule for reading this *fort/da*; it might provide us with a criterion for interpreting this untiring exclusion/inclusion. It is a question of another divide, within psychoanalysis or, in any case, a divide that seems somewhat different than the one I spoke of a moment ago between Freud, the psychologist of evolution, and Freud, the psychologist of individual history. I say "seems somewhat different" because the one perhaps leads back to the other.

The line of this second divide is, quite simply—if one can say this—death. The Freud who breaks with psychology, with evolutionism and biologism, the tragic Freud, really, who shows himself *hospitable* to madness (and I take the risk of this word) because he is foreign to the space of the hospital, the tragic Freud who deserves hospitality in the great lineage of mad geniuses, is the Freud who talks it out with death. This would especially be the Freud, then, of *Beyond the Pleasure Principle*, although Foucault never, to my knowledge, mentions this work and makes only a very ambiguous allusion in *Mental Illness and Psychology* to what he calls a death instinct, the one by which Freud wished to explain the war, although "it was war that was dreamed in this shift in Freud's thinking" (1962: 99; 1987: 83).

Death alone, along with war, introduces the power of the negative into psychology and into its evolutionist optimism. On the basis of this experience of death, on the basis of what is called in the final pages of *The Birth of the Clinic* "originary finitude" (1963: 199; 1975: 197)—a vocabulary and theme that then take over Foucault's text and that always seemed to me difficult to dissociate from Heidegger, who as you know is practically never evoked, nor even named, by Foucault[13]— Freud is reintegrated into this modernity, from out of which *The History of Madness* is written and from which he had been banished at regular intervals. It is by taking account of death as "the concrete a priori of medical experience" that "the beginning of that fundamental relation that binds modern man to his originary finitude" comes about (1963: 198, 199; 1975: 196, 197). This modern man is also a "Freudian man":

> the experience of individuality in modern culture is bound up with that of death: from Hölderlin's Empedocles to Nietzsche's Zarathustra, and on to Freudian man, an obstinate relation to death prescribes to the universal its singular face, and lends to each individual the power of being heard forever. (1963: 199; 1975: 197)

Originary finitude is a finitude that no longer arises out of the infinity of a divine presence. It now unfolds "in the void left by the absence of the gods" (1963: 200; 1975: 198). What we have here is, then in the name of death, so to speak, a reinscription of Freudian man into a "modern" grouping or whole from which he was sometimes excluded.

One can then follow *two* new but equally ambiguous consequences. *On the one hand*, the grouping in question is going to be restructured. One should not be surprised to see reappear, as on the very last page of *The Birth of the Clinic*, the name of Jackson—and, before him, Bichat, whose *Traité des membranes* (1827) and *Recherches physiologiques* would have allowed death to be seen and thought. This vitalism would have arisen against the backdrop of *"mortalism"* (1963: 147; 1975: 145). It would be a characteristic of the entire European nineteenth century, and it could be attested to just as well by Goya, Géricault, Delacroix, or Baudelaire, to name just a few: "The importance of Bichat, Jackson, and Freud in European culture does not prove that they were philosophers as well as doctors, but that, in this culture, medical thought is fully engaged in the philosophical status of man" (1963: 200; 1975: 198).

But there is a second ambiguous consequence of this relation to death as originary finitude. And so, *on the other hand*, the figure or face that is then fixed, and in which one believes one recognizes the traits of "Freudian man," comes to occupy a rather singular place with respect to what Foucault calls the analytic of finitude and the modern *episteme* at the end of *Les Mots et les choses* [*The Order of Things*] (1966). From the standpoint of a certain epistemological trihedron (life, work, and language, or biology, economy, and philology), the human sciences are seen to be at once *inclusive* and *exclusive*; these are Foucault's words (see 1966: 358; 1973: 347).

As for this inclusive exclusion, Freud's work, to which Foucault unwaveringly assigns a model that is more philological than biological, still occupies the place of the *hinge*; Foucault in fact speaks about the place and workings of a *"pivot"*: "all this knowledge, within which Western culture had given itself in one century a certain image of man, pivots on the work of Freud, though without, for all that, leaving its fundamental arrangement" (1966: 372; 1973: 361).

"Though without, for all that, leaving its fundamental arrangement": that is how everything turns round the event or the invention of psychoanalysis. It turns in circles and in place, endlessly returning to the same. It is a revolution that changes nothing. Hence this is not, as Foucault adds at this point, "the most decisive importance of psychoanalysis."

In what, then, does this "most decisive importance of psychoanalysis" consist? In exceeding both consciousness and representation—and, as a result, the human sciences, which do not go beyond the realm of the representable. It is in this respect that psychoanalysis, like ethnology in fact, does not belong to the field of human science. It "relates the knowledge of man to the finitude that gives man its foundation" (1966: 392; 1973: 381). We are far from its earlier determination as an analytic psychology. And this same excessive character leads psychoanalysis toward the very forms of finitude that Foucault writes in capital letters, that is, toward Death, Desire, Law, or Law-Language (see 1966: 386; 1973: 375). It would be necessary to devote a more detailed and more probing reading to these few pages, something I cannot do here. To keep to the surest schema, let us simply say that, from this point of view and to this degree at least, psychoanalysis, as an analytic of finitude, is now granted an intimacy with the madness that it had sometimes been conceded but had most often been emphatically denied in *The History of Madness*. And this intimacy is a sort of complicity with the madness of the day, the madness of today, "madness in it present form, madness as it is posited in the modern experience, as its truth and its alterity" (1966: 387; 1973: 375).

But let us not oversimplify things. What Foucault generously grants psychoanalytic experience is now nothing other than what is denied it; more precisely, it is the being able to see what is denied it. Indeed, the only privilege that is here granted to psychoanalysis is that of the experience *that accedes to that to which it can never accede*. If Foucault here mentions, under the name of madness, only schizophrenia and psychosis, it is because psychanalysis most often approaches these only in order to acknowledge its own limit: a forbidden or impossible access. *This limit defines psychoanalysis*. Its intimacy with madness par excellence is an intimacy with the least intimate, a non-intimacy that relates it to what is most heterogenous, to that which in no way lets itself be interiorized, nor even subjectified: neither alienated, I would say, nor inalienable.

> This is why psychoanalysis finds in that madness *par excellence* ["madness *par excellence*" is also the title given by Blanchot many years earlier to a text on Hölderlin, and Foucault is no doubt echoing this without saying so]—which psychiatrists term schizophrenia—its intimate, its most invincible torture: for, given in this form of madness, in an absolutely manifest and absolutely withdrawn form [this absolute identity of the manifest and the withdrawn, of the open and the secret, is no doubt the key to this double gesture of interpretation and evaluation], are the forms of finitude towards which it usually advances unceasingly (and interminably) from the starting-point of that which is voluntarily-involuntarily offered to it in the patient's language. So psychoanalysis "recognizes itself" when it is confronted with those very psychoses to which, nevertheless (or rather, for that very reason), it has scarcely any means of access: as if the psychosis were displaying in a savage illumination, and offering in a mode not too distant but precisely too close, that towards which analysis must make its laborious way. (1966: 387; 1973: 375–76)

This displacement, as ambiguous as it is, leads Foucault to adopt the exact opposite position of certain theses of *The History of Madness* and *Mental Illness and Psychology* concerning the couple patient-doctor, concerning transference or alienation. This time, psychoanalysis not only has nothing to do with a psychology, but constitutes neither a general theory of man—since it is above all else a knowledge linked to a practice—nor an anthropology (see 1966: 388, 390; 1973: 376, 378–9). Even better: in the movement where he clearly affirms this, Foucault challenges the very thing of which he had unequivocally accused psychoanalysis, namely, of being a mythology and a thaumaturgy. He now wants to explain why psychologists and philosophers were so quick, and so naive, to denounce a Freudian mythology there where that which exceeds representation and consciousness must have in fact *resembled*, but only resembled, something mythological (see 1966: 386; 1973: 374). As for the thaumaturgy of transference, the logic of alienation, and the subtly or sublimely asylum-like violence of the analytic situation—they are no longer, Foucault now says, essential to psychoanalysis, no longer "constitutive" of it. It is not that all violence is absent from this rehabilitated psychoanalysis, but it is, I hardly dare say it, a good violence, or in any case what Foucault calls a "calm" violence; one that, in the singular experience of singularity, allows access to "the concrete figures of finitude":

> neither hypnosis, nor the patient's alienation within the fantasmatic character of the doctor, is constitutive of psychoanalysis; . . . the latter can be deployed only in the calm violence of a particular relationship and the transference it produces. . . . Psychoanalysis makes use of the particular relation of the transference in order to reveal, on the outer confines of representation, Desire, Law, and Death, which outline, at the extremity of analytic language and practice, the concrete figures of finitude. (1966: 388–89; 1973: 377–78)

Things have indeed changed—or so it appears—between *The History of Madness* and *The Order of Things*.

From where does the theme of finitude that seems to govern this new displacement of the pendulum come? To what philosophical event is this analytic of finitude to be attributed—this analytic in which is inscribed the trihedron of knowledges or models of the modern *episteme*, with its nonsciences, the "human sciences," according to Foucault (1966: 378; 1973: 366), and its "counter-sciences," which Foucault says psychoanalysis and ethnology are also (1966: 391; 1973: 379)?

As a project, the analytic of finitude would belong to the tradition of the Kantian critique. Foucault insists on this Kantian filiation by specifying, to cite it once again: "We think in that place." Here is again and for a time, according to Foucault, *our* age, *our* contemporaneity. It is true that if originary finitude obviously makes us think of Kant, it would be unable to do so alone, that is—to summarize an enormous venture in a word, in a name—without the active interpretation of the Heideggerian repetition and all its repercussions, particularly, since this is our topic today, in the discourse of French philosophy and psychoanalysis and, especially, Lacanian psychoanalysis; and when I say Lacanian, I am also referring to all the debates *with* Lacan during the past few decades. This would have perhaps deserved some mention here on the part of Foucault, especially when he speaks of originary finitude. For Kantian finitude is precisely not "originary," as is, on the contrary, the one to which the Heideggerian interpretation leads. Finitude in Kant's sense is instead derived, as is the intuition bearing the same name. But let us leaves all this aside, since it would, as we say, take us a bit too far afield.

The "we" who is saying "we think in that place" is evidently, tautologically, the "we" from out of which the signatory of these lines, the author of *The History of Madness* and *The Order of Things*, speaks, writes, and thinks. But this "we" never stops dividing, and the places of its signature are displaced in being divided up. A certain untimeliness always disturbs the contemporary who reassures him or herself in a "we." This "we," our "we," is not its own contemporary. The self-identity of its age, or of any age, appears as divided, and thus problematic, *problematizable* (I underscore this word for a reason that will perhaps becomes apparent in a moment), as the age of madness or an age of psychoanalysis—as well as, in fact, all the historical or archaeological categories that promise us the determinable stability of a configurable whole. In fact, from the moment a couple separates—from the moment, for example, just to locate here a symptom or a simple indication, the couple Freud/Nietzsche forms and then unforms—this decoupling fissures the identity of the epoch, of the age, of the *episteme* or the paradigm of which one or the other, or both together, might have been the significant representatives. This is even more true when this decoupling comes to fissure the self-identity of some individual, or some presumed individuality, for example, of Freud. What allows one to presume the non-self-difference of Freud, for example? And of psychoanalysis? These decouplings and self-difference no doubt introduce a good deal of disorder into the unity of any configuration, whole, epoch, or historical age. Such disturbances make the historians' work rather difficult, even and especially the work of the most original and refined among them. This self-difference, this difference *to self* [*à soi*], and not simply *with self*, makes life hard if not impossible for historical science. But inversely, would there be any history, would anything ever *happen*, without this principle of disturbance? Would there ever be any event without this disturbance of the principality?

At the point where we are, the age of finitude is being de-identified for at least one reason, from which I can here abstract only the general schema: the thought of finitude, as the thought of finite man, speaks *both* of the tradition, the memory of the Kantian critique or of the knowledges rooted in it, *and* of the end [*fin*] of this finite man, this man who is "nearing its end," as Foucault's most famous sentence would have it in this final wager, placed on the edge of a promise that has yet to take shape, in the final lines of *The Order of Things*: "then one can certainly wager that man would be effaced, like a face drawn in sand at the edge or limit of the sea" (1966: 398; 1973: 387). The *trait* (the trait of the face, the line or the limit) that then runs the risk of being effaced in the sand would perhaps also be the one that separates an end from itself, thereby multiplying it endlessly and making it, once again, into a limit: the self-relation of a limit at once erases and multiplies the limit; it cannot but divide it in inventing it. The limit only comes to be effaced—it only comes to efface itself—as soon as it is inscribed.

2. I'm finished with this point, and so I should really finish it up right here. Assuming that I haven't already worn out your patience, I will conclude with a second indication as a sort of *postscript*—and even more schematically—in order to point once again in the direction of psychoanalysis and to put these hypotheses to the test of *The History of Sexuality* (1976–84).[14]

If one is still willing to follow this figure of the pendulum [*balancier*] making a scene before psychoanalysis, then one will observe that the *fort/da* here gives a new impetus to the movement, a movement with the same rhythm but with a greater amplitude and range than ever before. Psychoanalysis is here reduced, more than it ever was, to a very circumscribed and dependent moment in a history of the "strategies of knowledge and power" (juridical, familial, psychiatric) (1976: 210; 1978: 159). Psychoanalysis is taken by and interested in these strategies, but it does not think them through. The praises of Freud fall decisively and irreversibly: one hears, for example, of "how wonderfully effective he was—worthy of the greatest spiritual fathers and directors of the classical period—in giving a new impetus to the secular injunction to study sex and transform it into discourse" (1976: 210; 1978: 159). This time, in other words, in reinscribing the invention of psychoanalysis into the history of a disciplinary dynamic, one no longer indicts only the ruses of objectivization and psychiatric alienation, as in *The History of Madness*, and no longer only the stratagems that would have allowed the *confinement without confinement* of the patient in the invisible asylum of the analytic situation. This time, it is a question of going much further back, and more radically than the "repressive hypothesis" ever did, towards the harsh ruses of the monarchy of sex and the agencies of power that support it. These latter invest in and take charge of sexuality, so that there is no need to oppose, as one so often and naively believes, power and pleasure.

And since we have been following for so long now the obsessive avatars of the Evil Genius—the irresistible, demonic, and metamorphic returns of this quasi-God, of God's second in command, this metempsychotic Satan—we here find Freud himself once again, Freud, to whom Foucault leaves a choice between only two roles: the bad genius and the good one. And what we have here is another chiasm: in the rhetoric of the few lines that I will read in a moment, one will not be surprised to see that the accused, the one who is the most directly targeted by the indictment— for no amount of denying will makes us forget that we are dealing here with a trial and a verdict—is the "good genius of Freud" and not his "bad genius." Why so? In the final pages of the first volume of *The History of Sexuality*, the accusation of pansexualism that was often levelled against psychoanalysis naturally comes up. Those most blind in this regard, says Foucault, were not those who denounced pansexualism out of prudishness. Their only error was to have attributed "solely to the *bad genius* [*mauvais génie*] of Freud what had already gone through a long stage of preparation" (1976: 210; 1978: 159, my emphasis). The opposite error, the symmetrical lure, corresponds to a more serious mystification. It is the illusion that could be called emancipatory, the aberration of the Enlightenment, the misguided notion on the part of those who believed that Freud, the *"good genius"* of Freud, had finally freed sex from its repression by power. These

> were mistaken concerning the nature of the process; they believed that Freud had at last, through a sudden reversal, restored to sex the rightful share which it had been denied for so long; they had not seen how the *good genius* of Freud had placed it at one of the critical points marked out for it since the eighteenth century by the strategies of knowledge and power, how wonderfully effective he was ... in giving a new impetus to the secular injunction to study sex and transform it into discourse. (1976: 210; 1978: 159, my emphasis]15

The "good genius" of Freud would thus be worse than the bad one. It would have consisted in getting itself well placed, in spotting the best place in an old strategy of knowledge and power.

Whatever questions it might leave unanswered—and I will speak in just a moment of one of those it suscitates in me—this project appears nonetheless exciting, necessary, and courageous. And I would not want any particular reservation on my part to be too quickly classified among the reactions of those who hastened to defend the threatened privilege of the pure invention of psychoanalysis, that is, of an invention that would be *pure*, of a psychoanalysis that one might still dream would have innocently sprung forth already outfitted, helmeted, armed—in short, outside all history, after the epistemological cutting of the cord, as one used to say, indeed, after the unravelling of the navel of the dream. Foucault himself during an interview seemed to be ready for some sort of compromise on this issue, readily and good-spiritedly acknowledging the "impasses" (this was his word) of his concept of *episteme* and the difficulties into which this new project had lead him (see Foucault 1980: esp. 196-97). But only those who work, only those who take risks in working, encounter difficulties. One only ever thinks and takes responsibility—if indeed one ever does—in the testing of the aporia; without this, one is content to follow an inclination or apply a program. And it would not be very generous, indeed it would be especially naive and imprudent, to take advantage of these avowals, to take them literally, and to forget what Foucault himself tells us about the confessional scene.

The question that I would have liked to formulate would thus not aim to protect psychoanalysis against some new attack, nor even to cast the slightest doubt upon the importance, necessity, and legitimacy of Foucault's extremely interesting project concerning this great history of sexuality. My question would only seek—and this would be, in sum, a sort of modest contribution—to complicate somewhat an axiomatic and, on the basis of this perhaps, certain discursive or conceptual procedures, particularly regarding the way in which this axiomatic is inscribed in its age, in the historical field that serves as a point of departure, and in its reference to psychoanalysis. In a word, without compromising in the least the necessity of reinscribing almost "all" psychanalysis (assuming one could seriously say such a thing, which I do not believe one can: psychoanalysis *itself*, *all* psychoanalysis, *the whole truth about all* psychoanalysis) into a history that precedes and exceeds it, it would be a question of becoming interested in certain gestures, in certain works, in certain moments of certain works of psychoanalysis, Freudian and post-Freudian (for one cannot, especially in France, seriously treat this subject by limiting oneself to a strictly Freudian discourse and apparatus), in certain traits of a consequently non-globalizable psychoanalysis, one that is divided and multiple (like the powers that Foucault ceaselessly reminds us are essentially dispersed). It would then be a question of admitting that these necessarily fragmentary or disjointed movements say and do, provide resources for saying and doing, what *The History of Sexuality* (*The Will to Knowledge*) wishes to say, what it *means* [*veut dire*], and what it wishes to do (to know and to make known) with regard to psychoanalysis. In other words, if one still wanted to speak in terms of age—something that I would only ever do in the form of citation—at this point, here on this line, concerning some trait that is on the side from out of which the history of sexuality is written rather than on the side of what it describes of objectifies, one would have to say that Foucault's project belongs too much to "the age of psychoanalysis" in its possibility for it, when claiming to thematize psychoanalysis, to do anything other than let psychoanalysis continue to speak obliquely of itself and to mark one of its folds in a scene that I will not call self-referential or specular but whose structural complication I will not here try to describe (I have tried to do this elsewhere). This is not only because of what withdraws this history from the regime of representation (because of what already inscribes the possibility of this history in and since the age of Freud and Heidegger—to use these names as mere indications for the sake of convenience). It is also for a reason that interest us here more directly: what Foucault announces and denounces about the relation between pleasure and power, in what he calls the "double impetus: pleasure and power" (1976: 62; 1978: 45), would find, already in Freud—to say nothing of those who followed, discussed, transformed, and displaced him—the very resources for the objection levelled against the "good genius," the so very bad "good genius," of the father of psychoanalysis. I will situate this with just a word in order to conclude.

Foucault had clearly cautioned us: this history of sexuality was not to be a historian's history. A "genealogy of desiring man" was to be neither a history of representations nor a history of behaviours or sexual practices. This would lead one to think that sexuality cannot become an object of history without seriously affecting the historian's practice and the concept of history. Moreover, Foucault puts quotation marks around the work *sexuality*: "the quotation marks have a certain importance," he adds (1984: 9; 1985: 3). We are thus also dealing here with the history of a word, with its usages starting in the nineteenth century and the reformulation of the vocabulary in relation to a large number of other phenomena, from biological mechanism to traditional and new norms, to the institutions that support these, be they religious, juridical, pedagogical, or medical (for example, psychoanalytic). This history of the uses of a word is neither nominalist nor essentialist. It concerns procedures and, more precisely, zones of "problematization." It is a "history of truth" as a history of *problematizations*, and even as an "archeology of problematizations," "through which being offers itself as something that can and must be thought" (17–19; 11–13). The point is to analyze not simply behaviors, ideas, or ideologies, but, first of all, these *problematizations* in which a thought of being intersects "practices" and "practices of the self"—a "genealogy of practices of the self" through which these problematizations are formed. With its reflexive vigilance and care in thinking itself in its rigorous specificity, such an analysis thus calls for the *problematization of its own problematization*. This latter must *itself* also question itself, and with the same archaeological and genealogical care, the same care that it itself methodically prescribes.

When confronted with a historical problematization of such scope and thematic richness, one should not be satisfied with a mere survey, nor with asking in just a few minutes an overarching question so as to insure some sort of synoptic mastery. What we can and must try to do in such a situation is to pay tribute to a work that is this great and this uncertain by means of a question that it itself raises, by means of a question that it carries within itself, that it keeps in reserve in its unlimited potential, one of the questions that can thus be deciphered within it, a question that keeps it in suspense, holding its breath [*tein . . . en haleine*]—and, thus, keeps it alive.

One of these questions, for me, for example, would be the one I tried to formulate a few years ago during a conference honoring Foucault at New York University.[16] It was developed by means of a problematization of the concept of power and the theme of what Foucault calls the *spiral* in the duality power/pleasure. Leaving aside the huge question of the concept of power and of what gives it its alleged unity under the essential dispersion rightly recalled by Foucault himself, I will pull out only a thread: it would lead to that which, in a certain Freud and at the center of a certain—let's say for the sake of convenience—French heritage of Freud, would not only not let itself be objectified by the Foucauldian problematization but would actually contribute to it in the most determinate and efficient way, thereby deserving to be inscribed on the thematizing rather than on the thematized border of this history of sexuality. I thus have to wonder what Foucault would have said in this perspective, and were he to have taken this into account, not of "Freud" or of psychoanalysis "itself" in *general*—which does not exist any more than power does as one big central and homogeneous corpus—but, for example (since this is only one example), about an undertaking like *Beyond the Pleasure Principle*, about something in its lineage or between its filial connections—along with everything that has been inherited, repeated, or discussed from it since then. In following one of these threads or filial connections, one of the most discreet, in following the abyssal, unassignable, and unmasterable strategy of this text, a strategy that is finally without strategy, one begins to see that this text not only opens up the horizon of a beyond of the pleasure principle (the hypothesis of such a beyond never really seeming to be of interest to Foucault) against which the whole economy of pleasure needs to be rethought, complicated, pursued in it most unrecognizable ruses and detours. By means of one of these filiations—another one unwinding the spool of the *fort/da* that continues to interest us—this text also problematizes, in its greatest radicality, the agency of power and mastery. In a discreet and difficult passage, an original drive for power or drive for mastery (*Bemächtigungstrieb*) is mentioned. It is very difficult to know if this drive for power is still dependent upon the pleasure principle, indeed, upon sexuality as such, upon the austere monarchy of sex that Foucault speaks of on the last page of his book.

How would Foucault have situated this drive for mastery in his discourse on power or on irreducibly plural powers? How would he have read this drive, had he read it, in this extremely enigmatic text of Freud's? How would he have interpreted the recurring references to the demonic from someone who then makes himself, according to his own terms, the "devil's advocate," and who becomes interested in the hypothesis of a late or derived appearance of sex and sexual pleasure? In the whole problematization whose history he describes, how would Foucault have inscribed this passage from *Beyond the Pleasure Principle*, and this concept and these questions (with all the debates to which this book of Freud either directly or indirectly gave rise, in a sort of critical capitalization, particularly in the France of our age, beginning with everything in Lacan that takes its point of departure in the repetition compulsion [*Wiederholungszwang*])? Would he have inscribed this problematic matrix *within* the whole whose history he describes? Or would he have put it on the other side, on the side of what allows one on the contrary to delimit the whole, indeed to problematize it? And thus on a side that no longer belongs to the whole nor, as I would be tempted to think, to any whole, such that the very idea of a gathering of problematization or procedures, to say nothing any longer of age, *episteme*, paradigm, or epoch, would make for so many problematic names, just as problematic as the very idea of problematization?

This is one of the questions that I would have liked to have asked him. I am trying, since this is, unfortunately, the only recourse left us in the solitude of questioning, to imagine the principle of the reply. It would perhaps be something like this: what one must stop believing in is principality or principleness, in the problematic of the principle, in the principled unity of pleasure and power, or of some drive that is thought to be more originary than the other. The theme of the *spiral* would be that of a drive duality (power/pleasure) that is *without principle*.

It is *the spirit of this spiral* that keeps one in suspense, holding one's breath—and, thus, keeps one alive.

The question would thus once again be given a new impetus: is not the duality in question, this spiralled duality, what Freud tried to oppose to all monisms by speaking of a dual drive and of a death drive, of a death drive that was no doubt not alien to the drive for mastery? And, therefore, to what is most alive in life, to its very living on [*survivance*]?

I am still trying to imagine Foucault's response. I can't quite do it. I would need him to take it on himself.

But in this place where no one can answer for him, in the absolute silence where we remain nonetheless turned toward him, I would venture to bet that, in a sentence that I will not construct for him, he would have associated and yet also dissociated, he would have placed back to back mastery and death, that is, the same—death *and* the master, death *as* the master.

NOTES

On 23 November 1991, the Ninth Colloquium of the International Society for the History of Psychiatry and Psychoanalysis devoted a conference to Foucault's *Histoire de la folie* to mark the thirtieth anniversary of its publication. This essay, which was given as a talk at that conference, was published in French in *Penser la folie: Essais sur Michel Foucault* (Paris, 1992).

1. *Ed:* In December 1981, Derrida was invited by a group of intellectual-dissidents from Prague, Czechoslovakia, to deliver a lecture, and was later arrested. The best précis of the affair is recorded in the "Curriculum Vitae" prepared by Geoffrey Bennington:

   1981: With Jean-Pierre Vernant and some friends, [Derrida] founds the Jan Hus Association (help for dissident or persecuted Czech intellectuals) of which he is subsequently vice-president. The same year, goes to Prague to run a clandestine seminar. Followed for several days, stopped at the end of the week, finally arrested at the airport, and, after a police operation on his suitcase in which they pretend to discover a brown powder, he is imprisoned on the charge of "production and trafficking of drugs." (Bennington and Derrida, 1993: 334)

   Of his Kafkaesque experience Derrida himself writes: "[W]hen I said that I had never seen the drugs that were supposed to have been discovered in my suitcase before the customs officers themselves saw them, the prosecutor replied: 'That's what all drug traffickers say'"(Derrida 1992a: 218).

   Foucault was among the first intellectuals to sign a petition against the Czech action, and spoke on the radio on Derrida's behalf—acts that helped mend the rift that developed in the wake of their personal and professional differences. Derrida's release was, though, mostly effected by the speedy intervention of the French government under Françoise Mitterand (who was pressed on the matter by his close advisor, the leftist philosopher Régis Debray).

2. *Trans:* Derrida refers here and throughout to the original edition of *Folie et déraison*. The book was reprinted with different pagination in 1972 and included as an appendix "Mon corps, ce papier, ce feu," Foucault's response to Derrida's "Cogito et histoire de la folie," a lecture first given in 1963 and reprinted in 1967 (translated in Derrida 1978: 31–63). A much abridged version of *Histoire de la folie* appeared in English as *Madness and Civilization* (1965).

   Since Derrida refers to the unabridged text of 1961 and works with the original title throughout, we have referred to this work as *The History of Madness* (or in some cases, *The History of Madness in the Classical Age*). Wherever possible, we have given references to both French and English texts. Since all other texts of Foucault cited by Derrida have been translated in their entirety, we have provided both French and English page references. Translations have been slightly modified in several instances to fit the context of Derrida's argument.

3. *Ed:* square brackets within quotations indicate Derrida's remarks throughout.

4. *Trans:* See "Propos sur la causalité psychique" and "La Science et la vérité," *Ecrits* (Lacan 1966: 209, 219–44). The latter has appeared in English (1989: 4–29).

5. *Trans:* This final chapter of *Histoire de la folie* is not included in *Madness and Civilization*.

6. *Trans:* This is the case for the French versions but not for the English.

7. One will note in passing that we have here, along with very brief allusions to the *Three Essays on the Theory of Sexuality, Introductory Lectures on Psycho-Analysis*, and a couple of individual cases in *Mental Illness and Psychology*, and a reference just as brief to *Totem and Taboo* in *The Order of Things*, one of the few times that Foucault mentions a work of Freud; beyond this, he does not, to my knowledge, cite or analyze any text of Freud, or of any other psychoanalyst, not even those of contemporary French psychoanalysts. Each time, only the proper name is pronounced—Freud, or the common name—psychoanalysis (see Foucault 1987: 31; 1973: 379).

   Discovery is underscored by Foucault, along with *return* and *language*. Freud is the event of a *discovery*—the unconscious and psychoanalysis as a movement of *return*—and what relates the discovery to the return is language, the possibility of speaking with madness, "the possibility of a dialogue with unreason."

8. "Mon corps, ce papier, ce feu" was first published in *Paideia* (Sept. 1971) and was reissued as the appendix to the 1972 edition of *Histoire de la folie*.

9. "And so laws keep up their good standing, not because they are just, but because they are laws: that is the mystical foundation of their authority, they have no other. . . . Anyone who obeys them because they are just is not obeying them the way he ought to" (in Derrida 1990: 939; Derrida's French text appears on facing pages). Elsewhere, Montaigne had mentioned the "legitimate fictions" on which "our law" "founds the truth of its justice" (ibid). And Pascal cites Montaigne without naming him when he recalls both the principle of justice and the fact that it should not be traced back to its source unless one wants to ruin it. What is he

himself doing, then, when he speaks of "the mystical foundation of its authority," adding in the same breath, "Whoever traces it to its source annihilates it" (ibid)? Is he re-founding or ruining that of which he speaks? Will one ever know? Must one know?

Power, authority, knowledge and non-knowledge, law, judgment, fiction, good standing or credit, transfer: from Montaigne to Pascal onto others, we recognize the same network of a critical problematic, an active, vigilant, hypercritical problematization. It is difficult to be sure that the "classical age" did not thematize, reflect, and also deploy the concepts of its symptoms: the concepts that one will later direct toward the symptoms that it will one day be believed can be assigned to it.

10. Insofar as, and to the extent that, it follows Jackson's model (for the "stroke of genius" also consists in escaping from this), psychoanalysis is *credulous*, it *will have been* credulous, for it is in this that it is outdated, a credulous presumption: "it believed that it could," "Freud believed." After having cited Jackson's *The Factors of Insanities*, Foucault in fact adds (I emphasize the verb and tense of *to believe*):

> Jackson's entire work tended to give right of place to evolutionism in neuro- and psycho-pathology. Since the *Croonian Lectures* (1874), it has no longer been possible to omit the regressive aspects of illness; evolution is now one of the dimensions by which one gains access to the pathological fact.
> A whole side of Freud's work consists of a commentary on the evolutive forms of neurosis. The history of the libido, of its development, of its successive fixations, resembles a collection of the pathological possibilities of the individual: each type of neurosis is a return to a libidinal stage of evolution. And psychoanalysis *believed that it could* write a psychology of the child by carrying out a pathology of the adult. . . . This is the celebrated Oedipus complex, in which Freud *believed* that he could read the enigma of man and the key to his destiny, in which one must find the most comprehensive analysis of the conflicts experienced by the child in his relations with his parents and the point at which many neuroses became fixated.
> In short, every libidinal stage is a potential pathological structure. Neurosis is a spontaneous archeology of the libido. (1962: 23–26; 1987: 19–21)

11. For example: "It is not a question of invalidating the analyses of pathological regression; all that is required is to free them of the myths that neither Janet nor Freud succeeded in separating from them" (1962: 31; 1987: 26).

12. A literally identical schema was at work a few pages earlier: "Psychology can never tell the truth about madness because it is madness that holds the truth of psychology." It is again a tragic vision, a tragic discourse on the tragic. Hölderlin, Nerval, Roussel, and Artaud are again named through their works as witnesses of a "tragic confrontation with madness" free of all psychology (1962: 89; 1987: 74, 75). No reconciliation is possible between psychology, even if analytic, and tragedy.

13. Except perhaps in passing in *Les Mots et les choses*: "the experience of Hölderlin, Nietzsche, and Heidegger, in which the return is posited only in the extreme recession of the origin" (1966: 345; 1973: 334).

This ponderous silence would last, I believe, right up until an interview that he gave not long before his death. Faithful to the Foucauldian style of interpretation, one might say that the spacing of this omission, of this blank silence—like the silence that reigns over the name of Lacan, whom one can associate with Heidegger up to a certain point, and thus with a few others who never stopped in France and elsewhere, to dialogue with these two—is anything but the empty and inoperative sign of an absence. It *give rise* or *gives the place* [*donne lieu*], on the contrary, it marks out the place and the age. The dotted lines of a suspended writing *situate* with a formidable precision. No attention to the age or to the problem of the age should lose sight of this.

14. *Histoire de la sexualité* is the name given by Foucault to his entire project on sexuality, of which three volumes have now been published [and translated into English] (1976/1978; 1984/1985; 1984a/1986).

15. It is perhaps appropriate to recall here the lines immediately following this, the last in the first volume of *The History of Sexuality*. They unequivocally describe this sort of Christian teleology or, more precisely, modern Christianity (as opposed to "an old Christianity") whose completion would, in some sense, be marked by psychoanalysis:

    the secular injunction to study sex and transform it into discourse. We are often reminded of the countless procedures which an old Christianity once employed to make us detest the body; but let us ponder all the ruses that were employed for centuries to make us love sex, to make the knowledge of it desirable and everything said about it precious. Let us consider the stratagems by which we were induced to apply all our skills to discovering its secrets, by which we were attached to the obligation to draw out its truth, and made guilty for having failed to recognize it for so long. These devices are what ought to make us wonder today. Moreover, we need to consider the possibility that one day, perhaps, in a different economy of bodies and pleasures, people will no longer quite understand how the ruses of sexuality, and the power that sustains its organization, were able to subject us to that austere monarchy of sex, so that we became dedicated to the endless task of forcing its secret, of exacting the truest of confessions from a shadow.

    The irony of this deployment is in having us believe that our "liberation" is in the balance. (1976: 210–11; 1978: 159)

    Some might be tempted to relate this conclusion to that of *The Order of Things*, to everything that is said there about the *end* and about its *tomorrow*, about man "nearing his end" right up to this "day" when, as *The History of Sexuality* says, "in a different economy of bodies and pleasures, people will no longer quite understand how," and so on. It is difficult not to hear in the rhetoric and tonality of such a call, in the apocalyptic and eschatological tone of this promise (even if "we can at the moment do no more than sense the possibility [of this event]—without knowing either what its form will be or what it promises" [1966: 398; 1973: 387]), a certain resonance with the Christianity and Christian humanism whose end is being announced.

16. The following analysis thus intersects a much longer treatment of the subject in an unpublished paper entitled "Beyond the Power Principle" that I presented during this conference at New York University, organized by Thomas Bishop, in April 1986.

the witch
metapsychology

Rodolphe Gasché

translation by Julian Patrick

11

Editor's Note

In this essay on Freud's *Beyond the Pleasure Principle* (1920), Rodolphe Gasché explores a number of themes which occupied him over 20 years ago. At that time he was very interested in psychoanalysis—in the "theory of the phantom" and, more particularly, in the logic of psychoanalytic discourse—and wrote two major essays in addition to "La Sorcière métapsychologique," both concerning Freud's *Gradiva* study. One of these, called "Phantasme et temporalité," was never published, while another appeared in Italian translation (1977: 125–64). Gasché presented "La Sorcière" at a 1974 conference on the theory of textuality in Urbino, Italy.

According to Gasché, "La Sorcière" was intended as a first chapter to a book-length study of Freud's *Beyond* that he never completed. "The book," Gasché reports, "was to center on the death drive, not only on its primordiality with respect to life and the pleasure principle, but especially on how life is but a function of death, a doubling of death, in the service of the death drive. In addition, I wanted to show that this principle is also operative on the argumentative and textual level of Freud's text." The appearance of this essay in English is long overdue and will be rewarding reading for those interested, first, in one of Freud's most obscure texts, and second, in its analysis by one of the most thoughtful proponents of deconstruction anywhere.

RODOLPHE GASCHÉ is Eugenio Donato Professor of Comparative Literature at the State University of New York at Buffalo. He is the author of *Die hybride Wissenschaft: Zur Mutation des Wissenschaftsbegriffs bei Emile Durkheim und Claude Lévi-Strauss* (1973), *System und Metaphorik in der Philosophie von Georges Batailles* (1978), *The Tain of the Mirror: Derrida and the Philosophy of Reflection* (1986), and *Inventions of Difference. On Jacques Derrida* (1994). He is currently completing a book on the work of Paul de Man tentatively entitled *Wild Cards*.

JULIAN PATRICK teaches in the Literary Studies Programme, Victoria College, University of Toronto, and is an Associate Professor of English and Comparative Literature. He has published essays on Shakespeare, modern poetry, literary theory, and achitecture, and is working on the emergence of representation as a concept in the early modern period.

TRANSLATOR'S INTRODUCTION
Julian Patrick

The extended analysis of Freud's *Beyond the Pleasure Principle* that follows was written in the early 1970s in Paris, during a very fertile period for psychoanalytic writing. One has only to mention, among many, many others, Derrida's seminal work of that time, the writing associated with André Green's seminar, the hot pursuit of Lacan's texts in the wake of the 1966 publication of the *Ecrits*, Lyotard's turn toward psychoanalysis in many occasional essays, the advent of a philosophically acute feminist psychoanalytic criticism, symbolized by Luce Irigaray's early work, and the beginning, in the post-1968 milieu, of the philosophy of psychoanalysis as an academic subject. Gasché's essay fits in well with this list of proper names. From an utterly unsentimental, post-Freudian perspective, the essay interrogates Freud's philosophical claims in *Beyond*—among them, his use of theoretical science, especially the philosophy of biology, the coherence of his constantly shifting instinct theory, his dualisms and analogies (and the analogism of psychoanalytic theory in general), the function in his text of philosophy's own proper names (Kant, Schopenhauer, Nietzsche), the use and misuse of Plato and, perhaps most important, Freud's unconscious deployment of/entrapment by what Gasché calls the "veiled nudity of the instinctual structure of language."

It is not, however, for its easy assimilation to lists of this kind that Gasché's generation-old essay asks to be read now, but rather for its uncanny belatedness, contemporary relevance, and predictive force. To assess this claim, one might recall both the early power of *Beyond the Pleasure Principle* to shock and scandalize the devoted, and the continuing challenge of its current reception. It is well known that orthodox Freudians, whether clinicians or philosophical analysts, have very little use for this text, unlike its near contemporary, *The Ego and the Id,* where some of the "findings" of *Beyond* are toned down and rendered systematic. Their rejection is due not only to the fact that Freud here appears to jumble his earlier instinct theory almost beyond recovery, nor to the text's apparent flirtation with many of the positions attacked in the *Three Essays* of 1905 (popular or folk attitudes to life, sexuality as essentially a procreative force, etc.), but also to its philosophical style, its unique blend of speculative voyaging (beyond the portals of the known, conceptual world, one might say), its oddly insistent rationalizations, and constant self-undermining—in a word, its pursuit of its own fatality, like Ulysses in Dante's great canto. If analysts, generally, want no part of this, the currently fashionable assimilation of Freud's text as a narrative myth of the meaning of narrative, performed by Peter Brooks and others, is as scandalous in its own recuperative tale-telling as is philosophy's fastidious rejection. This is because such readings must ignore, without accounting for, the faultlines, omissions, lacunae, gaps, and leaps in reasoning that obscure and darken, but also make up, the most prominent figure in this predominantly figurative writing. The cost of such an assimilation is very great, because it weaves its own counter-tale by refusing to read the textuality of Freud's text.

It might be suggested that, had Gasché's essay been widely disseminated in the quarter century since its writing, it would be possible to imagine a considerably more nuanced version of the Scylla and Charybdis (that is, rejection and pyrrhic assimilation) I have outlined. Gasche's essay permits us to escape from this ineluctable choice, to beat the bounds, by thoroughly analyzing the middle space of the many representations of death in Freud's text, including and especially the uncanny effects of unlikeness.

Gasché's essay presents itself primarily as an analysis of how "speculative, metaphysical discourse is . . . subdued to the very structure of its 'object': the unconscious, the repetition compulsion, the (death) instinct." Starting from a discussion of Freud's relation to the theoretical discourse of science, Gasché shows how, step by step, Freud is led and leads himself towards uncertainty. He does so by pursuing what emerges as the virtually unrepresentable object of his investigations, namely, the unconscious in its relation to the death drive. In its service, Freud's theoretical discourse becomes dismantled—by uncertainty, unceasing analogism, endless substitutions, and replacements, and by a kind of romance voyaging in and out of the apparently safe harbors of other philosophies, finally to be replaced by a discourse appropriate to the death drive itself, a discourse which, like the organism, must die in its own way. In its clearest form, this is the discourse of unlikeness, of dissimilation, which seeks to uncover resisted and occluded figures of the dissimilar within the homogenizing effects of analogies, dualisms, and every other discursive strategy that would strive to assimilate the othering quality of the discursive effects of death to the systematizing, re-presencing effects of the life force. The effects of the dissimilar are perhaps most tellingly symbolized in the inability of Freud's writing to find an appropriate resting place, a place where the results of its reasoning would be final. The presence/absence of such an unquiet grave suggests vividly the extent to which *Beyond the Pleasure Principle* stages unconsciously the putting to death of discourse. In such a death, of course, the loser is the winner, since what is gained in such a "failure" is the gradual, but unmistakeable, emergence of the figure of Freudian desire.

A note on the translation: it is striking how often over the last thirty years, translators of French philosophical prose have been constrained to apologize for keeping too close to the syntax of the original, so unlike Freud's practice as a translator, for instance, or that of the English *Standard Edition*. In respecting, so far as is possible, the syntax of the original, one is hoping, of course, to carry over into English, at the cost of some awkwardness, the myriad small connections in the thinking of the original that a radically revamped syntax might obscure, or distort. This translation is no exception, perhaps especially in its respect for a more paratactic style than would be usual in English, and in its retention of many long sentence fragments. Not only is French prose more tolerant of what in English would be treated as a solecism, but Gasché's use of sentence fragments is of obvious thematic relevance to his argument.

The witch metapsychology! Without metapsychological speculation and theorizing—I had almost said "phantasying"—we shall not get another step
forward.

—Freud, "Analysis Terminable and Interminable"

TO RESIST WANTING TO READ IN A TEXT what has already governed its theoretical interest requires more than a detour. The reasoning that follows is
worth at least as much for the reading of *Beyond the Pleasure Principle*, a
decisive text inasmuch as it seems to inaugurate a turning point in Freudian
thought, as for what is written here, notwithstanding a reliance on Freud's text to
the point of being only a commentary on it. This will to adequation, however, is
misleading. An inevitable deception, it will serve to produce an effect of unlikeness
in the hand-to-hand struggle with the text from a resistance that, though based on
the phantasmatic "structure," puts in play not the phantasm as itself—there could
never be one—but one of its figures: the representation of death is always other.

To read the text of Freud, displacing its specificity by a certain blindness concerning its theoretical requirements, reinscribing this specificity within a "logic"
always particular to the phantasmatic space, is to read it within an optic that it
opens on the void, on the gap between theoretical discourse and speculation. A gap
that does not at all permit the elaboration of a theory of reading or of writing, but
into which will be drawn, to the point of confusion, both Freud's deep prejudices
and our own. Now, the phantasmatic is the space in which representation is fragmented. The regression that befalls it is never the same insofar as it is repetition.
Whence the difference in the confusion.

Let us begin, therefore, by repeating what relation there is between the exact sciences and speculation—as it has been sketched prior to the text we're going to be
dealing with here—so that we may start reading it at the point of the modification
it has already undergone in *Beyond the Pleasure Principle*.

Let us pretend to be interested, at first, in epistemological questions.

I.

And let us remember what Freud wrote, six years before the appearance of *Beyond*,
concerning the relation between speculation and science, in a text entitled *On Narcissism: An Introduction*:

It is true that notions such as that of an ego-libido, an energy of the ego-
instincts, and so on, are neither particularly easy to grasp, nor sufficiently
rich in content; a speculative theory of the relations in question would
begin by seeking to obtain a sharply defined concept as its basis. But I am
of opinion that that is just the difference between a speculative theory and
a science erected on empirical interpretation. The latter will not envy speculation its privilege of having a smooth, logically unassailable foundation,
but will gladly content itself with nebulous, scarcely imaginable basic concepts, which it hopes to apprehend more clearly in the course of its development, or which it is even prepared to replace by others. For these ideas

are not the foundation of science, upon which everything rests: that foundation is observation alone. They are not the bottom but the top of the whole structure, and they can be replaced and discarded without damaging it. (SE 14: 77)[1]

There are several points to be brought out in the passage cited: the observation of empirical facts, and not certain synthetic or directive ideas, is the base on which science is built. Ideas or speculations form the upper part of the scientific building and rely on empirical foundations in such a way that the former can be substituted and removed without the slightest damage to the building itself which, in turn, seems able at first to do without them. Thus, the relation between the exact sciences and theoretical speculation appears to be one of pure contingency and not one of necessity, because speculative ideas can be deliberately replaced by others. The relation between empirical science and speculative theory, such as it is sketched in the passage in question, suggests that the latter is more of the order of a metatheory, which has its base not in the domain of empirical facts, but uniquely in the order of concepts—that is to say, that speculation or the theoretical order is founded on a rigorous network of clear and distinct concepts. This difference between the two systems explains the contingent relation between the two discourses. But the two orders are superimposed on one another and are named reciprocally. Where, then, do fundamental ideas come from, those scarcely perceptible ideas with which science is initially satisfied, and *vice versa*—what is the origin of the ideas and concepts upon which metatheoretical speculation strives, for its part, to bestow a form that is logical and even rigid?

To make precise this relation/non-relation between the two orders, as well as the way descriptive science has of thinking and developing, it will be necessary to return to another metapsychological text from the year 1915, "Instincts and Their Vicissitudes." Freud here challenges, in a peremptory fashion and from the first sentence, any idea that science is founded on "clear and sharply defined basic concepts." The observation in question is not only valuable for the advent of a science, but, though this point is brought out less clearly, is equally important for the perfected state of a scientific structure: "The true beginning of scientific activity consists rather in describing phenomena and then in proceeding to group, classify and correlate them" (*SE* 14: 117).

The impossibility of starting off from definite concepts, prior to any observation, is controlled from the outset by a certain inductive reasoning of science, a procedure which only anticipates the concepts to be found and defined, more or less rigorously, in the course of work. Now, Freud never sank to an empirical positivism that would think of itself as being able to start without any theoretical presuppositions, as if the facts themselves had hidden their own conceptualization:

> Even at the stage of description it is not possible to avoid applying certain abstract ideas to the material in hand, ideas derived from somewhere or other [*irgendwoher*] but certainly not from the new observations alone. Such ideas—which will later become the basic concepts of the science—are still more indispensable as the material is further worked over. (*SE* 14:117)

The advent of an exact, empirical science, which rests on an assemblage of materials produced by observation, must therefore take a route that moves between induction and deduction, even for the simple description of facts. Is it then a certain precomprehension, still in an unelaborated state, that structures the sensory material and which will become more precise as and when the science advances, in a way that results, finally, in an ensemble of basic concepts? Have we here a hermeneutic circle, where one would always already know in advance what one would find? Up to a certain point the text lets us think so. Let us insist, however, on Freud's remark that the "certain abstract ideas," which are already applied at the level of simple description, do not procede from deep within and do not arise from an intuitive understanding of the phenomena in question.[2] They take their origin, on the contrary, *from somewhere or other*. Thus their provenance proves to be indeterminate to the highest degree. The indefinable origin of "these certain abstract ideas"—where "certain" emphasizes again their vague character—will result in their being in turn indefinite and poorly delimited: "They must at first necessarily possess some degree of indefiniteness; there can be no question of any clear delimitation of their content" (*SE* 14: 117).

The indefiniteness and undecidability of their content arise as much from their shadowy origin as from the fact that they seem to have been taken from the material of experience that, nonetheless, is subject to them. The relation between the abstract ideas and the phenomenological material to be described and classified is therefore heterogeneous (paralleling the non-relation between the empirical and theoretical modes). This state of affairs can only be remedied by a reiterated multiplication of references to the material provoked by observation, a process by which one agrees provisionally concerning the meaning of these ideas.

Reference to the material and to the experience to be described and analyzed then becomes the necessary condition for the transformation of the abstract and indefinite ideas into concepts appropriate to the specific domain of the science being worked out, as if, by a repeated and persistent operation of reference, these ideas were to lose the indecisive character of their vague and inexact origin. Now, this procedure cannot succeed unless the abstract ideas have, despite their origin *from somewhere or other*, a close relation to what they are supposed to structure:

> Thus, strictly speaking, they are in the nature of conventions—although everything depends on their not being arbitrarily chosen but determined by their having significant relations to the empirical material, relations that we seem to sense [*erraten*] before we can clearly recognize and demonstrate them. (*SE* 14: 117)

But, if there is intuition and hermeneutic precomprehension, it is not because these ideas are already the essence of phenomena that science has before its eyes, ideas which one should only apply rigorously to the exhibited material of observation. On the contrary, what turns out to be necessary is a revision, a modification, of ideas received *from somewhere or other*, so as to make them more apt for the work of structuration. The important relation between abstract ideas and the raw material consists then in the susceptibility of ideas to being altered by the incessant confrontation with the data of observation. In this way only—and this reveals one reason why ideas can be borrowed from an uncertain origin—what seems to lend itself out as convention will be likely to become a basic concept:

> It is only after more thorough investigation of the field of observation that we are able to formulate its basic scientific concepts with increased precision, and progressively so to modify them that they become serviceable and consistent over a wide area. Then, indeed, the time may have come to confine them in definitions. The advance of knowledge, however, does not tolerate any rigidity even in definitions. (*SE* 14: 117)

To say that ideas borrowed *from somewhere or other* are conventions is to remark once again on their more or less heterogeneous character in relation to the material to be analyzed, and to evoke a certain contradiction that affects them not only with respect to what they are applied to, but equally between them, their indeterminate origin leaving implied that they come from different domains. To make possible a repeated comparison with the material, they have been detached in large measure from their origin and thus have lost their contradictory aspect. The alteration, the modification they have undergone, sanctions the rupture, deepens it, and in a way procures for them a certain homogeneity, permitting them to settle things between themselves in a non-contradictory manner. The difference persists, however, despite all these modifications that partly eliminate the extraneous connotations of the basic ideas, modifications by whose erasure the ideas should be able to be transposed into concepts appropriate to the domain to be described. Concepts that are really appropriate and specific are, as Freud says, always in suspension, for they can be removed by each new advance, namely, by every discovery at the level of the potent and unshakeable foundation of science; in other words, by observation and experience.

Despite all the breaks and modifications, concepts remain in a provisional relation with the material. Therefore, psychoanalysis can never have a language that would be truly its own, that would be established once and for all. It is scientific progress, certainly, Freud is invoking here, but this is clearly not the principal reason.

Let us delimit a little more closely this apparently undecidable place, which has been floating in obscurity till now, the place of this *somewhere or other*. It is again in "Instincts and their Vicissitudes" that we find a first location or domain that will nonetheless not be unexpected, lending itself well to deductive operations. A place that, by its specific, scientific (etc.) character, makes an odd contrast with the abstract cast of the ideas that come from it:

> In the course of this discussion [which has to do with the nature of the instincts—R.G.], however, we cannot fail to be struck by something that obliges us to make a further admission. In order to guide us in dealing with the field of psychological phenomena, we do not merely apply certain conventions to our empirical material as basic *concepts*; we also make use of a number of complicated *presuppositions* [*Voraussetzungen*]. (*SE* 14: 119–20)

If the origin of ideas and of basic concepts appeared to remain vague, and if that seemed to be a matter of course, it was because the modification of imported terms was more important. The precision of the place of the borrowing, which is announced in the word presupposition, is going to complicate things considerably, however: the *somewhere or other* proves to have, in effect, the nature of a presupposition. We propose to bring forth throughout the text the logical and spatio-temporal character of this *pre-* [*Vor*] for reasons that will be clarified when useful. The presupposition signifies a place and time prior to the field of psychology and not solely an indifferent or vague space and time of the sort from which certain abstract ideas originate, ideas without connection to the field from which they have been borrowed and specifically directed toward important relations with the material to be analyzed, but rather a place and time of excess that seems, because of its antecedent quality, to overflow the domain and discourse of psychology itself: "We have already alluded to the most important of these presuppositions, and all we need now do is to state it expressly. This presupposition is of a *biological* nature . . ." (*SE* 14: 120).

Before the supplementary recognition, the biological has therefore *already* shaped the metapsychological text. With this biological we are in the presence of a first delimitation, both of the place and of the discourse about this earlier place from where the transference prevails. Now, as the term presupposition shows, there is not only deduction pure and simple of a few ideas coming from this domain, but a quality of antecedence, of being before this place and its discourse. This anteriority is the foundation for a profound kinship, differences notwithstanding, between the two domains, and it supports the requirement of an important signifying relationship between ideas and their material of application. The anteriority takes the form of a certain authority which makes the kinship possible. This anteriority could be understood as the overflowing of the biological into the psychological, as the inscription of the psychological within the domain of the biological. Now, it cannot be a question of reducing an ensemble of complex phenomena to phenomena of a simpler order. We must emphasize first that the presupposition is also transformed in idea, into an idea which, like others already mentioned, achieves the status of a basic concept only by its eventual modification:

> We have already alluded to the most important of these presuppositions, and all we need now do is to state it expressly. This presupposition is of a *biological* nature, and makes use of the concept of "purpose" (or perhaps of expediency) and runs as follows: the nervous system is an apparatus which has the function of getting rid of the stimuli that reach it, or of reducing them to the lowest possible level; or which, if it were feasible, would maintain itself in an altogether unstimulated condition. Let us for the present not take exception to the indefiniteness of this idea. . . . (*SE* 14: 120)

The transference does not operate only *from* a presupposed domain, but the domain is also transferred—in a movement that resembles the transference of abstract ideas—*into* the psychological, into its discourse, as a result of which it is transformed there into an idea, into a representation indistinguishable from the others. The domain, despite its origin which, from this point forward, will be well defined, finds itself affected by the transference of an indeterminateness that was not originally its own. Freud urges us for the time being [*vorläufig*] not to be put off. By being carried into the interior of discourse on the psychological, the biological is modified: up to that point an anterior outside, it finds itself altered to become an internal *Voraussetzung*, an exterior interior of the psychological itself.

Be the new indeterminateness as it may—it is an indeterminateness as much of ideas as of presuppositions—Freud insists that we must not cut it short immediately, must maintain it in an indecisive state for as long as possible. This is an inevitable move, to avoid falling back into an exterior anteriority, into an antecedence not represented by the psychological and its discourse. This effort to retain the indeterminate and to defer all fixation by granting priority to a solution for psychological problems (a solution, however, that will not work without using borrowed ideas) characterizes a whole stratum of Freudian discourse.

Confusion, therefore, of the *somewhere or other* with the place of the biological and, let us add immediately, with the physiological. But, far from having exhausted all the resources of this undecided place, we now find it necessary to arrange yet another region for it, one no less heavy with consequences. And this will be in a text overburdened, overdetermined by references to biology—namely, *Beyond the Pleasure Principle*—where it will be possible to locate, by following these references closely, another point or place from which certain analogies will be employed.

In grappling with this metaphorical reserve, a different light, different from that by which we have understood biological facts till now, will illuminate in return the status of the reference to biology. The domain in question is that of popular opinion. Freud straightaway grants it an explanatory value for the scientific investment proper to psychoanalysis, a value whose status does not seem to be distinguished all that much from the scientific domain mentioned before. To clarify the reference to popular opinion, let us return to the discussion concerning the distinction between the instincts. The analysis of transference-neuroses obliged Freud to work out a difference between the sexual instincts, defined by their relation to an object, and other instincts, difficult to detect, that he called ego-instincts. This distinction, an abstraction composed entirely of interpretation and hypothesis, obtruded itself from the domain of observation alone. To shed some light on the obscurity cloaking not only the identity of or the difference between these two sorts of instincts, but principally the nature of this last—that of the ego-instincts, always a provisional term—Freud finds himself, for lack of something better, constrained to recur to popular opinion:

> Psychoanalysis, which could not escape [*entraten*] making *some* hypothesis [*Annahme*] about the instincts, kept at first to the popular division of instincts typified in the phrase 'hunger and love'. At least there was nothing arbitrary in this; and by its help the analysis of the psychoneuroses was carried forward quite a distance [*ein ganzes Stück weit*]. (*SE* 18: 51)[3]

Psychoanalysis, in the embarrassment of not being able to do without [*entraten*] some supposition or other, to protect itself at least with an approximate knowledge, is forced to image, to guess at [*erraten*] a provisional solution. Since total obscurity veils the nature of the instincts, some sort of hypothesis, without any particular value in itself, is better than no hypothesis at all. To guess implies here a recurrence to the already guessed, to the already known in popular belief. Such belief has the advantage of leading at least *ein ganzes Stück weit*, even if the value, the explanatory weight, is limited enough. It leads only up to a certain point, because the popular conception, owing to its distinction between "hunger and love," implies that the two opposed instincts are divided between the self-preservation of the ego on the one hand, and, on the other, sexuality understood only as the reproduction of the species.[4] A distinction which, because of a common denominator—the preservation of the life of the individual or of the species—is not really a distinction at all. It opens only towards the thought or practice of a more radical difference.

Freud underlines the difficulty of giving an account of instincts in the psyche other than those supported by the libido. He attributes the problem to our insufficient knowledge of the ego. Thus the distinction between the ego-instincts and the sexual instincts is far from definitive. The observation reveals, in effect, that there must be many more instincts that do not fuse with those that belong to the preservation of the ego or of the species.

The distinction itself, which provisionally fills in for our lack of knowledge, is taken from the familiar opposition between "hunger and love." The question to be raised would therefore be the following: is not the quasi-impossibility of demonstrating the non-libidinal instincts imputable precisely to the application of a known and familiar grid? Two specific moments in *Beyond* will help to define the problem. The first moment concerns precisely the libidinal instincts and other instincts, supposed to be unconnected to the first:

> We suspect that instincts other than the libidinal self-preservative ones operate in the ego, and it ought to be possible for us to point to them. Unfortunately, however, the analysis of the ego has made so little headway that it is very difficult for us to do so. . . . The difficulty remains that psychoanalysis has not enabled us hitherto to point to any [ego-] instincts other than the libidinal ones. That, however, is no reason for our falling in with the conclusion that no others in fact exist. (*SE* 18: 53)

This remark comes at a moment when Freud has already displaced the opposition between "hunger and love." For the application of a grid, of a network of (binary) oppositions, constantly erases the oppositional character of the instincts so that only one point remains in common: one libido, unique and unifying.

The second point concerns the death drive. Freud had followed very closely the thesis put forward by biology that an internal tendency conducts living beings irrevocably to death: now, this tendency, immanent to the living, had been determined by biologists such as Weismann as a late emergence within evolution, which had become necessary and rational for reasons of adaptation to external conditions. Death, therefore, did not by any means obey a tendency that was really intrinsic. Life and death are not the terms of a radical opposition, but of a subsidiary oppositional couple dominated by one of the terms exclusively, that is, by life. Thus the conception of a scientific, biological order undeniably approximates familiar representations about death. Freud writes: "[A]n account of the origin of death such as this is moreover far less at variance with our habitual modes of thought than the strange assumption of "death instincts" (*SE* 18: 47). Scientific hypotheses, quite as much as popular representations, only conduct the analysis of observed facts (as well as observation itself) to a certain limit—the boundary of analysis and observation—which is that of deductive ideas. In this way every strange fact, every sight of another (of other instincts) that cannot be reduced to habitual ways of thinking is permanently dismissed. To re-discover libido everywhere, in the sexual instincts as well as in the ego-instincts, to understand death as an adaptation imposed by the survival of the species, implying that the life instinct is in no way affected by other and different forces—all of this shows clearly that these conceptions, despite their claimed dualism, prevent a decisive result being reached. Scientific and popular conceptions reunite on a common point, a point where dualism is obliterated, where their representations are close together [*viel näher*], where familiarity has erased difference.

It is against the proximity of the presuppositions of biology and of common sense, which first served as explanatory schemas by reason of their conceptual dualism, and to which it is necessary to recur for lack of something better, that Freud has written the text of *Beyond*. Thus, at the conceptual level (but is it still a question of concepts?), Freud will propose with ardor and a certain audacity conceptions which no certainty can help. For the indeterminateness resulting from the transfer of scientific notions and familiar representations will be substituted a radical indeterminateness; to hypotheses familiar from science and close to common sense will be opposed conceptions that are strange and even disquieting; and to the proximity of the habitual, the far reaches of myth and oriental philosophy.

The operation following the first transference of abstract ideas will be performed by bringing out within the known, the ordinary, the familiar, something like the outline of the other. It is only here that the modification of the imported, the recasting of inherited concepts, will take place decisively, and by means of an unexpected displacement. If the traditional concepts—such as, for example, the notion of Eros in the sense conferred by the poets, but also notions coming from psychoanalysis, primarily the pleasure and un-pleasure principle (an apparently unshakeable principle, authorized up to this point without the slightest reserve)—make us find again in the material submitted to them what one would *want* to find there, then by all the evidence psychoanalytic research ends inevitably in comforting results. The disquieting and strange that will be put into relief within the familiar and the near at hand, or rather which, by destabilizing them, will be inserted there, opens out within the faultline of the known, having already undermined it from the very beginning. This disquieting presence will be produced by Freud by means of a whole series of operations of which the most conspicuous and insistent will take place in the "logic," in the writing, in the very texture of the text of *Beyond*.

Throughout his exposition of Weismann's theses, Freud reveals without really saying it explicitly a certain impotence on the part of science to account for life and death. Not only does the discourse of biology appear profoundly divided on this subject (between Weismann's theses and the refutations of other researchers), but the impotence of science shows itself perhaps most obviously at places where it is not even able to call into question the hypothesis of the death drive. It is exactly this incapacity that becomes then for Freud a supplementary reason to develop his thesis, which thus will lose any real support in the order of the sciences. Or we can say it this way: with the impotence of science, the development of the notion of the death drive becomes even more pressing. In the absence of any conviction, the taking into consideration of instincts other than the libidinal[5] becomes open to extended exposition:

> Even before we had any clear understanding of narcissism, psychoanalysts had a suspicion that the 'ego-instincts' had libidinal components attached to them. But these are very uncertain possibilities, to which our opponents will pay very little attention. (SE 18: 53)

Freud therefore is not going to develop directly instincts other than the libidinal. On the contrary, the uncertain possibility pointed to is akin in a certain way to the familiar representation of a subsidiary opposition between life and death, or of the primacy of life over death. Intervening at a moment when the familiar dualism has shown itself insufficient to take account of observed facts, the hypothesis of libidinal components in the ego is going to invalidate precisely the inherited dualism between "hunger and love." The hypothesis in question will breach the classical opposition between the self-preservative and the sexual instincts. But this invalidation is not a return to an indifference, to an identity of the instincts. The operation consists in deferring the dualism, in displacing it, in putting it off. The introduction of libidinal elements into the ego, although it makes it extremely difficult to demonstrate that the ego has a non-libidinal part, will have the advantage of lending itself well to the elaboration of a more radical dualism after the fact. He would thereby gain exactly the aspect of unpredictability and strangeness suggested. Refusing thus the ease and certainty from which the familiar dualist conceptions profit, Freud assumes the right, against all likelihood, to put into practice a further step into the provisional. The step shows itself to be necessary because the habitual dualism rests on the restriction of sexuality to the reproductive function. To linger there would imply a falling back into erroneous conceptions of sexuality that psychoanalysis has come to weaken. It is only by forcing the extension of sexuality, under pain of erasing the dualism completely, that a now decisive dualism will be taken into account.

Let us read the following passage from "Instincts and Their Vicissitudes":

> I have proposed that two groups of such primal instincts should be distinguished: the *ego,* or *self-preservative,* instincts and the *sexual* instincts. But this supposition has not the status of a necessary postulate, as has, for instance, our assumption about the biological purpose of the mental apparatus; it is merely a working hypothesis, to be retained only so long as it proves useful, and it will make little difference to the results of our work of description and classification if it is replaced by another. (SE 14: 124)

In addition to the remarks that we have already taken as evidence, we see here that the substitution for the traditional dualism of a dualism that stands out more clearly is prescribed from the moment when usefulness of another order than that which characterizes the march of science on this side of the pleasure principle becomes vital to the research. The extension of sexuality will make the replacement of the initial opposition useful and necessary as a means of escaping the always menacing and even inevitable falling back into a banal dualism, or yet again, into a Jungian monism.

This substitution, however, which is only looked forward to and not put into practice in the text of "Instincts and Their Vicissitudes," is deferred, for a classification of the instincts cannot be undertaken entirely apart from the material of observation. At the risk of repeating ourselves one more time, let us take up again the debate concerning the indispensable transference of hypotheses that makes such a classification possible from a place other than the psychological, in the hope of weakening little by little the unflagging recourse to science. The biological, once again, will come to prescribe the analytical discourse in the form of a presupposition:

> . . . I am altogether doubtful whether any decisive pointers for the differenti-
> ation and classification of the instincts can be arrived at on the basis of work-
> ing over the psychological material. This working-over seems rather itself to
> call for the application to the material of definite assumptions concerning
> instinctual life, and it would be a desirable thing if those assumptions could
> be taken from some other branch of knowledge and carried over to psychol-
> ogy. (SE 14: 124)

And:

> The contribution which biology has to make here certainly does not run
> counter to the distinction between sexual and ego-instincts. Biology teaches
> that sexuality is not to be put on a par with other functions of the individual;
> for its purposes go beyond the individual and have as their content the pro-
> duction of new individuals—that is, the preservation of the species. It shows,
> further, that two views, seemingly equally well-founded, may be taken of the
> relation between the ego and sexuality. On the one view, the individual is the
> principal thing, sexuality is one of its activities and sexual satisfaction one of
> its needs; while on the other view the individual is a temporary and transient
> appendage to the quasi-immortal germ-plasm, which is entrusted to him by
> the process of generation. The hypothesis that the sexual function differs
> from other bodily processes in virtue of a special chemistry is, I understand,
> also a postulate of the Ehrlich school of biological research. (SE 14: 124–25)

Nothing new apparently in this recourse to biology. Having undergone a first explanatory sketch on the basis of a familiar idea, the dichotomy between "hunger and love," the distinction between self-preservative and sexual instincts—an outcome of the conflicted analysis of the transference neuroses—finds itself validated by the contributions of biology. It is a substitution that is added to the first one and thus completes the initial transference, in order to produce a more assured certainty. The known, the familiar, the idea of the primacy of life over death are not unsettled in any way by this. And moreover, it is not science alone that prompts Freud to defer in this way the radical dualism he is looking forward to, for once scientificity is well established (and even if it only bears on limited conceptions) and pursued to its end, *speculation* becomes indispensable.

It has been prepared for surreptitiously by this transference of scientificity *into* metapsychological discourse. The fundamental presupposition of biology, not being of the order of a working hypothesis, is subjected in effect by its transference, by its representation within analytic discourse, to a modification that undermines its scientificity.

The question remains, however, of its importing and effective implantation within metapsychological discourse. From Freud's perspective, characterized theoretically by the discovery of the very overflowing of sexuality, this cannot be the thematic of the assertions of biology, which run exactly counter to the psychoanalytic discovery. What Freud retains of scientificity, of biology as a leading science or, let us say, what functions effectively in his text, will only be certain purely formal indicators that science has put at his disposal.

The instincts, for example, as Freud defines them, are representations of excitations that have their source in the body. Representation, that is to say, belongs to the domain of the mind, strictly speaking, while excitation by contrast is physiological. Characterized in this way by having two faces, they are "limit-concepts" [*Grenzbegriff*]. Now, instincts can only be apprehended as mental representations. The excitations that are supposed to be carried across remain beyond reach. Nevertheless, by employing concepts drawn from physiology to describe the instincts as representations, Freud can use them only as an assemblage of formal marks. Features such as the impetus, aim, object, and source of the excitation introduced into the analysis of the instincts must subsequently undergo a metaphorical transformation as well as a stripping of their original content.

Without pursuing this analysis here, let us remark simply that the borrowing within a domain other than the psychological of a *set* of formal distinctions is inevitable from the moment that psychoanalysis decides not to make do with an agglomeration of crude facts. In this manner, the transference guarantees a hold over the facts collected and a minimum of scientific formality. Thus the biological orientation, for example, is not exhausted in the suppression of tension, pure and simple, as the initial concept suggested, but, beginning at least with the text of *Beyond*, in maintaining it for the greatest enjoyment of the tension itself. The dualism inherited from biology and founded on the opposition of the individual and the species is radicalized with the dissolution of the reproductive function of sexuality, by an inscription of life (and of biology with all that it implies) in death.

The fact of such a utilization of a science adapted to the needs of analysis, exploiting it up to a certain limit only, manipulating its procedures and its concepts, shows that scientificity is always already shaped in this utilization by *speculation*. It is not a question, therefore, of a simple reversal of the dichotomy, but of a mixture, of a perfusion of the opposition science/speculation, which contrasts profoundly with the theses announced at the beginning.

II.

Let us define a little more closely this extraordinary discourse called speculation.

In *Beyond*, evoking the obscurity that perpetually cloaks the nature of the instincts, Freud goes so far as to valorize even the merest of incidental ideas [*Einfall*]: "In the obscurity that reigns at present in the theory of the instincts, it would be unwise to reject any idea [Fr. Trans: *la moindre idée survenant incidemment*] that promises to throw light on it" (*SE* 18: 53).

The explanatory value derives its emphasis not only from the sudden occurrence of such an idea, through the unexpected light that it promises, but also from the fact that the sudden indication is, as the German term *Einfall* suggests, a happening, an interpolation, an irruption or breach in the discourse in question. The power of such an incidental idea results moreover from that which comes from a *somewhere or other*, but this time from a place that, insofar as it is a presupposition, is already inscribed in the beyond of the dichotomy: leading sciences versus metatheoretical or philosophical speculation.

The existing obscurity of the theory of the instincts remains opaque despite the introduction of the opposition between life instincts and death instincts. For, having already displaced the earlier opposition between the ego-instincts and the sexual instincts, this later opposition ends up, nevertheless, by making the life instincts prevail, by all its explanation via the biological sciences, and by the attempt to found the opposition on biology. However, what Freud was looking for was a way to reconstitute the original opposition he had left behind, that he had dropped in the hope of finding another that would be sharper, more radical, and more decisive. That the incidental idea, the isolated, exemplary idea has to do with an example, and that the example is that of another opposition—the ambivalence between hate and love affecting object relations[6]—is not arbitrary. In fact, it leads on to primary sadism, to the force of destruction and aggression that facilitates the relation to an object, in whose wake what will come to slip through after the fact will be only affection towards the object. The same example will later lead to the supposition of a primary masochism. This example, which gives prominence to an unheard of force of destruction, is an example undiscoverable within the register of the biological sciences. It belongs to another order, to the order of an interpolation and, beyond that, is recognizable only as an incidental idea.

The *Voraussetzung* of which the example is but an index, and which from now on is going to regulate the movements of the text of *Beyond*, is a presupposition of metapsychological discourse (of which this one here will be the representation), a presupposition which structures it from an earlier time to the time proper of its discursive elaboration, from a time neither logical nor spatio-temporal in the sense in which this presupposition would have already obviously existed in another discourse. Or again, the presupposition in question that structures the metapsychological quest is a before that is constituted only in the elaboration of the metapsychological and speculative "science," for which it provides a place, a time, and a "logic."

It is mainly because of the ineffectiveness of the established sciences, of the vague notions of common sense, of the impossibility of starting only from the material of

observation, that Freud will give a different status to metapsychological speculation. But we must also be aware that the necessity of speculation is based on the
object itself of psychoanalysis, which is certainly not an object in the traditional
sense, not allowing itself to be clearly objectified, but occurring rather, in the psy-
choanalytical situation for example, as a lacuna, omission, or fault within the discourse: this "object" is the unconscious. If the unconscious is one of those
presuppositions of analytical and metapsychological discourse, then evidently it is
a question of an earlier state of which no scientific discourse had given an explicit
sign until now, these discourses always obeying the rules and dominant logic of consciousness. Thus all the deductions that one can make from these discourses remain
necessarily inadequate: as a consequence, they will have only a provisional status,
even though we have already suspected that the fact that they must be replaced cannot be reduced only to their unsuitability, but that it is dictated by the very nature
of the object of metapsychological discourse.

Chapter Four of *Beyond* begins in this way:

> What follows is speculation, often far-fetched speculation [*oft weitaus-
> holende Spekulation*], which the reader will consider or dismiss according
> to his individual predilection. It is further an attempt to follow out an idea
> consistently, out of curiosity to see where it will lead.
>
> Psychoanalytic speculation takes as its point of departure the impres-
> sion, derived from examining unconscious processes, that consciousness
> may be, not the most universal attribute of mental processes, but only a
> particular function of them. (*SE* 18: 24)

Freud's liberalism here should not mislead us. It has everything to do with the
nature, let us say the expressed form, of speculation. As it is a question of bringing
the death instinct to the fore (which we know never shows itself in a pure state, its
appearance remaining always doubtful), the tolerance invoked by Freud concerns
exclusively its representations, and not the "source" from which these developments draw their vigor.

In the passage cited, Freud mentions curiosity, *Neugier*, the ardent desire for the
new, the unappeasable desire that incites him to follow an idea to the end, to its
extreme consequences. Curiosity, in effect, has been one of the most conspicuous
ideological motifs of the birth of science. It should be noticed, though, that this
motif cannot account for the arguments elaborated in *Beyond*. When he has concluded the debate over the death instinct, Freud writes this:

> It may be asked whether and how far I am myself convinced of the truth of
> the hypotheses that have been set out in these pages. My answer would be
> that I am not convinced myself and that I do not seek to persuade other peo-
> ple to believe in them. Or, more precisely, that I do not know how far I
> believe in them. There is no reason, as it seems to me, why the emotional fac-
> tor of conviction should enter into this question at all. It is surely possible to
> throw oneself into a line of thought and to follow it wherever it leads out of
> simple scientific curiosity, or, if the reader prefers, as an *advocatus diaboli*,
> who is not on that account himself sold to the devil (*SE* 18: 59).

Freud adds that scientific curiosity excludes all sentiment, even all belief. Now, if curiosity were purely scientific, it would have to be crowned with a pleasure bonus and would not be without affect as a consequence. In "Formulations on the Two Principles of Mental Functioning," Freud notes that science is the first to get the better of the pleasure principle but remarks immediately that it yields an intellectual pleasure and the promise of a practical gain in addition (*SE* 12: 222). If, therefore, in *Beyond*, curiosity has nothing to do with affect, we must conclude that it is not scientific curiosity merely, and that the lack of sentiment results from the fact that an affect of a different nature is at stake. Hence curiosity would be following another motif. It would perhaps be a demoniacal motif (remember that Freud several times designated the compulsion to repeat with this word), of which the devil's advocate would be the representative, in the figure of a witch not entirely abandoned to the devil, since science always gets itself involved throughout this project. The witch metapsychology, emphasized in the epigraph, is thus revealed as the hybrid product of a scientificity denuded of affect and without advantage: a scientificity that this time would have radically overcome the pleasure principle, and a demoniacal curiosity prompted also by a beyond of the pleasure principle stronger than the pleasure imputed to properly scientific discourse.

Metapsychological discourse is directed at the silent, subterranean work of the death instinct: hence, the pleasure linked to metapsychological speculation will also be unobtrusive, the imperceptible work of the death instinct manifesting itself only in its repetition through isolated examples and never in a pure state. Freud's pleasure, quite as much as the status of metapsychological discourse, is affected by the exemplary and the temporary, remaining essentially incommunicable and having to forego any hope of persuasion at the level of examples, which can always turn out to be motivated by the pleasure principle and the life instinct. And assuming the role of devil's advocate, to be summoned to defend a thing unworthy of being defended by proposing objections to and disputing the unreserved acceptance of the pleasure principle in psychoanalysis (this is how the text of *Beyond* begins)—is this not to expose himself to incredulity and incomprehension, thus furthering, more or less without knowing it, as a thing unquestionable, the very universality the devil's advocate wanted to challenge?

The text of *Beyond* is the scene of this (dialectical?) conflict between the witch and the man of science, taking shape in the figure of the devil's advocate. This struggle would perhaps be dialectical to the extent that the man of science would seem always to win. Now, the text is also a struggle of the two instincts that he dramatizes: the death instinct and the life instinct. Since the latter is the only one to show itself to the senses, since it seems to take charge of the pleasure principle, since it assumes the function of countering any possible agreement on the evidence of a contrary tendency that might weaken the apparent primacy of this principle, the silent work of the death instinct has perhaps appealed to the dialectic in question from the outset.

In a surreptitious fashion, the fatal movement that leads to the condemnation of the devil's advocate and his presuppositions will find itself frustrated. The game of question and answer which appears at the end of the exposition, emphasizing the servitude of the life instinct with regard to the death instinct, is a simulated game.

Throwing doubt on all the preceding development, Freud partly diverts the massive resistance imposed on the acceptance of a repetition of the repetition compulsion and of the death instinct. What has been advanced concerning their nature, what has been reiterated about it, is something one finds difficult to believe, as long as it has not been lived through and committed to memory. The experience of the repeated is always resisted, a supplementary reason for the earlier exposition being speculative. Nevertheless, Freud plays the game of question and answer, dismissing the necessity of the affect and the need for an immediate experience of the lived: he suggests that it is a question simply of developing arguments in a purely scientific project to stimulate at least an intellectual interest. By means of a semblance of scientificity, by a simulacrum of coded argumentation, he circumvents, though in an evidently limited fashion, any affective resistance, repudiating even the idea itself of such a development:

> I do not dispute the fact that the third step in the theory of the instincts, which I have taken here, cannot lay claim to the same degree of certainty as the two earlier ones—the extension of the concept of sexuality and the hypothesis of narcissism. These two innovations were a direct translation [*direkte Uebersetzungen*] of observation into theory and were no more open to sources of error than is inevitable in all such cases. It is true that my assertion of the *regressive* character of the instincts also rests upon observed material—namely on the facts of the compulsion to repeat. It may be, however, that I have overestimated their significance. And in any case it is impossible to pursue an idea of this kind except by repeatedly combining factual material [*blob Erdachtem*] with what is purely speculative and thus diverging widely from empirical observation. The more frequently this is done in the course of constructing a theory, the more untrustworthy, as we know, must be the final result. (*SE* 18: 59)

Because observation is determined by the hypothesis of a life instinct, of a universal Eros (the enlargement of the notion of sexuality and narcissism, even though both will be inscribed in the death instinct), one can translate facts into theory immediately for lack of any resistance from what one calls a fact. No obstacle stands in the way of the theory's certainty, so much so that the theory does not have to submit to the detours that constrain the death instinct and its discourse. The theory is trying to establish the universality of the life instinct, the perfectibility of the instincts as well as the immortality of the germ-plasma in the light of an anticipated presence—of which it is the witness *qua* theory—and encounters no opposition. It cannot shock, nor can it be a stumbling block. Now, this desire of theory to generate the translation of facts directly is an illusion to the extent that it must repress a certain aspect, a certain face of the facts, but especially of the facts that might make difficult an instantaneous translation without detour. Freud evokes these facts when he says that the hypothesis of the regressive character of the instincts also rests on material furnished by observation. Not all the examples that Freud puts forward, and which are capable of demonstrating the existence of phenomena of the repetition compulsion and the death instinct, yield themselves to immediate translation.

Though always appearing motivated by the pleasure principle and the life instinct, an irreducible remainder is left behind. The remainder in question, contrary to the observable life instincts, is not progressive (is not aimed at any perfectibility), is a remainder that does not open out toward apprehension in the light of theory, and which, because of its regressive aspect, will require another enactment. The representation in question eludes clear and distinct certainty and could be understood, at the very most, as a counterpart to the theory. At the very most, for this remainder, irreducible to the theoretical, does not reveal itself in just any light. *Hence it requires a mode of interpretation in which the speculative no longer plays a role complementary to the theoretical, but in which the speculative erodes the theoretical to the point where it is inscribed, as a restricted domain, within its "logic."* The weakening of science that ensues implies a dislocation of the exclusive and fundamental value of observation, of the status of objective fact and of the logic proper to theoretical discursivity. The eventual overestimation of the facts concerning repetition does not consist therefore only in the possible exaggeration of their significance, but is directed just as much at the nature of the fact itself. To be observed is what characterizes the life instinct. The apprehended fact, always overestimated, becomes then an excrescence having to do with the supposedly progressive nature of the life instinct and of the discourse that takes it in charge, namely, theoretical discourse. By contrast, the death instinct works in silence, imperceptibly: not giving rise to facts, it regresses towards a beyond of the observable. Such is the major reason why facts are necessarily overestimated from the perspective of the death instinct. In the abyssal speculation from which only specters of death will arise, facts become subject to the same regressive movement that characterizes the nature of the death instincts: they become like specters, leaving their objective character behind them.

Thus pure reflection (in all senses of this word) [*blob Erdachtem*] assumes a primacy over observable facts, a prevalence to which the repeated process of grafting testifies. A combination of facts with reflection, reiterated on several occasions [*mehrmals nacheinander*], modifies the facts in the direction of a regressive perspective, in a manner that produces the strange and the removed, the *weit . . . enfernt*. The *mehrmals nacheinander* breaks down the uniqueness and unity of the direct and immediate combination between the effective value of a fact and the idea that the theoretical approach makes of it: that is, the possibility of a translation without delay, just a simple carrying-across, so as to make the repetitive appear suddenly within the very thematic of repetition.

Freud's speculative, metapsychological discourse is, as a consequence, subdued to the very structure of its "object": the unconscious, the repetition compulsion, the (death) instinct. It shows its discontinuous nature in leaps and jumps, in bounds and rebounds, in detours and returns of all sorts, the purpose being to subvert the different forms that the *Darstellung* [presentation/representation] of these "objects" takes. The movements in question shape the text, without, for all that, being set out in a network of definitions. This operation becomes inevitable from the moment at which one decides not to stop the regressive movement to which the death instinct, with its endless reiteration, attests. Therefore, the death instinct cannot be a scientific object to the same degree as the life instinct (as long, to be sure, as this latter is not yet weakened by the death instinct). The non-objectivizable nature of this non-object, fleeing, in the name of its regressive movement, without ceasing, without any possible place to stop, the dead products of its *Darstellung*, remaining like the traces of its impossible representation,[7] displays itself only in the interval of different repetitions. It is not only all certainty that thus collapses in this circumstance; the degree itself, or margin, of uncertainty remains impossible to determine.

Freud's breaking off at the end of his argument, before he proposes his critical remarks, is not a final result [*Endergebnis*] in the strict sense. The breaking off, and even its result, can only be provisional, for the process of combination, of repeated grafts, is not limited theoretically by an agency internal to the repetition. A result so much less definitive that the successive movement of combination provokes a growth, a fatal augmentation of uncertainty. Irrevocable, ineluctable uncertainty, to which has just been added as a supplement complete doubt in knowing whether one has guessed correctly or shamefully lost one's way, a doubt so powerful that it even abrogates all the rights of intuition: "One may have made a lucky hit or one may have gone shamefully astray [*in die Irre gegangen sein*]" (*SE* 18: 59).

The breaking off, the interruption of the exposition concerning repetition and the life and death instincts, "mimics" a final result, which is nothing, however, but a figure articulating a non-object. The pretense of making critical observations bathes this apparent result in a critical light after the fact, in the light of theory. The breaking off constitutes a well drawn figure, resembling an experience, on which the light of critique can halt in its turn. Precisely because of the uncertainty, of the fugitive and fictive character of the result, this breaking off does not equally leave the light of theory intact. Freud writes:

> Since we have such good grounds for being distrustful, our attitude towards the results of our own deliberations [*eigenen Denkbemühung*] cannot well be other than one of cool benevolence [*ein kühles Wohlwollen*]. (*SE* 18: 59)

And again: "I hasten to add, however, that self-criticism such as this is far from binding one to any specific tolerance towards dissentient opinions" (*SE* 18: 59).

The critical remarks function to cut short any divergent opinion that might come from elsewhere. It appears, then, that the critical supplement, which seemed to be concerned with the final result, stigmatizing the undeniable uncertainty, is in fact a criticism addressed to the theoretical function itself. The critical supplement makes noticeable the undoubtedly provisional character of the final result, necessarily provisional, but not invalidating in any way the "logic," doubtful in itself, from which the result comes. Each representation of the death instinct, of the repetition compulsion, is in effect problematic; each *Endresultat* of their representation constitutes only a mixture motivated by the two originary instincts. The movement of these two articulated instincts, invalidating any stopping at a definitive result, is in effect the most powerful demonstration of the beyond—of the beyond of the pleasure principle, of the laws that regulate scientific discourse.

There is nothing astonishing, then, if it is language precisely as a network of concepts that is being questioned:

We need not feel greatly disturbed in judging our speculation upon the life and death instincts by the fact that so many bewildering and obscure processes occur in it—such as one instinct being driven out by another or an instinct turning from the ego to an object, and so on. This is merely due to our being obliged to operate with the scientific terms, that is to say with the figurative language [*Bildersprache*], peculiar to psychology . . . We could not otherwise describe the processes in question at all, and indeed we could not have become aware of them. The deficiencies in our description would probably vanish if we were already in a position to replace the psychological terms by physiological or chemical ones. It is true that they too are only part of a figurative language; but it is one with which we have long been familiar and which is perhaps a simpler one as well.

On the other hand it should be made quite clear that the uncertainty of our speculation has been greatly increased by the necessity of borrowing from the science of biology. Biology is truly a land of unlimited possibilities. We may expect it to give us the most surprising information and we cannot guess what answers it will return in a few dozen years to the questions we have put to it. They may be of a kind that will blow away the whole of our artificial structure of hypotheses. (*SE* 18: 60)

The oddness and impossibility of a concrete presentation seems here to be imputed to the scientific nature of the language used: the figurative language of depth psychology, searching and probing the depths and not the surfaces exposed to more or less common knowledge. But certainly, that is not the whole story: the lack of transparency in language that is metapsychological but also scientific in Freud's sense of the term results precisely from the appropriateness, from the appropriation of a language from the object that is proper to it. Thus appropriateness excludes the claim of universal comprehension. Besides, and however paradoxical this may appear, the appropriateness is rendered opaque by the figurative nature of this language, however proper it may be, deferring in this way the appropriateness of the object itself. As figurative language, a particular scientific language is a rebus that cannot be deciphered by recourse to what the images represent on their own: the figures, the objects, etc. On the contrary, the displaced transparency of a scientific language proper to a particular region of knowledge requires substitution or interpretation by another language.

The interpreting language at Freud's disposal is that of biology. Now, it is precisely from this language that Freud, in *Beyond* and elsewhere, has hastened to make such massive borrowings that one is inclined to think he has entirely biologized his own discourse to the detriment or profit of his domain and of its science— this language of biology is the origin of a supplementary uncertainty in speculative discourse. The supplementary interpretation serves only to obscure the meaning of the discourse to be interpreted.

By emphasizing the necessity for an interpretation, by another language, of scientific knowledge and of the language, of psychoanalysis, we can understand better the inevitable exigency of the borrowing, an exigency based on the impossible and delayed transparency of a literal language. The ineluctable necessity of substitution and of interpretation by means of other pre-established discourses is outlined the moment that analytic discourse is displaced towards metapsychological speculation from a science with exclusively empirical pretensions and determined by an objectifiable object (which, in all rigor, it has never been). Speculation cannot lay claim to such an object: what it is supposed to account for are rather processes [*Vorgänge*], conflictual movements that are not exhausted in naming the objects they set in motion and present. The insistence on figurative language clearly makes evident the fleeting character of the terms that sustain the movements in question. In *The Interpretation of Dreams*, Freud makes the following observation concerning figurative language, especially the rebus: "If we attempted to read these signs according to their value as images instead of according to their signifying references, we should clearly be led into error" (*SE* 4, 277, trans mod.).

The images claim a connection with what they are supposed to signify. Now, what is true of dreams is no less true of the figurative discourse of metapsychology: signifiers only signify other signifiers. If the images of metapsychological discourse require an interpretation that substitutes biological terms or images for the network of a properly psychoanalytic language, no greater transparency for the interpreted language would evidently result. On the other hand, the employment of biological discourse tends rather to blur the clarity and augment the uncertainty already proper to metapsychological discourse itself. It is out of the question that a science that deals with complex processes (biology and physiology) could shed a clarifying light on a domain appreciably more complex still. Besides, the uncertainty of such a science as biology, and what it is expected to contribute, only increases the current precariousness and cannot much dissipate the doubts that reign at present in psychoanalysis.

In trying to determine why psychoanalysis must refer to biology and its language one cannot, therefore, cite as one's authority the argument that biology possesses a greater scientificity. Meanwhile, what one needs to try to define is the internal, intrinsic claim of an interpretation and of a substitution of metapsychological language— namely, of speculative science—by another language that, notwithstanding its deep-seated uncertainty, has the advantage of being a bit more familiar than the first.

The same "logic" of replacement directs the retrograde movement towards the language of physiology and chemistry. The return in question promises, according to Freud, a probable, though not certain, elimination of the faults of metapsychological language. The advantage of the figurative language of chemistry consists in its simplicity, in its long-standing familiarity, though it too is only a figurative language. By descending through the hierarchy of the sciences step by step with Freud, one approaches again the non-place, the somewhere, the *somewhere or other*. This non-place then proves to be the reservoir of possible substitutes, distinguished by their familiar character.

Now this metaphoric reserve becomes a recurring term. This time it is a question, however, of a recurrence that is not governed by a need to structure the material of observation, but that arises from the need to reinterpret what has been interpreted with the help of ideas deduced and modified in confrontation with the material of experience.

It should be observed that this return to the simple, the familiar, the point of departure does not leave intact the discourses belonging to the reservoir. In other words, the transference of the figurative language of biology, physiology, and of chemistry *into* metapsychological discourse brings back again, in a contrary gesture, the modifications they have come to designate in these scientific discourses themselves. Resorting thus once more to the reserve in the need to reinterpret metapsychological discourse, the earlier discourses undergo a supplementary interpretation in their turn. This interpretation after the fact of discourses serving metapsychology makes these become like languages that are saying the impossible, of which metapsychology was the first attempt at articulation. Considered as king pins, these discourses that appear simple and familiar make up an integral part of metapsychological discourse, and they are affected by the same strangeness as metapsychological considerations strictly speaking. Another reason for the substitution, the reinterpretation, is suggested from then on: under the cover of a glorified scientificity, metapsychological discourse—needing transparency and linguistic material and lacking concepts—appropriates images and languages in order to wear them away and obliterate them in the impossible representation of modifications for which it should be accounting.

We can add a third determination for the necessity of substitution and interpretation. The regression through the stages of the hierarchy of the sciences towards a simple and familiar level is not governed solely by a need to wear away concepts and to put them *en abîme* in order to reinterpret the domains of biology, physiology and chemistry. Nor is it regulated uniquely by a desire for a more rigorous scientificity, for greater security in thinking, for an unshakeable certainty; but rather, by a desire to restore, at the level of the textuality of *Beyond*, what the instincts are tending towards: the inorganic for which chemistry is the ultimate signifier, under the domination of the repetition compulsion and the death instinct as they are at work in this text.

Freud writes concerning the conservative character of the instincts:

> [I]t must be an *old* state of things, an initial state from which the living entity has at one time or another departed and to which it is striving to return by the circuitous paths along which its development leads. If we are to take it as a truth that knows no exception that everything living dies for *internal* reasons—becomes inorganic once again—then we shall be compelled to say that '*the aim of all life is death*' and, looking backwards, that '*inanimate things existed before living ones*'. (*SE* 18: 38)

The goal of the replacing function of metapsychological discourse is, in the perspective envisaged here, its substitution by the language of chemistry, representing the inorganic state, death, in the order of discourses. Therefore, this substitution is not the simple replacement of metapsychological language; chemistry, even a more evolved chemistry, will not take over from metapsychology. Every organism having its own way to die, metapsychology also has its own unique way of producing in itself its regression towards its simplest, most familiar, and most certain discourse: that of a chemistry adapted to the specific requirements of a language that has modified it for its needs and its own regressive perspectives. It is a question of repeating in metapsychological discourse languages that—from the point of view of a living person, speaking and imagining his earlier state according to the laws of the conservative instincts—relate to this first state: the biological, the physiological, the chemical. Or again, it is a question at the level of scientific, metapsychological discourse—always a figurative discourse—of regressing to a language whose images are the simplest and most familiar representations of the initial state of death.

The reversal of the relation between the exact sciences and speculation that *Beyond* undertakes then becomes more clear. The completely speculative inscription in metapsychology of the sciences mentioned is such that the initial deductions, quite as much as the return to an earlier state that these discourses express, unsettle the scientificity of these discourses. Moreover, what has functioned as a metatheory, loosely overhanging the empirical science of psychoanalysis, is transformed in its turn into a discourse that comes together in a very particular mixture, composed of a phantasmatized scientificity[8] and of speculations that shape the facts in the course of submitting them to modifications that are no less phantasmatic. Strictly speaking, there is no reversal, but rather a recasting and resumption in a framework that does not bring about the unity of scientificity and the speculative, but which is above all a middle space [*mi-lieu*] in which the always occurring game of their union and separation originates. Namely a middle space which incessantly delays establishing the purity of the sciences through what they have come to respond to— the phantasmatic question about origin and end—and which delays metatheoretical and philosophical speculation by introducing crude facts into it, like strange and irreducible bodies that tirelessly come to trouble them.

III.

Metapsychological speculation is haunted, in effect, by what Freud calls the "ultimate things, the great problems of science and life." In saying this, he is referring not only to philosophy, but to what, in the manner of a blindspot, marks philosophical discourse without its knowing it: the phantasm. In *Beyond*, philosophy is summoned, but in vain, to respond to the meaning [*Bedeutung*] of the sensations of pleasure and unpleasure we experience:

> ... [W]e would readily express our gratitude to any philosophical or psychological theory which was able to inform us of the meaning of the feelings of pleasure and unpleasure which act so imperatively upon us [*für uns*]. (*SE* 18: 7)

Even if the impressions [*Eindrücke*] on which the pleasure principle is based leap to the eye so obviously [*augenfällig*] that it is scarcely possible not to see them, if these visible, felt traces give rise to the construction of a pleasure principle—one of Freud's first speculative constructions—even so, the meaning of these impressions, of the observable facts which they concern, is not clarified. It is very much a question of establishing the meaning of impressions, of sensations of pleasure and unpleasure, and not that of speculation (the pleasure principle). The impressions in question make possible the construction of the pleasure principle, which is the speculative rule for them and of which they are the effect, but what they signify *for us*, for a subject who represents himself by means of language, remains totally unknown. It is a task for explication that philosophy will have to sort out, and which it is not fulfilling despite its pretention to originality and priority. As well, the insufficiency in question leads Freud to lose interest in the eventual relationship of his thesis on the pleasure principle with an historically determined philosophy. But philosophy, for Freud, despite its incapacity to pronounce on the question of the phenomena indicated, becomes a part of the non-space from which ideas indispensable to metapsychological speculation are drawn. The reduction of philosophy to a domain of reference, to a reservoir of metaphors, to a region divided up by the fact that Freud refuses to rely on a well established philosophical system, both weakens and provokes the priority and originality recommended by philosophy. *Nor will philosophy escape the destiny inflicted on the sciences of being made use of and used up in the web of metapsychological discourse.*

On the first pages of *Beyond*, Freud writes that in his psychoanalytic work he is aiming neither at priority nor originality. This implies that even metapsychological speculation—to the extent that it shuffles the materials of observation unceasingly, where it is always ready to substitute new ideas for its ideas—has nothing definitive about it, in the sense of an original response to the desire for subjective comprehension of the significance of the phenomena analyzed. At a pinch, its originality could only be that of an original borrowing, inasmuch as it might adhere to a particular philosophical system, to a philosophy that would think the origin in a manner both fresh and original. Never paying attention, however, to such a significance, metapsychological speculation gives up altogether a final response to major questions. The borrowings and their successive multiplications endlessly displace any possible stopping at a specific significance. Mixed with large questions about the origin of life and death, metapsychological discourse, as an exhaustive description (through its topographical, dynamic, and economic viewpoints), cannot claim priority and originality, because it is going to have to give an account of the origin of originality and priority, an origin, however, whose mode will no longer be that of a definitive pronouncement.

Why then would Freud appear grateful to a philosophical system that would bring him an answer as to the significance of the sensations of pleasure and unpleasure? Would it not be because he could then have a response for his own use that, by its necessarily subjective and imaginary nature, could be submitted to metapsychological treatment?

Nietzsche, whose decisive importance for Freud is well known, appears in the text of *Beyond* without, however, being named, on the occasion of a reference to "the eternal return of the same" (see *SE* 18: 22). On this subject, it is astonishing that the recourse to "lofty thought" comes in a context in which Freud is talking about utterly banal phenomena of repetition. In effect, it is a question of a series of examples of people continually deceived by repeated, fateful setbacks, examples belonging to the experience of daily life. If the Nietzschean thought of the eternal return arises precisely on this occasion, a mere banal reflection on unsurprising facts, then we must believe that for Freud the idea of "the eternal return of the same" has an explanatory value of the same order as what it is clarifying here: it is not more surprising than the facts to which it refers and which it does nothing but duplicate. Compared to the repetition compulsion and to what is reiterated in regressive repetition—death—the thought of the eternal return, a thought so close to Freud that it can seem to be Freud's, is nevertheless nothing but a deceptive figure. A philosopheme such as Nietzsche's in no way overtakes the belief in fate in the Freudian design, which common sense calls on in similar cases. In the argument of *Beyond*, the lofty thought of Nietzsche becomes only a sort of coin in exchange, a mere coin among others. Now if, despite everything, an interchange between Nietzschean philosophy and the speculation of Freud remains undeniable, it is not to be found at the level of declaration and of citation, but in a movement common to the two texts, *Beyond* and of *Zarathustra*, namely, in the fundamental impossibility of saying in a clear and distinct manner, of summarizing in *one* figure, the thought of return.[9]

What about Schopenhauer? After the reply, addressed to Weismann, that the forces of the death instinct are already right at work in the life of protozoa, after having reprivileged the dualistic conception of the two sorts of original instincts, Freud writes this:

> There is something else, at any rate, that we cannot remain blind to. We have unwittingly steered our course into the harbour of Schopenhauer's philosophy. For him death is the 'true result and to that extent the purpose of life,' while the sexual instinct is the embodiment of the will to live. (*SE* 18: 49–50)

The passage cited is preceded by the refutation of Weismann's thesis concerning the immortality of the protozoa. Biology has demonstrated its incapacity to reject the supposition of a death instinct intrinsic to living matter from the moment of its origin. This powerlessness then becomes for Freud the negative condition for starting the speculation rolling again. For, notwithstanding the facts that he (along with other researchers) opposes to Weismann's theses, the facts themselves could not be relevant. Their irrelevance emerges with evidence of an opposition that Freud constructs on this occasion, between manifest signs of death [*manifeste Aeuberung des Todes*] and internal, latent processes pressing towards death. The first, the manifest signs, are acquired late, while the latter are earlier, innate to living matter. The distinction in question is not based on the facts that Freud has used to refute the thesis of immortality: it is only the negative character of certain facts that has made it conceivable.

Freud revalorizes after the fact the distinction between soma and germ-plasm. Here he emphasizes the striking likeness [*auffällige Aehnlichkeit*] to his distinction between the life and death instincts. But in fact, if there is an analogy, is it not exclusively in the idea of a dualism in general, to which the two sets of oppositions would only be bearing witness? One would be thus led to affirm that anything dualistic could do the job. Therefore, the taking up again of the Weismannian dualism is not a return to this author's mode of enunciation, a mode that Freud has not ceased refuting throughout the preceding. On the contrary, this reprise splits Weismann's dualism. That is to say that, rejected initially for its lack of a clear contrast, the Weismannian dualism is undermined by a dualism more radical still, which not only splits the opposed terms with more vigor, but which, with the opposition between the manifest exteriorization and latent impulsion of the death instinct, dualizes the very terms of the originating opposition:

We may pause for a moment over this pre-eminently dualistic view of instinctual life. According to E. Hering's theory, two kinds of processes are constantly at work in living substance, operating in contrary directions, one
constructive or assimilatory and the other destructive or dissimilatory. May
we venture to recognize in these two directions taken by the vital processes
the activity of our two instinctual impulses, the life instincts and the death
instincts? (SE 18: 49)

A proper name, that of Weismann, is replaced by another, the name of Hering.
Is there development, or simple analogical substitution? Or do these two conceptions, those of Hering and those of Weismann, function in the text to exclude one
another, the one representing principally the constructive and progressive tendency
(the thesis of the immortality of the germ-plasm), the other going rather in a direction already opposed? A displacement of the limited dualistic conception of Weismann towards a balanced dualism, giving equal importance to assimilatory and to
dissimilatory tendencies, has certainly taken place. The response to the question of
a possible identification of these two tendencies with the Freudian dualism remains
again in suspense, however, for as elegant as Hering's dualism may be, it has not yet
been shaped by the distinction between manifest sign and imperceptible impulsion
of death.

If assimilation means rendering similar, and if dissimilation (in German, *Dissimilation*) implies differentiation, difference, and if this last marks a movement of
deanalogization, then the so-called striking analogy between the Freudian conception of the nature of the instincts and the dualism of Weismann or of Hering ought
necessarily to be dissimilated. This will take place surreptitiously. Being the characteristic, in the sense attached here to this term, of a textual practice that, by the
play of substituting analogies, provokes their subversion from another register—
that of a radicalized and generalized dualism—the dissimilation in question happens noiselessly. This practice—interior to language, to its structure—that pulls to
pieces the dualisms of the two authors named, so that they appear like belated manifestations of the undermining impulse in the substitutive structure of language, is
the erosion of analogism, insofar as it would be the mimesis of an earlier plenitude.
*Dissimilation is, at the level of the text, the silent and imperceptible work of the
death instinct.*

The work of death happens in silence. In order to fill this gap, to say it in the
very impossibility of saying it—for it invalidates every expression, linguistic or
other, every possible signification—all analogies are good so long as they are ceaselessly replaced, unceasingly dissimilated. By this bias alone—and let us not forget
that the term, dissimilation, is only a figure, no less an analogy—the metapsychological text, whose discourse has to do with the repetition of death, "manifests" this
death and its silence in submitting itself from the outset to the "laws" that govern
the instincts.

On the other hand, what do they do, the philosophers and certain psychoanalysts as well? They invent new distinctions and metaphors for their own pleasure,
busying themselves [*wirtschaften*] in manipulating them "and juggled with them
like the ancient Greek natural philosophers with their four elements" (*SE* 18: 51).
With psychoanalysis, they have in common the profusion of distinctions, the pro-

duction of substitutes, in order to saturate a domain where one marks time in complete obscurity. But the philosophers try to fill in the hole, to cover it over, to muffle the silence in the jumble of productive significations. They make use of the substitutive nature of language as it suits them and unknown to themselves are subjected to its ascendency and its dissimilating structure. By the denial or repression of this undermining activity, they are subject to the lure of signification. On the other hand, metapsychological speculation produces an effusion of substitutes, but doesn't retain them long enough to establish significations. Through its elaboration of a radical dualism, and its always already undermining of the set of oppositions produced by the philosophers, it gets at the veiled nudity of the instinctual structure of language. It does not reach it through the enunciation of this dualism, but insofar as it repeats, through its consuming and dissimilating of the analogies it finds ready made or which it invents in its turn, the instinctual structure of language. In this repetition, by this return to the fatal anteriority of signification, metapsychological discourse prepares for its own exhaustion. Thus it does not represent, it does not signify this approximative activity the philosophers busy themselves with; it demonstrates the work of the instinct in the putting to death of signification and of representation.[10]

In return for which, metapsychology can go to the point of accommodating itself, without the sin of arbitrariness, to the very material of familiar beliefs. From this point of view, it can equally do without any philosophical reflection of its own: it finds it always already elaborated somewhere, even though it is powerless, as are other discourses, to respond to the large questions. It finds it ready for the work of misappropriation.

After the developments that we have put forward, the name of Schopenhauer arises. Just like the others, his proper name is only a piece of money to spend. It is worth our while, nonetheless, to stop a moment at this name, so that we may analyze the stunning metaphorics that emerges with him, and finally, because we find ourselves at a decisive turning point in the text that announces itself as follows: "Let us make a bold attempt at another step forward" (SE 18: 50).

After the elegant dualisms of Weismann and Hering have been advanced, the Schopenhauerian dualism turns up: one dualism more, but a dualism where the accents have perhaps been displaced. If the dualism of Weismann was limited because he privileged the life instinct, and if that of Hering balanced the two terms of the opposition, Schopenhauer's dualism lends itself to reinforcing the primacy of the death instinct. With him, this appears to be the "true result" of life. The conception in question seems to have something in common with that of Freud insofar as it would perhaps already obey the distinction made between manifest death and its latent work. It is to the will to live (in the sexual instinct) that the act of incarnation [Verkörperung], and therefore, of manifestation, is imputed. It is the will to live that again puts flesh on death, which is then able to take on the apparition of a manifest sign. Death, on the other hand, is defined by Schopenhauer as result and telos. The "true result" would then manifest death as a last compromise of death with life, as an incarnation that signifies again the primacy of the force of life. The purpose [Zweck], on the other hand, the telos, would be understood as the silent work of the death instinct, playing around with its incarnation in the manifest sign under the apparent primacy of the life instinct. All that remains clearly undecidable, if one keeps strictly to the text of Freud alone.

But what matters is that Schopenhauer's philosophy represents a harbor for Freud where his speculations can end up [*einlaufen*]. As if Freud, wandering on the seas, lost amid the uncertainties of speculation, has been conducted without perceiving it to a secure place, that of a particular philosophy. Towards a port, notwithstanding the diverse wanderings, whose bay would have always already embraced him. Towards a harbor that understood his speculations even before their beginning and which marks them with originality after the fact. Does the wandering that led him as unexpectedly [*unversehens*] to the harbor of Schopenhauer's philosophy, to the conception of a philosophical dualism (that by its ambiguity, however, remains very close to Hering's), does it guarantee indemnity, does it assure the safe and sound passage of the traveller? In this way, Freud would not be susceptible to any reproach, all that he had advanced up to that point being already canonized. No recourse properly speaking to philosophy therefore, but an unwished for result, unknown to Freud and, consequently, all the more reassuring! Always already supported by philosophy, the arbitrary and fantastical speculations of metapsychology would see themselves justified after the fact. The harbor of Schopenhauer's philosophy seems then to promise nothing less than an intact disembarking on well established ground.

Now, Freud will immediately propose an audacious step forward, one step more and leading further [*weiter*]. Would this be a step onto the continent of the terra firma of Schopenhauerian philosophy, or would it be rather a question of a step leading beyond the dichotomy: wandering on a sea, wandering that leads the traveller always without his knowledge to the shore of terra firma and the assurance of stepping on this earth? Namely, beyond the dichotomy of an opposition whose terms are equivalent, imbricating itself in a well balanced interdependence?

The one step beyond, following the entry [*einlaufen*] into port, could be of such a sort that this engagement would only be provisional [*vorläufig*]. The ambiguity of Freud with regard to Schopenhauer shows well that he is going to take a supplementary step in and outside this philosophy, thus leaving the promised terra firma. In effect, the step sketched in the rest of *Beyond* is a step that, after developing unprecedented speculations concerning the transposition of narcissism to cellular life, ends up after some detours in another harbor, already less reassuring—namely the myth of Aristophanes in the *Symposium*. Thus, Schopenhauer will only have been the springboard on which one never again falls back once the leap has been taken. But this springboard will have been useful for, and will have been inscribed in, the wasting and consuming movement of speculation.[11]

Without knowing it, the text makes its way accordingly, wandering *hither and thither*, towards the harbor of a predetermined philosophy to leave as soon again with a bold step, not guided by whatever intuition this might be, along doubtful paths. It is that the text, obsessed by wandering, abandons the impartiality whose sign would be intuition.

I do not think a large part is played by what is called "intuition" in work of this kind. From what I have seen of intuition, it seems to me to be the product of a kind of intellectual impartiality. Unfortunately, however, people are seldom impartial where ultimate things, the great problems of science and life, are concerned. (*SE* 18: 59)

Being impartial, intuition is not particularized and divided up among different responses to the choice of routes to take. It is a function of the intellect, of the faculty of understanding that aspires to impartiality, to the certain, and, as a consequence, to plenitude. The impartiality of the intellect presupposes not only a non-divided intuition, but also a renouncing of all decisions. Thus, in the debate concerning the last things, it abstains from opting for some primacy or other and refuses a particular perspective, concealing itself in this way within the inevitable wandering of which choice is composed. To pursue an idea to its utmost end, to expose oneself in this manner to incredulity, to the practically unavoidable possibility of an unfortunate setback, is no longer to have anything to do with intuition and impartiality. They lack this curiosity that Freud had instanced. Arising from a set purpose in the debate surrounding the great questions, curiosity is not uniquely the index of purely scientific research, which clearly must abandon all partiality. The curiosity that pushes Freud to pursue certain ideas right to their extreme consequences comes then from an elsewhere, from a beyond of scientific research, intellectual impartiality, and intuition. It results from a *predilection*, from a prejudice accorded certain questions, the great questions: "Each of us is governed in such cases by deep-rooted internal prejudices [*innerlich tief begründeten Vorlieben*], into whose hands our speculation unwittingly plays [*unwissentlich in die Hände arbeitet*]" (*SE* 18: 59).

It is to these deeply-rooted prejudices that this type of facilitation returns, and, without his knowing it, makes Freud make his way along the wandering paths of speculation. The speculations, moreover, those that have been mastered again and known, at least to a certain degree, play unwittingly into the hands of the author's profoundly buried prejudices. Nevertheless, the speculations are not more scientific, in the proper and rigorous sense; rather, they belong to the order of fantasy, but a fantasy that obeys a phantasmatic structure. The introduction of the Platonic myth is the index of this in the text.

In context, it is a question of making the cohesive force of Eros correspond to the repetition of an earlier state. Freud writes:

> In quite a different region [*an ganz anderer Stelle*], it is true, we *do* meet with such a hypothesis; but it is of so fantastic a kind [*von so phantastischer Art*]—a myth rather than a scientific explanation—that I should not venture to produce it here, were it not that it fulfils precisely the one condition whose fulfilment we desire [*wenn sie nicht gerade die eine Bedingung erfüllen würde, nach deren Erfüllung wir streben*]. . . . What I have in mind is, of course, the theory which Plato put into the mouth [*durch*] of Aristophanes in the *Symposium*. (*SE* 18: 57)

The recourse to this myth was essential, for it was necessary to answer the question about the origin of sexual difference and copulation. Science had virtually nothing to say on the subject. Now, a fantastic thesis, issuing from the mouth, emitted by the voice of Aristophanes, is a way of throwing "a ray of a hypothesis" [*der Lichtstrahl einer Hypothese*] into the darkness that repeatedly overcomes the question. In reality, it has to do with a hypothesis, with defending the question, with an underpinning of scientific and philosophical discourse that will sustain and subtend them. It is the reason why Freud notes that the response comes from elsewhere, out of a different place [*an ganz anderer Stelle*], to clarify with its light the obscurity of the origin. This elsewhere, this place, this position are themselves already hypotheses to the extent that they re-establish a state (by repeating the myth) anterior to the discourse that is examining the origin, that is, philosophical discourse and, to a certain extent, scientific discourse as well. The hypothesis then satisfies one condition, it fulfils it [*erfüllen*], and is also a condition of the fulfilment [*Erfüllung*] towards which Freud's text leads and yearns [*streben*]. It is to the myth that this fulfilment is imputed, a myth that explains in its way the drive and desire for an earlier state. The fulfilment of the drive and likewise the fulfilment of the explanatory condition towards which Freud's text leads consists in a return to an undifferentiated state (lack of distinction between the sexes; undecidability between science and myth) and is connected to the dead time of myth that science, as already a metapsychology, ought to take into consideration in order to reduce the obscurity and silence that surround the origin. At least two sorts of lights, then, are being interposed: a light of death and a light of life. One is that of the speculative point of view, the other belongs properly to theoretical discourse. The first is a strange, disquieting light, the other, clear and reassuring. Let us read the following passage:

> The hypothesis of self-preservative instincts, such as we attribute to all living beings, stands in marked opposition to the idea that instinctual life as a whole serves to bring about death. Seen in this light [*schrumpft, in diesem Licht gesehen, ein*], the theoretical importance [*die theoretische Bedeutung*] of the instincts of self-preservation, of self-assertion and of mastery greatly diminishes. They are component instincts whose function it is to assure that the organism shall follow its own path to death [*den eigenen Todesweg*], and to ward off any possible ways of returning to inorganic existence other than those which are immanent in the organism itself. We have no longer to reckon with the organism's puzzling determination (so hard to fit into any context) to maintain its own existence in the face of every obstacle. (*SE* 18: 39)

The light that Freud speaks of here is that of the *pre*-supposition [*Voraus-setzung*] that all instinctive life is in the service of death. Of a death whose work remains unperceived [*unauffällig*]. What appears, what becomes perceptible [*es muß ... auffallen*], in the light of this presupposition is nothing other than the discrete work of the death instincts in their effects. In the light evoked, nothing will happen for all that to bring objective facts into broad daylight, the death instinct not being observable, the effects remaining always ambiguous. It makes a radical contrast with the light that is the condition, the element and the product of the theoretical. On the contrary, it is a light that will make vanish, or rather, will shrink [*einshrumpfen*] both the instincts of self-preservation insofar as they are derived from the life instinct and the facts themselves. In the light of the presupposition of a death drive, of the repetition compulsion, what is carried into effect is the atrophy of the theoretical and of the significance to which it gives birth. For what is mirrored, reflected in the disconcerting light of the presupposition, regresses to an etiolated state of deteriorating alteration. This light is the light of speculation.

The light of theory, of scientific discourse, is not instinctive like the first. By contrast, it belongs to the order of "intelligent inclinations" [*intelligentes Streben*]. Among the instincts, it is the sexual instincts that are clarified by the light of theory: "The sexual instincts, to which the theory of the neuroses gives a quite special place [*Sonderstellung*], appear under a very different aspect [*in ein ganz anderes Licht rücken*]" (*SE* 18: 39).

The sexual instincts appear to repeat and to prolong life indefinitely. But, even before restricting considerably the significance of this supposition, Freud notes that the sexual instincts may only work to prolong the path leading inevitably to death. That the sexual instincts have been able to occupy this special place results from the fact that they have been put there by the discourse of the theory [*Lehre*] of the neuroses, although, as one knows, it is a discourse inspired by familiar ideas about sexuality. Therefore, as he goes along, Freud brings about a decisive displacement of the facts apparently established and acquired concerning sexuality. In the light of speculation, the special place of the sexual instincts collapses, as well as the theoretical discourse that has granted them this status. If theoretical discourse is founded on an intellectual predisposition [*Streben*]—which obliges us to notice that *streben* signifies also "to buttress," "to prop up," a movement by which theoretical and scientific discourse substantiates, supports the sexual instincts as if it sought to preserve, to re-establish the earliest propping [*Anlehnung*] of the sexual instincts on the ego instincts, to avoid the dissolution, the uncoupling of the two sorts of instincts and the forced entry of the sexual as phantasm, extending beyond the purely reproductive function of sexuality—in that case, it must be considered one of the substitutes for repression of the instincts, of their regressive aspect.

It is uniquely in the strange light of speculation and of its presuppositions, a light which focusses on the algebraic sign x that the instincts represent, that their "real" nature can appear.

Bathed in this unusual light, the life instincts cease to play the role of peace breaker [*Störenfried*] that they represent as much in psychic life as in the theoretical discourse charged with giving an account of them:

> Another striking fact is that the life instincts have so much more contact with our internal perception—emerging as breakers of the peace and constantly producing tensions whose release is felt as pleasure—while the death instincts seem to do their work unobtrusively. (*SE* 18: 63)

The strange light of the hypothesis makes a *tabula rasa* of what absorbs the theoretical, of what troubles its reasoning [*empfindliche Störung unseres Gedankenganges*], of the pleasure that science experiences again in its work, in order to displace it at once beyond the pleasure principle. What lies beyond the philosophic and the metatheoretical speculative is the myth, which thus responds to the desire for a certain silence of scientific discourse, fulfilling in its work the loss of profit and the victory over the pleasure principle. Therefore, the myth will be this disquieting light that for a moment will throw light on obscure origins. The myth will have the power to pierce the darkness because it is spoken: words of *Aristophanes* who brought a light regarding origins while distinguishing himself by his prophetic force; words, therefore, that will definitely re-establish the silence by making the repetition of the death instinct be repeated. In other terms, the myth repeated by Freud, and which he draws from an earlier scene than scientific discourse strictly speaking, a fantastic and phantasmatic myth representing a primitive scene—the separation of a unity that afterwards tends to reconstitute itself—(is) the repetition in a figure which, as an image, illuminates and makes visible that aspect of the origin that cannot be spoken of except in figures or in scenes. As a consequence, the mythic light reestablishes the obscurity, its word reinstates the initial silence, having suspended it and displaced it for an instant only. In the slender break that separates the two obscurities, the initial obscurity and the obscurity after the illumination, the presuppositional, parenthetical hypothesis looms up, like a flash [*Lichtsrahl*] that repeats death in its obliteration. By the division that is reiterated and that reiterates obscurities, the phantasmatic hypothesis becomes the lot of scientific discourse and exploits the repetition compulsion as the repetition of the death of this discourse. The way scientific discourse finds of dying in its own way [*der eigene Todesweg*] is its reinscription within the order of the phantasmatic, within the regime of a certain mythic quality, which is not the myth of the philosophy or of the science which would have preceded them as their disfiguration.

Let us take up again the *profound prejudices* thanks to which Freud has justified his speculations. Deeply established prejudices [*Vorlieben*, in the German text], whence the speculations play the game behind the subject's back. There, where it is a question of clarifying the great questions of life and death, each and everyone is haunted by the prejudices in question. They thus require a mistrust, an attitude of calm benevolence [*kühles Wohlwollen*] with reference to them, which extends also to the very intellectual efforts themselves [*die Ergebnisse der eigenen Denkbewegung*].

Now, the *Vorliebe* is what also precedes actual love, its earlier state. Love, as much in its aspect as love of the self, or as object love, flows as libidinal energy in tracks opened up originally by hate.[12] The primordial anterior of love would then be aggression, destruction, hate, etc. They constitute the earliest time, the *Vorzeit* of love and of the sexual instincts. The time of love, of the sexual instincts and of the life instinct, is thus preceded by an earlier time whose representations are united with deep prejudices. But, contrary to science that stops at a non-instinctual state of sexuality in reducing it to reproduction, to an instinct of the conservation of the individual and of life, prejudices regress precisely towards the instinctual, namely to the repetitive nature of the instinct. It is by the repetition of a state prior to sexual tension, subjected to the pleasure principle, that this latter is overcome in the direction of a pleasure hand in glove with death. Yet a pleasure whose ultimate satisfaction consists in deferring itself/in making itself different [*se différer*] in the repetition of the tension.

The time anterior to the *Vorliebe*, marked by partiality and from which the speculations flow, does not have as its simple purpose to make the whole scientific edifice collapse at one blow. In the course of maintaining the tension between them,

it is going to delay both the subsiding of this edifice and the straightforward fulfill-
ment of the mythic silence. The text of *Beyond* is arranged in this hybrid state
between, on the one hand, a scientificity continuously obsessed by silence and, on
the other, an obscurity varied by figures or interpretations.

LET US TRY TO MAKE OPERATIVE—now that the mechanism is in place—a series of signifiers that continuously mark the text of *Beyond*: the provisional, the vacillating,
the patient.

Before committing himself to a discussion of the possibly progressive character
of certain instincts (other than the conservative instincts), Freud writes:

> [F]or the moment it is tempting to pursue to its logical conclusion the
> hypothesis that all instincts tend toward the restoration of an earlier state of
> things. The outcome may give an impression of mysticism of or sham pro-
> fundity; but we can feel quite innocent of having had any such purpose in
> view. We seek only for the sober results of research or of reflection based on
> it; and we have no wish to find in those results any quality other than cer-
> tainty. (*SE* 18: 37)

A note at the bottom of the page warns the reader that eventually such an
extreme way of conceiving the conservative character of the instincts will be toned
down. Nevertheless, nothing of the sort happens, and, on the contrary, this aspect
will become more insistent when the subject is the repetitive nature of the sexual
instincts. For Freud, speculation and its development are in the service of a larger
certainty. The correction that is later brought to speculation suggests that here it is
a question only of heuristic theses that will require verification and limitation by the
material of observation. On the contrary, the extreme theses will not be falsified,
nor toned down, nor limited in the text of *Beyond*, but will be extended more
widely. Therefore, the promised recasting of the thesis by means of the material of
observation doesn't come about, for the thesis is so extreme that it renews itself at
each confrontation with new material of observation.

If, therefore, there is a place to speak of certainty, it is here that we should pin it
down. The requirement of a wider certainty must be understood as the power to
repeat the same thesis. A thesis like this can only belong to the order of speculation.
In its successive realizations, each one more radical than the last, it in no way abandons its "profound," even its slightly mystical, aspect.

From the beginning, therefore, there is a kind of seduction, a temptation to trap
oneself [*verlocken*] into following the paths of wandering deliberately. These ways,
and the results to which they lead, are evidence of a certainty—of a certainty that
is nevertheless the product of the uncontrollable reappearance of these results after
each new confrontation with the facts. This certainty, moreover, in itself uncertain,
is a "provisional certainty" [*vorläufig*]. The reason for it being so must be imputed
to the fact that absolutely nothing is known of what the speculation is supposed to
be giving an account. It is the big X, the original chiasmus, the bar that crosses out
all knowledge about the nature of the instincts, about the nature of excitatory phenomena in the elements of psychic systems, the shortcoming of a well defined, clear

and distinguishable object, that makes all speculation, however certain it may be, remain nonetheless indefinitely provisional and indeterminate:

> The indefiniteness of all our discussions on what we describe as metapsy-
> chology is of course due to the fact that we know nothing of the nature of the
> excitatory process that takes place in the elements of psychic systems, and
> that we do not feel justified in framing any hypothesis on the subject. We are
> consequently operating all the time with a large unknown factor [Fr.
> Trans.: "*un grand X*"], which we are obliged to carry over into every new for-
> mula. (*SE* 18: 30–1)

Therefore, there is no object that might serve to validate speculative considerations once and for all. The emptiness of the knowledge they are concerned with will
repeat itself ceaselessly in each new construction—reason enough why speculations
are based only on their substitutive, progressively radical movements—incorporating and manipulating all the available material in its regressive movement. It is only
by locating and repeating their movements in different facts that the speculations
are assured of a certain certainty. It is also provisional, however, for sidestepping
the big X is also their product. Because one must serve as a substitute for the other,
metapsychological speculations work to break the object down. They are caught
between two provisional arrangements: one that aims at and anticipates a presence—the impossible chance arrival of the object X—and another that runs [*läuft*]
before [*vor*] even the possibility of representation. This last provisionality is bound
by its very nature, because it belongs to the primary process, to all that has been
said concerning the character of the instincts. This implies a repetitive character,
one that tends to re-establish a prior state, to return to what takes place before the
process, before the *Vorgang*.

What leads metapsychological speculations, originating in profound prejudices,
to be engulfed immediately in an earlier time, only to set out again by representing
themselves in figures and new constructions, is the fact of their not being bound, of
their looking for an immediate satisfaction, obeying the economy of the primary
process. It is what gives them their floating character. The wandering, floating
aspect, the fact of not being bound, no longer shares the fragile relation of metatheoretical speculation to scientific empiricism. Strictly speaking, it is beyond that
dichotomy and all that it implies. For metapsychological speculations do not float
above established empirical facts; rather, they propel and set the facts going by a
process of brewing them together, using them up, consuming them as representations of the big X, perpetually different and deferred. They consume them as they
are themselves engulfed.

Speaking then at the beginning of *Beyond*, of the most obscure region of psychic
life, Freud remarks that the vaguest and most indeterminate suppositions [*Annah-
men*] are best suited to prepare an approach to this fleeting domain:

> This is the most obscure [the meaning of the feelings of pleasure and unplea-
> sure—R.G.] and inaccessible region of the mind, and, since we cannot avoid
> contact with it, the least rigid hypothesis [Fr. trans: *une hypothèse aussi*

vague et générale que possible], it seems to me, will be the best [*so wird die lockerste Annahme, so meine ich, die beste sein*]. (*SE* 18: 7)

The most vague and indeterminate supposition defers certainty; it belongs to the order of speculation. It will not bring a definitive solution to the great questions. It is nothing but the always provisional substitute for such a response, a substitute that is therefore indefinitely replaceable. Scientific progress, then, is nothing other than this infinite movement of substitutions of always provisional responses. Patience, then, is indispensable, a patience that will have no limit. Let us read, at the end of *Beyond*:

> We must be patient and await fresh methods and occasions of research. We must be ready, too, to abandon a path that we have followed for a time, if it seems to be leading to no good end. Only believers, who demand that science shall be a substitute for the catechism they have given up, will blame an investigator for developing or even transforming his views. (*SE* 18: 64)

What is not bound as supposition, what has no basis in any belief, what witnesses solely to profound prejudices in the resolution of the great problems is what lends itself very particularly, however paradoxical this may appear, to substitution and expenditure.

The remark about the necessity for vague suppositions is followed by the development of the first speculative thesis, namely the pleasure principle:

> We have decided [*entschlossen*] to relate pleasure and unpleasure to the quantity of excitation that is present in the mind but is not in any way "bound"; and to relate them in such a manner that unpleasure corresponds to an *increase* in the quantity of excitation and pleasure to a *diminution*. (*SE* 18: 7–8)

If "decided" [*entschlossen*] is the contrary of *verschlossen*, of "reserved," of "restrained," then the decision in question obeys the acceptance of a floating supposition in theoretical discourse, similar in this way to the apparatus not being able to avoid the irruption of a quantity of unbound energy that requires to be discharged in order to be able to return after to a state of instinctual silence. Now, the instincts only keep silent for a little while before appearing again with renewed vigor. Patience is indispensable as well with regard to their definitive reduction in the silence of death. What is instinctively seductive [*verlocken*] about getting oneself trapped into adopting, into introducing vague [*locker*] suppositions into discourse, is the pleasure in what is vague, in digression, in wandering. Wandering, being always in a position to dispense with the accepted suppositions, is quite obviously governed by the pleasure principle; but it is a pleasure without profit. It is born of the tension that defers its immediate abolition, following in that fashion the proper manner for theoretical discourse to be engulfed by its own death, to waste away in non-significance.

The detours that lead theoretical discourse to its death are the paths of wandering, of the infinitely provisional. It can only attain this death by limping. The text of *Beyond* breaks off by being conciliatory over the slowness of scientific progress, which is that of a course full of obstacles, towards [*vorlaufen*] a "knowledge" of death in the phantasmatic framework, and towards the abolition of theoretical discourse in the mythic silence. Attesting to this silence are the *Vorlieben*, the prejudices that already shape the text of *Beyond* in silence, and which reduce it, which try to reduce it to silence in a certain writing and a certain speech, which is only its effect. Consolation comes, incidentally, from a writer:

> What we cannot reach flying, we must reach limping.
> . . . .
> The Book tells us it is no sin to limp.

NOTES

1. *Trans:* Occasionally, the English translation has been modified to correspond to Gasché's argument, and very occasionally the text of the French translation of Freud has been provided to bring out a sense that the English translation characteristically abridges.

2. We refer here to what Freud says about intuition in the last pages of *Beyond the Pleasure Principle*.

3. Let us remark again that it is sufficient that the important relations between ideas and material are not arbitrary, even though they are unimportant in themselves. The fact that there was a familiar interpretation, a popular representation, is already enough to validate their explanatory effect.

4. Let us add here that for this conception of sexuality, popular belief and science rejoin another kind of belief, not less popular, if you will, to which Freud from time to time is inclined to grant a separate status—that of the poets, namely, the conception of Eros and its cohesive force. We know that throughout *Beyond* this cohesive force will be debated, will be put in doubt, by the simple fact that, after a long detour, it is reattached to the principle of repetition and to the death drive.

5. Instincts whose existence had already been suspected by Freud a long time before the introduction of narcissism, and which, under the impact of borrowed grids, had to remain in suspense.

6. The opposition between hate and love, the incidental idea, comes already from a beyond of what one might properly call philosophy. It descends from mythic, presocratic philosophemes, more precisely from the philosophy of Empedocles. In this respect, we refer to the text of Sarah Kofman, "Freud and Empedocles" ([1969] 1991).

7. Not only these varied and successive representations, but also the ceaseless repetition of one of these particular and concrete representations.

8. Since the discourses used within metapsychology are being summoned to respond to the always phantasmatic question of origin and end.

9. In this regard, one should read Bernard Pautrat, "Nietzsche Medused" ([1973] 1990).

We skip over the references to Kant in the text of *Beyond*, which would require a more extended treatment than we can produce here.

10. For a more exhaustive analysis of the destabilization of signification and of representation, one reads the decisive texts of Jacques Derrida, "Freud and the Scene of Writing" ([1967] 1978), and Jean-Michel Rey (1974), especially the chapter, "De la dénégation."

11. Let us add a supplementary remark concerning the references invoked by Freud. A reading that would compare what the discourses from which Freud draws the master pieces of his construction "actually" contain would easily be able to show that he impoverishes considerably the complexity of the texts. This has already been noticed several times: by Lacan in the seminar of 1973/74, concerning Weismann [Seminar 21, *Les non-dupes errent*]; by Laplanche concerning the way Fechner is used ([1970] 1976), as well as Breuer's discovery of bound and free floating energy. Schopenhauer will not constitute an exception, nor, according to us, will the treatment of the Platonic myth, which Freud subjects to cuts that are far from being innocent. Without doubt such a work of comparison is not without importance, as long as it does not serve to accuse Freud of dilettantism, of bad faith, of inexactitude: these are academic judgements *par excellence,* keeping watch over the specificity and complexity of the so-called thought of the authors. Such a work that, for obvious reasons, cannot be undertaken here, would nevertheless provide a measure to evaluate more precisely the interested reduction of the discourses Freud uses to exchangeable coins that, like agreements only children know how to make, are going to give rise to phantasmatic scenarios; the words in question will not get a hearing in such scenarios except by the expedient of certain indices, marks that are perceived and retained. (See Jean Laplanche and J.-B. Pontalis, "Fantasme originaire, fantasmes des origines, origine du fantasme" [1964]). We are not insinuating by this that metapsychological discourse is a phantasm, but that it is partly linked with one insofar as it tries to respond to certain large questions concerning precisely the origins of life and death. By broaching this essentially phantasmatic question, it obeys the "logic" of the phantasm, at least to a certain extent. But if the phantasm, in the three major primitive scenes—seduction, parental coitus, castration—has to do with the origin of life, the difference between the sexes, etc., it is at the same time the repression of this origin or difference. The concrete phantasms conceal precisely the difference, the breaching, the violence of the facilitation, the predominance of hate, of aggression, etc. The violence and the original separation which, as origins, belong just as much to the order of the phantasm, achieve a particular emphasis, however, in a discourse *on* the phantasm, which is the discourse (the more complete discourse) of metapsychology, by the revelation of surplus repression of which the last representation is death, on the one hand, and the setting to work of the force of dissimilation at the level of textuality itself, on the other. It is finally on death, as representation and silent, unrepresentable work, that the responsibility falls for the separating power, the expense, the reduction of complexity to its simplest expression—to the "simplification by excess," as Bataille would say. Death in Freud's text is not uniquely a theme, and certainly not a theme among others that would immediately invoke another theme as equivalent, namely life, the major theme, occupying the position of full, intact presence. In relation to life, death only lets itself be

understood by absence, lack, default, etc. Death, as the drive towards death, is the reiterating and regressive movement which, by its differentiating action, not only defers the realization of life (in immortality), but which defers also, in becoming the slave of the life instinct, its own abolition, immediate and without detour, in nothingness. Thus *death*, in its nature as a drive, shapes the life drive every bit as much as the death drive.

It is this movement that we are able to read in a text like that of *Beyond*. It shapes it throughout its presentation. The final result of such a movement can never be other than a provisional [*vorläufig*] precursor of a goal which, insofar as it is regressive, is always already a forerunner. In the tension that keeps the final goal in suspense, the *Endergebnis*, the drive is at work. The drive is always the death drive no matter how it reveals itself. In what is provisional—for example, the separation between the death drive and the life drive—it will have left its trace after the fact.

12. We refer here to the final pages of "Instincts and Their Vicissitudes" (*SE* 14).

basta così: **12**
mikkel borch-jacobsen
on psychoanalysis
and philosophy

interview by Chris Oakley

Editor's Note

Having tied psychoanalysis to the coattails of the French intellectual elite, Lacanianism in the 1960s and 1970s became what Mikkel Borch-Jacobsen calls the "official philosophy of France." This meant that psychoanalysis became at once the heir to and cutting edge of Kojève's influential reading of the "subject" in the decentering terms of negation.

In this interview with Chris Oakley, Borch-Jacobsen outlines his own relation to this tradition, which at one point hinged on his deconstructive work on Freud and mimesis. He explains that he is no longer very compelled by his early work, not only because psychoanalysts themselves are "immune to logical argument," but because his early consideration of psychoanalysis finally implied a critique of the poststructualist view of subjectivity within which he worked. Borch-Jacobsen discusses his growing dissatisfaction with deconstruction and the "closure of representation" within which so many are trapped.

Borch-Jacobsen also explains in detail his more recent views on psychoanalysis. For example, he argues that Freud's rejection of hypnosis was tied to his rejection of the seduction theory of 1897. But instead of following either the Freud of sexual fantasy (psychoanalysis proper) or the Freud of seduction, he thinks we must return to the "hypnotic origins" of psychoanalysis in the history of medicine. This interview is an excellent introduction to important and controversial aspects of French philosophy and psychoanalysis, and to Borch-Jacobsen's provocative thoughts in this regard. It should attract a wide readership across disciplines.

MIKKEL BORCH-JACOBSEN is a Professor of French and Comparative Literature, University of Washington, Seattle. His books include *The Freudian Subject* (Stanford, 1988), *Lacan: The Absolute Master* (Stanford, 1991), *The Emotional Tie: Psychoanalysis, Mimesis, and Affect* (Stanford, 1993) and *Remembering Anna O.* (Routledge, forthcoming). He is currently preparing a book on Freud's seduction theory, as well as a collective volume on the historiography of psychoanalysis (with Sonu Shamdasani).

CHRIS OAKLEY is a psychoanalyst working with the Philedelphia Association in London. He is a contributor to *Thresholds Between Philosophy and Psychoanalysis* (Free Association Books), and writes extensively in many psychoanalytic journals.

Chris Oakley: There almost seems to be a general will to ignorance in psychoanalytic circles concerning the relationship between psychoanalysis and philosophy. This began with Freud, but can even be found with Lacan where, for instance, he said he wanted his teaching to have an absolute rupture with philosophy. So my opening question is this: Does psychoanalysis need philosophy? And if it does, why?

Mikkel Borch-Jacobsen: My gut response to your question would be: No, psychoanalysis doesn't need philosophy, quite the contrary! I think Freud was right when he said that psychoanalysis doesn't have anything to do with philosophy; you know, in this wonderful passage in *The Ego and the Id* where he states that people trained in philosophy are quite simply unable to understand what the unconscious is all about (see *SE* 19: 13). I agree with him: philosophy, at least the philosophy of consciousness and of the subject that goes from Descartes to phenomenology (and beyond), can only prevent us from understanding what is at stake in psychoanalysis. From this vantage point, psychoanalysts don't need more philosophy—they need *less* of it.

The problem with my gut response is that you don't get rid of philosophy that easily. When you try to ignore it, it comes back with a vengeance and what you end up with is simply bad philosophy, sloppy ontology. I'm not just thinking of the rank and file psychoanalysts, whether they be British or American; I'm thinking of Freud and of psychoanalysis as a whole. For you could equally well argue that Freud, precisely because he was not philosophically trained, was all the more prey to an implicit philosophy. Take for example the concept of "representation" [*Vorstellung*], which is so important in Freud's work: as soon as you speak of "unconscious representations," you inject into "the unconscious"—whatever that may be—a concept that is precisely at the very basis of the philosophy of consciousness. Just think of the Cartesian *cogito*: I am inasmuch as I think or, if you prefer, inasmuch as I have *cogitationes*, ideas, representations. The Cartesian subject is nothing but the series of representations in which it con-sciously appears to itself. Conversely, when there is no consciousness (like in sleep, for instance), there is no subject, no *ego*, because there is no representation. Representation is the locus of consciousness, in the sense that the subject is always co-posited with it and, in fact, is nothing else but this *con-scienta* (the I always "accompanies" its representations, as Kant would say). To speak of *unconscious* representation, as Freud did, is therefore a complete contradiction within the Cartesian tradition. And that is why some philosophers dismiss the Freudian unconscious with a sleight of hand: for them, it is simply "absurd" to speak of a representation that isn't conscious. You may think, of course, that this only proves that philosophy is hopelessly "resistant" to the notion of the unconscious. But, on the other hand, if you take this notion seriously, you'll have to admit that Freud could have hardly chosen a more unfortunate term than "representation" to express what he meant by "the unconscious." The concept of "unconscious representation" may be an embarrassment for philosophy, but it is no less of an embarrassment for psychoanalysis. For how are you going to explain that a representation is not conscious, that is to say, *is not represented*? Because it is represented somewhere else, "in the unconscious," on an "other scene"? But then you reintroduce the very idea you were trying to get rid of—that of a subject *to* which representations appear. Whether you like it or not, this is exactly the structure of con-sciousness, of the co-position of the subject *with* all its representations. To baptize this subject "the unconscious" doesn't change anything with regard to the age-old problematic of the subject of representation; it only gives it a new twist.

This means, to answer your question, that you have to be philosophically informed to disassociate Freud's intuitions from the philosophically laden concepts in which he tried to express them. Psychoanalysis certainly doesn't need philosophers to put a gloss on its concepts, or to provide it with some "ontological" foundation. But it does need philosophers to help it extirpate itself from philosophy. Let me go a bit further, since I want to be absolutely clear about this: this also means, I think, that psychoanalysis needs philosophers to help extirpate itself *from itself*, from this dubious philosophy of the unconscious we call "psychoanalysis." For it is not only the concept of "unconscious representation" that is steeped in the philosophy of consciousness and of the subject; it is psychoanalysis as a whole, as I have tried to argue in *The Freudian Subject* (1988). In this respect, I fully agree with Michel Henry's diagnosis in *The Genealogy of Psychoanalysis* (1993): namely, that Freud is the "ultimate heir" to Descartes, and that psychoanalysis is the ultimate, if paradoxical, form of the philosophy of consciousness. Of course, I know that this may be hard for many people to swallow, and that it runs against all accepted tenets about the relationship between psychoanalysis and philosophy—especially in France. Lacan, for instance, claimed that psychoanalysis irreversibly "subverted" the Cartesian subject. Similarly, Althusser peremptorily declared that Freud had founded a new *science*, thus breaking once and for all with philosophy and its degraded offspring, psychology (1993). So let me just say at this point, to clear the ground before we move on, that these vocal declarations of rupture with philosophy appear to me as rather elaborate forms of denial—especially in the case of Lacan. Nobody was more Cartesian, *rigorously* Cartesian, than Lacan!

CO: Why is it that so many French thinkers—Sartre, Merleau-Ponty, Ricoeur, Deleuze, Derrida—engage with, and are entangled in, psychoanalysis? Is this broad interest in psychoanalysis really just an effect of Lacan's particular initiatives?

MB-J: I don't think so. Obviously, Lacan is a major figure in this "French-Freudo-philosophical" connection, but he is not the only one. Historically speaking, Lacan was by no means the first French intellectual who tried to mix psychoanalysis and philosophy. Think not only of Georges Politzer, but also of Georges Bataille, who put Freudian concepts to use in his early "sociological" writings of the thirties. And we have recently learned that Alexandre Kojève started writing an essay on Hegel and Freud as early as 1936 (see Auffret 1990: 447). Sartre's work on "existential psychoanalysis" in *Being and Nothingness* appeared before Lacan actually started his teaching. There is, I think, much to be said about Sartre's influence on the early Lacan. Merleau-Ponty, another friend of Lacan's, was elaborating his own phenomenological reading of Freud at the same time, as his courses at the Sorbonne amply testify (see Merleau-Ponty 1988). So let's not write an exclusively Lacanocentric history of the relations between psychoanalysis and philosophy in France. French philosophers and intellectuals were interested in Freud well before Lacan's teaching began to attract people outside psychoanalytic circles. Lacan certainly exploited and amplified this trend, but he didn't initiate it. Now, why French philosophy has been so hospitable to psychoanalysis in the first place—I really don't know. I don't have a definite answer to that question.

CO: But the odd speculation?

MB-J: Well, it seems to me that this is somehow related to the major changes that affected the French philosophical scene in the thirties. Before that, as Roudinesco (1990) has shown, psychoanalysis made its way into France mainly through psychiatry and literature. Philosophy, which plays an important role in French intellectual life, remained allergic to it. French philosophy was dominated at the time by a kind of neo-Kantian rationalism (Léon Brunschwicg), and there was simply no room for psychoanalytic ideas. Of course, there was always Bergson, who represented an important counterweight to neo-Kantianism; but Bergson never really reached out for psychoanalysis. As for Janet—who was more of a psychologist, but could still be considered a philosopher—he had his own reasons to reject psychoanalysis, since he had a priority dispute with Freud. So there was no philosophical host culture for psychoanalysis.

All of this changed dramatically over the thirties, mainly because of Kojève's famous lectures on Hegel's *Phenomenology of Spirit*, which acquainted the new philosophical generation not only with Hegelian dialectics, but with the young Marx and Heidegger's existential analysis of *Dasein*. You may ask what in the devil this has to do with psychoanalysis? Well, what is crucial here is Kojève's redefinition of subjectivity in terms of radical negativity, because this is precisely what made possible the reception of psychoanalytic ideas by French philosophy. What Kojève introduced into French philosophy was a fascination with negativity in all its forms. Indeed, the philosophy of the subject becomes in Kojève's hands a philosophy of negativity, or better yet, of the subject as negativity. Why is that? Because consciousness, in Kojève's "anthropological" reading of Hegel, can be a truly human consciousness only when it negates itself as an animal body, when it accepts to risk its own life for no reason, in a gratuitous "struggle to the death for pure prestige." In other words, the very essence of consciousness is to be found in negativity, death, and suicide; quite paradoxically, the Kojèvian subject becomes a subject only when it vanishes, when it negates itself in order to become something other than what it is. Hence the themes of death, of the Other, of desire, of desire of the desire of the Other, of lack-of-being, of absence-to-self, of transgression, and so forth—themes that have literally dominated the French philosophical landscape ever since.

Because of Kojève, then, everybody was toying with the idea of a "subject" that does not coincide with itself, that "is not what it is and is what it is not" (I am quoting Kojève and Sartre quoting Hegel). This idea of a de-centered subject is not something that Lacan invented in the fifties, for you find it expressed in numerous ways before him—especially in Sartre. Read Sartre's "existentialist" descriptions of the "for-itself," and you'll see that they all rest on this Kojèvian idea: "human reality" is never present to itself because "presence to self," as Sartre explicitly states in *Being and Nothingness*, implies a self-negation, a non-coincidence with self.[1] Now, it is easy to understand why such a philosophy of the de-centered subject would be more hospitable to psychoanalysis than before. The ideas that consciousness is not transparent to itself and that the ego is not "master in its own house" suddenly didn't seem so absurd anymore. Quite the contrary, it made a lot of sense. And thus the philosophic "subject" was ripe for the psychoanalytic take-over to follow. If you add to this the fact that the phenomenological-existential mood of the time relished in the description of "concrete" behaviours, states of mind and affects, you will understand why people started to read Freud with new eyes. That doesn't mean, of course, that this new philosophical reading of Freud was in any way faithful to psychoanalytic theory. Sartrian "bad faith," for example, is obviously not the same thing as Freudian repression, and Heideggerian-existentialist themes like "angst" or "being-towards-death" should not be confused with psychoanalytic "anxiety" or "death drive." And you can say the same thing about Lacanian notions like "desire," "subject," "truth," "intersubjectivity," "lack," and so forth. These are philosophical concepts and, as such, have much more to do with Kojève, Sartre or Blanchot than with Freud. What distinguished Lacan from his more orthodox Freudian colleagues is that he fully understood that the future of psychoanalysis in France depended upon its acceptance by the intellectual elite, and that this required a reformulation of its concepts in terms of a philosophy of negativity and of the de-centered "subject"—be it at the price of discarding most Freudian tenets (just think of the desexualization implied in the Kojèvian notion of "desire"). This is what Lacan's famous "return to Freud" was all about: it was a highly strategic move that enabled Lacan to sell Freud to the philosophers, while at the same time selling philosophy to the psychoanalysts under the same, good-old-Freud label. This strategy proved to be incredibly successful, as we know, and it provides a key to the enormous impact of psychoanalysis on French thought and culture. Because of Lacan's *philosophical* "return to Freud," psychoanalysis has become the dominant theory in France; the fact is you can hardly be a philosopher or an intellectual there without dealing somehow with things psychoanalytic. Which simply means that psychoanalysis, thanks to Lacan, is now the official philosophy of France.

CO: And presumably it also operates the other way—that it is inconceivable to be a true "psychoanalyst" in France without having a interest in philosophy.

MB-J: Absolutely. You know, I now live in the United States, and most psychoanalysts over there couldn't care less about Hegel, Heidegger, or Husserl. But when I go back to Paris, it's just the opposite. My psychoanalyst friends hardly read Freud anymore, but they know everything about Blanchot, Derrida, or Lévinas. That's what they talk about.

CO: Some of us wish that were true here in London.

MB-J: Well, as you say, the grass is always greener on the other side. Having been a part of this French psycho-philosophical culture, I tend to be a little less enthusiastic about it. Not that I want to advocate philosophical ignorance. As I said, psychoanalysis does need philosophy—but only to *get rid* of it, not to drown in it! In this respect, I think Lacan did psychoanalysis a disservice when he injected it with massive doses of Hegel, Heidegger, and Kojève. Of course, it all depends on what you expect from psychoanalysis. If you want to transform it into a vast "cultural" enterprise, then philosophy is certainly what you need—at least in France, where philosophy, thanks to the *classe de philosophie*, still has a dominant position in intellectual life. As for myself, I believe that psychoanalysis should have more modest claims. I view psychoanalysis mainly as a therapeutic technique that came out of the practice of hypnosis in the late nineteenth century. We too often forget that curing, or at least changing people, is what psychoanalysis is really about. Does psychoanalysis really change people? And if it does, how does it work? What is efficacious—and why? Quite frankly, I find these modest, "technical" questions much more *philosophically* interesting than the pseudo-philosophy that you can so easily build upon Freudian texts.

CO: Is it possible to trace a rough genealogy of your itinerary? Where did it begin? Sonu Shamdasani mentioned to me that you were once involved with translating Freud's early texts on hysteria, which you read against the Freud-Fliess correspondence. Were these the origins of your interest in psychoanalysis and philosophy?

MB-J: I did translate and annotate with two friends some of Freud's "pre-psychoanalytic" writings on hypnosis and hysteria that were not available in French at the time, back in the late seventies.[2] But my interest in psychoanalysis dates from much earlier on, when I started studying philosophy in the wake of May '68. This was the heyday of Lacanian psychoanalysis, and young intellectuals were all frantically reading the *Ecrits*. So I just did what everyone else was doing at the time: I followed the crowd, went religiously to Lacan's seminars, and participated in various Lacanian study groups and colloquias. I even ended up teaching briefly at the Department of Psychoanalysis of the University of Vincennes in the mid-seventies, when it had become a stronghold of Lacanian orthodoxy. The only difference was that my mentors at the University, Philippe Lacoue-Labarthe and Jean-Luc Nancy, happened to be more Derridian than Lacanian—which probably saved me from becoming just another Lacanian clone. Together they wrote a little book on Lacan, *The Title of the Letter* ([1973] 1992), which was the first rigorously philosophical reading of Lacan; this gave me the critical distance I needed. Nancy and Lacoue-Labarthe were also working at the time with Derrida on the notion of mimesis, so I began to read Freud through that angle. That was what really started it all.

CO: Can you say something about your work on mimesis?

MB-J: If you insist, although I must say that this notion is not central to my thinking anymore. Mimesis is an age-old concept that stems from the Greeks, especially from Plato. As you know, Plato expels actors and poets from the philosophical "Republic" on the grounds that they are mere "imitators" and "mimeticians." This notion of "imitation" has subsequently played a very important role in Western aesthetics and philosophy, as well as in Christian theology, in pedagogy, and in theories of society. What I learned from Lacoue-Labarthe is that Plato, contrary to widespread interpretation, doesn't condemn "imitation" (or "art," or even "poetry") in general. Under the name of "mimesis," he actually condemns a very specific imitation, that of the actor—or, what is the same thing, of the tragic poet—who *mimes* different characters, who *identifies with* other people. And this condemnation of mimesis, before being a matter of "poetics" or of "aesthetics," is essentially philosophico-political in character. People who mime, says Plato, are dangerous to the body politic, for one never knows *who* they are: they transgress the "just" division of labor and identity, and therefore threaten to disrupt the social order. In other words, what Plato expels from the philosophical *Politeia* is exactly what René Girard would call "mimetic desire": it is the lack of identity and the potential violence that is implied in mimesis. And this violent expulsion of mimesis is of course also a way of acknowledging it at the very origin of identity. For why would Plato be so anxious to exert a political control over mimesis if identity wasn't something fundamentally labile, fluctuating, *alterable*?

I was struck by the deep similarity between Plato's philosophico-political condemnation of mimesis and the theory of identification set forth by Freud in *Group Psychology and the Analysis of the Ego* and other texts of the same period. Like Plato, Freud places the mimetic process at the very origin of personal identity (the ego is nothing else but the sum of its identifications) and of sociality (identification is what "binds" people together in groups and crowds). And like Plato, he simultaneously tries to control the dangerous lack of identity implied in the process of identification (a lack of identity that he very clearly links to hypnotic "suggestibility" and violence in crowds). Of course, Freud doesn't purely and simply *expel* identification from the psychoanalytic "Republic"—although you could say that he does expel hypnosis and suggestion. Being a late Cartesian, he does something else: he tries to ground identification—that is to say, mimesis—in a prior subjective "identity." In Freud, identification is usually conceived as the expression of a desire, that is, of a desiring *subject*, that predates it: I identify myself with this or that "object" *because* I love it. Or again, I identify myself with another *because* we both love the same person, or *because* of some other libidinal "analogy" between us. In other words, love ("object libido" in Freud's parlance) is always supposed to come before identification, either logically or chronologically, and you find this thesis reiterated by Freud time and again, especially with regard to the Oedipus complex. I cannot describe in detail here how this anti-mimetic theory of identification finally collapses in *Group Psychology*, bringing back to the fore the whole range of hyp-notic phenomena that Freud had so consistently tried to contain in theory, as well as in practice, since the mid-1890s. Let me just say that this reading of *Group Psychology* provided me with the starting point I needed. It made me understand that psychoanalysis as a whole was a powerful attempt at controlling, theoretically *and* practically, the mimetic phenomena that Freud was confronted with at the begin-ning of his career—hysteria, hypnosis, and so forth. Or, if you prefer, it made me realize that when Freud was speaking of unconscious "wishes," "thoughts," or "phantasies," he was unduly re-formulating in terms of a philosophy of the subject (or representation) a mimeticism that expressed, much rather, a radical absence of "subjective" identity. For example, instead of understanding the hysterical drama as a paradoxical "simulation" or "role playing" without subject—after all, it is not by chance that Breuer spoke of "catharsis"; mimeticism was obviously in the wings—Freud described it in terms of a hidden subject expressing unconscious wishes and phantasies through symptomatic identifications, dreams, behaviors, etc. In other words, Freud started his psychoanalytic career by reinjecting the whole problematic of the subject into phenomena that precisely eluded it. That was my initial project in *The Freudian Subject*: namely, to show the extent to which Freud remained a prisoner of the philosophy of the subject, in order to clear the ground for a refor-mulation of psychoanalytic conceptuality in mimetic terms. In this regard, I was pretty much following the path of the French "critique of the subject," with the only difference that I didn't think that psychoanalytic theory could live up to it. Does that answer your question?

CO: Yes it does—but I'd like to formulate another question. In response to your presentation of "The Oedipus Problem" (1994) at the Institute of Contemporary Arts in London, Michael Münchow posed a question to you which resonates with my own experience when I first entered an analytical setting: namely, what do you want of psychoanalysis? Do you have some other configuration, destination, or trance-formation in mind?

MB-J: At the beginning, my project was to "infiltrate" psychoanalysis, like a dou-ble agent, and change it from within. Remember, I was a trained "deconstruction-ist," and this is what the strategy of deconstruction is all about: you take a theory and use its own conceptuality to highlight its internal contradictions, aporias, etc. But when you engage in this kind of parasitic activity, you obviously run the risk of becoming yourself a victim of the conceptuality you feed upon. And this is the trou-ble with so many deconstructionist readings, whether they be of Hegel, Heidegger, or Freud: they simply cannot escape the problematic they claim to deconstruct. This has certainly been my feeling after a while. I grew tired of pointing out to psycho-analysts the inconsistencies in Freud or Lacan—especially since the psychoanalytic community as a whole is so incredibly immune to logical argument. I mean, psy-choanalysts are like Teflon—nothing sticks. You may prove, say, that Freud forged all his case histories—which actually wouldn't be so far from the truth—and these people will go about their business as usual. They simply don't care about the con-sistency of their own theory—much less, at any rate, than their "deconstructionist" critics! And that's why psychoanalysts like literary critics and philosophers so much: however critical they may be, they still legitimize psychoanalytic theory. So psychoanalysts are more than happy to let them take care of the theory, while they are themselves taking care of business. As you can see, I don't have many illusions any more about the psychoanalytic institution and the possibilities of internal transformation. More to the point, and to answer your question, I don't want anything of, or from, psychoanalysis anymore. I don't want to change it, I don't want to save it, I don't want to redeem it. *Basta così!* As I see it today, Freud's theories about the unconscious, the therapeutic rapport, and so forth, are quite simply misleading and don't get to the bottom of things. So I've started to formulate things rather differently now, without the help of psychoanalytic conceptuality.

CO: Could you expand upon the idea that Freud has taken us down the garden path?

MB-J: Well, I happen to believe that Freud took the wrong path when he decided to dispense with hypnosis, a fateful decision that marked the birth of psychoanalysis proper. Until that point, Freud was only one of the many psychiatrists or psychologists who used hypnosis with their patients. Everybody was experimenting with hypnosis at the time: Charcot, Richet, Binet, Bernheim, Delboeuf, Janet, Myers, William James, Flournoy, Schrenck-Notzing, Benedikt, Möbius, Krafft-Ebing, Moll, Dessoir, to name only a few. And all these people were toying with the idea of a "subconscious," "unconscious," or "co-conscious" activity of the mind which, in turn, they all saw as a *hypnotic* or "*trance*" phenomena. In this respect, Breuer's and Freud's first theoretical elaborations on the "splitting of consciousness" were hardly original; the same can be said about the various hypnotic techniques that Freud used with his hysterics. If you look at the chronology of things, you will see that Freud pretty much followed the "technical" trends of the time: after having been a Charcot devotee, he started using Bernheim's very direct "suggestive therapy"; then he had his patients re-live earlier traumas as Bourru, Burot, and Janet had done; and finally he used the "pressure technique" in keeping with Bernheim's then current ideas about the efficacy of *light* hypnosis. You could even argue that the method of "free associations," which is usually seen as a major innovation, is nothing but a variant of what Janet called "automatic talking"—itself a variant of the widely used "automatic writing." Anyway, all of these methods were intended to induce some kind of hypnotic or "hypnoid" state, as Freud himself admitted in *The Interpretation of Dreams* with regard to his "free associations" method (*SE* 4: 102).

As you know, Freud also claimed to have abandoned hypnosis at some point during the mid-1890s. I say "claimed," for I don't think Freud ever cleared the analytic situation from its hypnotic component. In fact, Freud only dispensed with the openly directive or "suggestive" technique of hypnosis—and even that is a matter for discussion in light of Freud's very authoritarian way of conducting analyses! But it cannot be disputed that this alleged break with hypnosis is of tremendous importance for the self-interpretation of psychoanalysis, since it is the very ground upon which Freud claims theoretical originality and practical superiority. Now, why

Freud initially decided to dispense with hypnosis in all its forms is a complicated issue, for the reasons later set forth by Freud himself are very diverse and sometimes quite simply contradictory. For instance, Freud would say in one place that he abandoned hypnosis because too many people resisted it; in another he would claim that it was because hypnosis didn't allow the resistance to manifest itself, etc. Also, the chronology is difficult to establish, for one never really knows what Freud means by "hypnosis." Did he mean the cathartic method, which would imply that the break occurred when he started the "pressure technique"? Or did he include the "*Druckmethode*" itself, which he described as a "light" or "mild" hypnosis and compared to hypnotic crystal gazing (*SE* 2: 107, 113, 271)? If so, the alleged break would have taken place later, when he decided to have patient's associate "freely," without pressing on their foreheads. As I see it, Freud's negative attitude towards hypnosis is directly related to the collapse of the "seduction theory" in 1897. Whatever the actual chronology of his therapeutic techniques may have been, Freud seems to have associated hypnosis—that is to say, in his mind, *suggestion*—with the memory of this painful episode. He says this in so many words in the *Autobiographical Study* (1925), when he states that *because of the technique he was using at the time*, that is, the "pressure technique," patients would come up with tales of "seduction" (*SE* 20: 33)—what we today call "sexual abuse." This is a very important statement, for here Freud acknowledges something that he vehemently denies most of the time (see *SE* 20: 35); namely, that he *suggested* the alleged memories of abuse. What happened in 1897, I think, is that Freud, after having announced publicly that he had discovered the "*caput Nili*" of hysteria, realized that his patients had simply complied with his own theoretical expectations—something his hypnotist colleagues, like Krafft-Ebing, Moll of Löwenfeld, had said all along.[3] In other words, he had made a fool of himself, exactly as his master Charcot did when he denied having "suggested" the clinical manifestations of the "*grande hystérie*," as Bernheim claimed. At this point, Freud had only two choices. He could either acknowledge the hypnotico-suggestive element in the psychotherapy of hysteria— which would have compromised his claims to originality, since this was hardly news for his post-Bernheimian colleagues. Or he could deny the whole thing— which he in fact chose to do. While carefully refraining from publicly acknowledging the collapse of his seduction theory for quite a while, he set out to silently reformulate it in terms of Fliessian infantile sexuality and the Oedipus complex, the argument being that his patients had unconsciously *wished* to be "seduced" by the father, the brother, and so forth.

Or again, instead of admitting that these stories of sexual abuse had been the product of the hypnotic technique that he was using, Freud decided to attribute them to the oedipal unconscious of his patients—that is to say, if you allow me to play on the ambiguity of this word, of his *subjects*. As we know, the whole psychoanalytic edifice rests on this reversal and it amounts, in my view, to a pure and simple *denial* of the role played by hypnosis and suggestion in the elaboration of the seduction theory. The "unconscious," wish-fulfilling phantasy, infantile sexuality, the Oedipus complex—all these concepts are direct, if clandestine, products of hypnosis and, therefore, have no more validity than, say, Charcot's "*grande hystérie*" or Janet's "psychological automatism." So it's pretty easy to understand why Freud so quickly disassociated himself from hypnotherapy after the seduction episode, and also why he would be so adamant about not having "suggested" the memories of sexual abuse; it was a way of exorcizing, quasi-magically, an enormous problem that could potentially invalidate all his theories. That's why I am saying that Freud took the wrong path at one point: instead of confronting the problem of hypnosis and/or "suggestion," which was so clearly at the basis of all the phenomena he was studying, he simply side-stepped it and then covered up his tracks. I suggest we do the opposite. Rather than sticking religiously to Freud's dubious theoretical constructions—which is what Jeffrey Masson and his feminist followers still do when they advocate a return to the initial seduction theory—let's try to understand something about their "hypnotic" origins. Clearly, it all started with the investigation of trance-like states, and this is, in my view, how we should reframe psychoanalytic theory and practice. It's not to Freud that we should return, whether it be Freud 1 or Freud 2, but to Bernheim, Delboeuf, William James, Janet and all these other people. They will probably not provide us with the right answers, but at least they had the right questions: What are the relations between hypnosis and hysterical phenomena, hypnosis and dream, hypnosis and "the unconscious"? Why and how does hypnosis cure certain people? What lies behind hypnotic "suggestion"? Is there anything like a hypnotic *state*? Those were the very important questions out of which psychoanalysis grew, and they are still waiting for answers—for psychoanalysis has simply prevented us from addressing them.

CO: Part of your initiative, then, is to reinstall trance into the heart of psychoanalysis. As you say, trance seems almost identical with transference, transference being a light hypnotic state.

MB-J: Yes, a light and very *controlled* hypnotic state.

CO: Like Freud, Lacan stated that trance states should be utterly excluded from the psychoanalytic encounter (1977: 49; see Borch-Jacobsen 1993: 194, n. 49), and you, I think, are quite right to find the absurdity of that. For it is here that the therapeutic efficacy occurs. But there is often no analysis of trance or of the dissolution of the transference.

MB-J: In my opinion, the dissolution of the transference is a false problem.

CO: Well, there's a question mark—since some of us argue that it is an impossible project, that transference cannot be dissolved.

MB-J: That's more or less what I *used* to say. In my essay "Hypnosis in Psychoanalysis" (1993: 39–61), which I wrote ten years ago, I argued that transference could not be dissolved. At the time, I was still in the business of "deconstructing" psychoanalysis, or critiquing it from within. More specifically, I wanted to show that although Freud had officially abandoned hypnosis, it came back with a vengeance in his own practice under the guise of transference. Basically, I described transference as a kind of "return-of-the-repressed," as a disguised form of hypnosis—a very light and controlled state of trance to be sure, a trance focussed on the person of a *silent* "hypnotist," etc., but a trance nonetheless. I therefore objected to the idea that psychoanalysis had once and for all broken off with hypnosis, with the obvious implication that the therapeutic results of psychoanalytic treatment were not due to the analysis of transference, but rather to the "hypnotic" element present in the transferential rapport. But because I was still working from within the psychoanalytic framework, I ended up arguing—contrary to what Freud had claimed—that transference (i.e., hypnosis) could not be "dissolved" at the end of the treatment. This was a typical deconstructive move that amounted to saying that psychoanalysis is interminable.

Today I would put things quite differently. I would say that transference is indissoluble and interminable *only within the psychoanalytic framework* or, if you prefer, only within the "closure" of its self-representation. It is only within the hypnophobic set-up of analysis that hypnosis takes the form of a "transference" that drags on and on. I mean, this is what the whole psychoanalytic business is about—eliciting the transference for the sake of dissolving it. No wonder it takes decades to achieve that goal! But hypnosis doesn't need to take this form, even though Freud and his followers have successfully managed to convince almost everyone that hypnosis is just another form of transference. Hypnotherapy can very well be conducted without any form of transference. What is so striking about hypnosis is that anyone can walk in and put you in a trance, whether it be deep or light. All it requires is that you go along with it. Clearly the person who hypnotizes you doesn't need to be a substitute for your father, mother, sister, or the big Other. Freud claimed that the hypnotist occupies the place of the ego ideal, like the *Füher* in crowds, and Lacan contended that he was the incarnation of the *object petit a* of phantasm, confused with the ego ideal. Maybe these are good descriptions of what happens in Freudian or Lacanian *analyses*, but they just don't make sense when applied to hypnosis at large. I have attended large seminars in Ericksonian hypnosis, during which people would randomly pick a partner and hypnotize each other to train themselves. The effects were sometimes quite striking—I can testify to that—and they obviously had nothing to do with transference, since people not only didn't know each other, but they also practiced on each other for only a few minutes at a time before swapping partners. I should also add that most of these people were beginners, which means that they could hardly be phantasmatically invested with the prestige of the analyst having undergone years of training in a psychoanalytic institute, or on Lacan's couch . . .

CO: So this would be in contradistinction to the Lacanian reading of what installs transference, which is the assumption of absolute knowledge, of the subject-supposed-to-know. Are you saying that trance states are not informed by that, and that they involve a radical cleavage from that particular understanding?

MB-J: Absolutely. You don't need to assume that the hypnotist knows everything about your unconscious or your desire. You don't even need to suppose that this person is a good hypnotist! This idea of an omnipotent and omniscient hypnotist is a caricature that has more to do with cheap novels—and probably also with Freud's personal relationship with Charcot—than with the actual practice of hypnosis. The only thing that really matters is the subject's willingness to play the hypnotic "game" with the operator, and the latter's ability to utilize and enhance the "rapport" thus established. The rest follows quite naturally. Let me add that you may produce a striking therapeutic effect in just one session, without doing any interpretation, perhaps even without talking. So you don't need to go through the whole process of eliciting the transference, analyzing the resistances, and so forth, like we find in the orthodox Freudian cure. You don't even need to speak or achieve the famous Lacanian "full speech"—although Lacan was clearly on the right path in his 1953 "Rome Discourse" when he emphasized the role of speech to the detriment of any "realistic" consideration. For it is quite true that the efficacy of the therapeutic "rapport" has nothing to do with retrieving memories of the past, or with adapting the ego to reality. It rests much more on the "here and now" of a performative and interactive—what Lacan called "intersubjective"—reconstruction of reality. In this respect, Lacan's practice was obviously much closer to the practice of any old hypnotist than to the orthodox, New York way of conducting analyses. After all, what's "full speech"—this intersubjective speech that *produces* rather than re-produces reality—if not a sophisticated form of suggestion? But as you suggested, Lacan chose to deny this, for reasons that were philosophical as well as "political." He even went so far as to solemnly *condemn* the use of hypnosis and of trance-like-states—which is too bad. For his own theories about "full speech" and the signifier would have made much more sense within a frankly hypnotic framework. Whether he knew it or not, Lacan was using hypnotic techniques.

Actually, I'm very struck by the similarity between Lacan's use of jokes and puns, and one of Milton Erickson's favourite methods of inducing hypnosis: namely, the "confusion technique" (1964).[4] When faced with a subject difficult to hypnotize, Erickson would engage in a wild series of puns and non-sequiturs that would usually place the subject in a trance. Now, isn't this what Lacan did too, in theory as well as in practice? When you empty words of their meaning—which is exactly what Lacan's successive theories of "full speech," the signifier, and *la langue* are all about—you inevitably create a hypnotic setting; and this can occur in an analytic session just as well as in a frankly hypnotic one. Within this setting, anything you say will do the trick—the more absurd, the better.

CO: Earlier, you mentioned the work of Michel Henry. I believe that Lacan played a part in the suppression of this work.

MB-J: That's true. When *The Essence of Manifestation* appeared in 1963, an impressive book of 900 pages, Lacan made fun of it. As a result, nobody read Michel Henry for two decades.

CO: In your book, *Lacan: The Absolute Master* (1991), you describe Henry's book as being the definitive commentary on the unconscious—yet this is relegated to a footnote. Still, from your involvement in the issue of the *Stanford Literature Review* (1989) dedicated to Henry's work, it is clear that he has played a tremendous role in your own work.

MB-J: You're right, Michel Henry's work is quite important to me. I read his *Essence of Manifestation* early on, when I was a student of philosophy, but at the time considered him as a rather old-fashioned phenomenologist—not as someone who might have an impact on my own work. That changed in 1985, when Henry published his *Genealogy of Psychoanalysis*. François Roustang immediately sent me a letter, saying 'Read this!', and I remember very well that I was quite stunned when I did. This was still "old-fashioned" Michel Henry, but here at last was a philosophical reading of Freud with which I felt in deep agreement. Henry's reading dealt with exactly the same issues that interested me at the time—affect, the non-representational stratum of the psyche—but with a depth and philosophical rigor that impressed me. I cannot really say that Henry influenced me, for in a way I simply recognized myself in some of his ideas. But there is no doubt that his book enabled me to sharpen my critique of psychoanalysis, and to formulate my own ideas much more rigorously. Henry also made me realize once and for all that my own critique of psychoanalysis implied a critique of the French "critique of the subject"—something I had been reluctant to admit until then. For these things I owe him a lot.

Now, to answer your specific question about the treatment of Henry in my book on Lacan, let me just say that my essay on the *Genealogy of Psychoanalysis* had appeared in French well before the book; so I had already paid my theoretical dues to Henry at the time. But you are right to point out that Henry is relegated to a footnote in this book, which doesn't do justice to the importance that he has in my own itinerary. He is not the only one in this respect; Roustang, for instance, is barely mentioned. But all this has to do with the reading strategy I developed with regard to Lacan. Contrary to what I did in my book on Freud, I didn't speak for myself in *The Absolute Master*. It's not just that I "deconstructed" Lacan from within—actually, I don't think this is a deconstructive reading—but that I am simply *not there* in the book. One of my Lacanian critics diagnosed my reading of Lacan as betraying voyeuristic tendencies (Doumit 1991: 276, n. 3), and although he hardly meant this as a compliment, he was not far from the truth. In this particular book, I just wanted to show how the Lacanian machinery works, without passing any judgement on it. I adopted a very pedagogical, even pedestrian approach to Lacan's work, with the idea that this was probably the worst blow you could inflict on his theories; that is, to make them understandable. So I tried to remain as "neutral" as I could and this is why I refrained from quoting too extensively my friends and theoretical allies. As Descartes would say, "*larvatus prodeo*," I advanced behind a mask.

CO: You kept your desire veiled.

MB-J: Exactly—although I think what I was doing was pretty obvious. When my book appeared in France, it was immediately and very violently denounced by Lacanians. Gérard Miller even went so far as to deplore that so many trees had been wasted on printing it![5] So people understood very well the implications of my demonstration. Still, the way the book is written is a little disturbing, and you're right to point it out.

CO: The title, I think, is the give-away; it's so saturated with irony. But could you elaborate more on the relation between your work and Henry's on this idea of trance?

MB-J: Let me say, to begin with, that I don't agree with Henry on everything. In my essay on his *Genealogy*, I was as critical as I was admiring. For example, I'm not quite convinced by his description of the original sphere of subjectivity in terms of "self affection" and absolute immanence to self. I have some quarrels with that, for I think he falls back here into a philosophy of the subject that he critiques so well the rest of the time. In my view, the non-representational sphere is not closed in *itself*, quite the contrary. But I fully agree with the critical aspects of Henry's work when he reproaches Western philosophy since Descartes for having been unduly reduced to being-represented by and for a subject. This is a very important state-ment—for it has nothing to do, despite appearances, with the Heideggerian critique of the "metaphysics of subjectivity" that has so dominated French philosophy from Kojève to Lacan. The Heideggerian critique of the subject is conducted from the point of view of the truth of Being and of *Dasein*, conceived of as always already ahead of itself, always already de-centered, always already removed from itself, etc. But for Michel Henry, this Heideggerian critique of the subject is itself the logical outcome of a philosophy of the subject that defines it in terms of representation, that is to say, in terms of transcendence. From the very moment the Cogito is uni-laterally interpreted as an "*I think*," the subject will indeed always already be "*over there*," in the objectivity of representation, and it will be unable to be its own foun-dation. In other words, Heidegger and the modern French critics of the subject who follow are themselves part of what they claim to critique, "subvert," or "decon-struct." To this, Henry opposes a critique of the subject (of representation) that is not conducted from the perspective of negativity, but from that of a radical *posi-tivity* which he calls "affectivity," "immanence," or "life."

My own interest in this reversal of perspective lies in the fact that it allows us to do philosophical justice to affect, the body, sensation—in brief, to all the non-rep-resentational aspects of human experience that the philosophy of the subject has so consistently avoided, neglected, or rejected, because it defines everything in terms of transcendence and representation. Again, I'm not really interested in Henry's notion of "self-affection" or "immanence." But I am clearly interested in the idea of a non-representational sphere of the psyche, and I fully agree with Henry when he claims that this is what the Freudian "unconscious" is all about. What Freud described as "unconscious *thoughts*," "repressed *ideas*," *Vorstellungsräsentanten des Triebes*, is precisely something that doesn't pertain to representation, something—and here I go back to what I said before—that has much more to do with hypnosis and trance-like states. Hypnosis (by which I mean the actual *experience* of hypnosis, not its study "in the third person") is precisely what allows us to access this non-representational sphere and describe it, "phenomenologically" so to speak. That is my tack on this whole issue of the "unconscious": what Henry describes in phenomenological terms as the essence of subjectivity and life, I would like to describe in the more modest terms of trance states. Interestingly enough, Henry is now working on a book on intersubjectivity in which, he tells me, he too addresses the issue of hypnosis.

CO: Much of this seems framed by the notion that there is a "closure of representation," and that the unconscious is "structured like a language." In the wake of Derrida's work, I still wonder if there is not a fundamental incoherence in saying that there something outside of representation. Does the potentiality for thought, for representation, spring from the irrepresentable? Although I like this idea, how do we really make sense of it? How can we ever have an *experience* of that—since it's outside representation? Or again, how can there be any sort of access to drive without there being any psychic representation of that?

MB-J: There are two aspects to your question. You're asking whether one can access the irrepresentable without its being psychically represented, by which I assume you mean: *represented in the form of representation*, of a *Vorstellungsräsentanten des Triebes*, as Freud would put it. Empirically speaking, it is clear that the two dimensions are most often present simultaneously; you may feel an affect *and* represent to yourself the cause of that affect. Or, if hypnotized, you may execute a suggestion *while* watching yourself doing it. But even if representation was always present, it wouldn't follow that there is nothing *but* representation. This is the properly theoretical aspect of your question: Can we have *any* experience that would not be representational? Lacan would say no. For him, like most other French "structuralist" or "poststructuralist" thinkers, human experience is exclusively that of discourse, language, and the symbolic. We can, therefore, simply not have a direct experience of what is beyond representation, whether it be the "real," affect, the body, or animality. However much we try, we will still *represent* it and thereby make it vanish—since discourse, language, and the symbolic irremediably *absent* what they represent. Behind this Lacanian theme and its French variations, like the Derridian "closure of representation," there is, once more, Kojève's anthropological reading of Hegel and its emphasis on the radical difference between man and animal, discourse and the real, history and nature, and so forth. What does all this mean? It simply means, for this French Hegelian-Kojèvian tradition, that there is only one kind of being, at least for the human subjects that we are, and that is being-represented, being-represented by a subject. For instance, when Lacan emphasized the radical ex-centricity and division of the subject, it is from the perspective of representation; it is because the subject is *only* representation, language, and discourse that it can never be identical to itself. The (human) subject will never be able to go beyond representation, because it *is* representation through and through.

Now, it is easy to see that this is a self-confirming theory. Once you've dogmatically decided that there is no other being than being-represented, then you will never escape the famous "closure of representation"—for clearly you cannot *represent* the irrepresentable. But what if being cannot be reduced to being-represented? For sure, as soon as you speak or write you are in the realm of representation. Does that mean that nothing happens outside that realm, in another scene? I would argue that representation is only one part of human experience, and a tiny part at that. Just think of it: in order to read, speak, or write, you have to move your eyes, tongue, or hand—which you do, most often, completely unaware. Likewise, you dream every night even though you might not remember your dreams. And you are constantly falling into trance-like states—for instance, when you are driving your car—even though you pay no attention to it. Does this mean that nothing ever *happens*, simply because we don't represent these events to ourselves? Suppose you can't paint a wall in red because you only have a can of blue paint at your disposal. Does it follow from this that the color red doesn't exist, and that the universe is *blue*? All of these arguments about the closure of representation rest on a quite senseless reduction of human experience to representation and ideality. But, as Charcot would say, *"Ça n'empêche pas d'exister."* So you can't account for the irrepresentable within a philosophy of representation? Well, then, try another philosophy for a change! What we need is a philosophy that accounts for experience, not one that *denies* it.

CO: In his response to Michel Henry's work, Roustang talks about the non-verbal rapport between the mother and her offspring—something that may be analogous to a trance state. In a Lacanian spirit, what prevents us from saying that there is nonetheless something of the order of language taking place within this scenario? Namely, of the order of language on two counts: one, that it is structured around the pleasure principle, and two, that it is engaged in a signifying intercourse.

MB-J: Who says that language and representation are not part of the human experience? Certainly not me. It is not because Lacan reduces everything to the symbolic and the signifier that we should deny the role of language. More to the point, since this is obviously what is at stake in your question, I think it would be just plain stupid to claim that language doesn't intervene in the therapeutic rapport. It clearly does, even in a very deep hypnotic trance. People speak, interact through language, so yes, speech is almost always in the picture. The question is, What speech?, What language? Remember that Lacan himself had to come up with a very specific and idiosyncratic theory of speech and language to account for what happens in the cure. Not only did he insist, like others, on the arbitrariness of linguistic signs and symbols with regard to reality, but he emptied the signifier of any signified—which was a way of stressing that the role of language within the therapeutic exchange has nothing whatsoever to do with meaning. As I said earlier, this is consistent with what happens in hypnotherapy: in a hypnotic state, any word will be effective as long as it intervenes at the right moment within the interaction between therapist and patient (which is perhaps what Lacan was getting at when he spoke of giving the right "punctuation" to the subject's speech). The efficacy of language and speech—the "power of words," as Freud said—therefore has nothing to do with reality, nor with meaning. Does this mean that the "signifier" is all-powerful and that its efficacy is purely symbolic, as Lacan believed? I don't think so. What is operative here is the hypnotic rapport, not speech or "symbolic exchange" per se. Hypnosis dramatically enhances the power of words—their "suggestive" power—and this has to do with the peculiarities of the hypnotic trance, during which words (but also gestures, mimics, sounds, etc.) become pure indexes of the experience itself. In this respect, the whole debate as to whether the cure operates with or without language seems to me to be a very artificial one.

CO: So was Lacan responsible for the dichotomization of affect and language, for this sort of dualism?

MB-J: Yes, and in this respect he was just following Kojève's "dualistic ontology." He is quite clear about it in the "Rome Discourse": if we psychoanalysts start to pay attention to affect, where will we go? "Keep going in that direction," he said, "and I dare say the last word in the transference will be a reciprocal sniffing" (1977: 57). In other words, we'll end up sniffing each other like dogs! Clearly, Lacan didn't want to allow this affective, hypnotic, and "animal" dimension to resurface within the psychoanalytic setting. I believe, like Roustang, that this was a mistake, and am convinced that—even in Lacan's own practice—things were much more complex and ambiguous than he would have it. Again, speech is powerful, but only inasmuch as it becomes "hypnotic" speech. This is also the problem I have with Lévi-Strauss when he stresses the purely "symbolic" nature of the cures performed by shamans, sorcerers, magicians, or psychoanalysts. You need only watch a sorcerer operate: he clearly deals with symbols, with what Lévi-Strauss and Lacan called "zero symbols" or "signifiers," devoid of meaning—*abracadabra*, etc. And what is important in these cures, according to Lévi-Strauss, is that these symbols will allow the integration of the patient's experience—his *affective* non-symbolized experience—into the symbolic order. In other words, the efficacy of symbols lies, for Lévi-Strauss, in the fact that they enable the sick person to have his or her experience recognized by the society in which he or she lives.

CO: Right—its recognition as inclusion, not as identification.

MB-J: Exactly, and again, there's no need to deny all of this. But Lévi-Strauss, in my view, misses the point entirely when he disregards the non-symbolic elements in these ritual cures, and especially the role played by trance-states. As I've tried to show in my "Mimetic Efficacy" (1993: 98–120) paper, most of these ritual cures involve some kind of trance state, whether it be in direct form—like when the patient or medicine man go into a trance—or in a more indirect, "symbolic" form—like when the cure involves some narrative of possession or dispossession of the soul. Trance is always present somehow, and it is easy to understand why: namely, because symbols and "signifiers" wouldn't be effective without it. Words and symbols are powerful only when they operate on another level than the purely linguistic one, when they stop being "mere" words, "mere" symbols. And this is precisely what the "trance logic" allows. Lévi-Strauss's structuralist theory of shamanism is very partial and doesn't account, in my view, for the very efficacy of symbols. The same could be said about the Lacanian cure, which is basically a Lévi-Straussian, structuralist version of shamanism for our modern societies: that is, it doesn't work; or, if it does, it does so for reasons that have nothing to do with the theory. So why should we cling to a theory that is so obviously at odds with the actual experience of the cure? Let's go back to the shamans—and let's do away with the structuralists!

NOTES

This interview took place at Sonu Shamdasani's home in London, 5 May 1993. In addition to Shamdasani, I would like to thank Steve Gans and Michael Münchow for their encouragements. All subsequent notes are Borch-Jacobsen's.

1. "In fact the *self* can not be apprehended as a real existent; the subject can not *be* self, for coincidence with self, as we have seen, causes the self to disappear. But neither can it *not be* itself since the self is an indication of the subject himself. The *self* therefore represents an ideal distance within the immanence of the subject in relation to himself, a way of *not being his own coincidence*, or escaping identity while positing it as a unity ... This is what we shall call presence to itself. The law of being of the *for-itself*, as the ontological foundation of consciousness, is to be itself in the form of presence to itself ... The presence of being to itself implies a detachment on the part of being in relation to itself" (Sartre 1966: 123–24).

2. Unfortunately, these annotated translations could not be published in a volume because of a veto by Jean Laplanche and Presses Universitaires de France, who owned the copyrights to three of these texts. Consequently, these translations are still dispersed in various French journals: *Cahiers Confrontation* 7 and 9, *Café* 3, *L'Ecrit du temps* 3, 6, and 7. One last text, *Psychical Treatment*, was published—but without its critical apparatus—by Laplanche himself in his edition of Freud (1984).

3. Here is, for example, what Albert Moll wrote about Freud's theories in 1909 (at a time when it was by no means clear for all of Freud's colleagues to what extent he had already abandoned the seduction theory): "I have been forced more and more to the conclusion that, notwithstanding all the other advantages of the psycho-analytic method, *the importance of the factor of sexual experiences in the causation of disease has been greatly over-estimated by Freud* [his emphasis]. Moreover, I believe that the cures effected by Freud (as to the permanence of which, in view of the insufficiency of the published materials, no decisive opinion can as yet be given), are explicable in another way. A large proportion of the good results are certainly fully explicable as the results of suggestion. The patient's confidence in his physician, and the fact that the treatment requires much time and patience, are two such powerful factors of suggestion, that provisionally it is necessary to regard it as possible that suggestion explains the whole matter" ([1909] 1912: 278–79).

4. On Erickson's work, see Ernest Rossi (in Erickson 1980), and Jay Haley (1973).

5. Review courageously signed "G.M." in *Science et Vie*, August 1990.

references

Althusser, Louis. 1969. *For Marx*. London: Allen Lane.

——. 1993. "Freud et Lacan." Originally published as *Ecrits sur la psychanalyse. La Nouvelle Critique*. December 1964–January 1965: 161–62. Paris: Stock/IMEC.

Althusser, Louis and Étienne Balibar. 1979. *Reading Capital*. Translated by Ben Brewster. London: Verso.

Anderson, Lorin. 1980. "Freud, Nietzsche." *Salmagundi* 47–48.

Andreas-Salomé, Lou. 1964. *The Freud Journal*. Translated by by Stanley Leavy. New York: Basic Books.

Anzieu, Didier. 1986. *Freud's Self-Analysis*. Translated by Peter Graham. London: Hogarth Press.

Appignanesi, Lisa and John Forrester. 1992. *Freud's Women*. New York: Basic Books.

Arendt, Hannah. 1963. *Eichmann in Jerusalem: A Report on the Banality of Evil*. New York: Viking Press.

——. 1971. *The Human Condition*. Chicago: The University of Chicago Press.

Assoun, Paul-Laurent. 1980. *Freud et Nietzsche*. Paris: Presses universitaires de France.

Auffret, Dominique. 1990. *Alexandre Kojève, La philosophie, l'Etat, la fin de l'Histoire*. Paris: Grasset.

Austin, John L. 1975. *How to Do Things with Words*. 2nd ed. Cambridge: Harvard University Press.

Avtonomova, N., ed. 1991. *Lacan avec les philosophes*. Paris: Albin Michel.

Bannet, Eve Tavor. 1989. *Structuralism and the Logic of Dissent: Barthes, Derrida, Foucault, Lacan*. Chicago: University of Illinois Press.

Baudrillard, Jean. 1976. *L'éxchange symbolique et la mort*. Paris: Gallimard.

——. 1988. *America*. Translated by Chris Turner. New York: Verso.

Beauvoir, Simone de. 1952. *The Second Sex*. Translated by H.M. Parshley. New York: Vintage.

Bennington, Geoffrey and Jacques Derrida. 1993. *Jacques Derrida*. Translated by G. Bennington. Chicago: The University of Chicago Press.

Bernheimer, Charles. 1992. "Penile Reference in Phallic Theory." *Differences* 4: 1 (Spring): 116–32.

Bertin, Celia. 1982. *Marie Bonaparte: A Life*. New York: Harcourt Brace.

Borch-Jacobsen, Mikkel. 1988. *The Freudian Subject*. Translated by Catherine Porter. Stanford: Stanford University Press.

——. 1991. *Lacan: The Absolute Master*. Translated by Douglas Brick. Stanford: Stanford University Press.

———. 1993. *The Emotional Tie: Psychoanalysis, Mimesis, and Affect.* Translated by Douglas Brick and others. Stanford: Stanford University Press.

———. 1994. "The Oedipus Problem in Freud and Lacan." *Critical Inquiry* 20 (Winter): 267–82.

Bottomore, Tom. 1984. *The Frankfurt School.* New York: Tavistock.

Bougnoux, Daniel. 1991. *Le Fantôme de la psychanalyse, critique de l'archéologie freudienne.* Toulouse: Ombres/Presse Universitaires du Mirail.

Braidotti, Rosi. 1994. *Nomadic Subjects: Embodiment and Sexual Difference in Contemporary Feminist Theory.* New York: Columbia University Press.

Brecht, Bertolt. 1979. "The Threepenny Opera." *Collected Plays* 2: 2. Edited by John Willett and Ralph Manheim. London: Eyre Methuen.

Brennan, Teresa, ed. 1989. *Between Feminism and Psychoanalysis.* New York: Routledge.

———. 1991. "An Impasse in Psychoanalysis and Feminism." *A Reader in Feminist Knowledge.* Edited by Sneja Gunew. New York: Routledge.

Brincourt, André. 1972. "Si l'avenir donnait tort à McLuhan." *Le figaro* 15 juillet.

Brown, Norman O. 1959. *Life Against Death: The Psychoanalytic Meaning of History.* London: Routledge.

Burridge, K. 1969. *New Heaven, New Earth.* Oxford: Blackwell.

Butler, Judith. 1986. "Sex and Gender in Simone de Beauvoir's *Second Sex.*" *Yale French Studies.* 72: 35–49.

———. 1987. "Variations on Sex and Gender: Beauvoir, Wittig and Foucault," *Feminism as Critique.* Edited by Seyla Benhabib and Drucilla Cornell. Minneapolis: University of Minnesota Press.

———. 1990. *Gender Trouble: Feminism and the Subversion of Identity.* New York: Routledge.

———. 1993. *Bodies That Matter: On the Discursive Limits of "Sex."* New York: Routledge.

———. 1994. "Gender as Performance: An Interview with Judith Butler." *Radical Philosophy.* 67 (Summer) 32–9.

———. 1995. "For a Careful Reading." *Feminist Contentions: A Philosophical Exchange.* Edited by Linda Nicholson. New York: Routledge.

Callinicos, Alex. 1985. *Marxism and Philosophy.* Oxford: Oxford University Press.

Castoriadis, Cornélius. 1987. *The Imaginary Institution of Society.* Translated by Kathleen Blamey. Cambridge: Polity.

Ceiman, Alberto S. 1992. "A Foundation for Psychoanalysis: Lacan, Reader of Freud." Presented at The American Academy of Psychoanalysis, Cancun, Mexico (December 4).

Châtelet, François. 1967. "Un nouveau faux prophète." *Le nouvel observateur,* 29 November–5 December: 36–7.

Chertok, Léon and Isabelle Stengers. 1992. *A Critique of Psychoanalytic Reason: Hypnosis as a Scientific Problem from Lavoisier to Lacan.* Translated by Martha Noel Evans. Stanford: Stanford University Press.

Chisholm, Dianne. 1994. "Irigaray's Hysteria." *Engaging with Irigaray: Feminist Philosophy and Modern European Thought.* Edited by Carolyn Burke et al. . New York: Columbia University Press.

Cixous, Helénè. 1980. "The Laugh of the Medusa." *New French Feminisms.* Edited by Elaine Marks and Isabelle de Courtivron. New York: Schocken Books.

Clifford, James. 1992. "Travelling Culture." *Cultural Studies.* Edited by Lawrence Grossberg et al. New York: Routledge.

Collingwood, R. G. 1956. *The Idea of History*. London: Oxford University Press.

Colton, Charles. 1882. *Lacon, Or Many Things in Few Words; Addressed to Those Who Think*. London: Longman, Hurst, Rees, Orme, and Brown.

Crews, Frederick. 1993. "The Unknown Freud." *The New York Review of Books*, 18 November: 58–66.

Crump, Thomas. 1981. *The Phenomenon of Money*. London: RKP.

Derrida, Jacques. 1967. *L'écriture et la différence*. Paris: Seuil.

——. 1978. *Writing and Difference*. Translated by Alan Bass. Chicago: University of Chicago Press.

——. 1983. "*Geschlecht*: Sexual Difference. Ontological Difference." *Research in Phenomenology* 13: 65–83.

——. 1987. *The Post Card: From Socrates to Freud and Beyond*. Translated by Alan Bass. Chicago: University of Chicago Press.

——. 1987a. "Women in the Beehive: A Seminar With Jacques Derrida." *Men in Feminism*. Edited by Alice Jardine and Paul Smith. London: Methuen.

——. 1988. *The Ear of the Other: Otobiography, Transference, Translation*. Edited by Christie McDonald. Lincoln: University of Nebraska Press.

——. 1990. "Force of Law: The 'Mystical Foundation of Authority.'" Translated by Mary Quaintance. *Cardoza Law Review* 11 (July/August).

——. 1991. "Eating Well, or the Calculation of the Subject: An Interview With Jacques Derrida." *Who Comes After the Subject?* Edited by Eduardo Cadava et al. New York: Routledge.

——. 1991a. "At This Very Moment In This Work I Am Here." *Re-Reading Levinas*. Edited by R. Bernasconi and Simon Critchley. Bloomington: Indiana University Press.

——. 1992. "The Law of Genre." *Acts of Literature*. Edited by Derek Attridge. New York: Routledge.

——. 1992a. "Before the Law." *Acts of Literatures*, Edited by Derek Attridge. New York: Routledge.

Desanti, Dominique. 1974. "Marshall McLuhan, prophète de la communication—Le met en garde—Attention: le dialogue ou la mort." *Argus de la presse*, 22 juillet: 40–41.

Descartes, René. 1985. *Discourse on the Method. The Philosophical Writings of Descartes*. Translated by Robert Stoothoff. Cambridge: Cambridge University Press.

Deutsch, Helene. 1973. "Freud and His Pupils: A Footnote to the History of the Psychoanalytic Movement." *Freud as we Knew Him*. Edited by Hendrick M. Ruitenbeek. Detroit: Wayne State University Press.

Dommergues, Pierre. 1969. "Marshall McLuhan en question." *Le monde*, 9 August.

Doumit, Elie. 1991. "Intervention." *Lacan avec les philosophes*. Paris: Albin Michel.

Dufresne, Todd. 1994. "Review of *Meeting Freud's Family*." *Journal of the History of the Behavioral Sciences* 30 (July): 257–59.

——. 1995. "Joseph Wortis: notorischer Anti-Psychoanlytiker," *Werkblatt*, 34: 90–118. "An Interview With Joseph Wortis." *The Psychoanalytic Review* 83(3), June 1996: 455–75.

Dumur, Guy. 1972. "La galaxie MacLuhan." *La nouvel observateur*, 401 23 juillet: 36–7.

Eastman, Max. 1962. *Great Companions: Critical Memoirs of Some Famous Friends*. New York: Collier.

Erickson, Milton. 1964. "The Confusion Technique in Hypnosis." *Advanced Techniques of Hypnosis and Therapy*. Edited by Jay Haley. New York: Grune and Stratton.

————. 1980. *The Collected Papers of Milton H. Erickson*. 4 vols. Edited by Ernest Rossi. New York: Irvington Publishers.

Erikson, Erik H. 1963. *Childhood and Society*. 2nd edition. New York: Norton.

Ferenczi, Sándor. 1988. *The Clinical Diary of Sándor Ferenczi*. Edited by Judith Dupont. Cambridge: Harvard University Press.

Ferguson, Ann. 1989. *Blood at the Root*. London: Pandora.

Fischer, David James. 1994. "Review of Jacques Lacan & Co.," *Psychoanalytic Books 5*, no. 3: 365–78.

Forrester, John. 1990. *The Seductions of Psychoanalysis: Freud, Lacan, Derrida*. Cambridge: Cambridge University Press.

Foucault, Michel. 1961. *Folie et déraison: Histoire de la folie à l'âge classique*. Paris: Librairie Plon.

————. 1962. *Maladie mentale et psychologie*. Paris: PUF.

————. 1963. *Naissance de la clinique: une archéologie du régard médical*. Paris: PUF.

————. 1963a. *Raymond Roussel*. Paris: Gallimard.

————. 1965. *Madness and Civilization: A History of Insanity in the Age of Reason*. Translated by Richard Howard. New York: Pantheon.

————. 1966. *Les mots et les choses: une archéologie des sciences humaines*. Paris: Gallimard.

————. 1973. *The Order of Things: An Archaeology of the Human Sciences*. Translated by Alan Sheridan. New York: Vintage.

————. 1975. *The Birth of the Clinic*. Translated by Alan Sheridan. New York: Vintage.

————. 1976. *La Volonté de savoir*. Vol. I of *Histoire de la Sexualité*: Paris: Gallimard.

————. 1978. *Vol. I of The History of Sexuality: An Introduction*. Translated by Robert Hurley. New York: Pantheon.

————. 1979. "My Body, This Paper, This Fire." Translated by Geoff Bennington. *Oxford Literary Review* 4 (Autumn).

————. 1980. *Power/Knowledge: Selected Interviews and Other Writings, 1977–1984*. Edited by Colin Gordon. New York: Pantheon.

————. 1984. *L'usage des plaisirs*. Vol. 2 of *Histoire de la sexualité*. Paris: Gallimard.

————. 1984a. *Le souci de soi*. Vol. 3 of *histoire de la sexualité*. Paris: Gallimard.

————. 1985. *The Use of Pleasure*. Vol. 2 of *History of Sexuality*. Translated by Robert Hurley. New York: Pantheon.

————. 1986. *The Care of the Self*. Vol. 3 of *History of Sexuality*. Translated by Robert Hurley. New York: Pantheon.

————. 1986a. *Death and the Labyrinth: The World of Raymond Roussel*. Translated by C. Ruas. Garden City, NY: Doubleday.

————. 1987. *Mental Illness and Psychology*. Translated by Alan Sheridan. Berkeley: University of California Press.

Fox-Keller, Evelyn. 1989. "The Gender/Science System: or, Is Sex to Gender as Nature Is to Science?" *Feminism & Science*. Edited by N. Tuana. Bloomington: Indiana University Press.

Freud, Sigmund. 1953–74. *Studies on Hysteria*. Vol. 2 of *The Standard Edition of the Complete Psychological Works of Sigmund Freud (SE)*. Translated by James Strachey. [1893–95].

————. *The Interpretation of Dreams*. SE 4, 5 [1900].

————. *On Dreams*. SE 5 [1901]: 636-86.

————. *The Psychopathology of Everyday Life*. SE 6 [1901].

————. "Fragment of the Analysis of a Case of Hysteria [Dora]." *SE* 7 [1905]: 7-122.

————. "Three Essays on the Theory of Sexuality." *SE* 7 [1905]: 125-243.

———. "'Civilized' Sexual Morality and Modern Nervous Illness." *SE* 9 [1908]: 179-204.

———. "On the Sexual Theories of Children." *SE* 9 [1908]: 205-26.

———. "Notes Upon a Case of Obsessional Neurosis [Ratman]." *SE* 10 [1909]: 155-249.

———. "Addendum: Original Record of the Case [Ratman]." *SE* 10 [1909]: 253-318.

———. "Psychoanalytic Notes on an Autobiographical Account of a Case of Paranoia." *SE* 12 [1911]: 1-82.

———. "Formulations on the Two Principles of Mental Functioning." *SE* 12 [1911]: 213-226.

———. "On the History of the Psychoanalytic Movement." *SE* 14 [1914]: 7-66.

———. "On Narcissism: An Introduction." *SE* 14 [1914]: 67-102.

———. "Instincts and Their Vicissitudes." *SE* 14 [1915]: 109-140.

———. "Thoughts for the Times on War and Death." *SE* 14 [1915]: 273-300.

———. *Introductory Lectures in Psychoanalysis*. SE 15, 16 [1916- 1917].

———. "A Child is Being Beaten." *SE* 17 [1919]: 177-204.

———. *Beyond the Pleasure Principle*. SE 18 [1920]: 7-64.

———. *The Ego and the Id*. SE 19 [1923]: 3-66.

———. "The Dissolution of the Oedipus Complex." *SE* 19 [1924]: 173-79.

———. "An Autobiographical Study." *SE* 20 [1925]: 3-74.

———. *Civilization and Its Discontents*. SE 21 [1930]: 64-145.

———. "Female Sexuality." *SE* 21 [1931]: 223-43.

———. *New Introductory Lectures on Psycho-Analysis*. SE 22 [1933]: 3-182.

———. "Analysis Terminable and Interminable." *SE* 23 [1937]: 211-53.

———. *An Outline of Psychoanalysis*. SE 23 [1940]: 141-207.

———. 1960. *Letters of Sigmund Freud*. Edited by Ernst Freud. Translated by Tania and James Stern. New York: Basic Books.

———. 1987. *A Phylogenetic Phantasy: Overview of the Transference Neuroses*. Edited by Ilse Grubrich-Simitis. Translated by Axel Hoffer and Peter T. Hoffer. Cambridge, MA.: Harvard University Press.

———. 1992. *The Diary of Sigmund Freud*. Edited and translated by Michael Molnar. New York: Scribner's.

Freud, Sigmund and Arnold Zweig. 1970. *The Letters of Sigmund Freud and Arnold Zweig*. Edited by Ernst Freud. Translated by Professor and Mrs. Robson-Scott. London: Hogarth Press.

Freud, Sigmund, and Carl Jung. 1974. *The Freud/Jung Letters: The Correspondence Between Sigmund Freud and C. G. Jung*. Edited by William McGuire. Translated by Ralph Manheim and R. F. C. Hull. Cambridge: Harvard University Press.

Freud, Sigmund and Wilhelm Fliess. 1985. *The Complete Letters of Sigmund Freud to Wilhelm Fliess, 1887–1904*. Edited by Jeffrey M. Masson. Cambridge: Harvard University Press.

Freud, Sigmund and Lou Andreas-Salomé. 1972. *Letters*. Edited by Ernst Pfeiffer. Translated by William and Elaine Robson-Scott. London: Hogarth Press.

Fromm, Erich. 1958. "The Human Implications of Instinctivistic 'Radicalism'." Edited by Irving Howe. New York: Grove Press.

——— 1959. *Sigmund Freud's Mission: An Analysis of His Personality and Influence*. New York: Grove Press.

———. 1973. *The Anatomy of Human Destructiveness*. New York: Holt, Rinehart & Winston.

Gallop, Jane. 1982. *The Daughter's Seduction*. Ithaca: Cornell University Press.

———. 1985. *Reading Lacan*. Ithaca: Cornell University Press.

———. 1988. *Thinking Through the Body*. New York: Columbia University Press.

Gariepy, Renault. 1967. "Etre ou ne pas être ... McLuhanien! Mais comment l'être?" *La presse*, 8 July.

Garric, Daniel. 1967. "'La galaxie de Gutenberg' de McLuhan." *Le figaro,* 12 December.

Gasché, Rodolphe. 1977. "Psicoanalisi 'come' letteratura." in *La Critica Freudiana*. Edited by Franco Rella. Milano: Feltrinelli.

Gatens, Moira. 1991. "A Critique of the Sex/Gender Distinction." *A Reader in Feminist Knowledge*. Edited by Sneja Gunew. London: Routledge.

———. 1996. *Imaginary Bodies*. London: Routledge.

Gay, Peter. 1988. *Freud: A Life for Our Times*. New York: Norton.

Genosko, Gary. 1993. "Freud's Bestiary: How Does Psychoanalysis Treat Animals?" *Psychoanalytic Review* 80(4): 603–632.

———. 1994. "The Paradoxical Effects of *macluhanisme*: Cazeneuve, Baudrillard and Barthes." *Economy and Society* 23, 4 (November): 400–32.

George, François. 1979. *L'Effet 'yau de poêle'*, Paris: Hachette.

Gheerbrand, Gilles. 1969. "L'image de M.McL. à travers la presse." *Pour comprendre M.McL.* Association de compagnons de Lure: Rencontres.

Godin, Jean-Guy. 1990. *Jacques Lacan, 5 rue de Lille*. Paris: Seuil.

Goux, Jean-Joseph. 1992. "The Phallus: Masculine Identity and the 'Exchange of Women.'" Translated by Maria Amuchastegui et al. *Differences* 4, 1 (Spring) 40–75.

Gray, Paul. 1993. "The Assault on Freud." *Time*, 29 November: 47–50.

Grigg, Russell. 1991. "Signifier, Object, and the Transference." *Lacan and the Subject of Language*. Edited by Ellie Ragland-Sullivan and Mark Dracher. New York: Routledge.

Grosskurth, Phyllis. 1991. *The Secret Ring: Freud's Inner Circle and the Politics of Psychoanalysis*. Reading, MA: Addison-Wesley.

Grossman, Carl and Sylvia. 1965. *The Wild Analyst: The Life and Work of George Groddeck*. New York: George Braziller.

Grosz, Elizabeth. 1990. "Conclusion: A Note on Essentialism and Difference." *Feminist Knowledge: Critique and Construct*. Edited by Sneja Gunew. London: Routledge.

———. 1990a. *Jacques Lacan, A Feminist Introduction*. London: Routledge.

———. 1994. *Volatile Bodies: Toward a Corporeal Feminism*. Bloomington: Indiana University Press.

Hacking, Ian. 1988. "Telepathy: Origins of Randomization in Experimental Design." *ISIS* 79: 427–51.

Haley, Jay. 1973. *Uncommon Therapy: The Psychiatric Techniques of Milton Erickson*. New York: Norton.

Haraway, Donna J. 1991. "'Gender' for a Marxist Dictionary: The Sexual Politics of a Word." *Simians, Cyborgs, and Women: The Reinvention of Nature*. New York: Routledge.

Heath, Stephen. 1989. "Friday Night Books." *A New History of French Literature*. Edited by Denis Hollier. Cambridge: Harvard University Press.

Heidegger, Martin. 1980. *Being and Time*. Translated by John Macquarrie and Edward Robinson. Oxford: Basil Blackwell.

Henry, Michel. 1993. *The Genealogy of Psychoanalysis*. Translated by Douglas Brick, Stanford: Stanford University Press.

———. 1989. *Michel Henry: Philosophy and Psychoanalysis*. Edited by Mikkel Borch-Jacobsen. *Stanford Literature Review*. 6:2 (Fall).

Herdt, Gilbert. 1980. *Herculine Barbin: Being the Recently Discovered Memoirs of a Nineteenth-Century Hermaphrodite*. New York: Pantheon Books.

———. 1994. *Third Sex, Third Gender: Beyond Sexual Dimorphism in Culture and History*. New York: Zone Books.

Hollingdale, R.J. 1973. *Nietzsche*. London: Routledge and Kegan Paul.

Homans, Peter. 1988. "Disappointment and the Ability to Mourn." *Freud: Appraisals and Reappraisals*. Vol 2. Edited by Paul E. Stepansky. New York: Analytic Press.

Ionesco, Eugene. 1973. "Macbett." Vol. 4 of *Plays*. London: Calder and Bryers.

Irigaray, Luce. 1985. *Speculum of the Other Woman*. Translated by Gillian Gill. Ithaca: Cornell University Press.

———. 1991. *Marine Lover of Friedrich Nietzsche*. Translated by Gillian Gill. New York: Columbia University Press.

Jacobus, Mary. 1981. "The Question of Language: Men of Maxims and *The Mill on the Floss*." *Critical Inquiry* 8, no. 2.

Jarry, Alfred. 1972. "Gestes et opinions du Docteur Faustroll, pataphysicien." *Oeuvres complètes I*. Paris: Gallimard.

Jay, Martin. 1993. *Force Fields: Between Intellectual History and Cultural Debate*. New York: Routledge.

Jones, Ernest. 1955. *The Life and Works of Sigmund Freud, Volume 2*: New York: Basic Books.

———. 1959. *Free Associations: Memories of a Psychoanalyst*. New York: Basic Books.

Jung, C. G. 1988. *Nietzsche's 'Zarathustra': Notes of the Seminar Given in 1934-39*. 2 volumes. Edited by James J. Jarret. Princeton: Princeton University Press.

Kardiner, Abram. 1977. *My Analysis With Freud: Reminiscences*. New York: Norton.

Kaufmann, Walter. 1980. *Freud Versus Adler & Jung*, Vol. 3 of *Discovering the Mind*. New York: McGraw Hill.

Kingsolver, Barbara. 1993. *Pigs in Heaven*. New York: HarperCollins.

Knockaert, Yves. 1988. *Third Interlude uit het ballet "MacLuhan et MacDonalds."* Bruxelles: CeBeDeM.

Kofman, Sarah. 1985. *The Enigma of Woman*. Translated by Catherine Porter. Ithaca: Cornell University Press.

———. [1969] 1991. "Freud and Empedocles." *Freud and Fiction*. Translated by S. Wykes. London: Northeastern University Press.

Lacan, Jacques. 1938. "La Famille." *Encyclopédie française*, Vol. 8.

———. 1949. "Cure psychanalytique à l'aide de la poupée fleur." Comptes rendu, réunion 18 Octobre. *Revue française de la psychanalyse* 4 (October–December).

———. 1953. "Le mythe individuel du névrosé ou 'Poésie et Vérité' dans la névrosé." Paris: Centre de la Documentation Universitaire. Mimeo.

———. 1957. *Le Séminaire. Livre IV. La Relation d'objet et les structures freudiennes*; 1956–57. "Comptes rendus" by J.-B. Pontalis. *Bulletin de Psychologie* 10.

———. 1961–62. *Le Séminaire. Livre IX. L'Identification* (unpublished).

———. 1964. "Préamble." *Annuarie de l'École freudienne* I.

———. 1966. *Ecrit*. Paris: Seuil.

———. 1968. "Introduction de Scilicet." *Scilicet*, no. 1. Paris: Seuil.

———. 1975. *Le Séminaire. Livre I. Les Ecrit techniques de Freud. 1953–54*. Paris: Seuil.

———. 1977. *Ecrit: A Selection*. Translated by Alan Sheridan. London: Tavistock.

———. 1977a. *The Four Fundamental Concepts of Psycho-Analysis*. Translated by Alan Sheridan, London: Hogarth.

———. 1978. *Le Séminaire. Livre II. Le Moi dans la théorie de Freud et dans la technique de la psychanalyse. 1954–55*. Paris: Seuil.

———. 1979. "The Neurotic's Individual Myth." *Psychoanalytic Quarterly* 48: 405–25.

———. 1981. *Le Séminaire. Livre III. Les Psychoses. 1955–56,* Paris: Seuil.

———. 1983. "The Meaning of the Phallus." *Feminine Sexuality.* Edited by Juliet Mitchell and Jacqueline Rose. New York: Norton.

———. 1988. *The Seminar, Book I: Freud's Papers on Technique, 1953–1954.* Translated by John Forrester. New York: Norton.

———. 1988a. *The Seminar, Book II: The Ego in Freud's Theory and in the Technique of Psychoanalysis, 1954–55.* Translated by Sylvana Tomaselli. Notes by John Forrester. New York: Norton.

———. 1989. "Science and Truth." Translated by Bruce Fink. *Newsletter of the Freudian Field* 3, nos. 1–2: 4–29.

———. 1990. *Television.* Translated by Denis Hollier, Rosalind Krauss and Annette Michelson. Edited by Joan Copjec. New York: Norton.

———. 1994. "Discussion." *Revue Française de Psychoanalyse Comptes Rendus.* 20 April–June.

Lanoux, Armand. 1973. *Marcuse et McLuhan et la nouvelle révolution mondiale.* Introduction by Jean Marabini. Paris: Maisons mame.

Laplanche, Jean. [1970] 1976. *Life and Death in Psychoanalysis.* Translated by Jeffrey Mehlman. Baltimore: Johns Hopkins University Press.

———. 1980. *La sublimation.* Paris: Presses Universitaires de France.

———. ed. 1984. *Résultats, idées, problèmes,* Sigmund Freud. Paris: Presses Universitaires de France.

Laplanche, Jean, and J.-B. Pontalis. 1964. "Fantasme originaire, fantasmes des origines, origine du fantasme." *Les Temps Modernes* 215 (April).

———. 1973. *The Language of Psycho-Analysis.* Translated by Donald Nicholson-Smith. London: Hogarth Press.

Laqueur, Thomas. 1994. "From Generation to Generation." Unpublished paper, N. E.H seminar on Embodiment, Santa Cruz (Summer).

Lauretis, Teresa de. 1990. "Eccentric Subjects: Feminist Theory and Historical Consciousness." *Feminist Studies,* no. 1: 115–50.

Lee, Jonathan Scott. 1990. *Jacques Lacan.* Amherst: The University of Massachusetts Press.

Levinas, Emmanuel. 1987. *Time and the Other.* Translated by R. Cohen. Pittsburgh: Duquesne University Press.

Lewis, Wyndham. [1914] 1981. *Blast 1.* Reprint. Santa Barbara: Black Sparrow Press.

———. [1915] 1981a. *Blast 2.* Reprint. Santa Barbara: Black Sparrow Press.

Macleod, H.D. 1872. *The Principles of Economical Philosophy,* London: [?].

Marchand, Philip. 1989. *Marshall McLuhan: The Medium is the Messenger.* Toronto: Random House.

Marcotte, Gilles. 1974. "Marshall McLuhan et l'énergie du banal." *Le devoir,* 15 June.

Mariet, François. 1977. "Le macluhanism dans l'education." *Le francais aujourd'hui,* 38 June: 47–52.

———. 1978–79. "McLuhan, prophète ou imposteur," *Millésime.* June: 107–109.

Marcus, Steven. 1984. *Freud and the Culture of Psychoanalysis: Studies in the Transition from Victorian Humanism to Modernity.* New York: Norton.

Marx, Karl. 1973. *Grundrisse: Foundations of the Critique of Political Economy.* Translated by Martin Nicholas. London: Berlin.

Mazlish, Bruce. 1968. "Freud and Nietzsche." *The Psychoanalytic Review* 55: 3.

McLuhan, Marshall. 1972. *McLuhan Papers.* National Library of Canada, Ottawa. Letter from McLuhan to Tom and Dorothy Easterbrook, Aug. 1, File 23–19.

————. 1987. *The Letters of Marshall McLuhan*. Edited by Matie Molinaro et al. Toronto: Oxford University Press.

McGrath, William J. 1986. *Freud's Discovery of Psychoanalysis: The Politics of Hysteria*. Ithaca: Cornell University Press.

Merleau-Ponty, Maurice. 1962. *Phenomenology of Perception*. Translated by Colin Smith. London: Routledge & Kegan Paul.

————. 1988. *Merleau-Ponty à la Sorbonne. Résumé de cours 1949–1952*. Paris: Cynara.

Mernissi, Fatima. 1987. *Beyond the Veil: Male-Female Dynamics in Modern Muslim Society*. Revised edition. Bloomington: Indiana University Press.

Mijolla, Alain de. 1993. "Freud, la biographie, son autobiographie et ses biographes." *Revue internationale d'Histoire de la Psychanalyse* 6: 81–108.

Moll, Albert. [1909] 1912. *The Sexual Life of the Child*. Translated by Eden Paul. New York: Macmillan.

Morrison, Toni. 1994. *The Bluest Eye*. New York: Plume.

Muller, John P. and William J. Richardson. 1982. *Lacan and Language: A Reader's Guide to Ecrits*. New York: International Universities Press.

Nancy, Jean-Luc and Philippe Lacoue-Labarthe. 1992. *The Title of the Letter: A Reading of Lacan*. Translated by François Raffoul and David Pettigrew. New York: SUNY.

Natenberg, Maurice. 1955. *The Case History of Sigmund Frued: A Psycho-Biography*. Chicago: Regent House.

Nietzsche, Friedrich. 1927. *The Philosophy of Nietzsche*, New York: The Modern Library.

————. 1954. *The Portable Nietzsche*. Edited and translated by Walter Kaufmann. New York: Penguin.

————. 1974. *The Gay Science*. Translated by Walter Kaufmann. New York: Vintage.

————. 1989. *Beyond Good and Evil*. Translated by Walter Kaufmann. New York: Vintage.

Nunberg, Herman and Ernst Federn, eds. 1962. *Minutes of the Vienna Psychoanalytic Society*, Vol. 1. Translated by M. Nunberg. New York: International Universities Press.

————. 1967. *Minutes of the Vienna Psychoanalytic Society*, Vol. II. Translated by M. Nunberg. New York: International Universities Press.

Olivier, Christiane. 1989. *Jocasta's Children: The Imprint of the Mother*. Translated by George Craig. London: Routledge.

Ortner, Sherry B. 1993. "Is Female to Male as Nature is to Culture?" *Women and Values: Readings in Recent Feminist Philosophy*. Edited by Marilyn Pearsall. Belmont: Wadsworth.

Pangle, Thomas. 1986. "The 'Warrior Spirit' as an Inlet to the Political Philosophy of Nietzsche's Zarathustra." *Nietzsche-Studien*. Berlin: Walter de Gruyter.

Paskauskas, R. Andrew. 1985. "Ernest Jones: A Critical Study of His Scientific Development." Unpublished Ph.D. Dissertation, Institute for the History and Philosophy of Science and Technology. University of Toronto.

Pateman, Carol. 1988. *The Sexual Contract*. Stanford: Stanford University Press.

Pautrat, Bernard. [1973] 1990. "Nietzsche Medused." *Looking After Nietzsche*. Edited by Laurence A. Rickels. Albany: SUNY.

Ragland-Sullivan, Ellie. 1982. "Jacques Lacan: Feminism and the Problem of Gender Identity." *SubStance* 36.

Reich, Wilhelm. 1973. "Reich on Freud." Edited by Henrick M. Ruitenbeek. Detroit: Wayne State University Press.

Reik, Theodor. 1954. *Listening With the Third Ear: The Inner Experience of a Psychoanalyst.* New York: Farrar, Strauss and Cudahy.

———. 1956. *The Search Within: The Inner Experiences of a Psychoanalyst.* New York: Farrar, Strauss and Cudahy.

Rey, Jean-Michel. 1974. *Parcours de Freud.* Paris: Editions Galilée.

Rickels, Laurence. 1990. "Psychoanalysis and TV." *SubStance.* 61: 39–52.

Rieff, Philip. 1959. *Freud: The Mind of the Moralist.* London: Gollancz.

Roazen, Paul. 1969. *Brother Animal: The Story of Freud and Tausk.* New York: Alfred A. Knopf; 2nd edition, with a new introduction, New Brunswick, NY: Transaction Books, 1990.

———. 1975. *Freud and His Followers.* New York: Meridian; reprint New York: Da Capo Books, 1991.

———. 1976. *Erik H. Erikson: The Power and Limits of a Vision.* New York: The Free Press.

———. 1985. *Helene Deutsch: A Psychoanalyst's Life.* New York: Doubleday; 2nd edition, with new introduction, New Brunswick, NJ: Transaction Books, 1991.

———. 1990. *Encountering Freud: The Politics and Histories of Psychoanalysis.* New Brunswick, NJ: Transaction Books.

———. 1991. "Jung and Anti-Semitism." *Lingering Shadows: Jungians, Freudians, and Anti-Semitism.* Edited by Aryeh Maidenbaum and Steven A. Martin. Boston: Shambala.

———. 1992. "The Historiography of Psychoanalysis." *Psychoanalysis in Its Cultural Context.* Edited by Edward Timms and Ritchie Robertson. Edinburgh: Edinburgh University Press.

———. 1992a. "The Rise and Fall of Bruno Bettelheim." *The Psychohistory Review* (Spring): 221–50.

———. 1993. *Meeting Freud's Family.* Amherst: University of Massachusetts Press.

Rose, Jacqueline. 1983. Introduction II to *Feminine Sexuality: Jacques Lacan and the École Freudienne.* Translated by J. Rose. Edited by Juliet Mitchell and J. Rose. New York: Norton.

———. 1989. "Where Does the Misery Come From?" *Feminism and Psychoanalysis.* Edited by Richard Feldstein and Judith Roof. Ithaca: Cornell University Press.

Roudinesco, Elizabeth. 1990. *Jacques Lacan & Co.: A History of Psychoanalysis in France, 1925–1985.* Translated by Jeffrey Mehlman. Chicago: The University of Chicago Press.

Roustang, François. 1982. *Dire Mastery: Discipleship From Freud to Lacan.* Translated by Ned Lukacher. Baltimore: Johns Hopkins University Press.

———. 1983. *Psychoanalysis Never Lets Go.* Translated by Ned Lukacher. Baltimore: Johns Hopkins Press.

———. 1986. *Lacan, de l'equiuoque à l'impasee.* Paris: Minuit.

———. 1990. *The Lacanian Delusion.* Translated by Greg Sims. New York/Oxford: Oxford University Press.

Rubin, Gayle. 1975. "The Traffic in Women: Notes on the 'Political Economy' of Sex." *Towards an Anthropology of Women.* Edited by R.R. Reiter. New York: Monthly Review Press.

Rudnytsky, Peter L. 1987. *Freud and Oedipus.* New York: Columbia University Press.

Rycroft, Charles. 1974. "Folie a deux." *The New York Review of Books.* 18 April.

Sachs, Hanns. 1945. *Freud, Master and Friend.* London: Imago.

Sartre, Jean-Paul. 1966. *Being and Nothingness.* Translated by Hazel E. Barnes. New York: Washington Square Press.

Schaeffer, Pierre. 1978–79. "Dialogue chaud et froid avec McLuhan." *Millesime* (June): 103–7.

Schneider, Monique. 1980. *La Parole et l'inceste*. Paris: Aubier-Montaigne.

Schneiderman, Stuart. 1983. *Jacques Lacan: The Death of an Intellectual Hero*. Cambridge: Harvard University Press.

Schor, Naomi. 1994. *The Essential Difference*. Edited by N. Schor and Elizabeth Weed. Indianapolis: Indiana University Press.

Schwab, Gail M. 1994. "Mother's Body, Father's Tongue: Mediation and the Symbolic Order." *Engaging with Irigaray: Feminist Philosophy and Modern European Thought*. Edited by Carolyn Burke et al. New York: Columbia University Press.

Shute, Jenefer. 1992. *Life-Size*. London: Martin Secker and Warburg.

Silverman, Kaja. 1992. "The Lacanian Phallus." *Differences* 4 no. 1. (Spring): 84–115.

Sommers, Christina Hoff. 1994. *Who Stole Feminism? How Women Have Betrayed Women*. New York: Simon & Schuster.

Spelman, Elizabeth. 1982. "Woman as Body." *Feminist Studies* 8, no. 1: 109–31.

Sterba, Richard F. 1982. *Reminiscences of a Viennese Psychoanalyst*. Detroit: Wayne State University Press.

Stoller, Robert. 1968. *Sex and Gender*. 2 vols. New York: Jason Aronson.

Strong, Tracy. 1988. *Friedrich Nietzsche and the Politics of Transfiguration*. Expanded edition. Berkeley: University of California Press.

Sussman, Henry. 1990. "Psychoanalysis Modern and Postmodern." *Psychoanalysis And. . . .* Edited by Richard Feldstein and H. Sussman. New York: Routledge.

Swales, Peter J. 1983. "Freud, Martha Bernays and the Language of Flowers, Masturbation, Cocaine, and the Inflation of Fantasy." Privately printed.

Szasz, Thomas. 1976. *Karl Kraus and the Soul Doctors: A Pioneer Critic and His Criticism of Psychiatry and Psychoanalysis*. Baton Rouge: Louisiana State University Press.

Torgerson, Douglas. 1987. "Political Vision and the Policy Orientation: Laswell's Early Letters." *Administrative and Policy Studies*. Working papers, Trent University.

Turkle, Sherry. 1992. *Psychoanalytic Politics: Jacques Lacan and Freud's French Revolution*. 2nd edition. New York: Guilford Press.

Vichyn, Bertrand. 1993. "La psychanalyse entre l'archéologie et l'histoire." *Revue internationale d'Histoire de la Psychanalyse* 6: 127–141.

Wallace, Edwin R., IV. 1986. "Freud as Ethicist." *Freud: Appraisals and Reappraisals, Contributions to Freud Studies*, Vol. I. Edited by Paul Stepansky. New York: Analytic Press.

Wagner, Roy. 1975. *The Invention of Culture*. Chicago: University of Chicago Press.

Watzlawick, Paul, et al. 1967. *Pragmatics of Human Communication: Study of Interactional Patterns, Pathologies, and Paradoxes*. New York: Norton.

Weiss, Edoardo. 1991. *Sigmund Freud as a Consultant: Recollections of a Pioneer in Psychoanalysis*. New Brunswick, NJ: Transaction.

Weizsaecker, Viktor von. 1957. "Reminiscences of Freud and Jung." *Freud and the 20th Century*. Edited by Benjamin Nelson. New York: Meridian.

Winnicott, Donald W. 1971. *Playing and Reality*. London: Tavistock.

Wittig, Monique. 1992. *The Straight Mind and Other Essays*. Boston: Beacon Press.

Wortis, Joseph. 1984. *Fragments of an Analysis With Freud*. New York: Jason Aronson.

Žižek, Slavoj. 1991. *For They Know Not What They Do: Enjoyment as a Political Factor*. London: Verso.

index of names